What people are saying a[illegible]

A captivating, unforgettable [illegible] production adventures from [illegible] Emmy Award-winning filmmaker. A mind-expanding filmic trek leading to professional acclaim and personal tragedies that stir the soul.
Paul Davids, Executive Producer of Showtime's Original Movie *Roswell*

Intensely Patriotic. A thrilling ride into the rich culture and diversity of Africa, its spiritual dimensions and alternative healing methods. It is also the story of one man's struggle with the immorality of apartheid. A prophetic and cautionary tale.
Corey Feldman, actor, singer, best-selling author, environmental activist

Forever in My Veins is a fascinating description of a middle-class white man's experiences in South Africa during the late forties and early fifties. Later in his life as a filmmaker he describes developing a chronic disease that, in the world of allopathic medicine, had no obvious cause or treatment. It's a compelling story of returning to his roots in Africa where he was able to find shamans who helped him deal with his illness. This is an intriguing weave of the connections between white and black cultures, ancient shamanic ways and natural healing contributing to the evolution of consciousness.
Dr. Gabriel Cousens, MD, MD (H), DD, Director, Tree of Life Foundation, Arizona

What a story! What a journey! What a glass so full of life and love, and not half-full of fear and regret! I will read it again to cry, laugh, gasp and celebrate.
Pieter-Dirk Uys, South African political satirist, international best-selling author

Forever in My Veins

How film led me to the mysterious world
of the African shaman

Forever in My Veins

How film led me to the mysterious world of the African shaman

Lionel Friedberg

BOOKS

Winchester, UK
Washington, USA

JOHN HUNT PUBLISHING

First published by O-Books, 2020
O-Books is an imprint of John Hunt Publishing Ltd., 3 East St., Alresford,
Hampshire SO24 9EE, UK
office@jhpbooks.com
www.johnhuntpublishing.com
www.o-books.com

For distributor details and how to order please visit the 'Ordering' section on our website.

ISBN: 978 1 78904 391 4
978 1 78904 392 1 (ebook)
Library of Congress Control Number: 2019945258

A CIP catalogue record for this book is available from the British Library.

Design: Stuart Davies

Printed and bound by CPI Group (UK) Ltd, Croydon, CR0 4YY
US: Printed and bound by Thomson-Shore, 7300 West Joy Road, Dexter, MI 48130

For Diana
Simon, Jessica, David and Amanda

Prologue

How often have you stared in hushed silence at something so breathtaking that your pulse races and words lose all meaning? Have you ever experienced an epiphany of discovery so dramatically profound that you are forever altered by the experience? I guess I've been lucky because I have. Those rare moments have led me to believe that anyone with the slightest degree of curiosity must surely realize that the world is a far more complex place than we can imagine. During my 75-year sojourn on this planet I've been exposed to innumerable wonders. I'm convinced that despite our scientific disciplines and our philosophizing we will continue to plumb depths so bewilderingly complex that we will always hunger to know more, to want to go further, to crave gazing upon vistas that may aid us in our comprehension of the mysterious ways in which the universe works.

Modern technology is continually giving us new tools to unlock secrets previously inaccessible to science. But many puzzles prevail. To find their relevance in an ever-increasingly sophisticated age we sometimes need to look over our shoulders, to peel back layers of time. Yet people tell me that dredging through the past is passé, outmoded, unfashionable. I disagree. I believe that in bygone times lie nuggets of buried treasure. Reaching back into the shadows and prying moments no matter how bizarre from one's former years and then examining them in the clear light of the present could teach us invaluable lessons about what may lie beyond tomorrow.

I make neither excuses nor apologies for being nostalgic in the pages that follow.

So, please, come exploring with me.

Introduction

The year was 1996. Life was good. I was busier than I had ever been. A National Primetime Emmy Award from the Academy of Television Arts & Sciences sat on my desk. Alongside it was a News & Documentary Emmy. On a shelf in my office was a collection of other accolades that included four Columbus International Film Festival statuettes. On a wall hung the American Association for the Advancement of Science (AAAS) Westinghouse Award for Best Science Programming on Television. On spots between bookcases were a dozen other certificates and plaques going back to my first big win for Best Documentary Television Series in 1976. When it came to nonfiction film production I felt that I was on top of the world. I was smug with confidence. I had an unabashed conviction that Hollywood lay at my feet.

And then, out of the blue, everything fell apart.

I was in the middle of producing a three-hour documentary special called *Who Wrote the Bible?* for The History Channel. Surrounded by mounds of research material, ancient texts and transcripts of interviews with Biblical scholars, historians, archeologists and philological experts I was putting the finishing touches to the final script when I decided to take an early break one evening. I shut down my computer, put my feet up after dinner and settled back to watch my favorite game show, *Jeopardy!* The kids were doing homework upstairs. My wife Diana joined me in front of the TV. It was another lovely warm summer Californian evening. I was wearing shorts. As the show got underway Diana glanced at my feet, leaned over and asked: "Why are your ankles so swollen tonight?"

I looked and thought, that's strange, they *are* swollen. I had never noticed it before. What was going on? Well, it didn't take long to find out.

A visit to my primary care physician revealed that the

swelling was due to fluid retention in body tissue. That could be caused by one of two things, a heart condition or failing kidneys. Within two whirlwind weeks I underwent a kidney biopsy and was diagnosed with a chronic and potentially fatal disease called idiopathic membranous glomerulonephritis. The nephrologist and pathologist labeled the condition 'idiopathic' because they had no idea what had caused it. All they knew was that my immune system was acting aggressively towards my kidneys and was trying to destroy them. My own body had turned against itself. The pundits had only one suggestion. I should immediately start taking heavy doses of drugs to suppress the immune system or my kidneys would shut down.

"And what if I don't?" I asked.

"Your kidneys will fail," they said.

"And then what?"

"You will have to start dialysis."

"And if I don't?"

"You will die."

Perched self-confidently at the pinnacle of a career spanning more than three decades I had to face up to the fact that my universe was about to change completely. How could this be happening? I was 51 years old and as fit as a fiddle. My nephrologist informed me that my immune system was behaving erratically because it was probably reacting to something that it didn't like within the bloodstream. He proposed that there might be a latent toxin that the immune system saw as a threat. But it was not sure what to target so it was going for an organ directly associated with cleansing the blood. It could have attacked my liver but it was aiming for the kidneys.

"But you have no idea why it's doing it?" I persisted.

"None," I was told. "Something has probably been lying dormant in your system for years. Have you ever had blood poisoning or been bitten by anything venomous like a spider or a scorpion?"

"Sure," I said. "All of the above. I made movies in a lot of weird places. I was cut, scratched, bruised and bitten more times than I can remember."

"What about snakes?"

"No," I responded. "That's the only thing that never happened. But as for noxious things and dirty places I've been stung and bitten by bees, bugs, wasps, spiders, ants, mosquitoes, jellyfish, bluebottles, Portuguese men o' war, everything. I was even bitten by a baboon once and suffered blood poisoning that laid me up for weeks. I've drunk brackish water in filthy places. I've swum in polluted rivers. I've eaten questionable foods. But all that was years ago. Why on earth should any of that trigger my immune system into behaving this way now?"

"Idiopathic," my nephrologist said, at a total loss for an explanation. "We simply don't know."

We were confounded as to why this ghastly disease had risen out of the darkness of nowhere and was suddenly threatening my very existence. And then it came back to me. I remembered. Of course! Why should I be so surprised?

Now please hear me clearly before I say another word. I don't believe in hocus-pocus nonsense or that rabbits can magically be pulled out of empty hats. I'm not prone to accepting the unproven. I'm open-minded, yes, but gullible, no. And yet the facts were indisputable. This awful illness and all its ramifications had been uncannily predicted—prophesied, foreseen, call it what you will—a long time ago in a place far, far away.

One

I was born in a city called Germiston in South Africa in 1944. When I was four years old we moved to the small town of Kempton Park, eighteen miles to the northeast of Johannesburg. Summer or winter every morning at six o'clock except Sundays there was the growl of a diesel engine and the squeal of brakes outside our house. Seconds later a clink of glass on the front porch indicated that a bottle of fresh milk had been deposited there. Belching thick black smoke that wafted through every open window and caught at my throat the delivery truck moved on to the next house. Shortly after that the sound of the front door opening meant that our 'house boy' John had collected the bottle. Twenty minutes later he tiptoed quietly up the hallway and placed a steaming cup of coffee on the night stands on either side of my parents' bed in the room next to mine. To keep the coffee hot the saucer was always turned upside down and placed on top of the cup. A half-hour later enticing aromas would tease my nostrils and coax me out of bed as John began preparing breakfast at the other end of the house. Sorghum-based *Maltabella* or oatmeal *Jungle Oats* porridge, scrambled eggs, fried tomatoes and onions, kippered herring fillets, grilled bologna, farm-style *boerewors* sausage, sautéed lamb kidneys, fried liver, toast, hot cocoa.

For middle class whites the South Africa of my youth was a very special place. Although many people had served alongside the Allies in World War II the conflict in Europe had been very far away and the country was short of nothing. It was a great place in which to grow up. We kids had all we could ask for: privilege, spacious neighborhoods, servants, well-stocked pantries, tree-lined streets where we could safely ride our bikes. There was an abundance of all things and much to amuse the restless soul of a growing and curious child. It was a Norman Rockwell world. Everyone seemed happy, at least everyone who was white. The school system was based on the British model and we received a fine, solid, disciplined education. There was always the prospect of boundless, promising tomorrows. There was nothing to fear. The future beckoned with promise.

But in our exclusively all-white domains we were isolated from more than 80% of the country's population. The laws of apartheid became official government policy in 1948 when the Afrikaner-dominated National Party won the general election and came to power. After that, regulations based on strict racial division governed every facet of life. The twain between black and white seldom met. The system was designed that way. We were not supposed to know what was happening on the other side of the tracks or beyond the outskirts of the city. Our only direct contact with black people was in our home where they worked as domestic servants or gardeners. In stores and markets they swept floors and unpacked crates. At gas stations they cleaned the windshield, checked the oil and pumped fuel, seldom receiving so much as a thank you, let alone a tip. In factories they played second fiddle to white overseers. In gold and diamond mines they toiled as laborers, burrowing deep into the earth to wrest treasures from the depths. In their segregated overcrowded schools—often in the shade of eucalyptus trees which served as makeshift outdoor classrooms—they were educated only to a level where they would remain unskilled and never in a position to become a competitive threat to their white masters.

It was not uncommon to see small gangs of 'boys'—actually adult black men—repairing roads. Wearing frayed denim shorts and often muscular and shirtless their feet were clad in homemade rubber sandals made from the worn treads of old discarded automobile tires. During their lunch breaks they sat cross-legged on the sidewalk and ate loaves of white bread that had been hollowed out. The interior was usually filled with Coca-Cola or fizzy green, red or bright yellow soda pop. The men were always cheery and smiling, even under the scornful watch of a white supervisor who sat apart from them, eating his own lunch of sandwiches, hard-boiled eggs and *droewors* (dried sausage) in the cab of a maintenance truck. After they had chomped down the last of their mulchy bread most of the men lit up a smoke hand-rolled from cheap pipe tobacco. If you passed them on the way to or from school they would acknowledge you by obediently nodding and then offering a polite greeting in Afrikaans: *"Móre, my basie."* ("Good morning, my young master.")

We all had black staff at home. Until I was three years old I was virtually brought up by a Zulu nanny whose name I can only recall as Mamingka, though I suspect that it was a nickname. She took care of me, wrapping me up in a grey blanket, tying it around her shoulders and waist and then carrying me on her back all day long, papoose style. She sang Zulu lullabies and hummed folk tunes while I dozed as she polished floors, made beds, dusted, cooked and hung up laundry on clotheslines in the backyard. My father, a watchmaker and jeweler by trade, was an immigrant from Latvia. He was the most scrupulously honest human being I have ever known. He was principled to a fault. As a result, he was taken advantage of by a string of deceitful business partners who maneuvered their way into and out of his life, absconding with money and forcing him to reinvent himself again and again. Because of his misfortunes we moved around a lot as he started new jobs or began different business ventures. During my childhood we lived in three different towns, in seven houses and four apartments, sometimes moving back to the same place we left only a couple of years earlier. I changed school eight times. This contributed to me being a dismally poor and miserable student, especially during my high school years. Because we moved around so much we had many servants. I vividly remember every single one of them. Mamingka, Lizzy, Anna, Lulu, Sophie, Lettie, John, David, Calvin, Betsy. Even today as I drift into sleep their smiling faces still hover over me, reinforcing the indelible imprint they left on my life.

It was illegal to take a black person in your employment to another town without going through hassles with the authorities at the local Department of Native Affairs. I often overheard my parents wrestling over servants' 'permits' and 'papers.' These had to be renewed every year. I grasped little of what it all meant, but permission to allow a black person to move from one magisterial district to another was nearly always denied. The dreaded 'Pass Laws' were a constant obstacle. Every adult black person, male or female, had to carry an identity document called a 'pass' at all times. If stopped by police, even while doing little more than pushing a white baby in a stroller along the sidewalk or mowing a lawn, he or she had to produce the necessary pass proving that they had permission to be there. If their papers were not in order they were in trouble. The victim would be thrown into the back of a police van and hauled off to jail until bailed out by an employer. Even worse, they could be forced to await deportation back to a designated tribal territory, often hundreds of miles away in rural areas far from the main cities and industrial areas. As a child I saw many arrests on the streets, most of them ugly. With few exceptions the police were rude and discourteous. I never understood why seemingly innocent people were suddenly stopped for no apparent reason, bombarded with questions—invariably in Afrikaans, the language of the whites who wielded the political power—roughly frisked and then tossed into those sinister unmarked police vans and driven off. Where were they going? What did they do wrong? Whenever I asked my parents about it I was told to, "Shush! Don't ask about such things. It's none of our business."

A servant in our home was always treated well but decorum and protocol were strictly enforced. During the years that I lived with my folks there was always a little brass bell conspicuously placed in the middle of the dining room table. About four inches high it was shaped like a 19th century British country milkmaid. Both arms were extended and the little figure's fingertips daintily held up her wide skirt as she lifted it in a sort of courtesy pose. It was a charming object. It was also the sound of mealtimes as far back as I can remember. How many servants had it summoned? The breakfasts, lunches, dinners, houses, apartments, towns, cities and even countries changed but the bell was always the same, always there, always under the watchful eye and control of my mother who rang it to request the next course at mealtime. "Ting-a-ling-a-ling." Woe to the man or woman in the kitchen who did not respond immediately. I still have it, perched on my bookcase in my office, and whenever I ring it—albeit very softly—a cavalcade of ghosts, memories and smells wafts from the shadows. For me, sounds more than anything bring the past back to life. So it is with that bell. But I wonder how all those servants felt when the "ting-a-ling-a-ling" commanded them to serve and do our bidding. Did anyone ever ask? Or care? Or even think about it?

No matter where we lived, as a youngster I would frequently spend time with each of our servants in their Spartan-like quarters. Their tiny rooms were usually behind the garage at the far end of the backyard or—when we lived in apartment buildings in cities like Johannesburg—in a tight cluster of cubicles built around the elevator machinery room on the rooftop. There was a closet-size bathroom with a shower that provided only cold water and on the floor was a ceramic slat with a hole in it that served as a toilet. Minuscule bedrooms always smelt of cheap soap, lantern oil and candle wax. The scent of skin lightening crème hung on the air. Those cremes were very fashionable, especially among women. Their purpose was to make complexions look lighter, less black. They are now known to have contained hydroquinone which reduced the skin's production of melanin for protection against the sun's ultraviolet radiation, with deadly results. Many people developed cancerous melanoma from them.

In 1955 we were living in a tall apartment building in the suburb of Yeoville in Johannesburg. We had a wonderful maid named Elizabeth. She lived in tiny quarters with all the other servants and maintenance staff up on the rooftop. As I was an only child and as both my parents were working, whenever I got home after the tram ride from school I would usually go up there with her. There were always long clotheslines of starched white uniforms, aprons and other laundry fluttering in the wind; shirts and skirts and underwear, dazzlingly clean in the bright summer sun, dancing like apparitions in the sky against a backdrop of high-rise apartment buildings, office blocks and water towers. Lizzy didn't mind me sitting in her tiny room with her as she took off her servant's cap, sat on the floor with her legs outstretched and then curled her frizzy hair. Like many servants, much of the time she walked around barefoot. The heels and balls of her feet were often callused and I was always intrigued to watch her slice away little slivers of hardened skin with a sharp razor blade.

In the dim, cramped servants' rooms in the backyards of houses there was always a lingering odor of purple-colored methylated spirits or paraffin. Those fuels were used to power a little brass *Primus* stove that sat on the floor. It was used for boiling water or cooking food. Servants were not allowed to cook for themselves in our kitchens, but they were given generous portions of the same things that we ate. However, they usually preferred simple indigenous foods like white corn flour (meal) and water that was slowly boiled until it formed a firm porridge called *putu* or *pap*. They always shared it with me. I'd go and perch on my haunches in their room and dig into the *pap* with my fingers, scoop out a chunk, roll it into a little ball, dip it into some thick gravy and chew. Sometimes, dried corn kernels were boiled in salted water to make what was called *kabu mealies*. I was especially partial to that, and I also loved a spinach-like dish they made by boiling wild *marog (Amaranthus hybridus)* leaves that they had gathered in the veld outside town.

Wherever they were, on the tops of buildings or in backyards, inside those little servants' rooms there was usually a give-away calendar from a dairy, corner grocery store or local gas station stuck to the wall. There was often a framed black and white portrait of parents or relatives taken in some faraway tribal village or *kraal*. Without exception, the bed was always raised eight to ten inches higher than its legs. Each leg was perched on a couple of bricks to make certain the mattress was as far above the floor as possible. This was because of the much-feared *tokoloshe*. Stories of this mythical being were many. When I heard them as a kid they scared the living daylights out of me but then the servants were equally terrified. Dismiss it as superstitious nonsense if you will, but to those people—and to me—it was very real. Legend has it that the *tokoloshe* prowled the night. Half human and half animal, about three or four feet tall, he was a deformed, withered and hairy little creature constantly in search of mischief or worse. He was described as red-eyed, hunchbacked, yellow-toothed and usually wrapped in baboon or hyena skins. Because he was so short the bed was always raised to keep the sleeper as high as possible and out of harm's way from him. Some said the *tokoloshe* had a long tail, whereas others said that it wasn't a tail at all but an abnormally long penis which he draped over his shoulder as he scuttled around looking for women to rape and men to taunt. There was not a tribe in southern Africa that did not subscribe to some or other form of belief in the *tokoloshe*.

The world of the metaphysical was fundamental to the African. It was a force, a power, a reality that bore down on all facets of life. Even though the majority of urban blacks belonged to a church or a group affiliated with Western religious belief they nevertheless adhered to an intense conviction that ancestral spirits and psychic forces influenced a person's day-to-day activities. An ancient link that connected them with these forces or protected them from harm emanating from the metaphysical world was the function of a shaman. And shamans were plentiful, even in urban areas. They had many roles. He or she was not only a conduit between the worlds of the living and the dead but also an agent of protection against sorcery and witchcraft. They were skilled healers during time of sickness or need. Because the laws of apartheid created such unbridgeable barriers between people whites who lived in urban areas knew absolutely nothing of this or indeed of black culture generally. Centuries-old spiritual beliefs and healing methods were dismissed as nonsense, thought of as little more than 'black magic,' the work of 'witch doctors.' When one of our servants became ill my parents would offer to take them to a white doctor or clinic but they invariably declined, saying they would prefer to consult a shaman, a person they referred to as a *sangoma*, *inyanga* or *ngaka*. The African paradigm of healing was very different to Western allopathic medicine. It was based on a complex system of herbs, plants and other organic material including animal parts. It also encompassed spells, chants and ritual baths. Though invariably dismissed as witch doctors—an inaccurate and misconstrued term—traditional healers often spent years at the feet of elder practitioners who taught them their craft. It wasn't only about medicine but about contact with deceased ancestors and the ability to divine events that lay in the future. *Sangomas* could be clairvoyants, diviners, fortune tellers, soothsayers, herbalists and, most importantly, mediators between the living and the dead, the physical and the spiritual. It was believed that there was good and evil in the metaphysical realm and that this could be funneled by many supernatural entities into the corporeal world.

It was the work of the *sangoma* to identify a source of illness or misfortune and to correct it with the tools at his or her disposal. Those instruments took many forms but the most common was a set of animal bones, shells, stones, pebbles, charms, talismans, amulets and a conglomerate of tiny objects that were used for divination, for peering into the unknown. As the *sangoma* sat on the floor on one side of a small grass mat or animal skin and his or her patient on the other, the bones and other paraphernalia were thrown onto the mat. The way in which they fell was believed to be influenced by the patient's ancestors. Depending on how items lay in proximity to one another and whether they were 'right side up' or 'upside down' gave them negative or positive connotations. Their pattern on the mat was 'read' or interpreted to find out what ailed the patient, what was causing infertility, who was responsible for stealing money or what supernatural forces were working against the patient. Medicines—called *muti* in vernacular African languages throughout southern Africa—were dispensed to heal an illness, bring on a dream, lure a lover, punish an adversary or neutralize a problem. These medicines were derived from fresh organic material or more commonly from substances that had been dried and ground up into powder form. Water from the ocean or 'sacred' springs was also important. Fats, oils and ointments were common too. The patient was told to either drink the *muti*, apply it to the skin, use it in a ritual bath or even bury it or hide it in a specific location. Belief in the *tokoloshe* was but one tiny aspect stemming from this multifarious belief in a supernatural universe that embraced both positive and negative energies as well as a plethora of benevolent or evil entities.

As a child I often wondered why some servants who secretly practiced as *sangomas* in the privacy of their backyard rooms without their employers' knowledge often had visitors lining up outside their doors, usually just before sundown or on Thursday afternoons. In those days Thursday afternoons were set aside as domestic workers' half-days off work. Our own servant often confided in me, telling me that so-and-so who worked next door or down the road was not only a cleaning lady, garden boy or cook but also a 'special doctor,' a *sangoma*. People would arrive at the *sangoma's* door looking ill or distraught, disappear inside his or her room for a half hour or so, then emerge clutching a small package wrapped in wads of old newspaper. They invariably looked somewhat relieved or more hopeful when they came out carrying those little parcels. What had happened? What went on behind the closed door? The master or madam of the house usually accused servants who received many visitors of running a brothel or of selling illegal substances such as *dagga* (marijuana) or a potent home-brewed alcoholic drink called *skokiaan*. Police raids usually turned up nothing more than rows of clay pots, tins and little bottles containing mysterious but by no means illicit powders, liquids, ointments, ground bark, leaves, twigs and herbs, plus a little mat on the floor on which lay a pile of harmless bones, shells and stones.

"Oh, just another stupid witch doctor," the police would report back to the employer. "Kaffir nonsense. Nothing to worry about."

You could not be more disparaging to a black person than to call him or her a kaffir. It was the ultimate derogatory term. The word owed its origin to the 16th century Arabic word *kafir* that meant infidel or disbeliever, but in South Africa during the apartheid era it was adopted by whites to vilify or humiliate black people. The everyday term for a black person was 'native.' "Have you paid the native for the garden work? Did the native deliver the parcel? There's a native at the back door looking for work." But if you wanted to be nasty or humiliate a 'native' you would switch to 'kaffir.' Most often when police stopped blacks in the streets to inspect their pass books they would refer to them that way. *"Ja, kaffir, wys vir my jou pass."* ("Yes, kaffir, show me your pass.")

Despite their arrogant condemnation of traditional black healers the term *'muti'* for conventional medicine was perfectly acceptable in the language of white society. As a child I remember my mother telling me to "take your *muti* like a good boy" whenever I had to swallow a spoonful of castor oil or cough syrup when I was off color. Got a headache? Sore throat? "Take your *muti*."

In the sixth grade we were introduced to a new subject at school, 'Race Studies.' Textbooks proclaimed that whites were superior to blacks, or *Bantu* as they were more appropriately called. Whites were depicted as the saviors of Africa, the civilizing force that would redeem the continent from its heathenism and backward primitivism. Other than the ancient Egyptians or 'ruthless and murderous' tribes such as the Zulu or Xhosa who had been in conflict with early white settlers, not a word was ever mentioned of the many African civilizations and empires that had existed on the continent for centuries prior to the arrival of Europeans. Tribal blacks were depicted as basket weavers adorned in loin cloths and beads, totally without a history.

Few whites bothered to enter the black man's world, let alone take the trouble to find out what was really going on inside those servants' rooms where *sangomas* practiced their craft. If they did, they would have been surprised to learn that they were tapping into metaphysical forces as ancient and as mysterious as Africa itself. Those people were practicing healing methods and dispensing medicines just as powerful as that of the white man. But in the apartheid days they were just plain 'kaffirs.' So, why bother?

Many years later in my professional career as a film maker I would personally encounter the enigmatic strangeness of the African shamanistic universe. Then, long after I had left South Africa and settled in the United States I would return to that world. My encounters with the spiritual realms of Africa would open up a whole new portal of consciousness for me. It would even play a role in saving my life. But, in the beginning all that lay in the future. I had no clue what was to come. I could not possibly foresee how one mystifying event after another would work its way into my life. Some of them would be enlightening, others terrifying. I would be exposed to things that would totally defy reason or understanding. I would meet practitioners who would give me insight into the extraordinary reality of supernatural domains and the potent healing power of herbs and plants. As the years unfolded I would begin to see the world anew. Much of what I would learn would shatter every convention that I had ever been taught or held to be true.

Two

My mother was born in a small town to the northwest of Johannesburg. She spent her childhood on a farm. The predominant language in most rural areas was Afrikaans but because she spent so much time playing with the black farmworkers' children she was proficient in vernacular languages such as Pedi, Sotho and Tswana. She rode a horse, had a pet sheep that slept on her bed, collected eggs from the hen house and nurtured a great love for animals. Empathy with animals was a trait that I inherited from her. During my youth we visited the Kruger National Park at least once a year. The southern gate of the park was only 300 miles from Johannesburg and the nearest rest camp just a couple of hours' drive from the entrance. In the span of five or six days it was possible to visit immense swaths of Kruger and stay in various camps. Those trips fostered a passionate obsession with wildlife and wild places in me. There was nothing more exciting than roaming the park on its network of narrow dirt roads in Dad's big Buick and seeing just about all the species of mammals, reptiles, birds and insects that it had to offer. When I was young the place was relatively quiet and uncrowded. Those were before the days of large-scale tourism that brought fleets of buses rumbling in convoys on a network of double-lane paved roads. It was still wild Africa. Less than a day's drive from Johannesburg and the other cities and towns of the industrialized Highveld you could be in another time, another era, another universe.

The smell of the bush was intoxicating. It filled you with a sense of wonder. The rivers and streams were clean and unpolluted. Mountain ranges lay across the grassy veld. Vultures and eagles swirled in warm upward drafts high above the acacia and baobab trees. On the outskirts of the park were clusters of African villages. Smoke rose from outdoor fires at dawn and dusk. Mists hung over streams where young girls collected water in clay pots and then marched back to their villages, laughing and joking all the way. The pots were always perfectly balanced on top of their heads. Young herd boys dressed in tattered shorts and flimsy old shirts or faded moth-eaten sweaters watched over goats and cattle grazing in the hills.

The experience of seeing all this gave me a wonderfully romantic vision of Africa. I saw it as a tantalizingly raw continent. There was an edginess to it all. Danger lurked everywhere. But it was invigorating. I believed that adventure and excitement lay beyond every valley and horizon. That attitude was reinforced by Hollywood and British movies of the time that I loved so much: *King Solomon's Mines, She, The African Queen, Where No Vultures Fly, Duel in the Jungle, Mogambo, West of Zanzibar, Stanley and Livingstone*. To my mind Africa meant high drama and mystery. There were always new things to explore, wild animals and unknown tribes to discover. The movies created that impression so of course they had to be true. Fantastic kingdoms, lost diamond mines, buried treasure, evil sorcerers, fierce warriors and vast ruins peppered the forests and filled the jungles. Fortunately, both my parents loved going to either four-wall cinemas or drive-in movie theaters so I was exposed to film from a very early age. I was so fascinated by it that I started making my own 8mm movies at the age of 11. My infatuation with the medium was the catalyst that eventually led me to a professional career in the motion picture industry. I would spend over 50 years in the entertainment business, first in Africa and then in Hollywood, initially as a cinematographer, then as a writer and director.

In 1956, when I was 12, one of the most influential films my buddies and I saw at a matinee performance one Saturday afternoon was the full-length documentary called *No Place for Wild Animals*. Originally a German film entitled *Keine Platz fur Wilde Tiere* made by Dr. Bernhard Grzimek and his son Michael in

Central and East Africa, it was not only an exposé of professional trophy hunting in Africa but an appeal to the world community to help establish well-managed wildlife sanctuaries and national parks throughout the continent. There was an ominous side to its message. The film predicted a day when growing human populations and urban development would squeeze wildlife from the land, causing many species to become extinct with just a few remaining numbers relegated to tiny preserves here and there. It foretold of a time when the Africa I loved so much would cease to be. Wild animals would no longer roam the grassy plains. They would be doomed by the sheer presence of humans. People would take over their natural habitats. Tribal villages would be replaced by concrete cities. I was shocked. In fact, the film was so disturbing that it sent me into a veritable catatonic state of depression for weeks afterwards. How could such a future ever be possible? How could this terrifying prediction ever materialize? Then, in 1959 the Grzimeks made another film, the iconic *Serengeti Shall Not Die*. The original German title was *Serengeti Darf Nicht Sterben*. A passionate appeal for African wildlife conservation, Michael Grzimek lost his life in an air crash during the filming but the movie brought the plight of Africa's wildlife to the attention of worldwide audiences. That film did it for me. Movies and animals became integral to much that defined me, becoming as potent in my life as the dust of Africa that was already ingrained in my veins. It was a continent that I loved and admired intensely. I was proud to be born there. Even though I was of white-skinned European descent I thought of myself as African as any of the black people around me. It was my home, my birthplace, my identity.

The biggest problem facing my family during the late fifties was my father's constant financial struggles. How Dad ever managed to make it through those troubling times I will never know. But he was always calm, always good-natured. The other matter that weighed down heavily upon us was the scourge of apartheid. During high school many of my friends and I had become aware that enforced racist divisions within society were not only wrong but downright evil. If you crossed a bridge over the railway tracks a six-feet high barrier running along the middle of the bridge divided the races, 'Whites' on one side, 'Non-Whites' on the other. Signs everywhere split people apart. Stores and banks had separate entrances for whites and blacks. No blacks were allowed inside white movie theaters or churches. Buses, trains, schools, libraries, hotels, parks, playing fields, hospitals, public restrooms and even beaches were strictly segregated. It was a ruthless system that divided the very soul of the nation.

A massive black demonstration against the vilified pass laws took place at Sharpeville, a township near Johannesburg on March 21, 1960. The result was terrible violence and bloodshed. Police opened fire on 20,000 demonstrators, killing 77 and injuring hundreds. But the government had become immune to local and international condemnation. To make it all seem more palatable to the outside world, and to ease the increasing worries of industrialists and businessmen within the country, the whole concept of racist division was given a new title: 'Separate Development.' Under this guise people were more rigidly fragmented and divided, supposedly in the interests of providing each racial group with 'opportunities to advance,' but strictly within their own delineated areas. It was little more than blatant segregation with a fancy name.

South Africa was coming under increasing international criticism. It was still a member of the British Commonwealth and subject to British rules and standards. Although it had its own Prime Minister and elected government officials Queen Elizabeth remained head of state. But as nationalism and independence movements began spreading throughout the once mighty British Empire, and as one European colony after another was offered independence, British Prime Minister Harold Macmillan flew out from London on a fact-finding mission to South Africa. On February 2, 1960 he made his famous "Wind of Change" speech in Cape Town. With it he warned of the consequences of South Africa's racist policies.

"The wind of change is blowing through the continent," he said. "Whether we like it or not, growth of political consciousness is a political fact."

Things were bound to change. He cautioned the government about the perils of retaining apartheid but it fell on deaf ears. Unfazed, the ruling National Party implemented even more draconian legislation to keep the races apart. It also severed its links with the British Commonwealth. During a nationwide all-white referendum the Afrikaans-speaking white majority voted in favor of South Africa becoming a republic. Now it would be answerable to no one. In addition, plans were drawn up to create ten 'independent homelands' or *Bantustans* within the country for the black population. Depending on a person's language, birth and tribal affiliation he or she would have to live in one of the homelands set aside for each of the ten major ethnic groups. Those territories were intended to be completely excised from South Africa itself. Each would have its own president, government, flag, national anthem and coat of arms. The only way that a person from a homeland could live and work in 'white' South Africa was if he or she was in possession of the necessary temporary residence papers. It was tantamount to the 'green card' system in the United States today, but there was never the prospect of permanent residence, citizenship or security of tenure. Upon retirement or completion of a job on a gold mine, factory, farm or in a white-owned home the person had to return to his or her officially designated tribal homeland. Even if a black person had been born inside 'white' South Africa he or she still did not have the right to remain there. Ultimately, return to the appropriately apportioned *Bantustan* was inevitable. The creation of these so-called 'independent' areas was going to require vast funding and sap the South African economy, let alone the political and social dissent that it was going to cause.

By the end of 1960 my parents had had enough. They believed that by severing its links with Britain and the Commonwealth the country would become unstable and dangerous. The establishment of the *Bantustans* would create chaos and lead to civil war. These latest apartheid concoctions were, they believed, a recipe for disaster. Revolution would not be far off. And then something else happened. With the little money he had managed to save up after his last venture ended in financial failure my father set up a small jewelry and watchmaking business on his own in the city of Germiston. I was thrilled when he asked me to help him design the logo and exterior signage for the shop. His first consignment of inventory—a quantity of costly Swiss wristwatches—arrived just three days before he officially opened the door to customers. The day after the delivery he was held up by two masked black gunmen. They took off with everything. His insurance coverage had not yet become effective and he was wiped out, financially and morally. His mind was made up. It was time to call it quits and leave the country. And so he answered an ad in the *Sunday Times* for a job as manager of a small jewelry store in the British Colony of Northern Rhodesia, far to the north. The territory was right on the border of the newly independent Republic of the Congo where the departure of the Belgians had already ignited a civil war. But Northern Rhodesia was part of a federation of three territories—Northern and Southern Rhodesia and Nyasaland—all still under stable British control. Peace still reigned within the Federation. My folks would take their chances with that. Whatever happened it would still be safer than remaining in South Africa. To my great relief my loathsome high school education was complete and so I accompanied my parents on their quest for a fresh start in the Central African tropics.

Three

Shortly after we arrived at our new home early in 1961 a company with shareholders based in Britain and South Africa established the first television station in Central Africa. Its location was in the Northern Rhodesian mining town of Kitwe. This was the center of a string of small copper mining communities isolated from the rest of the world by a tropical landscape made up of thousands of square miles of bush and mountains punctuated here and there by marshes, rivers and lakes. It was magnificent country with a sublime climate. But apart from sports and social gatherings, boating, fishing, golf and billiards, dart competitions and beer and pink gins at the local club at sundown, there wasn't much else for the well-heeled local white population to do in the evenings. They had money to spend. Lots of it. Copper prices were high so there was substantial earning power around. Every home had the latest car, boat or trailer parked in the driveway. Whites could afford long holidays abroad, expensive imported fashionwear, fancy watches, diamonds, jewelry, the latest kitchen appliances and all the trappings of a well-to-do community in Europe or North America. The problem was that they were stuck deep in the African bush. Apart from annual vacation time there was no escape. There was little else to do but spend lavishly and enjoy life at home. A commercial television service would address the requirement for entertainment at night plus act as a showcase to encourage the spending of high wages on a wide range of goods and services. It was a perfect combination. So the studios of RTV—Rhodesia Television—rose in the Kitwe suburb of Parklands to cater to those needs. Fate and fortune were in my favor as it was there that I got a job. Before my 18th birthday I was behind a television studio camera.

Although the rules of apartheid did not apply in Northern Rhodesia, in true colonial style the twain between the races did not meet. Black workers on the mines lived in separate 'native compounds,' far from white neighborhoods. In movie theaters they were allowed to occupy only the first two rows of seats in the auditorium and not allowed to sit among whites. Their earning power was way below that of whites. Apart from food and essential commodities few could afford the enticing products, luxury vehicles and vacation packages advertised on TV. The average rate that the station charged for a 60-second ad during a broadcast was £14.00. Thirty seconds went for £8.00 and £5.00 bought a 15-second slot. The type of entertainment on offer was aimed exclusively at whites. And so *Bonanza, Highway Patrol, Dr. Kildare, Playhouse 90, Naked City, Bewitched, Leave It to Beaver, Rawhide, The Beverly Hillbillies, Wagon Train, The Defenders, Victory at Sea, Hazel, The Honeymooners* and many other productions from the US shared the airwaves with *Noddy, Fireball XL5, Dr. Finlay's Casebook, Z Cars, Danger Man, The Larkins, The Saint, Hancock's Half Hour* and *Eric Sykes* from the UK.

Those were the days before videotape, let alone microwave towers and satellite communications systems. When the station opened in 1961 the United States had not yet even launched *Telstar*, the first of its experimental communications satellites. All of our programming was either live or on film. Live programming consisted of quiz shows, teenage dance competitions, variety shows, talks and interviews, the odd dramatic play plus two ten-minute live advertising programs every night for local businesses called 'Ad Mags,' and, of course, a nightly news bulletin. International news stories were culled from a wire services telex machine in the newsroom that had a regular habit of breaking down. Some stories were illustrated with short newsreel clips on 16mm film, often shown days or weeks after the actual event had occurred because we had to wait for the footage to arrive from abroad. Our small group of reporters interviewed an endless cavalcade of Saville Row-suited white and black politicians who came in to discuss calls for black independence from British rule.

I got to know local politicians as well as representatives from the Foreign Office in Whitehall and deputations from the UN in New York. Our studio crew were soon on first name terms with the man who would lead the territory to independence, Kenneth Kaunda. He could not be more charming. He was the epitome of a gentleman and an extremely erudite speaker. His insightful perception of the challenges that independence would bring never failed to impress journalists. For a kid like me it was fascinating. I was still green behind the ears, only just old enough to have a driver's license and yet there I was behind a TV camera training my lens on the faces of people who were rewriting history.

We relied heavily on what were dubbed 'musical interludes' in-between commercials and programs. These consisted of recordings of the latest pop songs or melodies from British and American rock 'n' roll groups. They were played over images of live fish swimming in a small glass aquarium. The tank itself was kept in a corner of the studio and I took it upon myself to become responsible for feeding its occupants. Alas, many of the fish often perished under the hot studio lights, their lifeless bodies floating on the surface while Petula Clark sang *Downtown* or Chubby Checker belted out *Let's Twist Again*.

Because RTV also owned studios in Salisbury (now Harare) and Bulawayo in Southern Rhodesia (modern-day Zimbabwe) our entertainment programming on film was flown up to the town of Ndola on a Central African Airways commercial flight every morning from the south. From there it was delivered to the station in Kitwe by road. It was a precarious arrangement. If flights were delayed or cancelled we had nothing to transmit that night. All we could do then was turn to our limited stock of documentaries and dated library programming or be resourceful and come up with some form of jerry-rigged live entertainment show to keep us on the air. The fish tank came in especially useful during those occasions.

Sometimes in-between live shows I'd sit on the front steps of the studio building to munch on a sandwich or sip a coffee. The stairway was also the favorite spot of the studio's black workers, particularly the cleaners and night watchman. They liked to hang out there and puff on cigarettes. Although I did not smoke at that stage I enjoyed their company. We would perch on the stairs under a humming neon light where moths and beetles fluttered and buzzed, or stand quietly under a soaring canopy of stars discussing what life would be like once independence came. The din of frogs and insects from the nearby bush filled the air. Those sounds intermingled with the strains of American and British television shows echoing from a TV monitor in the lobby. It was bizarre, a surreal mixture of very different worlds. The contrasts could not have been more acute. Neither world belonged to the other, yet they coexisted, caught up in a cross-cultural mélange in the balmy African night.

White audiences loved the programming that we provided. Indigenous black audiences were equally enthralled. Though few blacks owned their own TV sets crowds always gathered around monitors in densely packed 'beer halls.' By law alcoholic beverages could only be consumed by blacks in designated community centers. These were usually situated on mine property and were enormously popular. Patrons at these establishments were especially fond of the TV Westerns. Deep in the bush at mission stations and in small villages where electrical power was available large throngs gathered around TV sets that had been set up in the windows of country stores or at clinics, churches and social centers. Among the crowds of men were women with babies on their backs and children who understood little or no English. Few knew anything about the locations where the stories were taking place or the meaning of the shows' action or plot. But that made no difference. The little flickering black and white television screen was a window onto an incomprehensible and fascinating alien world. They adored it.

Colonialism was in its dying throes throughout Africa. The Federation of Northern Rhodesia, Southern Rhodesia and Nyasaland was coming apart at the seams. Local demand for independence from British rule was eventually met with agreement from London that Northern Rhodesia would gain autonomy under a black government in October 1964. This created the new Republic of Zambia. Soon afterwards Nyasaland became Malawi. But whites in Southern Rhodesia decided to rebel against Britain's insistence on majority black rule. They would wage a bitter war against black nationalist groups and freedom fighters for 14 years. 20,000 people would die in the fighting. White control would only be relinquished in 1980 with the establishment of the Republic of Zimbabwe under President Robert Mugabe.

After the creation of Zambia our station was nationalized by the state. It was now no longer part of the commercial white-controlled enterprise that had owned it. Any reference to the old name Rhodesia was dropped. The operation was renamed ZTV—Zambia Television. Programming quickly began to reflect the cultural, social and political changes that had replaced colonial times. Even during the transitionary period prior to independence educational broadcasts had commenced on weekday mornings. These were aimed at rural black schools and mission stations. Live afternoon broadcasts showcasing tribal music and dances for off-duty black mineworkers had begun as early as 1962. Those shows were to have a profound effect on me. For the first time in my life I came face to face with ethnic black culture. Unlike the divisive apartheid-imposed barriers that had separated me from any type of African heritage during my childhood in South Africa I was now exposed to troupes of performers that had been brought to the studio from remote tribal areas, often hundreds of miles away. There were 70 different tribes in the country. By train, bus, truck or convoys of vehicles they came: Lunda, Bemba and Tabwa from the north, Chewa and Senga from the east, Tonga, Leya and Lenja from the south, and Lozi, Lovale and Ndembo from the west. Every afternoon the studio was filled with musicians and dancers clad in cloths, animal skins, feathers, grass skirts, masks and colorful costumes. With the air conditioning straining to cope with the number of sweaty performers who filled the stage I trundled my camera on its wheeled dolly through groups of half-naked musicians who beat out rhythms on drums, rattles, coconut husks and sticks. They blew on reed instruments, whistles and animal horns. The frenetic energy that filled the studio was extraordinary. The marriage of the medium of television and the art of indigenous people who had been extolling life through their music, song and dance since time immemorial was intoxicating.

At the end of the day the studio was cleared for the live Ad Mag shows; the telecine equipment up in the control room was laced with film and by sundown things settled back for a night of Western cultural fare for white audiences. This consisted of comedies and crime dramas from London and Hollywood. It was an extraordinary time to be cutting one's teeth on television. I learned much about my craft during those few years. We had to improvise and make do with miniscule budgets and few resources. I became adept at lighting, composition, camerawork and set design. If something didn't exist, you created it. If a shot was deemed impossible by our small corps of technical engineers you simply put your head together with the studio crew and found a way of doing it. They were wonderful years.

At the time of independence in 1964 a middle-aged black woman who claimed herself to be a 'prophetess' rose up in the northeastern part of the country to oppose the policies of the ruling nationalist party, UNIP, or the United National Independence Party. This was the party led by President Kenneth Kaunda. Her name was Alice Lenshina. She pronounced herself head of what she called the Lumpa Church. The movement became very militant, refusing to pay taxes, distancing itself from the rule of law and not accepting the validity of UNIP to govern. Its behavior threatened the stability of a large region around the Chinsali district in the province of Muchinga. Rioting began and state troopers were called in to restore order. In the ensuing gun battles between members of the Lumpa Church, UNIP supporters and government forces nearly a thousand people lost their lives. Alice Lenshina was arrested and sentenced to prison. It was a tragic event that clouded the nationwide celebration of independence.

One afternoon at the TV station a new member of the broadcasting staff—the first black person to be hired for the role—was assigned the task of interviewing a traditional African diviner or medicine man. The intention was to ask him to forecast whether the Lumpa Church troubles had finally been put down. In Zambia a psychic practitioner was commonly known as a *shinganga* or *nganga*. This was someone who performed similar functions to the *sangomas, inyangas* or *ngakas* of South Africa. One weekday afternoon just before the commencement of the daily tribal music performance a very tall, dark-skinned solemn-looking and barefooted man wearing an array of animal skins, cocoon-rattle ankle bracelets, zebra tails, feathers and carrying a small bag made of antelope hide silently padded into the building and sat down in one of two armchairs in the studio. After welcoming him our interviewer Neb Jere sat down in the chair opposite him. Because his guest spoke no English the interview was conducted in the vernacular Bemba language.

"With the quelling of the Lumpa Church riots would peace finally come to the Chinsali district?" Neb wanted to know. The *nganga* opened his little antelope hide bag and took out what looked like four ivory-colored flat white sticks. He seemed to be going into some sort of a trance as he held them in his two hands and shook them, mumbling under his breath. Neither I, the other studio cameraman nor indeed the producer, director, audio technicians or engineers up in the control room could understand a word that was being said. Neither would any white viewers who were watching so Neb did his best to translate the proceedings into English. He explained that the little objects were the *nganga's* divining instruments. He had inherited them from his grandfather on his father's side. The old man had taken him under his wing when he was a teenager and taught him his craft as a *nganga*. The grandfather had 'passed' some years ago and was now in the spirit world. From there he acted as the *nganga's* ancestral guide to help him in his work. I was immediately reminded of the stories of ancestors and the role of the deceased in the affairs of the living that I had heard years ago as a child in South Africa.

The *nganga* tossed the objects—each one about eight inches long—into the air a number of times, always catching them in his cupped hands. Finally he let them fall to the floor. While the other cameraman held a wide shot of the two men as the conversation continued I zoomed into a close-up of the divination sticks lying on the floor. It was obvious that they were made of bone, chiseled into flat elongated strips probably from the femur or tibia of a goat or cow. Each one had a different pattern of symbols etched onto its surface. The *nganga* leaned over and peered at the sticks for about a minute or so, saying nothing while Neb shifted uneasily in his chair. Then he loudly clapped his hands three times in acknowledgement of the message that the sticks had revealed to him. Yes, the Lumpa uprising and the violence were over, he proclaimed. Peace would prevail in Muchinga province. There was nothing to fear. Alice Lenshina was no longer a threat to security. She would languish in prison for about eleven years and then be released. She would not rise to defy the state again. All was well. The only thing to be done now was to celebrate independence and rejoice in the newly attained freedom from colonial white rule. And with that the interview was over. The two men stood up, shook hands and the *nganga* left the studio. Then the rear doors of the big stage were opened and a boisterous group of tribal dancers and musicians poured in to set up their instruments to begin an afternoon of lively entertainment.

Between 1961 and 1963 news bulletins broadcast from the station depicted many stories about NASA's Mercury space program in the United States. From Alan Shepard's *Freedom* 7 Mercury Redstone suborbital flight to John Glenn, Scott Carpenter, Walter Schirra and Gordon Cooper's orbital missions everyone watched those first efforts that would one day make America a spacefaring nation. Wherever the signal from our transmitter reached—even deep into the bush—people had been witnesses to the Mercury space program. This included a small community of Kaonde tribesmen in a mountainous region far to the west. And there one man had proclaimed himself to be the head of the 'Zambia Space Academy.' He announced that it was to be the country's very own astronaut training and space exploration program from which graduates would be offered to NASA in the United States.

I can no longer recall the fellow's name but he arrived at the studio one afternoon with a large entourage. This included a group of women praise singers who trilled and ululated loudly as they piled out of a big beat-up and muddied Bedford truck that had brought them from their village deep in the forest. Flamboyant in his long flowing yellow and white robe covered in an embroidered pattern of stars and moons made of silver sequins and wearing a headdress of white and gold feathers he carried a wildebeest tail fly whisk. He was strikingly handsome and very serious-looking. It was hard to judge his age but I guessed he was probably in his late thirties. His fingers were covered in rings bearing large artificial 'precious' stones. Looped copper earrings dangled from his ears. Barefoot with rattles and beads tied around his ankles he swept his way into the studio, sat down on the chair reserved for interviewees, rearranged his flowing robe neatly over his crossed legs and waited to be questioned by a nervous-looking Neb Jere. Meanwhile, his assistants and 'astronauts in training'—a group of young males in their late teens, all barefoot and lavishly attired in various hides, skins, cloaks and robes—sat down quietly on the floor in the corner of the studio. They were surrounded by the women who continued to trill and ululate. After asking them to please remain silent Neb Jere began the interview. This time it was conducted in English as his subject spoke it perfectly.

"What are your hopes for Zambia's astronaut training program?" he asked, trying to keep as straight a face as possible amidst this assortment of people who didn't remotely resemble anyone or anything depicted in any of the NASA footage we had shown on the news.

"To go to the moon," the man answered matter-of-factly. He did not wince. That was his intention and that was precisely what he was going to do.

"Is the government funding you?"

"No."

"So where are you getting the money for your work?"

"We have collection boxes in the community. Everyone is contributing. And I am going to make an appeal to the United Nations."

"Yes, but for how much?"

"Enough."

Neb was at a loss for words. He soldiered on. "How do you teach your students to cope with zero gravity?" he asked.

"We put them in big empty metal oil barrels and we roll them down the hill," the self-appointed head of the Academy answered unflinchingly.

"Roll them down a hill in barrels?" Neb responded, desperately trying to suppress a laugh. "Aren't there any injuries?"

"Of course," was the reply. "But in science there is always a cost for progress."

It was priceless. If only we had had videotape back in those days to record the interview. It wasn't just that it was hilariously funny but that there was a naïve conviction that everything the man was saying he believed to be true. As indeed did all his young student astronauts as they gazed in awe at their teacher and leader sitting in the blaze of the studio lights.

What was it that Pliny the Elder once said?

Ex Africa temper aliquid novi.

Always something new out of Africa.

In 1964 I had bought a brand-new light blue Volkswagen Beetle. It was my pride and joy. Because my salary at the television station had never been substantial enough to allow me to rent my own place in Kitwe as well as afford a car I had been living with my parents in the town of Ndola. I had been commuting to Kitwe in my blue 'Bug' via a monotonous pavement road through the bush every day, returning home just after midnight. I will never forget those long nightly trips. There were hardly any other vehicles on the road. Much of the time all you saw were pairs of fiery eyes glaring at you in the middle of the road. They usually belonged to a wild jackal, bush baby or deer that had been mesmerized by the headlights. Honking the horn and flashing the lights usually made them dart away. On either side of the road was the intense darkness of dense bush and forest. Everything looked the same, just inky blackness on the sides and a long ribbon of road stretching ahead. You could get a vague fix on where you were because of the charcoal burners' villages hidden within the forest. There were about half a dozen places where the charcoal burners lived. These were men who plied their trade selling charcoal in the markets in town the following day. Their unseen presence created an assuring aroma. At least you knew that you weren't the only human alone in the vast emptiness of the African night.

By 1965 my days in Central African television were almost over. President Kaunda had issued an edict stipulating that all jobs in Zambia Television were to be taken over by blacks—'Zambianized' was the official term. Within six months all white staff members were to vacate their positions. We had a domestic servant at home by the name of David Phiri. Softly-spoken and ever-obliging, David had been in my parents' employ for nearly five years. It was David who always left something warm in the oven for me when I got back from work late at night. We were extremely fond of him. It was hard to judge his age but I guess he was about five or six years older than I was. He came from the Chewa clan far to the north. He had received some education in his youth so he could read and write. He was fascinated by photography so one year we gave him a 35mm camera for Christmas. He and I often sat under the mango tree in our backyard discussing photography, exposures and lenses. His dream was to one day have his own darkroom and processing equipment and go into business on his own as a wedding photographer. One afternoon when I wasn't on call at the studio I told him that I was thinking of returning to South Africa. He was more than a little upset. We had become close friends and confidants. He admitted that he would miss me if I left. I told him that I did not want to leave but that I had little choice now that the process of 'Zambianization' was taking away white jobs all over the country. My place at the TV station would soon be replaced by a local black person. He suggested that I see someone who could advise me on whether it was a good idea to return to South Africa or not.

"Like who?" I asked.

"I know someone," he said. "In the township. I will take you there."

He told me that he would accompany me to see a *nganga*. He said that the one he knew could see far into the future and would offer me guidance as to what I should do with my life.

On my next day off work David and I rattled our way along a series of rutted dirt roads in my Beetle to a small council house in the black township on the outskirts of town. I was expecting to meet a man but the person who opened the blistered and creaky unpainted door was a woman. She was old, short, wrinkled and an albino. Albinism is a genetic condition that produces little or no pigmentation in the skin. Though a native-born Bemba her skin was whiter than mine. Despite the warm weather she wore a full-length dark skirt with a heavy grey woolen shawl over her shoulders. No introductions were made and nothing was said as she showed us in to a cramped little room. The drapes on the single window were drawn and the place was dark and musty. It smelt of camphor, eucalyptus oil and *Vicks VapoRub*. A battered old couch was on one side of the room and a small wooden table and two folding chairs on the other. On a wall was a faded black and white photograph of the Victoria Falls on the Zambezi River and on the adjoining wall a large, dusty reproduction of a painting depicting *The Last Supper*.

On the cool concrete floor lay a woven grass mat about four-feet square in size. The old woman sat down cross-legged on one side of the mat and indicated that David and I should sit on the floor opposite her. She spoke no English. She glanced at me briefly and then exchanged a few short words in Bemba with David. She reached into the shadowed corner behind her and produced a small leather bag. She lay that before me and alongside it placed a yellow small plastic tub of tobacco snuff. She opened the bag, held it in front of me and indicated that I should take a pinch of the brown powder and sprinkle it into the bag. Then she said something to David and he translated, saying: "State your name into the bag and blow into it."

I muttered my name and blew. The *nganga* eyed me for a second and then smiled briefly before she turned the bag upside down and spilled about three dozen small objects onto the mat—mainly animal bones but also fragments of ostrich shell, tiny patches of hide, an eagle's talon, small stones, a pair of dice and old pre-independence silver and copper coins depicting silhouettes of Queen Elizabeth II. Then she leaned forward and began staring down at the pattern in which the little oracular objects had fallen. I was watching her eyes carefully. What was she seeing? In the dim light of the room her pupils were large. And then the strangest thing happened. Her pupils suddenly became constricted as though she had just seen something very bright. Her body physically jerked backwards and with a whimper she covered her eyes. Then she called something out in Bemba to David. He quickly grabbed me by the wrist and said: "She wants to know what all the big lights are."

I did not understand and whispered: "What lights?"

"The ones around you," said David. "She says you are surrounded by very big lights."

I thought for a second and then it hit me. Could she be referring to the banks of lighting in the studio at the TV station in Kitwe?

"Does she mean the place where I work?" I asked.

David said something very softly to her and she nodded in the affirmative. Then she leaned forward again to study the scattered objects. She began prodding at them with a long, wrinkled forefinger. Now she could not be stopped. She began cackling words and sentences at an alarming rate, almost as though she were reading from invisible notes. David had trouble keeping up with her but as she disgorged information he tried his best to stay abreast for my benefit. The information she was giving was astonishing. She said I would go back across the wide river to the south. In years to come I would be surrounded by even more big lights but that I would also spend much of my time outdoors. I would feel the rays of the sun on my skin often and see things that most people could not even imagine. I would travel through the great waterways and wild places of the world. One of them would be all white. There would be no color there, she said, shaking her head in disbelief at what she was seeing. "White. Only white," she muttered in Bemba.

She told David I would marry two times. I would have four children. I would nearly be killed by a "great angry beast" in the veld. I must be wary of the "big water." It would be very dangerous and try to destroy me. I would know distant places and towns and I would meet many important people. I would come face to face with someone who was once very close to "the most evil person who ever lived." She ran the back of her hand over her forehead when she said that, almost as if she was trying to ward off the evil that surrounded this person that I would meet. One day I would settle far, far away to the north, across "many big waters." The time would come when I would be stricken by a very serious sickness. It would bring me very close to death. On and on she went, for a full twenty minutes or more. I wished that I had been taking notes of her rantings. When she finished she leaned back, sighed, clapped her hands three times and whispered something to the rafters above us.

"She is saying thank you to the ancestors," David whispered. "Clap your hands three times."

I did so, in unison with David. Then he too looked up and said something in Bemba. I presumed they were words of gratitude so in English I softly uttered, "Thank you."

I wasn't sure exactly who it was that we were thanking but then I said: "Can I ask her something?"

David addressed the old woman and she nodded. "Yes, you may," he said.

I asked if I would ever be able to come back to Zambia again. I felt a great affinity with the country and I would like to return someday. David translated this for me and the old woman thought for a moment and then offered her response. David looked at me and said: "You will always be a part of Africa. It is in your spirit. You already have it. She says the sign of that is stamped on your skin. But to make sure that you come back you must bury something of personal value in the soil."

I nodded but I understood little of what he meant. Then,

without speaking, the *nganga* got up and smiled. She dusted off her backside, turned and disappeared through a doorway into an adjoining room. Nothing more was said. David explained that she must be exhausted from hearing the spirits of her ancestors and that we should go. I slipped a £5 note under the grass mat where the bones still lay and we left.

For days I pondered on what the *nganga* had said. The only thing that I could relate to was her remark that I had Africa stamped on my skin. That was true. I have an inch-long birthmark on my right ankle. At that time it was in the perfect shape of a map of Africa. I had been wearing long trousers when I had gone for the reading so how did she know that? But David had seen me in shorts many times. Could he have told her that? But then why would he? As for the rest, nothing made sense. Face to face with someone close to the most evil person who ever lived? What did that mean? A home far to the north across the big waters? An illness in the future? A place where there was no color? Almost lose my life to a great beast? The big water will try to kill me? What did it all mean? Nevertheless, I was convinced there was substance in what she had said. I felt that whatever she had seen or felt or had been told by her ancestors would surely come to pass. I was determined to heed her advice about burying something to ensure that I would always be able to return to Zambia. A week after the session with her I drove up a little-used narrow dirt road to a hill overlooking Ndola. Armed with a garden spade I dug a hole in the soft soil under a mupapi tree and buried a sealed tin box about six-inches square. It once contained a dozen *Uiltjie* Dutch cigars that my father constantly smoked as he toiled over tiny coil springs, cogs and wheels at his watchmaker's desk. But now it contained a passport-size black and white photograph of me, a silver neck chain and a little silver locket in the shape of Africa. I had acquired them a couple of years earlier and they were among my most prized possessions. I had wrapped them tightly in a blue and white hankie and, as advised by the old albino diviner, I committed them to the earth. It was my fervent hope that my links with the heart of Africa would forever remain strong and true.

Four

On my return to South Africa I got a job at one of the country's largest film production companies. To be honest, I only saw that as a stepping stone. My sights were set on higher places but I knew that I needed more experience before I could take the plunge. Ever since I saw Esther Williams in the movie *Bathing Beauty* as a very young child with my mother I was fascinated by Hollywood. I always wanted to work there. To me, Hollywood was holy ground, the inner sanctum of filmmaking. I began to lay plans to eventually get there, come what may.

Alpha Film Studios in Johannesburg had a large staff of local technicians and creative talents. There were also many who had been recruited from abroad. Ian Wilson, one of the cinematographers, was from the UK. He took a liking to me and quickly shuffled me under his wing. He was only five years older than I was but he was extraordinarily talented. And caring. He became one of the most influential people in my life, teaching me everything he knew about the intricacies of our craft. He drummed into me the fact that cinematography was a combination of science and art, especially in those days when film was still a complicated mechanical and photochemical process. Precision engineering, gears, wheels, optics, light, lenses, rolls of celluloid, thermodynamics and great vats of chemicals were combined in a carefully measured synthesis of shadows, light and composition to create moving images on the screen. Of the countless number of people that I worked with around the world in subsequent years, to this day I regard Ian as my tutor, my *mentor extraordinaire*, the man who gave me my career.

Another person at the studio who left an imprint on me was a young assistant director by the name of Bill Pullen. He and his wife Sybil were *satsangis* or followers of Swaminarayan Sanstha. This was a Hindu path of spiritual development started in India during the 18th century. Bill occasionally used to come over to my small apartment in Hillbrow in Johannesburg and describe in glowing terms the virtues of Hinduism. I must confess that I had a poor perception of what he was talking about or what the real appeal was. Not only was he very excitable but half the time he was stoned on weed. Though illegal and certain to get you locked up by the cops if you were caught smoking it the favorite joint at that time was rolled from what adepts called 'D.P.' or 'Durban Poison.' This was a potent marijuana leaf grown in the highlands around the sugar cane fields in the province of Natal. I took a puff of it once or twice, nearly coughed my lungs out so I preferred it when it was baked in brownies or brewed in a tea. Adding it to soup was effective too.

When I did finally begin to grasp a little of what Bill was trying to explain to me about the Hindu path I was very taken with the overall concepts practiced by his group. The most appealing of all was their conviction that mercy and compassion towards all sentient beings was essential. Naturally, Bill and his *satsangi* colleagues were all vegetarians, something that I first found not only odd but downright weird. Then, one afternoon during a break from shooting he and I had lunch together at a popular steakhouse up the road from the studio. He ordered a baked potato and salad. When I ordered my usual hamburger he flew into a rage.

"Do you know what you just ordered?" he hissed, saliva spraying all over me.

"A hamburger," I replied.

"Yes!" he yelled. "Dead meat!"

I had never thought of it that way. He ranted on.

"*Murdered flesh!* Murdered for *you!*"

I was shaken. But he was right. That night he and Sybil came over and explained the concept of karma to me.

"Not only are you depriving the animal of its life," they expounded, "but it died suffering and in pain. For you. Our

Swami teaches that you will one day be accountable for that. It's all about balance. And once you understand that reincarnation is one of the primary principles behind life you may start to see things differently. Even the Christian Bible says that you will reap what you sow. You will have to pay a price for your actions."

It all suddenly fell into place. It was like a collection of children's toy blocks with letters of the alphabet on them being tossed out of a box and as they clattered to the nursery floor they fell into an ordered sequence that spelt out complete sentences. It all made perfect sense. Reincarnation. Cruelty. Balance. Responsibility. Karma. I bought the message immediately. Next day I became a vegetarian and have remained so ever since. Ian and Bill. They changed my life.

In addition to shooting on the soundstage I spent a lot of time on location. That brought me into a head-to-head clash with apartheid in all its forms. The laws of segregation had become more rigidly applied since I had left the country for Northern Rhodesia. Absolute divisiveness was the order of the day. Whenever we traveled away from the studio white crews were accommodated in comfortable hotels; black members of the crew had to be accommodated separately, often in substandard quarters which they shared with the cleaning staff, cooks and waiters in the nether regions and unseen warrens of hotels. In small towns there was nowhere for them to stay so we had to put them up with black church groups, in local community centers or in rented rooms in black townships or 'locations' as they were called. On farms, in rural areas and especially in national parks it was worse. Sometimes they had to make do with tents. The awful feeling of false superiority that this generated within me was horrible. At mealtimes during filming blacks couldn't eat with us. There was always a separate area set aside for them. On some productions they weren't even fed the same food as we were. A lot of the time they received only a standard issue of *pap en vleis*, the stiff cornmeal porridge, gravy and meat that was a staple in tribal areas and popular among domestic servants. They even had to have their own utensils, plates, drinking fountains. White toilets were off-limits to them. They had to go shuffling behind alleyways to relieve themselves in dirty facilities labelled 'Non-Whites Only.' It was an impossible situation.

Nelson Mandela and the leaders of the African National Congress (ANC) were now locked away in prison on Robben Island with life sentences for 'plotting to overthrow' the white regime. The talk of the day was the coming bloodbath. Many whites were predicting a revolution within five years. Apart from the fear that this generated my overwhelming emotion at the time was one of guilt. Blacks were under curfew in white cities. In places like Cape Town Colored people—those of 'mixed blood,' born to a black mother and white father or vice versa—had been physically removed from urban areas. In Durban the entire Indian population had been thrown out of the city. The 'Group Areas Act' was slicing ever deeper into the fabric of society. It was intolerable. It was time to leave.

Early in 1966 I departed for North America by way of London. Because there was such a stigma against white South Africans due to the apartheid policies it was extremely difficult to get permission to live in the United States. The Canadians were more forgiving. They accepted me as an immigrant. So, from Montreal—where I worked for the prestigious National Film Board of Canada—I eventually got to Los Angeles.

The Americans had done much to condemn South Africa and its racist behavior. For years an endless tirade of criticism in the press and at the UN had issued forth from Washington. But after a four-day-long bus ride to LA from Quebec I was shocked to discover how racially divided America still was. Wasn't this supposed to be the bastion of democratic values? So why were those 'Colored Waiting Room' and 'Colored Restroom' signs all over the place? Why didn't I see black people driving around in automobiles in small towns? LA itself, probably one of the most liberal of America's liberal cities, was still very much a white-dominated enclave. Not to speak of Hollywood itself. With few exceptions the motion picture industry was a white industry. Most blacks were maids, waiters, laborers, baggage handlers, gas station attendants. There were still signs everywhere saying 'Whites Only' or 'Coloreds Not Served Here.' The body language of people spoke for itself. There was an aura of supplication, of submission, of suppression in the interface between blacks and whites. And all this in a country that was one of the most vociferous in the campaign of condemnation against South Africa. I could not believe the hypocrisy.

Nevertheless, Hollywood was enchanting. It was everything I hoped it would be. Ever since Orson Welles had called it "the biggest electric train set any boy ever had" this was where the hardware and the creative talents of the industry were clustered. I was awe-struck by the major studios, one more gargantuan than the other. They were filled with the magical tools of the trade. The massive soundstages, outdoor water tanks, backlots, gleaming trucks, lighting generators and camera cranes thrilled me. But Africa kept gnawing at my soul. One evening—after a long day spent with a camera crew on the set of a forgettable romantic thriller called *Caprice* featuring Doris Day and Richard Harris at the 20th Century Fox studios—I went to see *Born Free* at a theater on Hollywood Boulevard. I sobbed. The grasslands and hills of Kenya tore at my soul. The lions and other wild animals glared directly at me from the screen. It felt as though they were imploring me to come home. Throw in the hauntingly beautiful music score by John Barry and the lovely colonial and British accents of Bill Travers, Virginia McKenna and Geoffrey Keen and I was ready to heed the call. The American Civil Rights movement was not *my* struggle. The Selma to Montgomery march was not *my* fault. Vietnam was not *my* war. As much as I admired the efforts being spent to end the violence in Southeast Asia and to tear down racial barriers in the United States I could not be drawn into the conflict. I could not identify with it. I was a film maker. I was white. Opportunities had been thrown at my feet. And I loved America, especially Hollywood. But I was African, pure and simple. I had no choice. I had to return.

No sooner had I made the choice than I realized what a foolish mistake I had made. What was there for me, a young white man, in independent black Africa in the late sixties? My mission was to visit my parents in Zambia and then go back to South Africa. My burning desire was to make my own equivalent of a *Lawrence of Arabia*, but set in Africa. More than anything I wanted to make a movie about the 19th century slave trade and about one of the key figures who fought against it, the Scottish missionary and explorer Dr. David Livingstone. But what of apartheid that still ruled the south of the continent? That system was not a prerogative or fault of mine either. I suddenly abhorred the idea of going back. What had I been *thinking?* This became especially troublesome after my parents picked me up at Ndola airport. As we drove down Broadway, the town's main boulevard with its shadowed canopy of flame trees and jacarandas, I looked out of the window and felt repulsed by my stupidity. So much had transpired since I last saw my parents that I found I had little to talk to them about. I was a different person, a new man. I'd worked in Hollywood. I'd seen a big chunk of the world. New York, Paris, Rome, Munich, Athens. I'd had a steamy affair with a beautiful married woman who was going through a divorce in Toronto. And now here I was in the same old Ndola again. Nothing had changed. It all suddenly seemed so boring, so small and insipid. It was as though time had stood still. The street signs and the trimmed lawns looked exactly as I'd seen them when I left the country years ago. Even the same stray dog lay in the same spot of shade under the same tree. Seized with panic, I don't think I was the least bit pleased to see the house and my mother's garden and flower beds as the car pulled into the driveway. It was only when I saw our servant David Phiri's beaming face as he raced out of the house to greet me that I started feeling a little less insecure. We hugged each other like long-lost brothers.

A few weeks later I was back in Johannesburg. My good friend and mentor Ian Wilson was now living in London. He had been asked to shoot a full-length feature film in South Africa but commitments at Pinewood Studios prevented him for taking on the assignment. He suggested me for the job and, like miraculous manna descending from heaven, it was offered to me. So off I went, back to the land of my birth.

Five

I expected to find a depressed, demoralized and stagnant society reeling under the yoke of apartheid in South Africa. Instead, the country I came back to was thriving. Blacks were still deprived third-class people and economically depressed but wherever I looked I saw growing white affluence. Everywhere was urban construction and industrial development on a colossal scale. The country was producing most of what it needed, even its own line of automobiles with the help of foreign companies like General Motors. With French and Italian assistance military aircraft were also coming off local assembly lines. Less than four years earlier the United Nations Security Council had imposed an arms embargo against South Africa, but few countries heeded it. ARMSCOR, the state-owned armaments manufacturer, was gearing up to produce much of what the Defense Force required to implement apartheid and to defend it against anyone desirous of liberating the majority black population. At the government-run Pelindaba nuclear research center outside Pretoria atomic weapons were also under development and a small stockpile of low-yield nuclear bombs was being amassed. Whatever could not be made locally was easily available on world markets. The gold price was high. The strength of the Rand could procure anything. Under President Lyndon B. Johnson the United States, though still vehemently critical of South Africa's policies, was doing little to physically stifle apartheid. Besides, the US was still trying to deal with racial troubles of its own in the Deep South. With the exception of Scandinavia, most European countries also did nothing except utter words of criticism. So, as far as South Africa was concerned, it was business as usual.

In the sixties Johannesburg's skyscrapers thrust higher and ever more confidently into the African sunlight. The city reverberated to the continuous rattle of jackhammers and pneumatic drills.

Johannesburg was becoming a modern metropolis. Shopping centers, suburbs and highways sprang up all over the place. New factories spread across the landscape. Immigration was high. The government encouraged whites from Europe to make South Africa their home. From all over they came, Dutch, Germans, Italians, Britons, Greeks. Airfares were subsidized for these 'new' white South Africans. Because 'job reservation' laws prevented blacks from working in many sectors of industry and commerce almost unlimited opportunities existed for skilled white immigrants. Despite increasing international criticism of apartheid the Nationalist government, smug in the country's booming prosperity, thumbed its nose at the world. As those in authority saw things the threat to white domination lay not only from blacks within the country itself but from forces from the outside. But they believed that local blacks were so subjugated there was little chance of an internal uprising succeeding. The general feeling was that with the leaders of the African National Congress (ANC) safely locked up or in exile the police and the military were well prepared to deal with any attempt from within to topple the government.

Capitalizing on the Cold War, Pretoria bolstered its military muscle by proclaiming communism to be the most dangerous of all evils. Behind every potential black terrorist, they argued, loomed a Russian or a Chinese. Blacks were merely puppets on a string being manipulated from Moscow or Peking (as Beijing was then still called). *"Die swart gevaar"* ("the black threat") was merely a front for *"die rooi gevaar"* ("the red threat"). The Minister of Defense, Pieter Willem Botha—who would become Prime Minister in 1978 and State President in 1984—had this to say: "We must not forget that the final communist target in Africa is the Republic of South Africa. If the Suez Canal closed and if the sea route round the Cape came under communist control a great section of the West might be forced to surrender to communism. The Cape of Good Hope remains not only the good hope for our own Republic but a stable South Africa means a safe and more secure subcontinent. Whatever the attitude adopted against us by the present governments of the USA and Britain South Africa will not surrender. We have set ourselves the task to build South Africa into a bulwark and beacon of light under the Southern Cross."

It was the old Afrikaner philosophy all over again. Whites were the saviors of Africa. They were its sole source of redemption from evil forces both from within and outside the continent. With Bible, gun and apartheid neatly tucked under his arm the white man, especially the Afrikaner, would maintain a bastion of power.

The motion picture I was going to photograph played directly into this theme. Thanks to Ian Wilson I could not believe my good fortune and I began working on my first theatrical movie as Director of Photography before my 23rd birthday. *The Long Red Shadow* was, as the publicity material touted it, "A story as new as tomorrow's headlines." Centered around the romantic involvement between two young people who lived on neighboring farms it was the tale of an attempted communist takeover of a fictitious African country. The shoestring budget made for a difficult production. We faced a real challenge to make it look and feel bigger than the money allowed. Percival Rubens turned out to be a very talented director with a great visual sense. We worked extremely well together. On release the movie got fair local reviews and the photography was praised. Some distributors abroad thought they could make a few bucks out of it and called it "a daringly refreshing independent film from South Africa's fledgling film industry." It was accepted for showing at the Cannes International Film Festival the following year which probably helped launch my career as a theatrical Director of Photography.

While white theaters, especially the drive-in theater circuits, were filled with local product nothing was being made for black audiences. In those days, the black population simply did not exist as far as the film industry was concerned. That situation would only change with the advent of television years later, in 1976. In the meantime, there were lots of feature films, documentaries and commercials to photograph. My career began to blossom. I had also become the South African correspondent for the London-based annual *International Film Guide*. As a film maker I subscribed to a number of professional publications including *American Cinematographer*, France's *Cahiers du Cinéma* and the British monthly, *Films & Filming*. On one occasion I received a notice in the mail ordering me to see the local postmaster about "an important matter." When I went in to find out what was going on I was quietly ushered into the postmaster's office. He sternly told me that I was in contravention of the Immorality Act. What? What had I done?

"You are importing illegal and immoral material into the country," he said in a heavy Afrikaans accent.

When I asked him to please explain himself he opened a safe and pulled out an envelope. Then, holding it as though it were something that would contaminate him, he handed it over to me.

"I mean this," he said, an intense frown scrunching up his forehead. The envelope was addressed to me. From the label I recognized it as my monthly copy of *Films & Filming* from London. The package had been neatly slit open and the contents examined.

"I don't understand," I said.

"The pictures inside," the postmaster said, tapping his forefinger on his desk. "They're pornographic."

Pornography in South Africa was a sin as unforgivable as sex between a white and a non-white person. Neither were tolerated. I sometimes wondered how people even managed to procreate because of the strict Calvinistic approach to all things sexual.

"You can go to jail for importing filth like that," the man scowled at me.

I flicked through the magazine. There were harmless critical reviews of films currently in release in Europe, production reports, news of forthcoming releases and then I saw what he was referring to. Two of the pages contained black and white photographs of a new Polish film depicting a young couple making love. It was innocent enough. There was not a genital to be seen. But they were naked. Even worse, they were naked *together*. I was told that the magazine was to be confiscated and that I would be reported to the police if anything like this ever arrived in the mail again. After protesting and explaining that I was a film maker and a writer and that I actually needed this type of publication to keep abreast of my profession I was handed a pile of documents and application forms that would be "submitted to the proper authorities to secure special permission for the importation of the material in question."

My God, I wondered, didn't these people have better and more important things to do than rip open people's mail simply to find what in their opinion were lurid pictures? But then that was South Africa in the sixties. Big Brother had to be on the constant lookout for subversive and immoral material that might jeopardize the security of the state. I asked whether doctors and artists had to go through the same process. After all, they too dealt with nudity. My question was met with a singular lack of humor and I was ushered out of the office. So, once a year I had to go to the post office in whichever city I was living to sign those annoying application forms giving me special dispensation to import literature essential to my profession.

After shooting documentaries on topics that ranged from the manufacture of ball bearings, steel cables, pharmaceuticals and fertilizer to tuberculosis, family planning and organic farming in 1967 I was offered a particularly interesting assignment. A trio of wealthy Americans were flying out from California to go on a hunting safari in the neighboring Portuguese 'province' of Mozambique. They wanted a filmed record of their trip. Hunting animals was something that always repulsed me. I never quite knew what attracted people to this so-called 'sport.' How could anyone justify killing a defenseless wild animal with a high-powered rifle or a bow and arrow for fun? If this was a way for men or women to prove their machismo or virility or simply fantasize about increasing the size and efficacy of their genitalia I could think of a hundred better ways to do it without inflicting injury and death on an innocent creature doing little more than what nature intended it to do by following its instinctual behavior in the bush. Well, here was a perfect opportunity to find out what drove people to this madness. I would fly from Johannesburg to Lourenco Marques (now Maputo) in Mozambique, make contact with the safari company, then fly on to Beira where I would meet up with the hunters. The whole thing certainly appealed to the adventurous spirit within me. It carried with it shades of *King Solomon's Mines*, *The Snows of Kilimanjaro* and Hemingway's *Green Hills of Africa*.

Lourenco Marques was very popular with South African tourists. The warm waters of the Indian Ocean lapped at its shores. Mozambique, like Angola on the West Coast on the opposite side of the subcontinent, was an African possession of Portugal. As such they were regarded not only as colonies but as provinces of the motherland. Mozambique's largest city was famous for its freshly caught shellfish and prawns prepared chili *piri-piri* style. There were giant locally grown cashew nuts, *Laurentina* beer, bullfights, handmade glazed pottery and the more relaxed openness of its society compared to South Africa. While racial discrimination was as real here as anywhere else on the subcontinent no one would look askance at you if you had a black woman on your arm as you entered a striptease joint or a nightclub. And you needn't look over your shoulder in case you were seen slipping into a brothel with a hooker—white or black, female or male—in one of the many little arcades leading off Lourenco Marques' boulevards and sidewalks.

There were topless beaches and nudist resorts. There was sex across the color bar, a thing that would have got you locked up in South Africa. Lourenco Marques was a slice of Portugal basking under a hot African sun. Tall palm trees whispered in the breeze. Wide avenues were lined with outdoor restaurants, bars and coffee shops. Guitars and *fado* songs drifted amidst the laughter, clinking glasses and clatter of plates in taverns along the beachfront. For South Africans wishing to escape their rigid, stifling and regulated society this was paradise, the perfect place to get away from it all. Whenever you went across the border to Mozambique you simply said you were "going to L.M.," whether it was actually to Lourenco Marques itself or to one of the many popular vacation resorts like Joao Belo, Inhambane, Xai-Xai, Vilanculos or the islands of Bazaruto and Santa Carolina.

By 1960 local tribes in Mozambique had begun agitating for freedom and independence from Portugal. A large protest to the Provincial Governor resulted in soldiers firing on the crowd, killing scores. Exiled black Mozambican leaders hiding out in Dar Es Salaam set up a liberation movement called FRELIMO (the Front for the Liberation of Mozambique) in 1962. And so, another in a long list of African wars was ignited. But Portugal was tough on dissenters and freedom fighters. By the mid-sixties there were more than 70,000 Portuguese troops in the territory. Like South Africa, Portugal held onto power through subjugation of the local populace through the barrel of a gun.

As I flew from Lourenco Marques to the northern port city of Beira in the DETA Airlines Fokker Friendship airliner I looked down on virginal Africa. There wasn't even a road that connected Lourenco Marques in the far south to Beira, located halfway up the coast, a distance of about 470 miles. The countryside was magnificent, a blend of yellows, browns and greens clutching at the Indian Ocean on one side and spreading deep into thick and unspoiled vegetation on the other. I spent a couple of days checking out my gear in Beira while I awaited the arrival of the three hunters. We were going to be together for a month and I wondered what they would be like. I loved Americans, but these guys were going to shoot animals for trophies and for fun. What kind of people were they? What could possibly justify the enormous expense of coming out here to kill animals? My curiosity was answered one sunny morning as I stood outside the small single building that constituted the Beira International Airport and watched the TAP Portuguese Airlines Boeing 707 materialize out of the hot sky and plop down on the runway, blue smoke puffing from its tires. The aircraft had flown in from Lisbon where the Americans had made their connection from Los Angeles via New York.

The plane was filled with passengers but only three people emerged from the first-class section. Each one was dressed in khaki fatigues and sported expensive sunglasses. Clearly, these were my white hunters, all gung-ho and ready for action. Admittedly, they were a very nice bunch of guys. I'll refer to two of them only by their first names. Brooke was probably in his late thirties and Cal in his early thirties. If memory serves me correctly both were either stockbrokers or lawyers. The leader of the trio was 42-year-old Arthur 'Spud' Melin, president of the Wham-O Toy Company. All smiles and bursting with energy, he turned out to be a terrific guy. He was smart, well-informed and very funny. I learned that he was the mastermind behind some of the most successful toys in history. Spud and his partner Richard Knerr founded their manufacturing empire in 1948 with the introduction of a slingshot. According to Spud, he invented it to shoot bits of meat and liver into the air for his trained falcons back in San Bernardino, California. Kids started buying the slingshots by the dozen, bringing fame and fortune to the company. Spud later met a guy who had created a plastic flying disc called the *Pluto Platter*. The company bought the rights, modified the disc and renamed it the *Frisbee*. Once again history was made. When the two founders heard of Australian children using a bamboo ring for exercise in the late fifties they mass produced it in plastic and called it the *Hula Hoop*. It caused a sensation. 25 million of them were sold within four months of their introduction. The craze swept the world including South Africa. Even I had one as a kid.

Once all the baggage had been unloaded from the 707 the cargo hold was opened. Every single item that came out of it belonged to the hunters. There were boxes, satchels, trunks, cases and crates. These were packed to capacity with powerful hunting rifles, ammunition, telescopic sights and the paraphernalia of the hunter. Even the customs official was dumbfounded at the amount of stuff the men had brought with them. There was enough hardware and weaponry among them to fight a war. After a couple of hours the necessary paperwork and clearances were completed and we were free to go. Two twin-engine Beechcraft planes had been chartered to fly the group and all our equipment to Zinave, a hunting concession along the banks of the Save River in central Mozambique. The concession—one of the biggest in Africa—belonged to the safari operator, Safarilandia. Off we went, two airplanes packed with enough weaponry to turn the tide of battle that was raging between Portugal and FRELIMO. But that was not our purpose. Beira disappeared behind us as we flew through a beautifully clear sky to a dirt airstrip deep within the bush.

The men in charge of the safari were waiting for us at the airfield in two olive brown open-topped Toyota Land Cruisers. These vehicles were just beginning to find favor in Africa after years of domination by the British-made Land Rover. Wally Johnson was a blonde, good-natured kind of a guy. I'd place him somewhere in his early thirties. Ken Fubbs was the quieter one of the two. Dark haired, bespectacled, pipe-smoking, perhaps in his early forties. Both men were highly experienced in their profession, excellent marksmen, tanned, and casually dressed in khaki shirts and shorts. Sporting a very warm welcome they strode out to greet us. After the overtures it took three trips for both vehicles to carry all the equipment from the aircraft to the base camp. There we were met by at least twenty black men. Four of them were guides-cum-trackers who doubled as personal assistants to Wally and Ken, some were bearers, the rest employees at the camp. The place smelt of the sweet, freshly-cut thatch that was used for patching the grass roofs of the crude brick and mud-walled buildings. There was a large kitchen, four or five bungalows containing simple metal-framed beds protected by mosquito nets, a large recreation area with a bar and dining room, a bathroom with hot and cold running water and various huts devoted to skinning and packing parts of animals that had been shot. A small newly-built brick house stood in a clearing not far from the camp. Wally lived there with his curvaceous and attractive wife whose name I no longer remember. Where the black staff slept I have no idea.

The first night in camp was interesting. Sipping cocktails in the bar Spud presented me with a list of shots his advertising agency wanted me to get on film. Apparently the Wham-O company had bought a weekly half-hour of airtime on a local TV station in LA and the agency was hoping to air a documentary about the safari. The plan was to feature most of Wham-O's products in the film. When Spud showed the list to Wally, Ken and I we cracked up with laughter. The rough shooting script called for a Hula Hoop to be tossed around the neck of a giraffe, a *'Super Ball'*—basically a ball made of a synthetic compound that made it bounce higher and faster than a regular rubber ball—was to be given to troops of local baboons to see what they would make of it. Some weird stuff called *'Nutty Putty'* was to be given to monkeys and baboons to play with. The agency also suggested presenting slingshots to kids in local tribal villages to see whether they could bring down any birds with them. It was an ambitious list. And utterly ridiculous.

"No, Spud," I protested as diplomatically as I could. "This is

Africa, not a zoo or a Hollywood-trained animal farm. This stuff will never work. Let's just film you guys shooting animals with guns, OK?"

Ken and Wally agreed and we partied well into the night. After much discussion Spud, Cal and Brooke slowly recognized the naïve folly of what the ad agency was hoping to get out of the trip. Round about midnight we hit the sack, ready to take on the wilds of Africa.

The mornings were always the nicest times of day. The world was fresh and filled with promise. A low mist drifted through the bush, slowly dissipating as the rays of the rising sun filtered through leaves and scrub. We normally left camp at about 5.30 or six, the thorn trees and tall grass awash in golden light. Spud and I usually traveled with Wally and a tracker in one Land Cruiser while Brooke and Cal rode with Ken and a tracker in the other. A large four-wheel drive truck was always a short distance behind us. In it were the 'pick-up boys' whose job it was to collect the carcasses of shot animals and transport them back to the camp. We would follow winding dirt tracks or simply plunge through virginal wilderness, the tracker constantly on the lookout for animal spoor. The place teemed with wildlife or, as the hunters and even many people nowadays still call it, 'game.' I detest that word. It implies that all wild animals are the playthings of humans, the objects of our hunting urges. I find that offensive. Wild animals are wildlife, not 'game.'

There were countless herds of impala with their orange-brown hides and white underbellies, curving antlers, and tails that whirred like little propellers whenever they were nervous. There were enormous gatherings of zebra and wildebeest, two herbivorous yet very different mammals that always kept one another company. You'd never see one without the other. There were groups of buffalo, usually in the reeds near the rivers as the sun rose. Monkeys and baboons darted from branch to branch in the tall mopane, acacia, wisteria, weeping boerboon, kiaat, sweet thorn and syringa trees. Here and there the forest was broken by vast open tracts of yellow veld, dry riverbeds, low bush and heavy groves of candelabra trees. Antelopes included the fleet-footed lechwe or gemsbok with its distinctive grey coat, black underbelly and straight, graceful antlers. Its cousins, sable and roan antelopes, were also plentiful. These large creatures sported tall curving antlers, arced backwards over their sleek black or brown bodies. They were skittish and seldom seen in herds. There were smaller antelope, some no taller than eighteen or twenty inches, like the skittish little Livingstone's suni. Giraffes stared out at you across the trees as they chewed on thorns and leaves with their prehensile tongues. Warthogs often dashed across the dirt tracks, followed by a dozen squealing babies, their tails always pointing straight up in the air. Waterholes and rivers were the homes of hippos and crocodiles. Hyenas were seldom seen during the day but at night their hee-haw calls reverberated everywhere.

Often, even above the noise of the straining diesel engines and whining four-wheel drive transmissions of the Land Cruisers, you could hear elephants tearing bark from trees or pushing dead stumps over. When you actually came across the elephants your heart stopped beating. They were ageless creatures, sojourners on the planet surely originally from some mysterious and faraway place. They were immeasurably strong yet you knew in your heart that these were peace-loving, wise and gentle beings. I know this sounds childishly anthropomorphic, but believe me, elephants have characteristics that defy our understanding. They were always in herds and an incredible sight to behold. Bulls, cows and calves would stare at you with wise, all-knowing eyes, their ears stirring the air to capture your scent. There were the big cats: lion, leopard and cheetah. As the vehicles crashed through thicket and grass, porcupines, hedgehogs and guinea fowl would scatter, the latter taking to the air as it emitted a terrifying screech.

And into this lovely world we humans brought our weapons of destruction. The animals knew that. The mere sight of a convoy of vehicles would upset them. They knew the sharp crack of gunfire would soon follow and that one of their numbers would fall or leap away in agony. Not every bullet finds its mark, especially with inexperienced hunters untrained to hit the spot that brings a quick death. Each of the visiting hunters had expensive licenses allowing him to 'take' a certain number of each species but with no limitation placed on birds. Each of them could shoot one elephant, one mature buffalo and either a lion or a cheetah. Other species could be shot in larger numbers. It was Wally and Ken's job to ensure that the proper quota was adhered to. Each animal has a distinctive spoor and it was the job of the trackers to follow that of a wounded animal because, wherever possible, hunting ethics required that an animal be put out of its misery once it has been shot. Alas, this was something all too often ignored. I wondered how many animals slowly bled to death or suffered from excruciating injuries that had slowly become septic due to bullet wounds.

Before the first hunt took place we were obliged to visit the local chief and pay him our respects. Tribal etiquette required that we meet him and express our gratitude for hunting on his ancestral land. He was a member of the Shangaan ethnic group and was much respected by local tribes who lived in and around the hunting concession. He had five wives and at least twelve children that I could count. He was also a practicing *sangoma* so Wally and Ken asked him to read the bones for us and determine whether our planned hunts would be successful. On the morning that we visited him he was seated outside his personal hut surrounded by his large family. He was wearing a dirty white T-shirt and a dyed cotton cloth tied around his waist. As he sat cross-legged on the ground I could detect a large swelling in his lower abdomen. He was suffering from either a hernia or a severe case of testicular epididymitis in the scrotum. He was clearly in pain but did his best to conceal the fact.

His many wives passed around a large calabash containing homemade beer, a whitish sour-tasting yet nutritious thick liquid fermented from sorghum and corn. After pleasantries were exchanged the chief cast his set of bones onto an antelope skin that had been unfurled on the ground. Yes, he predicted, the hunts would go well. The white men from America would get what they came for. But there was a precautionary note in his interpretation of the bones. We needed to be wary of the elephants. Because of memories of previous hunts they were nervous, making them unpredictable and dangerous. And on this sobering note the meeting was over.

One day it was decided that we'd go after buffalo. Spud's animal fell instantly. He'd caught it straight between the eyes just below the horns; a perfect shot. I got it all on film, the heavy Arriflex camera balanced on my right shoulder like a rifle and a cumbersome rechargeable lead acid battery in a leather case slung over my left shoulder. Those were the days before nickel cadmium batteries, let alone the lithium ion variety used today. Cal's animal took three shots to die. Brooke kept missing and the chase went on until sunset. Finally, we found a group clustered together in a thick clump of reeds on the banks of the Save River. Peering through the finder of the camera I stood behind Brooke in the fading light.

Bam!

Half a horn blew away, exposing part of the animal's skull. It bellowed in pain.

Bam!

It fell to the ground but Ken quickly realized that it was only the front left leg that had been shattered.

Bam!

Blood started spurting from the animal's rump as it struggled to get back on its feet.

"Let me do it," Ken whispered.

"No," replied Brooke. "I've got to do it myself."

The light was almost gone. He aimed again.

Bam!

Another blood-spurting hole as skin and bone tore away from the animal's front shoulder.

"Shit!" hissed Brooke.

Bam!

A total miss.

Bam!

Another leg.

Bam!

I wanted to cry out. It was too awful to see the senseless suffering. I counted eight bullets and twenty minutes before the poor creature finally keeled over, its life drained.

The carnage was horrifying.

One day we were after wildebeest. After picking one out for Cal and following it in the Land Cruisers we were suddenly surrounded by a great herd of them. They were agitated and angry. I saw Ken stop his vehicle. Cal stood up, took aim and fired. The animal's lower jaw was blown away. It kicked up its hind legs, blood and saliva splashing everywhere, and ran. Ken jammed down on the gas, chasing it. It stopped under a tree, separated from the herd, panting frantically. Cal aimed again.

Bam!

A miss.

The animal darted off again but this time, blinded with pain, it crashed headlong into Ken's vehicle. Cal stood up, aimed, and shot. Jesus! Now it was hit in its back. Then Ken stood up and swiped the wildebeest's face with his rifle butt. I heard its skull crack. The animal staggered back.

And then... Bam!

Thank God, Ken had the mercy to shoot it between the eyes, putting it out of its misery.

"Don't worry," he called out to Cal, still standing and

sweating profusely. "You'll get your chance at another one."

The next day was the elephants' turn. Cal got his old bull easily enough. Ken, wearing his trademark khaki outfit and a dark brown baseball cap, had selected it from within a herd of about fifteen animals. One minute the huge creature was looking our way, then a shot rang out from Cal's high-powered rifle and the bull's legs crumpled. It fell with a mighty thud that sent dust and dried grass flying. The rest of the herd stood frozen, then started to run. But they did not go far. I wanted to sob as the younger bulls, followed by the cows and two calves, came back to the fallen animal. They caressed him with their trunks and then tried to push him back up onto his feet again. Ken had to fire into the air to disperse them so that the clean-up crew could cut out the tusks and chainsaw the carcass into pieces for transportation back to base camp.

Because this was the first elephant to be shot we had to observe another local ritual. Tradition demanded that the trunk be donated to the local chief that we had met earlier. The trunk was to be used as an offering of respect for hunting on his tribal land. That evening we all arrived at his village. Once again homemade sorghum beer was passed around. When the big earthenware pot of dried calabash containing the brew reached you, you were obliged to take a big gulp from it. Too much of it and you were soon on your ear, motherlessly drunk. Children were everywhere, tied in blankets on mothers' backs, playing around the huts, seated in wide-eyed groups on the fringe of the central clearing. The big highlight of the evening was the presentation of the elephant's trunk to the chief. This was regarded as a delicacy and an organ containing special *muti* or magical powers. The elephant was sacred to the tribe. It was believed that by ingesting its flesh people would become imbued with the creature's tenacity and strength. One thing is recognized throughout Africa; the elephant is king of the jungle, not the lion. It is the one being that cannot be harmed or brought down by any other, with the exception of man. The blood-stained trunk was ceremoniously handed over by Wally and Ken to the chief who passed it on to his primary wife. She in turn passed it on to the other wives and a few grown daughters who used pangas—large broad-bladed machete-like knives—to chop it into small round pieces. These were dumped into a big black iron pot of boiling water suspended above an open fire.

Then the drumming began. Teenage boys and girls were responsible for the music while the adults began to dance. Wally's trackers and support staff joined in the festivities and soon the forest reverberated to laughter, drumbeat and song. In deference to the occasion Spud, Brooke and Cal also got up to briefly stamp their feet and twist their bodies. I wished I had battery-operated lights or some form of illumination to catch all this on film but the slow color reversal film stock of the time and the lack of suitable lighting equipment made that impossible. I sat in a corner puffing away on my Camel cigarettes and downing mouthfuls of the local brew, observing it all through a haze. Once the trunk had been cooked I wasn't counting on having to partake of any of it but decorum and protocol overruled me. Fortunately, the beer softened the experience and I picked up a small piece of the meat when it was passed around, stuck it in my mouth and chewed. And chewed some more. I have never tasted anything so tough. Knowing that I was a vegetarian the five big white bwanas were howling with laughter as they watched me. After that, things in the village really began to get exciting. It was to be a feast. Large cuts of elephant meat were brought in and hung over the fire to roast. All the locals arrived to gorge on it and to take part in the festivities. The sound of mirth and merriment drifted over the bush as we headed back to our base camp late that evening.

Despite the brutality of what we were doing life at Zinave was fascinating. On some evenings after the hunt we'd flop down exhausted on wicker chairs and couches in the recreation room. Wally would enter the cool parlor, toss his red beret on the bar counter and yell out, "Cervejas!" ("Beer!")

Instantly, trays loaded with bottles of chilled *Laurentina* would appear. The day's activities would be discussed and every so often Wally's pretty wife would stride over from the house to join us. Now and then she would even stay for the evening meal but most of the time it was just us men. This was a safari where you roughed it during the day but where luxuries were never far away at night. You'd come back caked in dust and sweaty grime and then collapse into a hot bath. Then there was ice and martinis and hors d'oeuvres, always beautifully prepared by the black camp chef and his staff. Often the hunters and I would talk about the ethics—or lack of it—of killing animals for sport. But there was no persuading these guys that what they were doing was to me repulsively wrong. They'd laughingly slap me on the back or clink their glass against mine and tut-tut me to hush and forget about it.

"People have been doing what we're doing for millions of years, kiddo," they'd say. "Get real."

And that would be it. Next day, the rifles would be bang-banging away as usual.

For the hunters one of the highlights of the day was the stroll down to the river in the evening. There, high powered rifles with their long-range sights would be exchanged for shotguns. The guys would hide in the reeds as the sun sank beneath the horizon, taking pot shots at guinea fowl, francolin, quails and wild duck as they hooted and screeched overhead, going home to roost for the night. These were often drunken binges, the hunters slurping their bottles of *Laurentina* while the pick-up boys raced hither and thither to retrieve downed birds. Those not dead would have their necks wrung. The chef was particularly adept at turning the flesh from these carcasses into a tasty ground meat sauce that was spread on tortillas and served in the bar with cocktails before dinner. If the drink of the evening was scotch, martinis or vodka, the guy who shot the least number of birds was required to sign the liquor tab for that night. The result was that those little excursions down to the river turned into competitive bloodbaths. You had to bring down as many birds as you could or the bar tab was yours.

Often we left the vehicles to stalk animals on foot. When this happened I was assigned a bearer who carried the camera, battery, tripod and spare film magazines. Sometimes we'd camp out under the stars in sleeping bags, getting an early start back to the vehicles before dawn. The bush was magical at night. On moonless evenings the sky was brilliant with a firmament of silvery dots, all twinkling like lights on a Christmas tree. You could lie there for hours counting streaks of meteorites. There is nothing quite like a night in the African bush. You sense deep regions within your own soul that you were never conscious of before. Perhaps it is because our ancestors millions of years ago walked those plains and gullies, then looked up and wondered what the sky was made of. Perhaps we still have that memory etched within our consciousness. I was aware of something else too. There came a time, especially in lonely, wild, distant places, when we realize how frail, private and different we are. I felt that as I aged—and I was still only 23—there were some things I could never share with others. They were buried in some fathomless place within me. Perhaps 90% of who I was, was too personal, too precious, too private to share with anyone. Perhaps much of me—my beliefs, my longings—were shut off from the world. Maybe they were too painful to share. Thoughts like that made me feel fallible, vulnerable, exposed. And it wasn't confined, enclosed spaces that made me feel that way but the endless infinity of space opened up by the African night. Besides, few if any really understood me, especially when it came to interests that I had in psychic and spiritual matters, largely as a result of my exposure to that amazing Zambian *nganga* years before.

While Cal had got his elephant, neither Spud nor Brooke

had got theirs. One morning the trackers at base camp woke up Wally and Ken long before dawn. News had come in of a big elephant herd about an hour's drive away. It wasn't long before we were all in the Land Cruisers, our bones and teeth clattering as we bounced along a rutted track. Soon after sunrise Wally's assistant pointed to the ground. Elephant footprints. Yes, probably yesterday a big herd had passed this way. Eventually we had to leave the dirt track and crash our way through bush and open veld. We seemed to be driving for hours. I was always worried about my equipment. The vibration and violent motion could dislodge gears, unseat delicate mirrors in the reflex shutter viewing system of the camera or jam rolls of film in the magazines. Suddenly one of the trackers held up his hand and pointed at the grass. Wally and Ken hit the brakes. The tracker jumped down and looked up excitedly. He had found a big lump of elephant dung. Sticking his finger into it he pronounced that it was no more than a few hours old. The herd must be somewhere nearby. Wally and Ken fell into heated discussion and announced that it would probably be best to proceed on foot from there. The elephants were probably moving away because of the noise of the vehicles. When the big Bedford truck reached us with the rest of the team we began to walk. I made sure I had my cigarettes and water bottle with me. One man took the camera and a spare magazine of film while another carried the tripod, battery and shoulder-brace that I used for handheld shooting. The rest of the men carried rifles and ammunition.

"This one's for you, Spud," announced Wally.

So, this was to be Spud's big day to bag his big prize. With two trackers leading, their eyes peeled to the ground, we all followed in single-file formation. Crunching our way through the dried grass, Wally was behind the trackers, then Ken, Spud, Brooke, Cal, me and the bearers in the rear. Whispering back at us Wally said we should be able to catch up with the herd within an hour.

The hour passed slowly. And then another hour went by. By 11am Wally halted the search.

"Let's take a break," he suggested.

I was thankful for that. It gave me a chance to check on whether the camera was OK. It was also a good time to drink some water and take a leak. By noon we were walking again, the heat merciless. Sometimes we were in shade under a canopy of trees, but a lot of the time we were exposed to the sun's blistering rays. Every now and then the trackers would excitedly point out a new clump of dung, and each time it was obviously fresher than the previous one. We were clearly gaining on the herd. But by sundown they were still nowhere in sight. We had brought no food with us, no extra water, no sleeping bags and, worst of all, I had run out of cigarettes. Cal had helped me finish my pack of Camels long before we realized that we were going to have to spend the night sleeping in the bush. When Wally and Ken pointed out a spot where we could bed down in grass and twigs under a thick grove of trees I was dying for a smoke. So was Cal. Even Spud—who rarely lit up—announced a craving for tobacco. Wally called one of the bearers over, giving him instructions in Shangaan. The man looked over at us, laughed, and went about collecting handfuls of grass, dried leaves and, most surprising of all, selected sections from a pile of dried elephant dung. Picking through it he separated the fibers and then mixed them with some grass. This concoction was placed on dry leaves and then expertly rolled up into joints and, voila! Cigarettes, African bush style. When Spud, Cal and I lit up we all agreed that we'd never tasted a better smoke in our lives.

The big problem now was water. Once more the Shangaan bearers came to the rescue. Using Wally's maroon beret they scooped some filthy brackish-looking stuff out of a muddy water hole and squeezed it through the cotton fabric into our water bottles. It tasted awful but it cured our thirst. Night came quickly. Sitting down with my back against a tree I was engaged in a stimulating discussion with Wally and Ken about local lore and legend. The Shangaans are deep believers in the world of the supernatural. Even today, their shamans or *sangomas* are recognized as some of the most powerful in Africa. Translating from his tracker, Wally enthralled Spud, Cal, Brooke and I with interpretations of the Shangaans' vision of creation, their concept of a divine super-intelligent being who rules over the world yet is so remote and so mysterious that few can even conceive of him or it. Equally important was their profound respect for ancestral spirits. The ancestors were everything. They brought rain, wives, virility, happiness, disease, misfortune, money or good luck. They chose the gender of your unborn child, determined the measure of your days and influenced every aspect of your life. It was important to remain on good terms with your ancestors.

Finally, we all dozed off. It had been an exhausting day. Despite the lack of food or beds we were comfortable enough. In fact, I was enraptured by a sense of being swallowed up by the night. It was as black as pitch. Africa wrapped itself around us like a heavy cloak. You could literally feel the darkness. We had no flashlight among us. The sky shimmered above. The bush creaked and croaked to the sounds of cicadas, insects and frogs. Then, slowly, everything went silent. Wally and Ken's trackers suddenly materialized out of the darkness, agitated and whispering softly.

"Sshh!" Wally hissed at us.

"What's wrong?" Spud asked groggily.

"Quiet!" Wally spat back. "It's the elephants!"

"What about them?" Brooke whispered nervously.

"They're here," Wally responded. "The herd. They've completely surrounded us."

I could hear everybody's heart thumping.

"Don't say a word," Ken cut in softly. "And whatever you do, don't anyone *move*."

I suddenly became very frightened. We all sat there in the

darkness. You couldn't see a thing but, as we strained to listen, we could hear them, *feel* them. We could detect the elephants breathing and their low guttural rumblings. But there was an even stranger sound, a gentle whoosh as their ears fanned the air, analyzing our scent. A twig cracked here and there. It was unbelievable. They had crept up on us in perfect silence, an entire herd of elephants, encircling us like a silent army about to pounce on a sleeping encampment. We sat frozen in terror. I heard clicks from Wally and Ken's rifles. I knew they wouldn't shoot. It was impossible to see the animals and, besides, we'd be dead if they so much as tried to fire at them. After what seemed like an eternity Wally whispered: "They've come to warn us."

"About what?" I heard Spud whisper back.

"That they know we're after them," Wally replied. "I think they're telling us to back off. They could easily trample us to death right now but they're not. They want us to leave them alone."

We were stunned. I guess filled with awe would be a better expression. As this thought seeped in I became utterly amazed at their capacity to stealthily creep up on us like invisible ghosts in the night, silently proclaiming their space and their strength. We were in the presence of titans, unquestionably of immeasurable intelligence. They knew precisely what we were after but they had come to ask us to leave them in peace.

"Fuck, I've never known anything like this," I heard Ken whisper.

And so we sat there, petrified. Unbridled respect for the invisible giants was palpable from everyone, tracker and hunter alike.

About an hour before dawn there were muted sounds of grass crackling and twigs breaking. The elephants were leaving. When the sun came piercing through the thorns, shrubs and branches they had gone. They had vanished into the bush as mysteriously and unobtrusively as they had come. We all looked at one another, nobody saying a word. The trackers simply huddled nearby, waiting for Wally and Ken's instructions. Clearly, we had all been altered by the extraordinary night. Spud was the first to speak.

"Forget it, Wally," he sighed, shaking his head.

"What do you mean?" Wally asked.

"I don't want an elephant. Let's head back to the Land Cruisers."

"You don't want to shoot one?"

"After last night? You must be kidding."

Spud could not bring it upon himself to kill an animal that could so easily have destroyed him and yet did not. He had gained newfound respect for creatures that I know he did not have prior to that unbelievable experience. As much as I admired his decision I must confess that he surprised me. A competitive spirit is what drives most Americans. It pervades every aspect of life, from sport to commerce to science and entertainment. Who can get there first? Who can go faster? Who can make it bigger? Who can best outwit the other guy? Who can amass more money? Which team will take the trophy at the Super Bowl? Which movie can outdo all the others at the box office? Who will win the Presidential race for the White House? It's all about competing and winning. And you've *got* to win. Losing is not an acceptable option in American culture. I knew all this from my short time in America. It doesn't hide its competitive nature from the world. In fact, it's proud of it. With good reason too. Competition is the engine of invention and success. America was preparing to send men to the moon because it was in competition with the Soviet Union. Henry Ford invented the assembly line because he was in competition with other automobile manufacturers. Examples raced on and on through my mind but I never knew that the imperative to win could also be linked to such things as hunting.

Brooke, as American as apple pie, wasn't going to go home without bagging his elephant. So, a couple of days later it began all over again. This time, however, Wally and Ken chose a more northerly sector of the Safarilandia concession. Because of what had happened they were not prepared to go after the herd that had eluded us. The two white safari leaders whose livelihood depended on killing animals for trophy and for fun on behalf of their wealthy clients found it within their hearts to spare the elephants who chose not to trample us to death, but another herd would be fine. So off we went in the Land Cruisers and the Bedford truck in search of them. It did not take long to locate them. It was a hot and cloudless afternoon. There they were, a group of about twelve animals half-a-mile away from us, leisurely standing in the shade of a grove of acacia trees, twisting off leaves and branches with their powerful trunks. When Wally held up his hand bringing all the vehicles to a stop my heart sank. There were two calves in the herd. Surely to God the hunters weren't going to shoot into this closely-knit family group where a hierarchy maintained the protection of its young ones. But then I saw the animal that Ken and Wally had singled out for Brooke. It was an old bull, standing apart from the rest of the herd. It was decided that we would leave the vehicles and approach the herd on foot. High-powered rifles were loaded and cocked. I readied the camera. To make things as lightweight as possible I decided to forego using the metal shoulder brace. I pressed the start button and ran a few feet of film. The camera purred beautifully. Though dreading what was to come I was ready for action.

As this was to be Brooke's elephant Ken headed the group with Brooke next to him and me directly behind him. Wally, Spud, Cal, the trackers and assistants followed at a close distance. Taking into account the direction of the slight breeze that was blowing from the east Ken led us on a devious circular route so that the elephants wouldn't catch our scent. Cautiously threading our way through the dry grass and trying to conceal ourselves behind trees and bushes we inched our way towards the old bull.

He merely stood there, swaying slightly, as elephants do. I have no idea how old he was but as African elephants can live up to 60 or 70 years I guess that he must have been at least around half that age. His ears swooshed as he gazed into the distance, totally oblivious of our presence. My heart went out to him. If only he knew what was coming. I wished that the wind would change, that he would catch our scent and run for safety. But he merely stood there unknowingly awaiting his fate. At about a hundred yards from him Ken signaled Brooke to get ready to fire. I sensed his excitement as Ken came to stand beside him. Brooke lifted his rifle and aimed.

"Between the eyes," Ken hissed. "Don't miss."

Time stood still. Brooke centered his target in his telescopic sight. He was breathing heavily.

"Steady," Ken advised in a low voice. "Take a deep breath, hold it, then squeeze the trigger."

But Brooke's breathing only intensified with anticipation. He was like a man about to climax in a passionate sexual crescendo. Sweat ran from his face, trickling down his cheeks. A wet patch spread on the back of his shirt. I turned on the camera. The old elephant contentedly gazed at the far horizon. Jesus, Brooke, come on. Get on with it. And then…

Bam!

The bull elephant lifted his head and looked at us, trumpeting loudly. The bullet had missed its mark. The rest of the herd went berserk. Older elephants immediately encircled the two babies. They were all trumpeting. Brooke aimed again but he was shaking nervously.

"No!" yelled Ken. "They'll stampede!"

Sensing that the calves may be in danger there was no telling what the herd would do. Then, surprising us all, one of the cows, probably a mother, suddenly broke away from the other animals and came tearing towards us. We froze. Brooke pointed his rifle at her. Pushing him out of the way Ken shouted, "No! Don't!"

I realized that my camera was still running. What should I do? Turn and make a run for the nearest tree or stay where I was? I remained in place, simply because I was paralyzed. Then Wally suddenly appeared in my frame. I zoomed in slightly, losing him from the image in my viewfinder which was now filled with a rapidly advancing and very angry elephant. I twisted the lens barrel to keep the animal sharply focused. The ground was shaking violently as she approached. In the background I could hear Cal, Spud and the Africans shouting. Somewhere in there I could hear my name being called but the frantic babble of voices was lost in the onrushing thunder of elephant feet. The frame within my viewfinder was now just blurred eyes and trunk and tusks and dust and then…

Bam!

Everything froze. The ground stopped shaking. The image in my frame became still. My right eye was glued to the viewfinder and the film was still running but, slowly, I opened my left eye and refocused on the outside world. Next to me stood Wally, his rifle smoking. I could smell the acrid gunpowder.

Less than twenty feet in front of me the elephant towered, swaying slightly. A spot right between her eyes began to ooze blood. I couldn't move but I held the camera steady, still rolling, capturing it all. With the exception of the whirring of the motor and the sprockets of the film the world had gone silent. I could hear the cow breathing deeply, each breath becoming more labored. With a sickening feeling surging inside me I realized that she was staring straight at me. But with each passing second her breathing slowed as more blood poured down from that hole in her skull, trickled onto her tusks and ran down like a crimson rivulet along the length of her trunk. Her eyes held mine. And then there was a strange but peaceful glimmer in her stare. I felt her death. But I sensed too that she was somehow reaching out to me, perhaps even attempting to communicate with me. I could swear that I was aware of her soul as it wafted across space and time, brushing and mingling with my own. Then her eyes began to glaze over. Slowly, like a circus elephant about to perform some obscene trick for our amusement, she gently sank to her knees, her eyes still locked with mine. Her gaze never left me for a second, even as she rolled over, taking one last deep breath followed by a deep gurgling sound in her throat. And then it was all over. Turning off the camera I sank to the ground. I felt Wally's hand on my shoulder as my entire body began to shake. That beautiful creature before me was dead. But it could have been me.

That night at base camp I sat in a corner and nursed a beer. As I stared at the tiny golden bubbles rising to the surface the words of David Phiri's translation of that old female albino diviner in Ndola years ago reverberated in my mind.

"You will nearly be killed by a great angry beast," she had foretold.

Was that violent spectacle under the African sun today what she was referring to?

I had no doubt that it was.

1

2

3

4

5

6

8

7

9

10

11

12

13

14

15

16

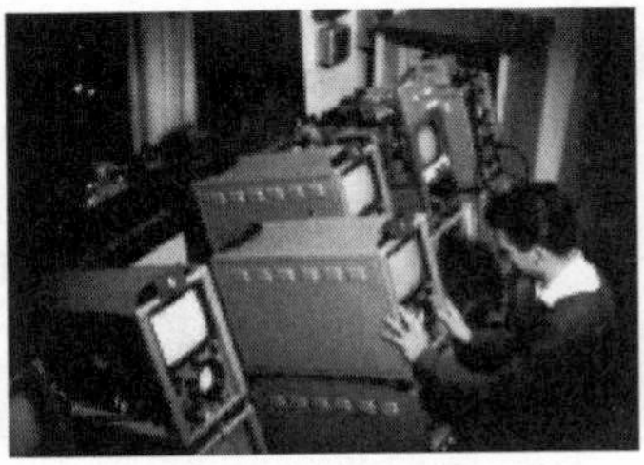

17

18

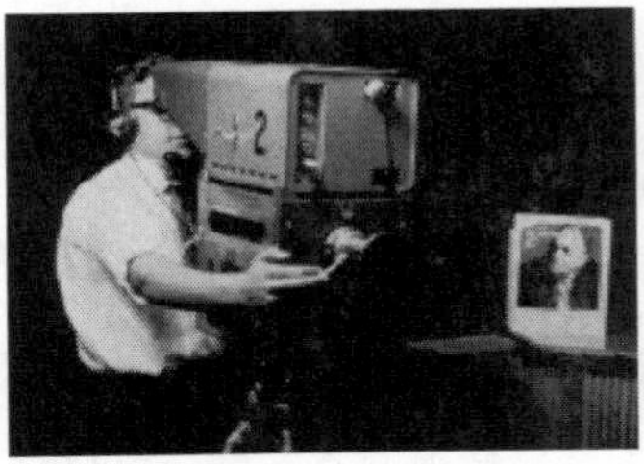

19

20

21

A PEEP BEHIND THE SCENES AT RTV STUDIOS

22

23

RADIO Guide

TUNING IN WITH M.T.P.

DAVID GRAY WARNS RTV

African programme is just not up to scratch

The forgetful dictator

Western Canadian humour

Boobs of the week

'Dior display' boosts standard of Topic

BY DAVID GRAY

24

Hire

TELEVISION SET

RADIO SET

KITWE

and Branches

MONDAY

June 24

RTV

FBC

TUESDAY

June 25

RTV

FBC

25

WEDNESDAY

June 26

RTV

FBC

THURSDAY

June 27

RTV

FBC

26

CLARKS

THOM'S

FRIDAY

June 28

RTV

FBC

SATURDAY

June 29

RTV

BRONCO BUSTER

FBC

SUNDAY

June 30

RTV

FBC

27

29

30

GOING OVERSEAS?

Take a ROOTES car in your pocket!

ROOTES

28

31

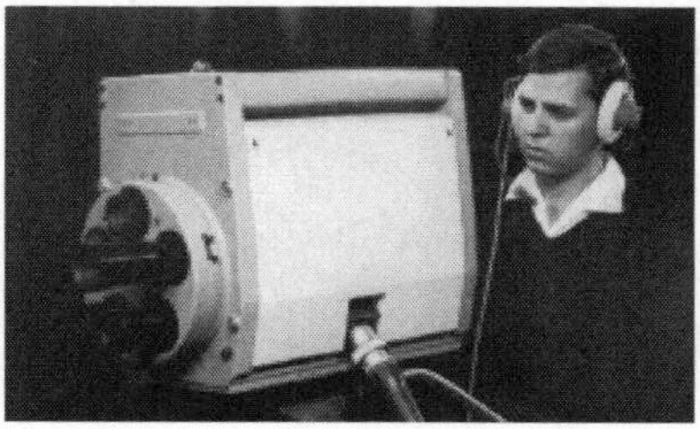

32

33

34

35

36

37

38

39

40

41

42

43

44

45

46

47

48

49

50

51

52

53

54

55

56

57

58

59

60

61

62

63

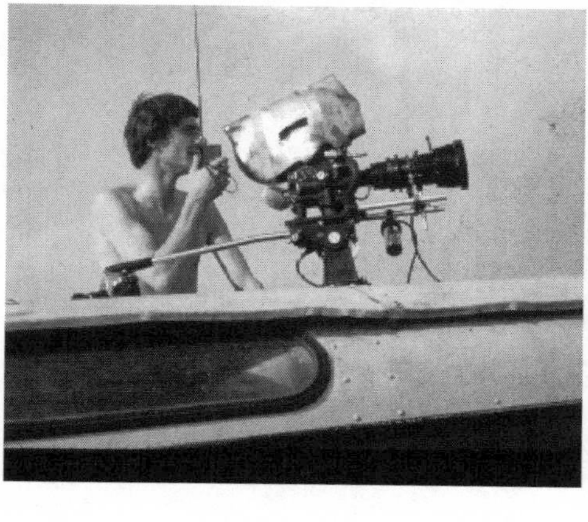
64

65

66

67

68

69

70

71

72

73

74

75

76

77

78

79

80

81

1. An iconic scene typical of South Africa during the apartheid era. Races were strictly segregated. The twain never met. Black people were relegated to the lowest rungs of society.
2. We white kids were constantly accompanied by our black nannies.
3. Age two, with Bapsie
4. Lettie
5. Age one, with mother and cousin Thelma. Bapsie and 'Mamingka' on right.
6. Age two, with Bapsie and 'Mamingka'
7. Age five. With 'Big John.'
8. On vacation at age 7 in Durban, Natal with Zulu rickshaw
9. As an amateur cinematographer, Northern Rhodesia, April 1961
10. With my beloved Paillard Bolex 8mm movie camera
11. Kitwe, hub of the copper mining district of Northern Rhodesia, 1961
12. Town center of Kitwe, Northern Rhodesia, 1961
13. Rhodesia Television (RTV) studios, Kitwe, Northern Rhodesia, 1961. The photo taken prior to Northern Rhodesia's independence from Britain and just before the breakup of the Federation of Rhodesia and Nyasaland. The 'R' for Rhodesia in the logo on the building would soon be dropped from the station's identity once independence was granted.
14. Main entrance to RTV studios, Kitwe, 1961.
15. Control room crew at beginning of RTV service. Vision Mixer Brian Heard, Producer/Director Hugh Duggan, Senior Producer/Director John Evans. Yours truly checking script in background. December 1961.
16. Control room, RTV, Kitwe. Control desk.
17. Camera control units (CCU) bay, RTV, Kitwe. Engineer Dave Hounsel at console.
18. Our trusty Philips telecine unit with its two 16mm film projectors. Much of our programming went out from this hard-working equipment. If it ever suffered a technical glitch we trained our cameras on a tank of tropical fish in the corner of the studio and played a 'musical interlude' while the problem was fixed.
19. Yours truly behind Camera 2 during the earliest days of RTV, Kitwe. A photograph of the Prime Minister of the Federation of Rhodesia and Nyasaland, Sir Roy Welensky, rests on display unit next to camera, waiting

to be featured during a political talk show telecast.

20. Cameraman Mike Yeats is on Camera 1. The cameras were built by our own engineers. They were based on a Vidicon picture tube platform mated to a 10:1 Pan Cinor zoom lens. Viewing screens were simply CCTV monitors bolted to the top of the camera unit. In the background is Floor Manager and Props Assistant, Darius Mumprokoso.
21. Behind my camera for the very first educational television program featuring a black presenter ever broadcast in Central Africa. RTV Kitwe, 1962. These programs were aimed at rural black schools in the Copperbelt region.
22. Article in local *Copper Post* mine newspaper taking readers behind the scenes at RTV studios, Kitwe. January 1963.
23. Newscaster Pat Rogers (center, smoking) interviews Northern Rhodesian black nationalist politicians Kenneth Kaunda (who would become president of the new Republic of Zambia after independence from Britain) and his opponent Harry Nkumbula. Pro-independence church minister Rev. Colin Morris on far right. RTV studio, Kitwe, 1962.
24. White-owned and run Copperbelt daily newspaper *Northern News* criticizes quality of African presenters on pre-independence RTV programming.
25. Images 25 through 27: *Northern News* newspaper lists programming for white viewers for week of June 24–30, 1963. (Note mixture of locally produced, British and American programming.)
28. Ad in *Northern News* for well-heeled Northern Rhodesian Copperbelt white mining community who often travelled abroad to Europe and the UK and shipped new cars back home to Central Africa.
29. Pending independence from Britain after the breakup of the Federation of Rhodesia and Nyasaland Rhodesia Television (RTV) became NRTV (Northern Rhodesia Television) in 1963. This was reflected in the on-screen logo used by the station.
30. After independence from Britain in October 1964 Northern Rhodesia became Zambia and the television service was renamed Zambia Television (ZTV).
31. The old RTV logo of the station was removed from the wall of the TV studio in Kitwe after independence.

32. New four-lens turret cameras were introduced after independence.
33. The latest image-orthicon zoom lens cameras from Europe soon replaced multi-lens turret studio cameras.
34. I returned to South Africa after Zambia gained its independence as all jobs held by whites at the TV station were replaced by blacks. Now I began my career as a cinematographer in the local film industry in Johannesburg.
35. On the soundstage of Alpha Film Studios, Johannesburg, 1965.
36. Lighting for motion pictures became my greatest passion.
37. With Directors of Photography Freddy Ford, BSC and Charles Minster at Alpha Film Studios, Johannesburg, 1965. Freddy was a renowned professional with international feature experience in London and Hollywood and was brought out to the Johannesburg studio on a long-term contract.
38. Filming German dramatic TV series *Diamanten sind Gefährlich (Diamonds are Dangerous)* for Zweites Deutsches Fernsehen (German Second TV Channel) on location in Kruger National Park, 1965. As color TV had not yet come to Germany the series was shot in black and white.
39. Ian Wilson, BSC, my very good friend and professional mentor to whom I owe my career in cinematography. He taught me more about lighting, lenses and camerawork than anyone else I ever worked with. A fine award-winning London-based cinematographer who came out to South Africa on a short-term contract, he gave me many of my first big breaks.
40. Taking time off on backlot No. 2 at Metro-Goldwyn-Mayer Studios, Culver City, Los Angeles in 1966. (1951's famous musical's Showboat moored on artificial lake in background.)
41. With multiple Academy Award-winning Director of Photography Leon Shamroy, ASC, on the set of *Caprice* at 20th Century Fox Studios, Beverly Hills, 1966. The film stared Richard Harris and Doris Day.
42. Back to South Africa to shoot the feature film, *The Long Red Shadow,* in 1967. Due to the influence of my mentor and friend Ian Wilson this was my first full-length movie as Director of Photography at age 23. The film was a romantic drama set against the background of a Communist takeover of a newly independent African country.
43. With director Percival Rubens (in hat) photographing a scene with actress

Gillian Claire for *The Long Red Shadow,* 1967.

44. Shangaan tribal chief and *sangoma* (shaman and traditional healer) meets hunting safari leader Wally Johnson at rural village in the Zinave hunting area, Central Mozambique, 1967. The purpose was to pay our respects to the chief for hunting on his ancestral tribal land.
45. Chief and *sangoma* foretells outcome of elephant hunt by reading his set of divination bones. His predictions regarding the hunt were uncannily accurate. He foresaw the coming dangers of the three white American hunters' quest to shoot elephants. The swelling in his lower abdomen was due to acute inflammation of the testes.
46. Some of the Shangaan *sangoma* chief's wives and children, Mozambique, 1967.
47. Safari leader Wally Johnson and tracker point out animal spoor (footprints) to hunter, Arthur 'Spud' Melin, in Safarilandia hunting concession, Zinave, Mozambique, 1967. Spud owned Wham-O Toys in Los Angeles and made his fortune by inventing and marketing the Hula Hoop, the Frisbee, 'Nutty Putty,' the Super Ball and other toys and sporting goods worldwide.
48. Giraffe, *Safarilandia* hunting concession, Zinave, Mozambique, 1967
49. Zebra, *Safarilandia* hunting concession
50. Tree full of baboons, *Safarilandia* hunting concession
51. Hunter and assistants prepare to skin a recently shot leopard. *Safarilandia* hunting concession, Mozambique, 1967.
52. Buffalo about to be shot during hunting safari in *Safarilandia,* Mozambique
53. Safari leader and professional hunter Ken Fubbs with buffalo just shot by Spud Melin, *Safarilandia* hunting concession
54. Male impala, *Safarilandia* hunting concession
55. Impala just shot by Spud Melin, *Safarilandia* hunting concession
56. Elephants on open plain at *Safarilandia* hunting concession
57. Elephant similar to the one that charged us after being shot at by hunters, *Safarilandia,* Mozambique, 1967. She was shot again and died just a few feet in front of me. I filmed the gruesome spectacle in its entirety, including her death.
58. Me behind movie camera with dead elephant after narrowly escaping her charge before she was shot by safari leader and professional hunting guide,

Ken Fubbs. The traumatic event was foretold in graphic detail by an albino female *nganga* (shaman) in Zambia over two years before it occurred.

59. With safari leader and professional hunter Wally Johnson after the elephant had been killed. Many shamans and *sangomas* in future years in various regions of Southern Africa told me that the spirit of the *ndlovu* (elephant) would remain with me all my life and will always protect me.
60. In the Okavango Swamps on location for documentary film for World Wildlife Fund. Moremi Reserve, Botswana, 1967.
61. Well and truly stuck in the swamp after our Land Rover was attacked by a lion. Director Graham Parker points to a possible way out. Moremi Reserve, Botswana, 1967.
62. Still stuck in the swamps waiting to be rescued after attack by lion. Yours truly on roof of Land Rover, Ian Wilson in foreground, director Graham Parker on right of vehicle. The heat was sweltering and tsetse flies and malaria a constant scourge.
63. Finally, a way out.
64. Ian Wilson filming from roof of Land Rover, Okavango, 1967. All camera units were in constant communication by radio.
65. Yours truly filming. Okavango Swamps, Moremi Reserve, Botswana, 1967.
66. Heat was a constant problem for the 35mm Eastmancolor negative film. Camera magazines always had to be specially shielded from the sun.
67. Legendary crocodile hunter and safari leader Bobby Wilmot—better known as the *Swamp Man*—holds juvenile crocodile, Okavango Swamps, Botswana, 1967.
68. Bobby Wilmot holds up recently hatched baby crocodile, Okavango Swamps.
69. Tswana woman and baby, Maun, Okavango Delta, Botswana, 1967
70. Young man, Maun, Okavango Delta, Botswana, 1967
71. Friendship. On street in the town of Maun, Okavango, Botswana, 1967.
72. Tswana family hut on the outskirts of Maun, Okavango, Botswana, 1967
73. Friendship. Tswana boys, Maun, Okavango, Botswana, 1967.
74. At age 24 I was Director of Photography on feature film, *Strangers at Sunrise,* 1968. Shot in South Africa, the story was set during the Anglo-Boer War between Britain and South Africa in the late 19th century. A high

budget production directed by Percival Rubens the film starred American actor George Montgomery, seated on far right. Assistant cameraman Ernest Kleynhans is on left of camera.

75. With American actors George Montgomery and Deana Martin, *Strangers at Sunrise,* South Africa, 1968.
76. Scene from *Strangers at Sunrise* on soundstage at S.A. Film Studios, Lone Hill, Johannesburg, 1968. Actors George Montgomery, Brian O'Shaughnessy, Roland Robinson. George Peters in background.
77. Filming documentary on board the 45,000-ton *Willem Barendsz* fishing factory ship in the Atlantic Ocean for BP Oil's *Panorama* cinema documentary series, 1968.
78. The documentary was shot on 35mm film for theatrical release.
79. Waiting to board a fishing trawler from the *Willem Barendsz* factory ship for a perilous journey of over 50 hours in a raging storm in the South East Atlantic, 1968. Despite the tempest we had a deadline to reach Walvis Bay in South West Africa (modern-day Namibia). The coming life-threatening storm at sea was also mysteriously foreseen by the Zambian *nganga* (shaman) many years earlier.
80. Fishing trawler similar to the Atlantic Endeavor that had to take us to Walvis Bay.
81. Danish skipper of the *Atlantic Endeavor* in whose hands our lives depended for the perilous, storm-tossed voyage to South West Africa. Despite our predicament the radio on his trawler was not operational. We had no way of sending out a distress call.

Six

Following my assignment in Mozambique I was hoping that my next job would be another full-length feature film, perhaps an adventure story or something light like a mindless romance or comedy. But in the freelance world you usually take the first thing that comes your way. There were no agents or artists' representatives in the film industry in South Africa in the mid-sixties. Jobs came by word of mouth or via reputation. Once again my old friend and mentor Ian Wilson in London came to the rescue. He had been contracted by a London-based company to photograph a documentary about the Okavango Swamps in Botswana. The movie was a promotion for the World Wildlife Fund (WWF) and was being sponsored by Coca-Cola in Atlanta. It would be shown on television in the UK and the US and distributed theatrically throughout the rest of the world. Ian wanted me to assist him. How could I possibly say no? Here was an opportunity to make a film with a positive and meaningful message about Africa's wildlife. Unlike the film I'd just worked on animals would not be depicted as simply 'big game' targets. The film would also look at the lives of the indigenous people who lived in and around the Moremi Reserve in Northern Botswana. The production was to be supported by the latest and best of everything. Part of the shoot would take place on houseboats and canoes in the swamps and the rest of it on land. Our safari leader would be Bobby Wilmot, a famous white hunter in that part of the world. In addition to the London crew we would have a substantial support team, mobile generators for charging batteries and for providing power at our various camp sites. We would also have every lens and fancy accessory for our 35mm movie cameras that Samuelson's the equipment rental company in London could provide. It promised to be a lot of fun. I eagerly hopped aboard the project.

The gateway to the Okavango Delta and Moremi Reserve was Maun. Today it is a thriving mecca catering to a popular tourist industry but in 1967 it wasn't much more than a dusty little settlement in the middle of nowhere. There was a trading store that also served as a post office. The single dirt road sported a butchery, a refueling station with two manually operated pumps, the bungalow-style Riley's Hotel and bar, a small public health clinic, a couple of mud huts and an outdoor market offering everything from woven grass baskets to goats to cash crops like tomatoes, potatoes and corn. Another dirt road ran from the village to an airstrip. The primitive field boasted a windsock that hung limply from the top of an unpainted pole and there was a single wood and corrugated iron hut that served as a departures and arrivals terminal. It also had a ramshackle outhouse for a toilet. Everything was unfenced. Kids, donkeys and stray dogs wandered around everywhere.

Originally inhabited by the Stone Age San people or 'Bushmen' Botswana was first known as the British protectorate of Bechuanaland. It gained its independence from Britain on September 30, 1966. Its first president was Sir Seretse Khama, grandson of Kgosi Khama III, ruler of the Bangwato people. The intrepid Dr. David Livingstone had spent time among them during his famous missionary travels in the 19th century. Seretse Khama was the first black leader to marry a white woman. She was Ruth Williams, daughter of a retired British army officer. Racists in South Africa and Rhodesia were incensed about having a mixed marriage couple as heads of state on their doorstep. Nevertheless, after much fuss and brouhaha the couple settled in and became the first family of what would become one of Africa's most stable and peaceful countries.

A rickety Botswana Airways DC-3 Dakota had flown us from Johannesburg to Gaborone, the capital of Botswana, and then to the towns of Mahalapye, Serowe and Francistown. After that it droned over the Kalahari Desert and the great Makgadikgadi

Salt Pans to Maun. When we arrived and loaded our gear into a fleet of Land Rovers we were met by smiling, friendly people. Small boys played with toy cars they had fashioned out of rusty wire and coat hangers. Women carried parcels on their heads and had babies tied to their backs. It was always refreshing to get out of South Africa and encounter black people who were not as suppressed as they were back home. Although signs of poverty were everywhere the locals were friendly, welcoming people. As a white South African I detected no feeling of animosity from them. Bobby Wilmot and his team drove us from Maun through magnificent forested wilderness towards the Okavango Delta. It was startling to see the difference in the landscape, especially after spending hours flying over yellow desert and scrub.

The Okavango Delta was unique. It was the largest inland delta in the world. Instead of flowing into the sea, an annual flood of fresh water flowed inland, spreading over 5,800 square miles of the Kalahari Desert into a maze of lagoons, lakes and channels. Countless islands within this enormous waterway created several ecosystems which were home to an enormous variety of animals including lion, leopard, elephant, giraffe, zebra, buffalo, hyena, antelopes and apes. It boasted over 550 species of birds. Crystal clear waters were home to crocodiles, hippos and many kinds of fish. The sharp scent of sage and swampy vegetation lingered everywhere. High canopies of shade and shelter were formed by ebony, wild fig, sycamore and sausage trees. Among all this forestation was the lovely malala palm. If you shut your eyes and imagined what the Garden of Eden might have looked like the Okavango would have probably fitted the bill perfectly.

Within this paradise was the Moremi Wildlife Reserve. Covering 1,160 square miles it was one of the world's most pristine wilderness areas. When we visited it nature's intricate web of life flourished without disruption. It was a place of islands covered in papyrus-like reeds, sandy riverbanks, grassy hills, floodplains, thick forests and lily-filled wetlands. Bobby

Wilmot knew the area like the back of his hand. He had spent decades in the delta hunting crocodiles and was simply referred to by everyone as 'The Swamp Man.' At age 50 he had already killed over 45,000 crocodiles, exporting their skins to France where they became fancy purses, bags, briefcases, wallets, belts and shoes. He once said: "Crocodiles are different to other creatures. It is the most brutal animal of all. It knows no mercy. I have never had a pang of regret killing one."

We bounced along furrowed tracks through forest and bush to his headquarters at Crocodile Camp. Traveling there took us through tsetse fly country. Every hour or so we had to stop at a corrugated metal shed, pull up inside and then remain in the vehicle while the doors of the shed were clanged shut. The guard on duty then sprayed the interior and exterior of the vehicle with a foul-smelling disinfectant. Before AIDS, the tsetse fly was the scourge of Africa. A bloodsucking insect that came in 21 different species, the larva developed inside the mother's body until it was ready to pupate in the soil. Although it was eventually eradicated in many parts of the continent a bite from the tsetse could transmit a dreaded single cell parasite called trypanosome. This attacked the blood and nervous system causing sleeping sickness. Even today, the disease affects as many as 500,000 people, at least 80% of whom will die. The tsetse's bite also causes nagana and other diseases that kill cattle and some wild mammals. At least three million cattle still perish from it every year.

There were no permanent buildings at Crocodile Camp. The place consisted of canvas tents and an exterior grass-walled shower cubicle where one of the camp attendants tipped buckets of fresh, filtered swamp water over you. There was also a small thatched outhouse with a simple wooden seat over a deep septic pit. Meals were cooked on outside fires. Sleeping quarters were simply hammocks slung between trees, each one wrapped in mosquito-proof netting. It was October and the nights were hot.

Mosquitoes were everywhere. Without those nets it would have been impossible to get any sleep. Our director Graham Parker always liked to get an early start in the mornings. Some days would be spent on large houseboats or outboard motorboats on the water, others on foot, but usually slicing our way through the bush in the trusty Land Rovers. I preferred the boats. That way, in between periods meandering under power through the maze of waterways, you could drift quietly, waiting to spot animals. It was a pleasure to be among so much wildlife with only cameras and no guns, although of course Bobby and his assistants always had a rifle or shotgun slung over their shoulders, just in case. Perched behind the gyro-stabilized camera and zoom lens I often hankered after Hollywood and took time off during those long waterway cruises to read Budd Schulberg's 1941 rags-to-riches novel about Hollywood, *What Makes Sammy Run?*

One morning Bobby Wilmot spotted a crocodile nest on the riverbank. Making sure none of the reptiles were around we splashed ashore, carrying cameras, tripods and batteries. I couldn't see where or what Bobby had seen until he dropped to his haunches near a sandy spot under a clump of reeds.

"This dark area means the area was recently dug up," he explained. "Crocodiles bury their eggs in the sand. Let's have a look."

With his bare hands he gently dug into the soft white sand, scooping it away. Sure enough, about nine or ten inches below the surface was a cluster of about 25 soft-shelled, whitish-brown, leathery-like eggs. Bobby lifted one out. As he held it in his hand so that we could get a close-up shot of it the shell of the egg began to move. A bulge here, then one there. Bobby smiled.

"This one's about to hatch," he announced.

He put the soft shell down on the sand and tore a little hole in it.

"I think the fellow inside needs some help," he smiled.

And then a wet claw appeared, ripping away at the rest

of the shell. It was unbelievable. Right before our cameras, in brilliant sunshine, we witnessed a new life entering the world. Emitting high-pitched screeches and glistening with fluid from the amnion sac in which it had developed the little crocodile, about nine or ten inches long, struggled to break through the egg. Then it twisted itself out, uncertainly balanced on its short legs and started crawling around, calling out to its mother.

"It'll eventually lose its voice," Bobby said as we all wondered at this miracle.

"And if we don't watch out," he added, "Mother will soon be here. They're very protective of their young."

We spent a few more minutes getting footage of the nest and the single small creature crawling around, and then Bobby covered the unhatched eggs with sand. But before we left he lifted the baby by its tail.

"They're vicious, right from the start," he said. "Watch this."

Breaking off a piece of dry reed he held it in front of the baby's face and the jaws immediately snapped around it. Prying open its mouth Bobby pointed out rows of the crocodile's tiny razor-sharp teeth.

"You don't want to get too close to this little guy," he added. "Once its mother gets here she'll carry it in her jaws to safety in the water and then release it. It will immediately start feeding on insects and small fish but it won't be long before it goes after bigger prey."

We left the baby squealing for Mom, stowed our gear back on the boat and puttered off into an estuary where a canopy of palms provided some welcome shade.

One day we were traveling around in the Land Rovers—we always used three vehicles, with camera crews split up amongst them—and I reached out of the window to get a light reading with my exposure meter. Before I knew it, a baboon came swooping down from the trees and grabbed it from my hand. We found the instrument two days later. It was in perfect condition, dangling from an acacia tree about a half mile away. Obviously the baboon couldn't make head or tail of it or it didn't taste good. On another occasion a large male lion jumped onto the roof of the vehicle Ian and I were traveling in with Bobby. The enclosed cab had a bench seat that could fit three. There was an open cargo deck in the rear. Although the camera had been rigged on a tripod there we managed to pull it inside the cab just in the nick of time and shut the windows. But this was a very determined lion. He clawed and tore at the roof until it began to rip open. Fortunately, Bobby managed to get the four-wheel drive system into gear very quickly and stepped on the gas, causing the vehicle to lurch forward. The lion fell off but he wasn't finished with us. He gave chase, swiping at the tires. Bobby drove us into a swampy patch and the lion stopped. Big cats, like all felines, don't like water. He stood watching us for about fifteen minutes and then sauntered off into the underbrush. Try as he might, Bobby couldn't get the heavy Land Rover to budge. We were well and truly bogged down in mud. We had to radio for the other two vehicles to come to our rescue. Finally, just before sundown, they found us and hauled us out of our predicament. That evening we celebrated our rescue by polishing off a bottle of Johnnie Walker Red Label.

The next morning I awoke with a terrible pain on the right side of my face. At first I thought it was a hangover but while brushing my teeth down at the river on the edge of our camp I realized that it was a toothache. Not only that but an abscess had flared above an upper molar. All that day I was in agony. We were bouncing around rattling our bones in the Land Rovers and the pain was excruciating. The right side of my face had turned ruby red and blown up like a balloon. I curled up in the tailgate area of the vehicle but every bump, every jolt, sent piercing stabs of pain through the right side of my face. That night back at camp Bobby asked his girlfriend Jillian, a retired nurse who had been living with him for the past couple of years and who was acting as crew medic, to take a look at my mouth.

"Jillie," he said—he always called her Jillie—"see what you can do."

Jillian lifted a hurricane lantern, peered into my mouth and gently prodded around the inflamed area.

"Ooh," she said, pulling a nasty face. "That must be terribly painful."

"Mmm," I mumbled.

"I think I've got some antibiotics," she said. "They should fix you."

She disappeared into the dark and fumbled around in the tent she shared with Bobby. A few minutes later she returned with two small brown bottles.

"Here," she said. "Take one of these every four hours, and two of these for pain whenever you need them."

I thanked her, downed a handful of tablets with some Johnnie Walker and crawled into my hammock.

The following day I woke up feeling even worse. Not only was the pain unbearable but I felt even more nauseous. While the others breakfasted I lay in my hammock. In the light of day I was able to read the labels on the two bottles Jill had given me. The painkiller was a simple form of aspirin but the antibiotic was something really potent. To my horror I discovered that it was more than three years beyond its safe shelf life. No wonder I felt like I was at death's door. I stayed in the camp that day, Jill and the cook regularly checking in on me. To Jill's consternation I was beginning to develop a raging fever. The pain was relentless, a fiery, burning, exploding torment in my mouth. I was blinded by it. Jill didn't know what to do. At about three o'clock I wandered over to the supply tent, tore open another case of Johnnie Walker and opened a new bottle. The pain was so bad that I had decided to drink myself into oblivion. It was the only thing that dulled my suffering. When Bobby, Ian and the rest of the crew returned to camp that evening I was numbed out of my agony, lying on a bench in the outdoor dining area with my head on Jill's lap, deliriously drunk. I heard them talking about radioing Maun and saying something about driving me into town where the doctor from the local clinic could take a look at me.

"If it's really serious," I heard Jill say, "we might have to fly him to the hospital in Francistown. I'm afraid of sepsis setting in."

I don't remember much more of what happened that night. All I can recall is that around midnight I found myself lying in my hammock, wearing nothing but my underpants. It was the pain that had woken me. Somebody must have put me to bed. Ian and I must have finished off an entire bottle of scotch. I looked over at his hammock and in the moonlight I could see him lying there, spread-eagled and stark naked. That was fine in the warm Okavango weather but not a good idea if the mosquito netting had not been pulled tightly around the cot. His wasn't. He could easily have been bitten to pieces, especially in areas of his anatomy where it would have caused particular discomfort. I got out of my hammock, tightened the net around him, then stumbled over to the dining area where yet another unopened bottle of Highland spirits sparkled in the moonlight. The entire camp was quiet and the central fire had long gone out. I downed half the bottle in one gigantic gulp. The rest of it is all a bit of a haze. I vaguely remember going back to my cot, fumbling around for something in my toilet bag, and then I recall going to one of the Land Rovers and searching for something amongst all the camera equipment. I then remember wending my way down to the water's edge carrying something heavy and falling into a boat. Clunk! Clatter! Bang! Splash! *Crash!* The rest of it is just a fog.

When I came to my entire body was on fire. And I couldn't see anything. Everything was white and blisteringly hot. It took me a few minutes to stop panicking and come to my senses. I looked at my watch. 12.30. It was way past noon the following day. The sun was beating down mercilessly on me. I was still clad only in my underpants. The fiery sensation was sunburn. I was adrift in one of the small rowing boats but I had no oars. I also had no idea where I was. I had cast myself adrift the night before and now I was lost somewhere in the swampy waterways of the Okavango. I was lying in the bottom of the boat, my left arm tightly folded around one of the heavy camera tripods and my right hand clutching my toothbrush. To this day I have no idea why I chose those two objects. Not a clue. I had a headache and a hangover the likes of which I would never wish upon my worst enemy. But I sensed something else. My toothache was gone. The abscess had burst in the night. My mouth tasted of a foul bitter substance mingled with a little blood. I reached overboard and scooped up some of the clear water and rinsed out. The taste of the cool sweet water and the relief from the pain slowly lessened my hangover but I was suffering terribly from the stinging rays of the sun. I was about to scoop up some more water to splash over myself when I suddenly saw two big yellow-brown eyes looking at me from just above the surface of the water, no more than five or six feet away. A crocodile. It seemed as big as a nuclear submarine. And then another one. And another. I was surrounded by them. What now? Without any oars I was helpless. And which direction was camp? Would anyone come looking for me? Why hadn't they found me already? I was doomed. And then I heard an outboard motor. I tried to shout but with my parched throat I could only manage a feeble croak. Summoning all my strength I took a deep breath and yelled at the top of my voice, "Help!"

Again, and again. Twenty minutes later, wrapped in a towel, I was being towed back to camp by a very jovial and relieved Bobby Wilmot and some of his camp staff. When Ian suggested we celebrate my rescue and recovery with another whiskey that night I politely refused. I'd had more than my fill. In fact, I didn't take another drop of alcohol for the rest of the shoot.

The following week was relatively uneventful. The abscess did not recur and life returned to normal. One night Bobby invited me to go crocodile hunting with him. I immediately took him up on his offer. I wanted to see how those prehistoric swamp-dwelling reptiles met their fate in order to satisfy the demands of the twentieth-century fashion industry. No one else expressed an interest in going and the producer and director decided that filming the hunt had no place in a conservation film so I would be unburdened by cameras and production equipment. Just after sundown Bobby, an assistant and I seated ourselves in a small outboard motorboat. Three of his trackers boarded a second boat. They took along a few coils of rope, some heavy nylon netting, a small hatchet, a large axe, four high-power flashlights and a couple of rifles. Putt-putting our way down the river from camp we entered a maze of winding waterways. Cutting the engines, both boats drifted. The sun had long gone and it was now dark. Bobby's assistant turned on one of the flashlights. He held it over the side of the boat just above the waterline, pointing it straight ahead. Bobby turned on the other one, doing the same on the other side of the boat. The men on the second boat duplicated the procedure.

"The light attracts them," Bobby whispered to me.

Both boats drifted silently alongside one another for about five minutes and then I heard a rippling sound up ahead. And then another one.

"They're coming," Bobby whispered.

The four bright beams of light cut through the darkness. It was not long before a pair of fiery eyes emerged from the water dead ahead of us. Attracted by the flashlight the crocodile moved swiftly towards our boat. Speaking softly to his assistant in Tswana Bobby told him to turn off the light.

"Too small," he murmured. "I'm only interested in the big ones."

As soon as we were engulfed in darkness I sensed the creature swim right past us. With the exception of a slight gurgling sound you could barely hear it. Then Bobby issued another soft command and the flashlights were turned on again. The beams immediately caught two more pairs of eyes up ahead. Bobby spoke in rapid but muted tones to his men.

He glanced back at me and said, "Watch out. We're going for the one on the right hand side."

Closer and closer the eyes came. This was a big one. Too big for my comfort. I inched over as far as I could to the left-hand side of the boat. Bobby's assistant put down his flashlight, stood up and picked up the axe. The other boat inched closer, all flashlights now on the one pair of eyes that Bobby had selected. The two brilliant eyes came gliding into the narrow gap between the two boats. As it did so the man with the axe lifted it high above his head and then whacked down as hard as he could. I heard an awful crunching sound. The water became a frenzy of twisting and churning. Instantly, the men from the other boat pulled up alongside us. Beams of light splayed across the water. I got drenched from all the splashing and thrashing but at least I could see what was going on. It was an ugly scene. The axe was wedged in the crocodile's skull, right between its eyes. A man on the other boat used his hatchet to gouge another hole in the creature's skull. In less than a minute it was dead. Using the nylon netting and ropes the men hauled the animal aboard the other boat. Then we turned around and headed for camp.

"Why the axe?" I asked Bobby on the way back. "Why didn't you just shoot?"

"Too dangerous and too noisy," he replied. "The sound scares off other crocodiles and in the darkness you may not hit him in the brain. That's the only place that'll kill him instantly. As you saw, to make sure he's dead we also use the hatchet to get into the braincase. Besides, if you shoot and hit him somewhere else on the body you'll ruin the skin and the price goes down. Simple economics. Don't spoil the merchandise."

During the course of production we spent a few days with a clan of San Bushmen. The script called for a sequence depicting their nomadic lifestyle and traditional hunting methods. These ancient people had wandered the Kalahari for well over 20,000 years. They were the last human remnants of the planet's Stone Age, the original inhabitants of Southern Africa. They lived in an area that spanned the subcontinent from the Atlantic to the Indian Ocean and as far north as Zambia. Their ancestral homelands were invaded by cattle-herding tribes about 1,500 years ago and then they encountered the racist discrimination of white settlers. After the arrival of the Dutch at the Cape of Good Hope in the 17th century they were hunted to extinction in the southernmost regions of the colony. Licenses to shoot Bushmen for sport in the Namib and Kalahari Deserts were still being issued by the South African government up to 1936. From an original population of several million their numbers were quickly reduced to less than 100,000. Today, there are probably no more than a couple of thousand of their descendants still living.

There were many different Bushmen people. After being eradicated or chased from their homes it is mainly the San who have survived. Their language incorporates a series of 'click' sounds. They have no written alphabet. Theirs is a hunter-gatherer society. In the 1960s they supported themselves in the Kalahari Desert and Okavango swamps through hunting skills and living off the land. The men produced their own spears, bows and arrows while the women gathered roots, bulbs, seeds and berries. Traditionally, they lived in rocky crevices or caves, or in temporary grass, twig and animal skin shelters. They were constantly on the move, foraging and hunting as they went. Unlike later tribes who moved into Southern Africa they made no pottery, using empty ostrich eggshells or animal bladders and body parts for storing water.

The hunt was always a crucial part of San culture. It embraced profound mystical significance. Their prey was always respected and held in high esteem. After a kill an all-night feast and trance-like dance ritual was held around a communal fire. The spirit of the animal was honored and thanks were offered to a divinity from which the San believed all life came. During a trance dance the men did the dancing while the women sang and provided rhythm through clapping, drumming and the shaking of rattles. Medicine men or shamans were the first to enter the trance state. It was said that their spirits traveled out of their bodies, connecting with ancestral entities and divine powers to heal people from sickness, foretell the future, control the weather and even ensure successful future hunts. The visions people brought back from trance states are what lie behind much of the Bushmen rock art that is found all over the subcontinent, some of it dating back at least 5,000 years. This art has been the subject of much study, but the images cannot be understood without taking the Bushmen's spiritual and metaphysical beliefs into account. Etched onto rocks or on cave walls the highly stylized and almost abstract shapes of creatures—both human and animal—are what the artist 'saw' during a trance or while he was having an out-of-body metaphysical experience.

One of our assignments during the shooting of the film was to follow a group of Bushmen during a hunt in the wetlands around the delta. We accompanied a half dozen of them as they pursued a herd of lechwe antelope. Expert at spotting tracks and keeping out of the wind the Bushmen wore only flimsy loin cloths and carried a spear, a bow and a quiver of arrows slung over their shoulder. They were as fast and as agile as the animals themselves. It was exceptionally tough keeping up with them. Ian was on camera with me behind, carrying the cumbersome wet cell acid battery in its leather case, a spare magazine of negative film and a couple of extra lenses. It was exhausting. Bobby Wilmot and the director followed about a half mile behind us in the Land Rover. The hunters shot an arrow tipped with poison derived from a combination of crushed insects, frog saliva and plants into the rump of a large male lechwe. They had to chase it until the poison took effect and brought the animal down. Breathlessly Ian and I kept up with them. We ran. We sprinted. We splashed through swamp and mud. And then the camera battery died.

"Go and get another one from the Landie, *quick!*" yelled Ian.

"I can't," I said. "We've used them all up. We're clean out of recharged ones."

Ian looked at me in disbelief. I thought quickly.

"Stay here," I said. "I'll be right back."

Running back to the Land Rover I told Bobby to kill the engine and pop the hood. Breathless and perspiring profusely, without explaining what I was doing I yanked the terminals off the big battery in the engine compartment, lifted it out of its rack and ran back to Ian. It felt like the thing weighed a ton. But it's amazing where strength and resilience come from when you're under pressure. Using a roll of 'gaffer tape' that every member of a camera crew always had tied to his belt, I jerry-rigged the camera cable to the heavy 12-volt battery and we were back in business. But the Bushmen and the injured lechwe were at least a half-mile away by now. Ian, with his long, thin, muscular legs sprinted across the swamp with me behind, the heavy Land Rover battery now perched on my head. How I kept up with him I shall never know, but we captured the entire sequence on film, right up until the moment the lechwe dropped and the Bushmen cut its throat and ritually removed its liver. When it was all over I collapsed into the thick muddy swamp, my heart pounding so hard that I thought it would burst from my rib cage. Ian lay panting nearby. Bobby and the director reached us shortly afterwards and helped us carry the equipment back to the vehicle.

I don't know what Bobby had thought about me ripping the battery from his Land Rover but he never said anything about it, not even as we relaxed around the fire that night and told our story to the rest of the crew. Despite his crocodile hunting Bobby was a very decent guy. He did his best to make an honest living out of his hunting activities, not for sport or to satisfy the bloodthirsty whims of wealthy clients. With deep blue eyes and a sun-dried skin almost as brown and leathery as the crocodiles he hunted he was a jovial and extremely obliging guy. Nothing was ever too much trouble for him. He did whatever he could to make our work in the Okavango as comfortable and as pleasant as possible. A year after the shoot I was saddened to learn of his unfortunate fate. The swamp he loved so much had finally got him. On December 19, 1968, he was out hunting crocodiles one night with the cook from his camp. Jill had remained behind in Maun. Stepping into a marsh he was bitten by a deadly black mamba snake. After an eight-mile dash back to camp by Land Rover he administered anti-snakebite serum but it was too late. Four hours later he was dead. The legendary 'Swamp Man' was no more.

Sadly, since we shot the film in 1967 the Botswana government has become particularly discriminatory towards the San Bushmen population. Those timeless nomads have been evicted from most of their traditional hunting areas and are restricted to only certain regions of the country. An intensive government-backed anti-Bushmen campaign got underway in 1986. Forced removals began in 1997. Those who remained in the Kalahari faced torture, restriction of hunting rights and the outright banning of the gathering of wild foods. Water pumps that had been established for them in the desert areas were destroyed. The argument presented by the Botswana government at the time was that the Bushmen needed to be assimilated into modern society and given access to proper education and health care. But AIDS, alcoholism and other social ills have taken the place of their nomadic and free-wheeling lifestyle. It is both tragic and ironic that a country which struggled for its own political independence from white domination eventually became intent on doing all in its power to bring one of the world's oldest and smallest groups of people to extinction. And as with the genocidal wars between the Hutus and the Tutsis in Rwanda or the mass murder of people by Islamic groups such as Boko Haram in Nigeria or Al-Shabaab in Kenya and Somalia, what is Africa and the rest of the world doing about it?

Nothing.

Seven

My career followed an interesting path after the Okavango project. This included the cinematography of a movie called *Strangers at Sunrise*. It was an ambitious feature film set during the Anglo-Boer War between Britain and South Africa in 1899. In addition to a large cast of some of South Africa's best actors the leads included American stars George Montgomery and popular singer Dean Martin's daughter, Deana. It was great working with Americans again. George Montgomery kept talking about how similar the Highveld countryside in South Africa looked like his native Montana. This film was followed by various commercials and documentaries. One of them was a film that I shot for the British Petroleum (BP) oil company. It was a theatrical documentary about the fishing factory ship, *Willem Barendsz*. Named after a famous Dutch whale hunter, the twin-funneled 27,000-ton diesel-powered vessel was originally built as a whaling factory ship in Schiedam, Holland in 1955. After ten years of service hunting and processing whales in Antarctic waters she came to South Africa in 1965 and was converted into a very different kind of factory ship. She sailed far into Atlantic waters for weeks at a time, hauling aboard catches of pilchards, anchovies and mackerel from a fleet of purse-seine fishing trawlers, processing the catch into dried fish meal, mainly for use as an agricultural fertilizer or for animal feed. It was one of the largest operations of its kind anywhere in the world. Only two of us made up the production crew. My assistant and sound recordist was Ernest Kleynhans, a guy I had known since the old days of RTV in Kitwe, Northern Rhodesia. Ernie and I had remained friends and often worked together.

The documentary we were shooting was part of a blue-chip series called *Panorama*, sponsored by BP Oil and distributed to cinemas throughout Southern Africa and to TV in Britain and

Europe. The plan was for us to remain on board the *Willem Barendsz* for about a week, gathering footage of the voyage and the operations on board. We were given a comfortable two-berth cabin with private bathroom in the officers' quarters on the port side of the vessel. The ship was large and jammed with equipment. It took forever to get from our cabin to the area where all the action took place. Huge vacuum pipes slung over the side of the ship sucked up the catch from the holds of the fishing trawlers, each one about 50 feet long and weighing about a hundred tons. The fish were then brought on board, and in cavernous areas below decks they were dried, crushed and packed into large sacks as commercial fish meal. The stench—infused with the smell of diesel fumes, oil and grease—was appalling. Fortunately, the crews' living quarters were all upwind in a seven-story high superstructure. Because she was once a whaler there was still a slipway in the stern where the carcasses of whales were once hauled aboard. From there they were flayed, dismembered and boiled, producing blubber, baleen and oil. I often used to go and sit behind the railing overlooking that slipway, watching the churning wake from the propellers, imagining the carnage of an industry that is now sadly making a vigorous comeback by nations as diverse as Japan, Norway and Iceland. I would often think back on how much Europe owed to those leviathans of the sea. Their baleen went into corsets, combs and jewelry, their fats into soaps and detergents. Their oils lit the palaces, streets, theaters and salons of Paris, Rome and London. But in 1968 the ship served a different purpose, harvesting protein from the ocean on an unimaginable scale, and all of it destined for animal feed and crop fertilizer.

One evening, with a gale howling outside, Ernest and I were sitting in our cabin cleaning our equipment and enjoying an after-dinner beer when there was a sudden rat-a-tat knocking at our door. It was one of the junior officers. The captain respectfully requested our presence on the bridge immediately, preferably with a camera. Our trusty Arriflex IIC movie camera was in pieces all over Ernie's bunk so we high-tailed it upstairs with a Pentax 35mm stills camera. The captain was an old Dutch salt of the sea. He was puffing away on his Meerschaum pipe as he waited for us in the warm bridge. Despite the weather it was pretty quiet up there. The gentle click and whirr of electronic instruments could be heard above the roar of the wind outside.

"Ah!" he said. "I want to show you something."

"What is it, Captain?" I asked.

"Have you ever seen St. Elmo's fire?" he asked, a sparkle in his eye. It was as though he was about to demonstrate some kind of magic trick to us. We shook our heads.

"Well then, come on," he said, opening the door to the flying bridge outside.

The wind took our breath away. It was a gale, with a stinging cold bite to it. I shivered. Ernie hesitated.

"Come on," coerced the captain laughingly. "There's nothing out there that's going to harm you."

We stepped outside, Ernest and I shivering, searching each other's faces for some clue as to what we might expect.

"Hold your arms out straight, like this," shouted the captain, as he thrust his own arms out sideways, in a stance reminiscent of the figure of Christ towering over Rio de Janeiro. As soon as he did this, something amazing happened. Long flaming streaks of blue light shot out from his fingertips, nose, ear lobes and hair. He was like an apparition from a fairy tale, a science fiction scene. It was unbelievable.

Laughing out loud he encouraged us to do the same. Hesitantly, Ernest and I extended our arms and zap! A buzzing blue ethereal glow immediately emanated from our fingers, faces and hair. It tingled slightly but was by no means uncomfortable. We were like three ghosts, all afire out there in the wind on the flying bridge. At first I was shocked, but soon we were all laughing, waving our hands and arms around, causing fireworks-like circles of blue and white light to surround us. I had never seen anything like it. The men inside the compass bridge had their faces glued to the window in the door, laughing and snapping photographs of us. The longer we stood there the more our hair stood on end, blue streaks shooting straight up as though we were about to be beamed up to the *Enterprise* starship. The science behind this phenomenon were discharges of atmospheric electricity caused by wind and stormy weather. St. Elmo's fire is a corona discharge, commonly observed on church steeples or belfries. But here we were, three mortals on the bridge of a ship in the Eastern Atlantic, and we had become disciples of St. Elmo, a corruption of the Italian name Sant'Ermo or St. Erasmus, the patron saint of Mediterranean sailors. They believe that the shooting streaks were a visible sign of St. Elmo's guardianship over them and their vessels. It was unforgettable. Back inside the warm compass bridge the captain said we must have been very blessed as he had only seen this three times in his 40-odd years at sea.

The next morning I knew that we would need that blessing. The captain summoned us up to the chart room and explained that a severe storm was heading our way. We were about 200 nautical miles off the coast of Angola. Our original production schedule depended on the *Willem Barendsz* putting in at the South West African (now Namibian) port of Walvis Bay for supplies within the next two days. We would disembark from there and fly back to Cape Town, pick up our vehicle and the rest of our gear and then return by road to Johannesburg. But that was not going to happen.

"I don't see us reaching land for another week or more," the captain explained. "Besides, there is a fleet of a dozen trawlers still out to sea and we cannot turn back until we've taken their catches on board."

My heart sank. Poor Ernest turned visibly pale. He was hoping to be home in Pretoria within five days to celebrate his wedding anniversary. The captain immediately sensed our disappointment. Puffing at his pipe he thought for a moment or two.

"Tell you what," he said. "There's a boat, the *Atlantic Endeavor*, due in tomorrow evening. It has a real character of a skipper, an old Danish fellow. His radio is out so we're not sure exactly when to expect him but I'm counting on sundown tomorrow. Once his load is aboard the *Barendsz* he is scheduled to head for Walvis. He's taking our mail with him and I'm sure you can hitch a ride. I know he won't mind."

Ernest and I looked at each other and we cheered up immediately.

"Fantastic, Captain," I replied. "That would be fine. Just fine. Thank you. Thank you very much."

He took another puff on his pipe, expelling a great cloud of sweet-smelling tobacco smoke in the chart room.

"But I must remind you about that storm," he warned. "The chances are that it will overtake you on the way back to Walvis. I have no idea how long your journey will be."

"How long would it normally take from this position?" I asked.

"Ag ja, well…" and he thought for a moment or two. "A day or two, maybe. In good weather."

Whatever would be would be. We were prepared to hitch a ride, no matter how long it took.

The Cape Town-registered *Atlantic Endeavor* with its bearded and middle-aged Danish captain and a crew of seven Colored deck hands pulled up alongside the *Willem Barendsz* at around four o'clock the following afternoon. A growing storm was already in the air. There was wind, a light rain and the sea was choppy. The two vessels banged and butted against one another as the vacuum pipes sucked the *Endeavor's* holds empty of fish. Ernest and I, with all our gear, paraphernalia and luggage, were lowered in nets slung from a crane on the *Willem Barendsz*. The minute our feet touched the pitching deck of the wooden-hulled trawler we knew we were in trouble. Unlike the big 27,000-ton monster we had just been on, this was a place that was wildly heaving and tossing like a bucking bronco. We had both been taking Dramamine to prevent sea sickness but I wondered whether it was going to be potent enough to stave off illness in this topsy-turvy vessel. The Colored crew helped us stow our things in the captain's sleeping quarters behind the little wheelhouse and then they retreated to their own cramped quarters in the forecastle directly behind the bow of the boat.

The captain wasn't much of a talker. Besides, his command of English was minimal. As soon as we were aboard he offered us a mug of hot coffee, threw the diesel engine into high gear, and muttered, "Ja, so, we go."

Thrusting the throttle all the way forward he turned the boat around and we were off, the towering mass of the *Willem Barendsz* soon little more than a grey blur barely visible behind us in the rain. Ernie turned various shades of green within the first hour. The rough weather made him terribly ill. He was constantly shoving his head out of the wheelhouse belching his guts out. By the time darkness enveloped the *Atlantic Endeavor* he was huddled in a fetal position on the captain's bunk. The captain himself said little and, whenever he did talk, I barely understood him. He hummed a lot of the time, his weather-beaten hands firmly gripping the wheel and his eyes—framed by crow's feet and long grey eyelashes—squinted down at the compass or stared into the darkness ahead. It was going to be a long night. And the weather was getting progressively worse.

By dawn we were falling into cavernous pits or rising up on mountains of water, topped by churning green foam. We were on a liquid roller coaster, a hundred feet up in the water one moment, then falling, falling, falling and crashing with a loud thud into deep valleys of ocean the next. I was surprised the vessel was holding up under the terrible pounding it was taking.

Wood creaked, metal groaned, machinery screamed as the diesel engine struggled to keep us moving forward. And through all of this the skipper said little, wrapped up in his oilskins, humming quietly, and drinking cup after cup of hot black coffee. I was amazed that I wasn't ill. Ernest had been reduced to a heap of blankets and rugs on the bunk in the murky recess behind us. I checked in on him often but he only moaned pitifully. The day was dark and unfriendly. Rain and crashing squalls swept over the decks. I had no idea how the Colored crew were doing up front. They couldn't emerge from their cramped quarters in the forecastle or they would have been instantly swept overboard. Just before sundown I asked the skipper when he thought we might reach Walvis Bay.

He merely shrugged his shoulders and muttered, "Ag ja… late."

I asked him whether he thought we shouldn't call up on the radio and tell them that we were on the way.

He looked at me, thought for a moment, then replied, "Ze radio has not vorked for zree veeks. Vhy it should vork now?" ("The radio has not worked for three weeks. Why should it work now?")

And then he looked away, continued humming and held fast to the wheel as we thudded, crashed and plowed through a sea angrier and more terrifying than any nightmare I had ever experienced. When night fell again we were still fighting our way through the turbulence. The windows on both sides of the wheelhouse were being attacked by pounding waves. We were wet. And cold. And miserable. And Ernest had not budged. At about 9pm that night the skipper looked at me and said, "I sleep now."

What? *Sleep?* Is the man crazy? Who's going to pilot the boat? He read my mind.

"Come," he said. "I show."

Planting me behind the wheel and the compass he showed

me how to maintain a grip on the cold, wet wheel.

"You hold," he said. "And you look."

He pointed down at the compass, barely visible in a half glow of failing electrical illumination. He tapped the compass.

"Here," he said. "*Only* here."

A dirty fingernail indicated the heading I was to maintain. I seem to recall that it was a south-south-easterly direction.

"*Only* here," he repeated.

And then he was gone, huddled on the bunk beside Ernest. Within minutes he was snoring.

The fate of all of us, ten souls, lay in my hands. I had not slept for over 36 hours. Time passed slowly. The coffee was cold. The sea was doing its best to bury us in a watery grave. Mountains of water loomed ahead, then valleys. Crash! Up, down, up. Vavoom! The wheelhouse protested with creaks and groans. The diesel engine strained. But I gripped that wheel and fought the Atlantic until my knuckles were white. I held on so tight that I *became* that wheel. And I kept a constant watch on our heading, not deviating from our prescribed route despite the sea's every effort to throw us off course. I was at war with some powerful opposing force, a demon that had taken the form of all that water around us. We were pitched in deadly combat, one against the other. My concentration was so intense that I developed a blinding headache. I wasn't going to survive this. None of us were. We were doomed. Just relax your grip and let the Atlantic take you, I thought. It's no use, no use at all.

And then I felt a tap on my shoulder. I nearly died of fright but as I looked around there was the skipper, smiling a mouthful of yellow teeth at me.

"Good," he said. "I take."

Then, patting me on the back he took over the wheel. It was long before dawn. His return had come just in the nick of time. I collapsed on the bunk next to Ernest and slept the sleep of a newborn babe. When I awoke I sensed that things were different.

It was quieter. The banging and crashing were gone. All I could hear was the gentle rumble of the diesel. And then I realized the pitching and rolling had stopped. I sprang from the bunk. It was still dark outside. I must have slept for hours. The skipper had turned on a bright light on the foremast. Its beam reflected off water as calm as a duck pond. And then, in the distance, I saw a flashing red light. And then more lights. I couldn't believe it. We were limping into Walvis Bay.

The deck hands had emerged from their quarters, chatting happily and smoking cigarettes as they readied ropes to tie us up alongside. As we approached the quay I could make out a gathering of people who had come to welcome us. The flashing red light belonged to an ambulance. Two people from a local newspaper were there. Flashbulbs popped. The rest is all confusion and haze. Apparently the *Willem Barendsz* factory ship had radioed that we were on our way. It had taken us over 50 hours to get there but we made it. We were treated like heroes. Before taking a car to Windhoek the following morning for our afternoon flight to Cape Town we learned that two of the trawlers supplying the *Willem Barendsz* with fish had gone down in the storm with all hands on board.

We had indeed been blessed by the fires of St. Elmo. Once again my thoughts went back to that dim room in Ndola so many years ago. What was it the old albino *nganga* had warned?

"Be wary of the 'big water,'" she had said. "It will be very dangerous and try to destroy you."

Now I knew what she had meant.

Eight

A string of feature films followed from 1968 to 1974, most of them forgettable. Directors invariably wanted to take short cuts. They did everything to avoid investing that extra little bit of time and effort to make a scene look better. Crews were continually rushed.

"Forget that additional light; it looks fine." "Leave the camera where it is and use the zoom. There isn't time to lay down tracks." "C'mon, it's great, let's just shoot."

Corner-cutting and penny-pinching were the rules of thumb. The sole object was to get as many camera setups a day as possible. The quicker you accumulated screen time the sooner editors could cut the movie and get it out on release. The industry was more like a high-speed assembly line. But what we really did was churn out garbage. Unless the picture was intended for the export market, the watchword of the faith among directors and producers at the time was, "Never mind. It's only for the drive-in."

And that was the truth of it. Most of the cheap musicals, comedies and silly dramas I worked on were intended purely for the lucrative local drive-in theater market. They were aimed at capitalizing on a thriving state-sponsored subsidy system. The government had introduced it to foster the creation of Afrikaans language films. Movies made in Afrikaans were subsidized with a much larger financial incentive from state-run coffers than English ones. On many productions we shot every scene twice, once in English and once in Afrikaans. This allowed for two separate language versions of the same show, bringing in two separate subsidies.

One of the pictures I photographed was a movie called *Piesang Strand* in Afrikaans or *Banana Beach* in English. It had a modest budget, a tight six-week shooting schedule and it made no pretensions of trying to be an artistic masterpiece. But we had a lot of fun making it. It was the story of two long-haul mainline passenger train conductors who become embroiled in a bank heist. Like so many contemporary films that come out of 'Bollywood' in India this one had everything in it—musical numbers, songs, chases, murders, blackmail, robbery, romance, shoot 'em ups, you name it. What made it especially enjoyable to work on was the fact that we shot a lot of it on sleeper trains and in exotic locations all over South Africa. The principal stars were two very talented white comedians who hailed from the stage and radio, Pip Freedman and Gabriel Bayman. They played Coloreds. It was typical of the times. A Colored person couldn't play a Colored. You had to cast a white man masquerading as one. Not only was it believed that white actors would give better performances but the logistics of dealing with an all-white cast and crew made everything so much easier, especially when so much of the movie was set aboard segregated state-run trains.

The director was David Millin. I was very fond of Dave and respected him enormously. My first film with him was a ridiculous piece of trivia called *Petticoat Safari* but he and I became very close friends. In 1970 I was hired to shoot one of the biggest pictures of my career for Millin's company. It was called *Shangani Patrol* and was the story of a tragic period in the history of neighboring Rhodesia during Victorian times when Britain marched across far-flung African territories to garner possessions for its empire. With a large cast of 23 principal players, numerous smaller parts and 3,000 black extras playing Matabele tribal warriors everything about this movie was big. The filming of *Shangani Patrol* took place on farms belonging to members of the Rosenfels family in the Matopos mountains of what was then still called Rhodesia, ten years before it became black-ruled Zimbabwe.

While we were shooting the picture Rhodesia was in its fifth year of unilaterally declared illegal independence from Britain under a white government led by rebellious Prime Minister Ian Smith. Black resistance fighters were on the prowl all over the country, murdering farmers, blowing up railway lines and shooting down commercial aircraft. We weren't in imminent danger at our location but, just in case, a small contingent of white Rhodesian troops was stationed near *Lydeard* farm, the main production center. There a diesel-powered electrical generating station, a large communal dining room, a bar, bathrooms, showers, bedrooms, dormitories and other facilities had been built to service the white cast and crew. In addition to guarding us from attack the troops served as extras in the movie. I was accommodated at *Stokestown* farm, a couple of miles away from *Lydeard*. This was the home of the matriarch of the Rosenfels family, a wonderful old lady we all affectionately called 'Gran.' Granny Rosenfels was a gem of a human being. I spent many a night in front of the fireplace with her in the living room of her ambling house that was filled with the bric-a-brac of decades of Rosenfels history. Despite her collection of books, African violets, a menagerie of dogs and cats, silverware and porcelain that dated back to the earliest white 'pioneers' who settled in Matabeleland she was a true lady of the African bush. She spoke all the local African dialects, knew every wild tree and flower by name, often gathered exotic bulbs, roots and wild mushrooms from the veld for dinner and adored her corner of the majestic Matopos mountain range. Slim, trim, in exceptionally good health, she wouldn't hesitate to rush out all on her own in the middle of the night to save one of her black staff from a snake bite or to help one of the farmhands' wives deliver a baby. Her staff adored her. Her sons and grandsons all had their own farms. *Lydeard* was run by Charley Rosenfels and his wife Pam. These farms were more like ranches in the Texan sense of size. *Lydeard* had many beautiful mountains and hills or *'kopjes'* on it. I grew passionately fond of one of them. On days that we weren't shooting I'd climb that *kopje* on my own and spend hours sitting up there gazing out at the endless expanse of the African wilderness, communicating with whatever wildlife, ghosts or ancestral spirits came my way. It was a magical place, a quiet domain of serene and absolute peace and solitude. One night at dinner Charley got up from one of the long trestle tables in the crew dining hall, tinkled his glass with a fork and pronounced that henceforth the hill would be known as *'Lionel's Mountain.'* What's more, for an annual fee of one Rhodesian dollar, I could lease it and call it my own for the rest of my life. I was deeply touched by this humorous but genuine gesture, so typical of the goodwill and warmth of the Rhodesian farmers. They always referred to us South Africans as "those crazy movie makers from the big city down south." The Rosenfels sons, grandsons and brothers were superb horsemen. They were in charge of animal wrangling on the picture. Many of the sets were built with their help. We simply could not have made the picture without them. *Shangani Patrol* opened to good reviews in South Africa, Rhodesia and neighboring territories. A deal to distribute the picture in the United States fell through because of legal wrangling over the music rights but on a trip to Los Angeles in 1971 I had been thrilled to see an enormous billboard promoting the movie on Sunset Boulevard.

By 1972 the so-called 'Bush War' between black guerrilla fighters and the white population in Rhodesia was intensifying. Robert Mugabe's 'freedom fighters' were launching deadly attacks against the country. But under the leadership of Ian Smith the whites steadfastly held on to the reins of power. Black majority rule was not a consideration for them. Many people were dying in bitter fighting, especially in rural areas along the Mozambique border. Yet despite the war that was ravaging the country in 1973 David Millin returned to Rhodesia to make *Die Voortrekkers,* the epic story of Dutch settlers who trekked away from British rule in the Cape of Good Hope in 1836 to found their own Afrikaner republics deep within the hinterland of South

Africa. Rhodesia was chosen as the location because of the cheap labor costs and availability of thousands of black extras that were needed to play Zulu warriors. War or no war, we would shoot all the battle scenes there. Returning to Rhodesia for the big action scenes for *Die Voortrekkers* posed a whole new set of problems. Many of the Rosenfels farms were now encircled by land mines planted by freedom fighters. It was dangerous. But life carried on.

Filming those two big pictures left me with everlasting memories. Bold and beautiful skies at night, the sheer majesty of the locations, farmers tilling their beloved land but struggling to hold on to colonial power, marvelous hours perched on top of 'my' *kopje* surveying the endless spread of Africa below, plus of course the sad images of countless disenfranchised black people who worked alongside us. Many of my memories have been scarred by the tragedies that befell the area after we completed shooting *Die Voortrekkers*. Two of Granny Rosenfels' sons—both farmers and fathers who became really good friends of mine—were killed by land mines. Others, including people who lived on neighboring farms and who helped on the productions, also died in that tragic and senseless war. Britain, together with the United States, Zambia and Tanzania, did everything possible to aid black nationalists in toppling Ian Smith's government to bring about majority rule. But despite all the trauma the movie itself turned out rather well.

I would go on to shoot 18 theatrical movies but documentaries remained my foremost love. After I saw Stanley Kubrick's *2001: A Space Odyssey* on the giant *Cinerama* screen in Johannesburg in 1968 I was seized with a need, a craving, a searing desire to make a nonfiction film about early man in Africa. The scenes of the hominids in *2001*—the *Dawn of Man* sequence—were breathtaking. They were supposedly shot on the African plains but really comprised of background 'plates' photographed in South West Africa (today's Namibia) and then re-photographed on a soundstage at MGM British Studios in Borehamwood, London. The sequence ignited my long-held interest in anthropology so I became determined to make a documentary about the renowned South African anatomist and anthropologist, Professor Raymond Arthur Dart. It was he who had found the first hominid fossil in Africa. In the absence of television the state-run Department of Information was one of the primary underwriters and distributors of documentaries which were made available to local distribution companies for showing in theaters. I took my idea for a film about Raymond Dart to them. I showed them my script and assured them that the film would paint a very positive picture of South African science. As the official mouthpiece of the government they would get good public relations mileage out of it. They were enthusiastic about the concept but would not put any money into the production.

"Our slate is full for the next three years. All of our finances have already been committed but if you produce the film we will distribute it for you. It's a fabulous idea."

Anxious as I was to make the film their word was all the incentive I needed. The Department of Information would distribute the film locally and I would retain all television and other rights overseas. I set up shop with my very good friend, stills photographer Sidney Yankelowitz. I had worked with Sid on a number of feature films. He would raise the funding and produce the film. We called it *The Turning Point*, playing on the theme that there was a time when primates splintered from the evolutionary tree, branching off to become hominids, the forerunners of modern humans and learning to use bone and stone tools and implements. That was one of the most significant 'turning points' in human evolution. Because it would be distributed theatrically we decided to shoot the film in 35mm and lavished everything we could on it including a fully orchestrated original music score by local composer Werner Krupski. With Professor Phillip Tobias of Johannesburg's

University of the Witwatersrand as our science and technical adviser we embarked on telling the tale of the man who found the first fossil and of what it represented.

Anthropologists and paleontologists had always thought that man had originated in Asia. But Africa and Dart were to prove them all wrong. In November 1924 Dart was gathering specimens in a limestone quarry at a place called Taung in the Northern Cape where a fossil of an ancient baboon skull had been found. He instructed his students and the quarry workers to look out for any other interesting animal fossils which he could discuss in his anatomy class as a professor at the University of the Witwatersrand. A couple of boxes of fossils were collected, crated and sent to Johannesburg. Going through the collection Dart recognized something that looked like the fossilized brain of an ancient primate. Putting it aside as possibly a small baboon or another species of ape the piece nagged at him. There was something odd about it. It had an uncanny resemblance to a small human brain. After chipping away at another lump of limestone Dart saw what appeared to be a cranium attached to a face and a separate jaw. When he joined the pieces together—brain, cranium, face and jaw—they made a perfect fit. But this was no baboon. The fossil was that of a young primate, maybe no more than three to five years old at the time of death. But what really surprised Dart was that even though it had a fossilized ape-sized brain—with a capacity of just over 400cc—its dental characteristics were not those of an ape. They were more like a human's. Examination also showed that the base of the skull was balanced on the vertebral column, providing unmistakable evidence about its posture. This creature walked upright on two legs. Dart considered it an intermediary between apes and humans, a 'missing link' as the local press dubbed it. He proclaimed that it lived somewhere between two and three million years ago, nicknamed it the Taung Baby, wrote a paper for the British scientific journal *Nature* and gave it the Latin name

Australopithecus africanus, 'australis' meaning south, 'pithecus' meaning ape, and 'africanus' for Africa. And so the 'Southern Ape of Africa' entered the vocabulary and consciousness of the scientific world.

But much of the international academic community shunned such thinking. Anthropologists vehemently resisted the idea that a human ancestor could have come from Africa. As far as the majority of scientists were concerned the furthest one could push back human history on the continent was to the time of the ancient Egyptians. Even the many stone cities and fortress-like structures such as Khami, Dhlo Dhlo and the great Zimbabwe ruins could not have been the handiwork of Africans, they argued. They had to be made by foreign invaders, perhaps even Phoenicians. But Africans? No way. They insisted that the indigenous people of the 'Dark Continent' were nowhere sophisticated enough to produce such structures without outside intervention. Even when questioned about Bushmen rock art very few experts would even consider that those ancient works depicting profound mystical motifs could have been created more than just a couple of thousand years ago. Before that? Out of the question. Europe and the rest of the world were simply not ready to accept the antiquity of man in Africa. That was the mindset that Dart was up against. Saddened by his rejection, Dart turned his attentions back to anatomy. He served as Dean of the department at the University of the Witwatersrand from 1925 to 1943. But one man did listen to his ranting and raving about Africa being the cradle of our species. He was the Scottish-born paleontologist, Robert Broom. Scratching around limestone quarries and caves during the thirties and forties Broom went on to discover many more Australopithecine fossils, most notably at Sterkfontein Caves just outside Krugersdorp, northwest of Johannesburg, and at field sites such as Swartkrans and Kromdraai. Now the world stood up and paid attention. The evidence was unmistakable. By the late forties, Dart and his claims were finally accepted. Africa, scientists conceded, was indeed the birthplace of humankind. The professor once again turned his attention to fossil hunting, uncovering other species showing that early humans walked the southern African landscape many millions of years ago.

Making *The Turning Point* was a fascinating experience. I first met Dart in 1970 in the office of Professor Phillip Tobias, the man who had taken over his position as professor of anatomy at the University of the Witwatersrand medical school. Short, stocky, white-haired, bright-eyed and with a piercing voice that hinted at his enthusiasm for all things, Dart was an extremely friendly and excitable man. He exuded an energy way beyond his 76 years of age. We sat down to chat over a cup of tea and, naturally enough, I brought up the subject of the fossil that started it all, the Taung Baby. Where was it? Would it be available for filming? Could he show it to us on camera once production got underway? Without saying a word Dart put down his teacup, sprang from his chair, rushed over to a safe in the corner of Tobias' office, whirled the combination lock and threw open the door. Then, very delicately, he removed a shoe box-sized container from within and brought it over to me. Opening the lid as carefully as though he were prying open a box of delicate Fabergé eggs he reached inside. And there, resting on a bed of cotton floss, was a fossil. He virtually tossed it into my lap and, had I not caught it, it would probably have gone rolling across the floor.

"You mean that?" he asked.

My God! I was holding the Taung Baby, the actual fossil. It was heavy, about the size of a grapefruit, approximately five inches long and four-and-a-half inches high. It was in three pieces but, like a tight-fitting jigsaw puzzle, it made up a single unit. The face and jaw were a greyish-white color and the fossilized braincase a dark brown. What was once a living, breathing being had become a lifeless, mineralized thing. But this was an object unlike any other on the planet. As I stared at it I looked into the deepest recesses of our human past. This baby, this small child, with its hollow eye sockets, peered back at me across 23 *thousand* centuries. Short of fingering a moon rock I knew that I would never again touch a physical object as rare, as meaningful as that again. Timidly and completely at a loss for words I handed it back to Dart. He returned it to its box and stowed it back in the safe.

I spent two weeks with Dart and his wife Marjorie at their apartment in Sandton, going through files, photographs and newspaper cuttings, gleaning precious moments from his past. It was fascinating. We would often spend hours in his living room as he pontificated on his beliefs that the Phoenicians had explored the interior of Africa long before anyone else. He was convinced that the Chinese had rounded the Cape of Good Hope centuries before the Portuguese. He was almost obsessed about that, often beginning a conversation in his comfortable armchair, then crawling over the carpet to me on his hands and knees, thumping the floor with his fists to emphasize various points, and ending up at my feet, staring up at me, exuberant and breathless. Seldom have I known anyone with such an extraordinary capacity to believe so intensely in the things that interested him or to get so worked up about a topic. His wife, Marjorie, would often try to calm him with a, "Now, now, Raymond, mind your heart," but it never worked. He was a furnace of energy and enthusiasm.

We took Dart to a place called Makapansgat, a yawning cave near Potgietersrus (now Mokopane) in what was then the Northern Transvaal province. Composed primarily of limestone, it had yielded over 100,000 fossils. Most of them were animals but many were *Australopithecines*. We worked with James Kitching, one of Dart's early researchers. During the sixties, he was the first person to find a fossil in Antarctica. We also filmed at various fossil sites with the brilliant Bobby Brain, then director of the Transvaal Museum in Pretoria. We spent an extraordinary weekend with him digging up fossils at Makapansgat. A fierce lightning storm one night turned the place into something straight out of Halloween. We huddled together as thunder rumbled. It shook the ground and echoed off the cave interior as sharp, bright bolts of lightning lit up the night sky. It was marvelously dramatic. I shot scenes of Brain and his assistants examining fossils around a hissing hurricane lantern as nature put on this spectacular display in the background.

By 1969 Raymond Dart had long retired from the University of the Witwatersrand. He divided his time equally between living in South Africa and the United States. He spent much of it lecturing, writing and acting as visiting professor at the Institute for the Achievement of Human Potential in Philadelphia. Founded by Dr. Glenn Doman, the goal of the institute—with branches worldwide—was to raise the intellectual, physical and social abilities of brain-damaged children. The institute helped victims to attain the maximum of their potential. Dart's work in unraveling how early hominids adapted to their environment and how they began to fashion crude tools from bones and stones was invaluable to the institute's work. It was amazing how successful it was. People learn to solve problems only when they are appropriately challenged.

When *The Turning Point* was finished a screening was arranged for the top brass of the Department of Information in Pretoria. They had requested a film of 40 minutes duration and that is what we delivered. After the end credits were over the curtains in front of the screen closed and the lights went up. To stunned silence. The man sitting next to me, a senior Afrikaans official in the department, cleared his throat. I looked at him. Then he coughed. He clearly did not know what to say, so I took the lead.

"What do you think?" I asked.

He coughed again. So did four or five of the other members of the audience. The Assistant Director of Information sitting in the row in front of me stood up. He straightened his dark flannel suit, turned around and in a very polite and low Afrikaans tone he said: *"Ons is jammer. Ons kan dit nie vertoon nie."* ("We're sorry. We cannot show it.")

"Why not?" I asked in English. "Didn't you like it?"

His reply was in Afrikaans again. *"Nee, nee, Meneer Friedberg. Dit was baie, baie goed. Maar jou prent is teen die kerk."* ("No, no, Mr. Friedberg. It was very, very good. But your film is against the church.")

"What?" I squeaked. "How come?"

The suited man shifted his beady eyes and announced that human evolution was not an appropriate subject with which the Department of Information could be associated. The film was anti-Bible, anti-Christian, anti-Dutch Reformed church, anti-Afrikaner and overtly heretical. I could not believe what I was hearing. Despite the fact that they themselves had seen the script, approved it, and assured me they would distribute the film because of its scientific content, now these self-same representatives of official government policy were throwing the age-old Creationist argument at me. I grabbed my film, and Sid and I stormed out of the theater.

Sid had invested a lot of faith and money in the project. And now this. There was only one recourse. We would have to try to sell it to television abroad. With a couple of cans of 16mm prints of the movie under my arm I set off on an around-the-world mission to find a distributor or a buyer for *The Turning Point*. But there were two things working against us. It was 1971 and South Africa's name stank more than ever all over the world. Few people would do business with us. And then there was the matter of the film's length. The Department of Information had requested a 40-minute film and that did not fit into the programming time slot of any television network. To accommodate commercials it either had to be 24 minutes long to go into a 30-minute slot, or 48 minutes to fit into an hour. In the end, we did manage to sell quite a few copies of the film but, financially speaking, we lost our proverbial pants. My heart broke for my partner Sid.

He had so much faith in the film and he had given his all to it. The oft-quoted lesson became abundantly clear. Never invest any of your own money in your own film. Despite the terrible disappointment Sid was a dear and wonderful friend. We remained lifelong buddies until he passed away in 2012.

The American premiere of *The Turning Point* was held at the Institute for the Achievement of Human Potential in Philadelphia. Raymond Dart and his wife Marjorie were in the audience. Both were happy about how the film depicted Dart's biography and the story of the little Taung Baby. Other major screenings included one for the staff of the Natural History museum of the Smithsonian Institution in Washington DC, one for the National Geographic Society and one at the annual dinner for Associates of the University of Southern California at the Century Plaza Hotel in Beverly Hills. Everyone liked the movie but the 'Made in South Africa' label had doomed it. In later years we were not the only ones to suffer from South Africa's political isolation. People around the world were also being deprived of good scientific and anthropological information because of apartheid. Years later, between April and September 1984 the American Museum of Natural History in New York held a wonderful exhibition entitled *Ancestors: Four Million Years of Humanity*. For the first time ever hominid fossils from all the major African sites were brought together for public exhibition. But because South African fossils were included in the displays many African governments boycotted the event. The result was that some of the most important discoveries including those from Olduvai Gorge in Tanzania were shown only as plaster casts. It was felt inappropriate to include them in the same gallery alongside the South African exhibits.

There was one episode in the story of *The Turning Point* that deserves special mention. Ten years before we made the film the American writer Robert Ardrey had published his milestone work on the early history of man, *African Genesis*. As he was a great admirer of Dart's it was arranged that I would spend two days with him at his home in Rome. We would show the film, drink wine, discuss possible sales outlets for the film and generally just shoot the breeze. And so it was that on a chilly day in March 1971 we gathered at a screening room in a narrow building above a travel agency on the fashionable Via Barberini in Rome. A group of Ardrey's friends and colleagues were there and we ran the print. They loved the show, especially Ardrey. I was thrilled. Here was a man who had begun writing plays for Broadway in 1936, penned many novels, then transitioned to Hollywood where he had written the screenplays for major motion pictures such as *The Four Horsemen of the Apocalypse, The Wonderful Country, Quentin Durward, The Green Years, Madame Bovary, The Three Musketeers* and, as his swan song, *Khartoum,* for which he had been nominated for an Academy Award for Best Original Screenplay in 1966. His nonfiction books on anthropology and human behavior, including *African Genesis, The Territorial Imperative* and *The Social Contract* had all become international bestsellers. I was encouraged by his reaction to the film. Perhaps a sale might still lurk somewhere in the world. I was yet to go to Germany, France, Denmark, England, the US, Japan and Australia, but, alas, that big sale never transpired. On our first evening in Ardrey's apartment in Trastevere, Rome, which he shared with his South African-born wife, Berdine Grunewald, a cat, libraries of books, antiques, paintings, sculptures and a formidable wine cellar, we got to talking about 'the business.' I was always anxious to make a film about the African missionary-explorer David Livingstone and as I adored Ardrey's screenplay for *Khartoum* which dealt with the last days of General Charles 'Chinese' Gordon during the British campaign against the Mahdi, the self-styled 19th century Islamic jihadist in the Sudan, I asked him whether he would be interested in writing the script. Large quantities of dry red Italian Chianti fueled his reply which was emphatically negative.

"I'm totally finished with screenwriting," he said. "What I'm doing now, writing about human history, is far too interesting, too rewarding for me to be bothered with movies anymore. It's not that films bore me. It's just that the film *business* bores me. I don't need its aggravations anymore. I'm tired of being fucked around by Hollywood. And I hope for your sake that you don't find yourself in the same position one day. Be careful, my friend, because you just might."

I sipped my wine. Ever since that night I have been thinking about what he said. Without any question, Robert Ardrey had learned his lesson well. I had just experienced my first brush with the coquettish world of film distribution and I too would learn many more bitter lessons about the egocentric and greed-driven industry in the decades that lay ahead.

Nine

Television finally came to South Africa in 1976. Prior to that the apartheid regime had regarded it as a dangerous threat. What would the black population think if they saw how people lived abroad? What incendiary intentions would it give them to see how multiracial societies functioned elsewhere? Blacks, browns, yellows and whites living together? In peace? Even falling in love and having sex and marrying one another? No way. Television was evil, a threat, a danger to the survival of the white man. But the clock could not be stopped. On January 5, 1976, the state-run South African Broadcasting Corporation (SABC) began nationwide transmissions of a tautly controlled and very conservative single television channel. At first programs were aimed exclusively at whites. It alternated between English and Afrikaans languages on different nights of the week. In 1981 another channel carrying programs for black audiences went on the air. In subsequent years more channels would be introduced but in the beginning it was essentially a pro-apartheid propaganda tool. It had a limited number of locally produced and imported shows to create the impression that it was an entertainment medium and, of course, there was always a lot of sport on it. South Africa has always been a sports-crazy nation. In those days the country was still banned from participating in the Olympic Games, yet another cost of the apartheid policies. Anything to do with sport—both local and foreign—was eagerly devoured by audiences, both white and black.

Prior to the commencement of the service the SABC began commissioning documentaries from local production houses. I had joined one of these companies as a director, writer and cinematographer in 1974 after becoming despondent about the atrocious theatrical features that I had been forced to work on. The company was Independent Film Centre (IFC). It was based at Lone Hill Studios in Johannesburg. It had been awarded a glut of shows on a variety of topics and there was one series that nobody was keen to work on. So I happily took on the assignment. It was to be a series of eight half-hour documentaries that would look at the various black tribes within the country. According to the brief from the SABC the programs were to introduce white audiences to the languages, culture, music, costumes, crafts and traditions of the country's ten different tribes. The Corporation's—in other words, the government's—belief was that most white employers knew little about their black workers and the series would make it easier for them to understand the differences between members of the various tribes and alleviate cultural and language difficulties in their relationships with black people. But, in retrospect, I wonder whether that was the real purpose. Perhaps the government had already seen the writing on the wall. Less than ten years after television was introduced Nelson Mandela would be transferred from his prison on Robben Island to the mainland and would secretly begin meeting with white Cabinet Ministers to determine the country's multiracial future. Perhaps the Afrikaner-dominated government and the ruling white political party, the Nationalists, were aware of the inevitable. Maybe they had already foreseen that the day would come when Nelson Mandela would be released as a free man, when apartheid would finally fall and when whites would be forced to hand over power to a democratically elected black government. Naturally, there was no hint or inkling of this when the television series was commissioned. At that time it was to be a cultural series only. But the producer Edgar Bold and I concurred that the shows should go further than what the SABC had requested. Here was an ideal opportunity for white South Africans to get to know their black neighbors like they had never been able to know them before. Here was a chance to break cultural barriers and set a tone of respect and understanding for the day when apartheid might end.

I called the series *The Tribal Identity*. It would be based on the writings, research and travels of 53-year-old Dr. Peter Becker, a retired schoolteacher turned anthropologist. With degrees in African languages, sociology, history, the classics and a PhD in anthropology his foremost love was pottering around the wilderness, camera and notebook in his satchel, recording the lives of the rural African. He had made numerous black friends over the years, many of them in high places within various tribal hierarchies. He spoke a few African languages fluently. A prolific author when we first met, Peter had already published 13 nonfiction books on African history with more in the pipeline. He had also traveled extensively in North America, the Middle East and to the islands of the Indian Ocean, writing about indigenous people.

Peter grew up on a farm that would eventually become the Johannesburg suburbs of Bryanston and Rivonia. Though he had two brothers they were much older than he was, so his playmates were the little African shepherd boys on the farm. Through them he learnt to speak Sindebele, South Sotho and Zulu. His boyhood hero was a farmhand, Sipho Mncube, an old black man who tended the cattle but who also practiced as a diviner and *sangoma*. Mncube entranced the youngsters on the farm with stories of great African chiefs and histories of the various tribes. Sitting around the fire outside the old man's hut at night Peter learnt about Shaka, legendary unifier and leader of the great Zulu nation, of Mzilikazi, founder of the Matabele dynasty, of Mosheshwe, creator of the Basutho nation, and of Mantatisi, queen of the Tlokwa people. In 1953 Peter began his professional research work, taking twenty years to cover all the major tribes of Southern Africa. Once, while consulting a Zulu *sangoma* he was told that his work would have far-reaching impact. He would open the way for one group of people to learn about another. Because of this the old *sangoma* dubbed him *Vulindlela,* a Zulu word meaning 'Opener of the Road.'

Peter and I hit it off right from the start. I was very excited about the prospect of spending over a year on this exciting project with him. Unfortunately, due to professional commitments as an advertising executive specializing in the African market, he would not be able to accompany us on all our location shoots. In fact, throughout the production he spent less than twenty percent of the time with us in the rural areas but he was always available in Johannesburg for discussions, to review dailies, look at edited sequences and provide guidance. We saw each other socially and, over the years, we became the very closest of friends.

One of my stops during the preparatory phase of the production was the Department of Bantu Administration in Pretoria, the government department responsible for all affairs pertaining to the country's black population. A liaison officer had been appointed to work with us. He was Mr. WA Meintjies, a tall, lanky Afrikaner with a sparkling sense of humor who went out of his way to smooth the production process. Although he toed the party line I liked him enormously. There were many hurdles to the project, the major one being that no cameras were ever allowed into the tribal homelands without the necessary government permits. Visitors could drive through those vast areas that dotted the entire map of the country but they had to remain on major roads. No detours were allowed. If anyone was caught in tribal territory without permission they were liable to arrest. There were reasons for this. Firstly, the government was terrified that conditions in these areas would be exposed to the world and, secondly, they wanted to control white contact with rural blacks because, to their way of thinking, sabotage, subversion and rebellion were constantly in the wind. Meintjies was the man who would issue us with permits for whenever and wherever we wanted to go. Each time a trip was planned he was to be informed of the names and addresses of all crew members. Provided the Bureau of State Security, or BOSS, had no files on anyone on that list the necessary permits would be issued. But they were not open-ended. They would stipulate precisely where we could go and how long we could spend in each place. Meintjies treated it all as a bit of a joke and we never experienced any problems but I was never sure how to read him. Whatever game he was playing he played it very well indeed. In fact, I never had any problems calling him up in the middle of the night from some God-forsaken one-horse town in the middle of nowhere to request an extension to our permit. Meintjies was always obliging and saw that I got what I asked for.

There was another reason why he was so essential to the project. Following the Yom Kippur War of 1973 and the worldwide reduction of oil supplies from the Middle East, South Africa had introduced fuel rationing. Meintjies was the one who got us the necessary paperwork to purchase additional gasoline while on the road and to even allow us to carry a few extra gallons on board the production van in case of emergencies.

There was one final hurdle for us. How would the leaders of the various black homelands receive us? After all, South Africa had been carved up into this crazy patchwork quilt of autonomous 'homelands' or *Bantustans*—ten in all. Many of the leaders of these territories were little more than stooges or puppets of the white regime. Basically, they did what they were told. With their own national flags, coats-of-arms, national anthems, newly-constructed legislative assembly buildings, fancy cars and police forces, they were quite happy to be propped up by Pretoria as figureheads of future republics that not a single nation outside South Africa itself would ever recognize. We knew we wouldn't have any objections from any of them. But there was one exception.

Prince Mangosuthu Gatsha Buthelezi was the political leader of the Zulus, by far the largest of all the Bantu groups, numbering about six million at the time. As head of the powerful Buthelezi tribe his position was hereditary and not merely bestowed upon him through the benevolence of the white-controlled Ministry of Bantu Affairs. He alone refused to be coerced into taking his people and their traditional homeland KwaZulu into the South African government's vision of independence. He was adamant that KwaZulu, previously known as Zululand and which occupied much of the province of Natal, would remain an integral part of South Africa itself. With his high public profile as the most powerful spokesperson of the country's entire black community—remember that Nelson Mandela and his associates were still incarcerated at the time—he was something of a thorn in Pretoria's side. He was regarded as an obstinate troublemaker who would simply not follow instructions. But there was little the government could do about it. They were hesitant to remove him from office and stir the up ire of the Zulu people. Simply by doing that would lead to the kind of conflict and bloodshed that the whites feared so much.

Peter Becker and Mangosuthu Buthelezi had been friends for over twenty years. They had initially met through Becker's association with the late Zulu king, Nyangayezizwe Cyprian Bhekuzulu. Buthelezi was the deceased king's cousin and a man close to his son, the present king, Zwelithini Goodwill kaBhekuzulu. Buthelezi grew up as a herd boy in the rolling green hills of Zululand, majoring in history and Bantu administration at the University of Fort Hare in 1948, at that time the only university in the country open to black students. After a spell working with a firm of attorneys in Durban he went to Mahlabatini in 1953 to take up his position as chief of the Buthelezi clan. When American director Cy Endfield made his epic motion picture *Zulu* in 1963—the story of the battle of Rorke's Drift in which 4,000 Zulus attacked a garrison of 130 British soldiers—Buthelezi was cast as King Cetshwayo. He played the part superbly well but it was politics and not movies where his future and his interests lay. Under the apartheid plan to create the independent Bantustans the KwaZulu Territorial

Authority was established in 1970 with Buthelezi recognized as its Chief Executive Officer. In 1976 he became its Chief Minister. But he resolutely refused to budge on the issue of accepting independence. We were unsure about how he would feel about *The Tribal Identity* so it was suggested I discuss the matter with him.

Our first meeting was something of a clandestine James Bond-like affair. Because of the sensitive nature of any encounter between the media and Buthelezi I flew from Johannesburg to Durban commercially and then chartered a small plane north to Eshowe deep in the heart of sugar cane country. There I met a local white farmer who drove me to Melmoth, about twenty miles to the northwest. In the secluded and comfortable confines of the home of a liberal and wealthy white English-speaking sugar baron, Buthelezi and I met, shook hands and faced one another over tea and cake in the library. He was dressed in a casual brown summer suit with a cravat, and had a string of colored beads and a large seed pod strung around his neck. In his closely cropped hair he wore a crane feather, the ancient symbol of his high tribal office. It was a cordial meeting. I was struck by the sincerity and intelligence of this articulate and friendly man. After a couple of hours of questioning I had his blessing to go ahead with the series, assuring me that from his perspective there would be no objection to filming in KwaZulu. I speak of KwaZulu as though it were a single, contiguous territory, but it was nothing of the sort. The conceivers of apartheid and the planners of the future map of South Africa had cut Zululand up into a mélange of no less than 43 separate pieces. And this morass was supposed to become an independent republic. It was actually rather comical, to say the least. But that's how things were. Before I left for my return trip to Johannesburg I put one final question to Buthelezi.

"How are you ever going to resolve the question of independence? What if the government forces you to accept it?"

He smiled and shook his head. He had a habit of talking with his eyes closed much of the time. It was as though he were reading from notes scribbled on the inside of his eyelids. It was a behavioral characteristic that I would get to know well over the ensuing years. Here was a man who thought and answered carefully. He tried to never speak *at* you, like so many politicians tended to do. His responses were carefully measured and his words neatly sculpted before anything left his lips.

"I'm as much a South African as you are," he said. "And it is not on the whim of any white Nationalist government nor anyone else that I and my people will forfeit our birthright as South Africans by accepting this pseudo-independence nonsense."

We shook hands and I left. I was aware that I had just met an extraordinary statesman, a man who had already single-handedly held down a massive black uprising against the white regime and who had prevented bloodshed from staining the political scene long before Nelson Mandela was released from prison.

On another occasion when I met him while hardliner John Balthazar Vorster was president—long before Pieter Willem Botha or Frederik Willem de Klerk occupied that office—Buthelezi told me: "Racial discrimination has to go. No stone should be left unturned to avert violence in this country. I believe that America is about the only outside force that can play any really meaningful role to get South Africans of all colors and creeds around a conference table. I believe the time has come for America to say to this government: 'If you don't go to the negotiating table to put aside your differences we can no longer support you.' If economic sanctions are the only tool left to avoid bloodshed and to prevent South Africans from slaughtering one another, I wholeheartedly support them."

I was thrilled to learn that he felt America held one of the major keys to solving South Africa's problems. Although I was happy to live in and be making films in Africa the United

States was never far from my mind or indeed my heart. I always knew the day would come when I might return there. I would interview Buthelezi on many occasions, sometimes in his office in the KwaZulu Legislative Assembly building, but most often at his home *KwaPhindangene* ('The Place One Returns To') on a hill overlooking the picturesque Ulundi valley deep in KwaZulu. This plain was where the final battle between the Zulus and the British had taken place on July 4, 1879. 20,000 warriors attacked a British force of 4,156 whites and 1,152 blacks employed by the Redcoats. The Zulus lost 1,500 men, the British only two officers and ten members of other ranks. After that battle the prolonged Zulu wars with Britain were over. After bitter fighting and loss of life the great Zulu nation was subjugated to the British crown. The Zulu king Cetshwayo was captured on August 28, 1879 and taken to Cape Town where he was imprisoned. In 1881 he was permitted to travel to London where he pleaded with Queen Victoria for clemency, promising that hostilities would never occur again. In 1883 he returned to Zululand and was reinstated as monarch. But after that white administration was the order of the day. British rule was eventually replaced by white Afrikaner rule, and that was that.

Under apartheid, Ulundi—not the battlefield itself but the veld nearby—was earmarked to become the new administrative capital of KwaZulu. It was here where Buthelezi would voice his most vehement criticism of government policy, pronounce his rejection of the idea of an independent nation, and constantly appeal for a democracy embracing all of South Africa's people. But the government stubbornly persisted in enforcing its *Bantustan* policies. On May 7, 1976 we filmed the official opening of the Legislative Assembly by the Minister of Bantu Administration and Development. The whole affair was something of a travesty. It was a ceremonial demonstration of white rule and willpower, replete with cavalcades of shiny black limousines and police on motorcycles rattling over potholes and dirt roads to the small temporary assembly building where South African and KwaZulu flags fluttered in the wind. Marching bands played military music. The whole thing reminded me of a circus coming to town with just a couple of differences. It was a stiff and pretentious affair, and no one was having any fun. No cheering crowds stood along the roadside, the whole place at that time being little more than a dustbowl. The most sophisticated building in town was a brand-new Holiday Inn, the world's smallest, planned to accommodate the few visiting dignitaries and other emissaries who would one day come to this seat of Zulu administrative rule. It was also the only establishment in town where you could get a nice chilled beer.

My visits to *KwaPhindangene* were always enjoyable. Mangosuthu Buthelezi's large, comfortable home was airy and modern, filled with a blend of Western and Zulu architectural styles and features. Furniture, art, cultural objects and overall design tastefully reflected both worlds. Mangosuthu and his wife Irene Thandekile—both devout Christians—were always wonderful hosts. I especially enjoyed the brief occasions I had meeting their children, Mandisi and Sibuyiselwe. In the early seventies Buthelezi founded Inkatha, a non-violent black liberation movement which immediately attracted a membership of over a million. It would grow in numbers very quickly and was particularly popular among the youth in urban black townships. Because of his power, his pacifistic beliefs and especially because he was the leader and spokesperson of the largest black group in South Africa I was convinced that Buthelezi would one day become president of a free and democratic South Africa. But back in those days it was impossible to foretell what the future held. To be honest, I for one never expected that Nelson Mandela and the other members of the African National Congress (ANC) would ever be released from prison. After his release from incarceration on Robben Island many years later Mandela and Buthelezi would have their differences. Mandela is a Xhosa, Buthelezi a Zulu. Zulus outnumbered Xhosas by about two to one. As a result of long-held historical differences between these two major groups reconciliation between them was difficult. In later years, during the campaign to elect South Africa's first fully democratic government in 1994, Buthelezi almost threatened to withdraw his Inkatha Freedom Party (IFP) from the elections. Inkatha was competing with the ANC, the party of Nelson Mandela. Due largely to Mandela's incredible charisma, his towering international fame and his all-abiding spirit of goodwill, by 1994 the ANC had become the most popular political organization in the country. At the last moment Buthelezi rescinded on his decision to boycott the elections, but when the final votes were tallied the ANC won more than 62% of the mandate with the IFP garnering just over ten percent. Bloody fighting between members of both parties broke out. Thousands died. Through the sheer persuasive force of their personalities and their remarkable leadership qualities, both Mandela and Buthelezi eventually galvanized their supporters, reining them in and turning them away from violence. When the country's new non-racist government finally took its place in parliament, Nelson Mandela became President and Buthelezi was appointed Minister of Home Affairs. When Mandela traveled abroad Buthelezi stood in for him as Acting President. But over the years the presidency eluded him. He would never make it to the top as Head of State.

Back in 1974 as I flew home to Johannesburg at sundown on the day that I first met Buthelezi I looked down on a land drenched in golden light. The magnificent valleys and hills of Natal stood out in stark clarity, amplified by lengthening shadows. This soon gave way to the grasslands and plateau of the Transvaal, and then the sun was gone. That sprawling domain beneath me was the home of a multitude of people, many of whose cultures were totally unknown to whites in urban areas. Perhaps *The Tribal Identity* would make a difference. Perhaps it would do something to help build bridges and span the cultural chasm that plagued the country.

The long line of kings who ruled the Zulu nation are known as *Ingonyamas* or Lions. The eighth direct descendant of the mighty Shaka who galvanized the nation into one of Africa's most formidable fighting forces was a man I would be privileged to get to know quite well. He was Zwelithini Goodwill ka Cyprian Bhekuzulu, son of the late King Cyprian. Peter Becker and King Cyprian were very close friends, so much so that when the king died in 1968 a delegation from the royal Zulu household approached Peter and asked him to accept the position of father-guardian to the king's 20-year-old heir-apparent, Prince Zwelithini. On October 29, 1969 the title was officially bestowed on Peter, an unprecedented honor for a white person. The two men—father-guardian and prince—developed a very close rapport. That bond became stronger after Zwelithini's coronation on December 3, 1971. The two men would see each other socially a few times every year, especially if Zwelithini had a pressing matter of state for which he needed advice or a sympathetic ear. In 20th century terms it was a strange relationship, a traditional tribal king and a white anthropologist. I would get quite a few opportunities to see them together. Our cameras would catch them wandering across the lawns of Peter's Bryanston home, locked in conversation, or Peter and the king sharing the African habit of sniffing pinches of the much-beloved tobacco snuff as they strolled together through the gardens of one of the monarch's rural palaces in KwaZulu.

The first time I visited King Zwelithini was in early 1975. It was at one of his royal residences near Nongoma, a small town in the heart of Zulu territory. Prior to the establishment of the KwaZulu Legislative Assembly at Ulundi, Nongoma was the administrative capital of Zululand. Our trusty Volkswagen Kombi minibus moaned and groaned its way along indescribably bad roads that wound through some of the most spectacular mountainous scenery in Southern Africa. But you couldn't see much of the countryside. It was raining heavily and the roads had turned into sluices of thick red mud. What made things especially treacherous were deep potholes, now hidden under water and sludge. Springs and shock absorbers labored under the strain. It took us hours to travel the 80 miles or so from the paved road at Melmoth. It was only in the late 1970s that KwaZulu's primary roads would be properly surfaced. Until then, they would merely be dirt tracks left to the mercy of weather and traffic, much of which consisted of little more than donkeys and ox carts as well as hopelessly overloaded and poorly maintained buses.

Our destination was *Dlamahlahla*, a modest 1920s vintage brick farmhouse surrounded by tall syringa and wattle trees. Though small and unimposing, *Dlamahlahla* was one of the king's royal 'palaces.' The rain had stopped as we approached the simple metal-framed wire gate. Geoff Collins, my loyal and trusty assistant and one of the nicest guys you could ever hope to meet, jumped out, swung the gate open and we drove up towards the outbuildings, cattle *kraal* and granary. As we approached the palace six *indunas* or senior Zulu regimental commanders dressed in full tribal regalia appeared out of nowhere. Each one held a spear, a large cowhide shield and a symbolic stick symbolizing his rank and office. They smiled, stamped their bare feet and started beating the spears against their shields in welcome. They looked absolutely splendid, symbols of something ancient, proud and powerful. Each one wore a headband of leopard skin. Some had feathers in their hair. One of the men had a pair of outstretched eagle's wings stuck into the rear of his headband. They all wore a variety of animal skins and furs around their waists, thin strips of hide and beads around their wrists, and beads and cocoon rattles around their ankles. Around their necks were strings of colorful beads. Slung across their naked chests was an assortment of intricately embroidered bands signifying their position as royal praise singers. Tribal royalty and chiefs went nowhere without a group of specially appointed men who constantly shouted out the greatness, lineage and accomplishments of their leaders. Other than acting as bodyguards, praise singing was the primary function of these six imposing warriors.

As we approached the porch of *Dlamahlahla* the front door opened and there stood the king himself, a tall, handsome 27-year-old direct descendant of the mighty Shaka. He was casually dressed in Western-style clothes, smiling and holding up his right hand in greeting. The praise singers immediately rushed to his side, thumping their shields and calling out the royal greeting, *"Bayete! Wena we Ndlovu! Bayete! Wena we Ndlovu!"* ("Hail! You are mighty like an elephant!")

We were ushered inside and introduced to the king's senior wife, the very beautiful Queen Sibongile. King Zwelithini had two wives at the time. He had married Sibongile first, therefore she was senior to the other queen who lived at another of the royal residences not far away. Apart from a magnificent beaded necklace and earrings, Sibongile was also dressed in Western clothing. She had remarkably smooth and alabaster-like light brown skin, a wonderfully sculpted face and the most perfect smile you ever saw. She was gorgeous. The royal couple invited us into the living room and we began to chat about the sequences we would be filming at the palace the next day. Both spoke perfect English and were enthusiastic about appearing in the documentary series, even though they were already highly accustomed to the media. During Zwelithini's coronation and again at his marriage to Sibongile camera crews and photographers from all over the world had descended upon them *en masse*.

We were due to stay at the Nongoma Hotel that night where we would meet Peter Becker who was driving down independently from Johannesburg. Next day's shooting would concentrate on scenes depicting the unique relationship between the two men. It was around midday when our conversation with the king about the arrangements for the filming was over, and the royal couple insisted we stay for lunch. The house was filled with an assortment of Western and Zulu artifacts including photographs or portraits of all of the king's ancestors. I noticed that the table in the small dining room had already been prepared for lunch. There was a place for all of us on the crew including, I was relieved to see, for our black camera assistant, Thomas Makhubela. Being a Zulu himself Thomas was especially honored to be here with us. After all, this was his monarch and he merely a humble subject. But Zwelithini was extremely courteous and treated him as an equal. He showed us to our places. In respect of Zulu custom, Queen Sibongile would not be dining with us. She would eat elsewhere with her female retinue, though where exactly I wasn't sure. Each place at the table had a floral pattern china plate turned upside down. Next to the plate were all the necessary cutlery and a tall glass into which a couple of colored paper napkins had been carefully folded. Some of them had Christmas motifs printed on them and others said, "Happy Birthday." There was a bottle of soda pop at every place, each one a different color and flavor: red, green, yellow, orange, dark cola. In the center of the table was a large, ornate arrangement of plastic flowers. Clearly, someone had gone to a lot of trouble to prepare for our visit.

Servants only appeared once we had seated ourselves at the table. Steaming bowls of food were brought in. They represented traditional Zulu dishes in addition to regular Western fare. Meats, vegetables, *putu* or *pap* (stiff cornmeal porridge described in previous chapters), fruits and desserts. There was no particular order to what one ate first. I noticed that Zwelithini the *Ingonyama* or Great Lion began his meal with stewed peaches and then went on to the *putu,* meats and gravy. There was more than ample quantities for a vegetarian like me although the king found it very peculiar that I did not partake of any of the meat dishes. He wasn't offended, just very surprised that here was a man who didn't eat any meat. During the course of the meal barefooted servants, bowing reverently whenever they approached the king, constantly bustled silently around us, removing dishes and bringing in new courses. A dog sauntered in and lay under the table. Then a white hen appeared, cluck-clucking her way into the dining room, pecking at crumbs and scraps that had fallen to the floor. Nobody paid the slightest attention to the animals. Having them there seemed to be perfectly normal. I was especially pleased when a friendly long-haired grey cat padded in, purring loudly and rubbing itself against my leg. All things were in harmony here. It was wonderful.

The conversation eventually turned to a problem that the king was having with his 16mm film projector. Although *Dlamahlahla* was supplied with electricity those were the days before the SABC's new television service had gone on the air and, besides, the TV signal would never reach this far deep into KwaZulu territory. Apart from SABC radio, 16mm films were the only form of entertainment available. The king subscribed to a lending library service in Durban. Twice a week, a few cans of film—usually comedies or Westerns—would be delivered by mail to his office in Nongoma. Geoff Collins and our sound recordist Henry Prentice looked into the projector problem after lunch, discovering that the machine needed nothing more than a new projection lamp and a photoelectric light bulb for the sound playback system. I promised Zwelithini that I would send him a few of each as a gift just as soon as we returned to Johannesburg, a prospect which clearly pleased him.

Later that day it started drizzling so we headed off to Nongoma, checking in to the somewhat dismal and rundown Nongoma Hotel. It was an all-white establishment and our black assistant Thomas Makhubela had to be content with sharing a small, smelly room in the servants' quarters near the coal-fired boiler room that provided the few white guests' bathrooms with hot water. Peter Becker arrived just after sunset and we went into the noisy, smoke-filled pub to have a pre-dinner drink. It was filled with white civil servants employed at the local regional administration offices, a couple of road construction workers, one or two traveling salesmen doing the rounds of general dealers deep in the mountains and a handful of Afrikaans cattle farmers. Every single one of them seemed to be chain-smoking pungent unfiltered cigarettes. The place was buzzing. Much of the talk centered around whether KwaZulu should be forced to accept independence or not. The Afrikaans farmers were very vocal about where they stood in the argument.

"Just tell that Buthelezi to go to hell," one of them pronounced after his fifth or sixth Castle Lager beer. "Pretoria should put its foot down with him."

"Ja," said another. "Jesus, man, who do these kaffirs think they are?"

A few heads nodded. Others did not. From somewhere in the smoke-filled room an English voice piped out, "Watch out what you say, old chap. These are Zulus. Don't muck around with them or you know what'll happen."

And then a lot of shouting and bantering ping-ponged around the room. I looked at Peter who sat there silently puffing on his corncob pipe. He merely winked at me and smiled. No, this was one argument we weren't going to get involved in. Slowly nursing my beer I was particularly fascinated by an 18-feet long python skin and a withered, dried elephant penis that had been suspended from a wooden frame above the bar counter.

The rain stopped later that night and filming went well at *Dlamahlahla* the next day. We wrapped by mid-afternoon and the king asked Peter whether he would like to see his new palace. It was being constructed for him by the KwaZulu legislative authorities about ten miles away. Naturally, we were all anxious to see it. I was invited to travel with the king and Peter in the royal car, a large maroon Chrysler New Yorker Brougham limousine that had been specially imported from the US. It gleamed and glistened. Its uniformed chauffeur was constantly wiping off dirty marks or shooing flies away from it. The Zulu royal standard flew from a short chromium staff on the front left fender. The crew followed behind us in the production vehicle. As I sat in the wide back seat, comfortably wedged in between King Zwelithini and Peter I noticed something strange dangling from the rear view mirror in front. It looked like a brown shriveled leather balloon. I leaned over to Peter, subtly pointing to it and frowning as if to say: What the dickens is *that*? He laughed. There was no need for secrecy or formality so he asked Zwelithini himself to explain it to me. I was told that the king always needed to have something symbolizing the presence of his ancestors wherever he goes. Many people, not only royalty, devoutly follow this ancient spiritual tradition. According to Zulu custom the symbol selected is most commonly the dried gallbladder of a specially sacrificed goat. After being treated with special *muti* or medicine by a *sangoma* the bladder becomes the temporary dwelling place for the ancestral spirits. Apparently, Zwelithini had many of these bladders hanging in various places. Even when he traveled abroad one of those little dried gallbladders would be tied to the overhead reading light panel above his seat in the first-class cabin of an airliner. As we drove along the wet and muddy roads people would see the royal car and hail their beloved *Ingonyama*. Men on bicycles, little boys tending cattle in the fields, women carrying boxes and bottles on their heads and babies on their backs, all would stop, respectfully bow their heads, reach out with their right hands and yell, *"Bayete!"* as we passed. After about fifteen minutes we turned off onto a little dirt track riddled with stones, potholes and more pools of muddy water. But it was all very deceptive. Nothing could prepare me for what was to come.

We passed an area where at least a dozen big yellow trucks were parked. But our chauffeur kept on going, approaching the rim of an escarpment overlooking a seemingly endless lowland. I clutched the seat in front of me as we pulled up dangerously close to the edge. When we got out of the car I was stunned by the scene. The view was breathtaking. Way beyond us was a sweeping valley of green grass and forest. Within this magnificent plain was the curving arc of a swiftly flowing river. Just below where we stood on a wide rocky outcrop a sprawling ultra-modern new brick and concrete palace was taking shape. White and black workmen—bricklayers, glaziers, painters, plumbers, tilers, electricians—scrambled all over the structure. When it was finished its panoramic windows, balconies, porches and patios would surely make it one of the most unique royal homes anywhere in the world. It is here where the *Ingonyama* would take up residence after his marriage to his third wife, Queen Mantfombi, a princess of the Swazi Royal family and daughter of King Sobhuza II of Swaziland (modern-day eSwatini). It was customary for Zulu royalty to marry Swazi royalty, cementing the close cultural, historical and traditional bonds between the two nations. In time, King Zwelithini would marry a total of six wives, each holding court in her own palace. But nothing would equal the splendid structure that I watched being built that day.

That evening over dinner at the hotel Peter mentioned that he knew a very powerful *sangoma* who practiced in the area nearby. Would we like to visit her? I saw it as a wonderful filming opportunity. Two of the episodes of *The Tribal Identity* would be devoted to mystical and spiritual matters. They would also encompass investigations into traditional healing and divination techniques as well as customs concerning death, the afterlife and the ancestors. We had not as yet shot anything on those topics so, yes, I was eager to meet her. And so it was that the next morning Peter's car and the production van pulled into a little *kraal* situated atop a windy hill. It was not a pretty area. The entire countryside was pockmarked with soil erosion. Lack of fuel and electricity and a burgeoning rural population had caused every tree in the district to be chopped down for firewood. Overgrazing by cattle, sheep and goats had denuded the landscape of grass. All the life-sustaining topsoil had been swept away by wind and rain.

I do not remember the *sangoma's* name. Hundreds of tiny white ceramic beads had been woven into her hair which had been plaited into thin strands and smothered in some kind of foul-smelling animal fat. On the crest of her head was a veritable bouquet of dried goat gallbladders. Long strands of red and white beads and strips of fur dangled from her neck. Bare breasted, she wore a dark black leather skirt over which hung an elaborately decorated beaded apron. On her wrists were bracelets and bangles of strips of animal hide, copper wire and beads. Around her ankles were tied at least two or three dozen dried cocoons and seed pods which rattled loudly. She held a wildebeest tail switch. Her cheeks were smeared with ochre and it was hard to judge her age but I guessed she was probably in her mid-forties or early fifties. She lived in the little settlement with her unemployed husband, two other female *sangomas*, a couple of younger men and women, a few teenagers and at least a dozen small children and babies. Their *kraal* was a mixture of huts made from timber, dried mud bricks and thatching grass. A tiny enclosure made of sticks and wire netting held a few thin cows and goats. There were a couple of mangy and pitifully underfed dogs lying around. Roosters pecked at whatever they could find in the grassless, muddy veldt.

Methods of divination among the Zulu vary but the most common form is the throwing of bones, just as I had witnessed with the old albino *nganga* that I consulted in Ndola all those years ago and with the Shangaan chief in Mozambique. The *sangoma* normally asks a patient or client to take a pinch of snuff, drop it into a small leather bag, state his or her name into the bag and then blow into it, just as I had witnessed before. Her little bag contained an array of animal bones as well as stones, shells, pebbles, coins and other small items that she used to foretell the future or determine the nature of an illness.

I was hoping to film the Zulu *sangoma* reading the bones for Peter in the little courtyard outside her hut but it started to rain again. There was no electricity within miles and due to a shortage of power outlets at the Nongoma Hotel our battery lamps had not been charged. Filming was therefore out of the question. Peter and the *sangoma* sat inside her *ndumba* or divination hut for about a half-hour or so, chatting away in Zulu. I left them alone. Peter was a spiritual man with a very deep understanding of the beliefs and traditions of tribal Africa. He was a font of knowledge about the important role that the ancestors played in the thinking, behavior and aspirations of black people. He approached the subject with unreserved humility, seldom sharing what he knew with his white compatriots. This was not because of an aloofness nor for selfish reasons but simply because he had tremendous respect for Africa's ancient ways and for the very important place of the *sangoma* in black society. He was never without his own set of divining bones and was very adept at reading them. He was always interested in comparing his set to those of professional diviners and to learn new interpretative techniques from them.

It began to rain quite heavily and I was debating whether to leave and head to our next location. The roads would be difficult and dangerous. Peter was going to head back north to Johannesburg in his own vehicle and would soon hit pavement again but the crew and I were going in the opposite direction, traveling on a lot of dirt roads before we met the highway to Durban which we were hoping to make by nightfall. As I sat in the production vehicle with the crew discussing what we should do Peter waved to me from the *ndumba*. I got out, ran because of the falling rain, then stooped under a low arch to enter the hut. I was told to kneel, clap my hands in respect of the ancestral spirits dwelling there and then sit down cross-legged on the floor. It was dark inside and the place was filled with many unrecognizable smells and objects. It was all a little unnerving. As I searched the gloomy walls of the circular structure I could make out a pile of pots, calabashes, canes, bottles, rusty tins, small boxes, animal tail whisks, hides, bark, stones, dried frogs, snakeskin, feathers, goat and monkey skulls, colorful but faded cotton cloths, all manner of things, but there were many items I simply could not identify. Peter wanted to know whether I wished to have my bones read. He had told the *sangoma* about our intention of capturing something of Zulu culture and conveying it to the world, and she expressed a desire to meet me. With Peter interpreting she said she would be happy to foretell the future for me. I was delighted at the invitation. Did I have a question to ask of her? I couldn't really think of anything so I asked whether the work we were doing—the making of the television series—would be successful. I was handed the bag of bones, told to blow into it, state my name, ask the question—all in English—and then empty the bag onto a little grass mat on the floor. I did as requested. An assortment of knuckle bones and other odd-looking little objects fell onto the mat. The *sangoma* picked up a little stick. She began prodding at some of the items. She reached down and carefully turned one or two of them over, then lay them down again exactly as they had fallen. When she began speaking in Zulu, with Peter translating into English, she used the stick to point out certain patterns in the way the bones lay. Without repeating everything back to me in English Peter was obviously having the deeper meanings of the pattern explained to him. The *sangoma* hardly ever looked up at me, concentrating only on the objects on the mat.

It was raining heavily outside now. The drops made a thumping sound on the thatched roof of the hut. The beginning of the reading was mildly interesting. I was told that what we were doing would be well received by many people, more than we could ever meet personally. Well, that made sense. Even though the *sangoma* had no concept of television she was right. Of course we couldn't possibly personally meet our audience. She said that the work would sometimes be difficult and that I would see things I had never seen before. Well, that was interesting too. But all of this could have been guesswork or, I suppose, applicable to just about anyone. But then the reading began to enter a deeper, stranger level. She told me that I was an only child. My father had passed away. I had been married but was now without a wife. This was all true. My first marriage ended in divorce and I would not marry my second wife for another five years. How did she know all of that? Had Peter told her anything about me? No, I thought. Why would he? And then it really got interesting. She said I had nearly died from a very serious illness when I was young, around two or three years of age. True. I had been pulled back from the maws of death when I had diphtheria at the age of three and almost succumbed to the affliction. Peter didn't know that. And then she said that I had "lived across the great river" and "traveled far beyond the big water." The Zambesi perhaps? My years in Zambia? As for the "big water" was this a reference to my ocean voyage to England and then my flight to North America? Or was she referring to that terrifying filming trip along the coast of Angola? Of course, I couldn't help recalling what the albino *nganga* in Ndola had also told me long before any of those events even came to pass. With Peter translating the *sangoma* went on. She told me I was very close to Africa. At one point Peter struggled with an interpretation that eventually came out as, "You have Africa *on* you."

My God, I thought. There it is again. My birthmark. The small birthmark on my right ankle that was in the perfect shape of a map of Africa. Although Peter had seen it many times she had not. I was wearing jeans that day, not shorts. Then the woman found something in the bones that she hadn't seen before. Looking straight at me and almost shoving her stick into my face me she barked out a string of words, one of which sounded like, *"Ndlovu."*

Peter struggled with the interpretation. But even I recognized it as sounding similar to what the praise singers had called out to King Zwelithini, *"Wena we Ndlovu!"* ("You are mighty, like an elephant!")

Peter looked puzzled and asked her a question. She excitedly pointed at the bones with her stick, agitated that he couldn't comprehend what she was saying and again tried explaining what she was seeing. When she was finished she stared at me, almost in wonderment. Peter looked at me oddly.

"I don't know what to make of it," he said. "But she says you have the spirit of an elephant with you."

It was unbelievable. The old albino woman in Zambia had told me that I would almost be killed by a great beast. That was long before my experience in Mozambique with the white hunters and the shooting of the elephant. I shifted uneasily. This was too much. I asked Peter to kindly request more details from her. Once again she pointed out a pattern in the bones but poor Peter was mystified. He couldn't make head or tail of her ramblings.

"All I can tell," he said, "is that she says mixed in with your ancestors and other protective spirits around you there is the essence of a great she-elephant. I really don't know what that means."

But I did. It was uncanny. I instinctively *knew* that the elephant that had died in front of me that day in Mozambique was still with me. I felt her presence often, usually when I was endangered or threatened by anything, no matter how trifle. It was as though she was protecting me. She had become part of me. I had never told anyone about it. I had kept that belief solely to myself. But there it was, clearly revealed in the *sangoma's* set of bones.

The rain was pelting down heavily as we said goodbye to Peter outside the *kraal*. He drove off in one direction and we in the other. Sitting behind the wheel of the van and staring ahead at the atrocious road as the wipers struggled to keep the rain off the windshield I felt numb. That woman had tapped into something undeniably profound in my past. Long after midnight that night in my comfortable double bed on the twelfth floor of a luxury hotel on the Marine Parade in Durban I was still wide awake, pondering on the mystery of it all. Could it be explained? Could anyone unravel the enigma of how a clump of dried bones and stones and dusty little items in an antelope hide bag could spill out onto a shredded mat on a floor and reveal such unknowable things? What I could not foresee that night is that I would be given the exact same messages by no less than three more *sangomas* in completely different places in the years ahead.

Ten

A place of verdant beauty stretched along South Africa's eastern seaboard. It lay between the cities of East London and Durban. About 200 miles of it was known as the Wild Coast. Rolling hills covered in grassy pastures met rocky cliffs, rivers, lagoons, long sandy beaches and tidal pools. All of this was lapped by the Indian Ocean. It was the traditional homeland of the Xhosa and Pondo people. Many different tribes made up the Xhosa-speaking group, one of the largest being the Thembus. It was in the little hamlet of Mvezo in Thembuland that Nelson Mandela was born on July 18, 1918. Under apartheid the area was known as the Transkei, the Xhosa-speaking people's officially designated *Bantustan* or homeland. Led by Kaiser Matanzima, a controversially appointed Chief Minister propped up by the South African government, Transkei was the first of the black homeland territories designated to become 'independent.' The date was set for October 26, 1976. Supported by Pretoria and by local chiefs who had been coerced to cooperate with the government, Matanzima had usurped the rightful Thembu Paramount Chief Sabata Dalindyebo in a bitter contest for leadership. He would become Transkei's first Prime Minister and eventually its President. In preparation for this fiasco—at great expense to the South African taxpayer—the government had requisitioned all white farms, trading stores and property in Transkei's rural areas, making them available only to local blacks through an organization called the Xhosa Development Corporation. But few Xhosas could afford to purchase property. Whatever was left over from the days of white occupation was slowly going to wrack and ruin. Vacated farmsteads and trading stores were everywhere. Apart from major towns like the capital Umtata the Transkei had virtually been emptied of white residents.

The Xhosas had a proud and colorful heritage. They were renowned for their hospitality. The Transkei was a place I got to know and love. I filmed there often in 1975 for *The Tribal Identity*, becoming familiar with many of its back roads and byways. Dirt tracks where cattle and other domestic animals wandered took you through some of the loveliest scenery imaginable. Round mud brick huts dotted the landscape. Their thatched roofs were topped by magic charms and seashells, talismans as protection against lightning and witchcraft. There was always an element of the supernatural hovering over people's lives. Most doorways faced eastwards towards the rising sun as a welcoming gesture to good spirits and benevolent forces. Cattle *kraals* and pens for goats, sheep and pigs were near every family's hut. It was the duty of the *kwedinis* or young prepubescent boys to take the cattle out to graze during the day. Though poverty was obvious everywhere the Wild Coast seemed like an idyllic place. People were happy there. My all-abiding memories are of smiling faces, laughing children, bright sunshine and spectacular hills of brilliant green. I often had the urge to stop the vehicle, jump out, lay down and, like a small child, roll down those sloping thick carpets of grass, coming to rest in a gulley, a stream or the sands of a wide and deserted beach.

Dress and adornment in that part of the country were very different to what one saw elsewhere. Whereas the Zulus made extensive use of beads, feathers and animal skins, the Xhosas wore woven cloths and thin blankets. The home-dyed blue, orange, brown and fawn-colored fabrics were works of art. They were covered in designs, one more ornate than the next. Women wore black, orange or purple turbans. Red ochre and white clay played a dominant role in makeup and adornment, especially during rituals and ceremonies. Men and women puffed on long-stemmed hand-carved pipes. Young girls could often be seen wandering along pathways playing a bowed musical instrument called a *Mqangi*. This was a simple, single-stringed little contraption. One end of the bow was clasped between the teeth while a simple stick was maneuvered backwards and forwards across a copper wire, the other hand putting pressure on the string to change pitch.

In Umtata I had found what in the film industry is known as a 'fixer.' This is someone who knows the local area and people well, and who can act as guide, translator, trouble-shooter and production assistant. He was a good-humored middle-aged retired guy by the name of Viv White. Viv was born in the Transkei, knew all the local customs intimately, and spoke the language fluently. He and his wife Marion had once lived in the little town of Elliotdale, deep in Thembu territory, but because they weren't black they had to sell up everything and move to Umtata as the Transkei was slowly being prepared for independence. Fortunately, Viv was granted permission to make use of his vacation cottages which he no longer owned but was permitted to lease at a nominal annual fee until independence was official. These were little whitewashed concrete and brick buildings situated on a remote and quiet beach called Mpame. It was a perfect spot, close to a river and a lagoon. There was ample fresh drinking water, a deep pit toilet, a portable electrical generator, and a wood-fired stove. It made for an ideal production base. What's more, the place was looked after by Ernest, a tall, cheerful thirty-year-old Xhosa man in Viv's employ who lived nearby with his two wives and five kids.

Between Viv and Ernest we had access to local chiefs, headmen and villagers. The two of them acted as guides and interpreters. Ernest saw to it that one of his wives or children always kept an eye on things at Mpame, as well as ensuring that a fire was going and water was on the boil when we got back from a heavy day's filming. Evenings were the best of times. We invariably returned caked in dust and sweat and would simply head for one of the tidal pools, throw off our clothes and jump in and soak. Many tidal pools along that wonderful strip of coastline were filled with marine life—lobsters, sea urchins, tiny colorful fish, clams, mussels. We would sometimes watch women and young girls in their lovely blankets come down to the shore at low tide to gather seafood which they carried back to their villages in plastic buckets propped on their heads. Oysters clung to the rocks and were easily available. The Xhosas were one of the few coastal people I met in my travels who also relished octopus, creatures plentiful in those waters.

We filmed sequences covering the entire gamut of tribal life from the cradle to the grave. Few events were as fascinating as traditional rites of passage for young women and men in preparation for adulthood and marriage. Unlike white society, sex was not a taboo subject in tribal areas. It was openly acknowledged that we humans are sexual creatures and that sex and procreation play an important role in human affairs. Sex education and initiation into an active sexual life was openly discussed. For Xhosa males, circumcision was an essential feature of that process. This ritual was practiced to a lesser or greater degree by other tribes, including the Zulu and the Venda, but the Xhosa circumcision procedure was widespread and unique in many ways. It was usually carried out when young males were well into their teens or early adulthood. When Viv introduced me to 17-year-old Taushile Debeza it was late autumn, just after the crops had been harvested. He lived with his parents and family in a small cluster of huts about an hour's drive from Mpame. At that time of year his duties tending fields and flocks were minimal so his father had arranged for him to leave home and partake in what is known as the *AbaKwetha* initiation ceremony. This was an ancient rite marking an adolescent male's transition to manhood. On the prescribed day, Taushile and two other local young men, both his age, gathered together to say goodbye to their mothers and female relatives. Then they were accompanied by their fathers and male adult family members and taken to a local *ingcibi* or *sangoma* for the *ulwaluko* ceremony. Here the boys were stripped naked. They would not be permitted to wear a single item of clothing for the next four weeks. Skilled in the use of a sharpened knife blade the *ingcibi* deftly performed the surgery. Fortunately for the three boys it was only a partial circumcision. Most of the prepuce or foreskin of the penis was left intact, leaving much of the glans still protected by a sheath of protective skin. They were lucky. The prepuce keeps the glans lubricated and is densely packed with nerves. It is extremely sensitive and serves a crucial role in providing sensation and pleasure during the sexual act. It is now generally acknowledged that men who have had the entire foreskin removed experience far less pleasure during sexual stimulation and intercourse than their uncut counterparts.

The cutting was a bloody and painful process. No anesthetic was used. The boys were strictly forbidden to show even the slightest hint of pain. They were not permitted to wince or blink, let alone cry out or murmur. Doing so would indicate cowardice. No stitches or blood coagulates were used other than an herbal paste derived from local trees and bushes. This was smeared onto the wound. Clutching their bleeding penises the boys were then daubed from head to toe in white clay made from powdered sandstone. White was sacred in many tribal groups. It was believed to please and appease the ancestors. It symbolized purity, spiritual cleansing and metaphysical protection. Now, as initiates, the boys were known as *Kwethas*. Their only possessions during the next four weeks would be a single grey blanket and a tin can slung from a cord around their neck containing the white clay. This is how they went about their daily routine, white ghost-like figures clad in blankets.

Immediately following the ceremony the three boys—all in pain but doing their utmost not to show it—took leave of their male relatives and were placed under the control of an *ikhankatha,* or overseer. I do not recall his name but he was a man who appeared to be in his late twenties. Specially trained by the tribal elders his functions were many. He led the boys off into a secluded valley, about a two hours' walk from the *sangoma's* kraal. There, near a stream, a special grass hut had been built for them. This was the *AbaKewetha* lodge. The *kwethas* would live there in complete isolation for four weeks, occasionally to have contact with visiting adult male relatives but never to be seen by a female. If a woman or young girl was spied on the crest of a hill or seen wandering along one of the pathways near the lodge the *kwethas* had to hide or immediately cover themselves with their blankets. Concealing their faces when a woman was around was essential because it was forbidden to reveal their identities. To do so would show disrespect for the ancestors and therefore compromise the boys in the spiritual and metaphysical realm.

The overseer was skilled in herbal medicine. He kept careful watch over the *kwethas'* wounds as they slowly healed, teaching the boys how to apply a daily dressing of various leaves and plants collected from the surrounding bush. It was also his task to maintain discipline during the long period of seclusion. It was almost a prison-like existence. The accent here was on hardship and austerity. The *ikhankatha* always carried a cane and was required to punish the boys by beating them if they broke a code of behavior based on modesty, supplication, respect and self-reliance. His duties included teaching them to hunt, to live off the environment by gathering edible fruits and to become as self-sufficient as possible. There was little wildlife around. Population pressures had long ago emptied the Wild Coast of once-plentiful wild mammals, but there was always the odd heron, pheasant, deer or fish that could be caught and barbecued. In keeping with the rules of the lodge, the *kwethas'* diets were extremely frugal. They had been provided with a supply of dried corn on the cob that they roasted over a fire. This was their staple food during the long, cold month that they spent at the lodge. The overseer also had the sacred task of instructing Taushile and the other two *kwethas* in matters pertaining to tribal traditions, sex, courtship, marriage and parenthood. This lay at the core of the initiation process. I often admired this opportunity for the young men to learn about their future lives as adults. I thought about how much teenagers in urban areas around the world could have benefited from a similar period of instruction, instead of resorting to peers or hearsay for information. Today, of course, a lot of kids in Western societies are often exposed to sex on the Internet but most of it is pornography with little of value to prepare them for responsible adulthood. When those young *kwethas* left the lodge nothing would be a mystery to them. They would have an understanding of a woman's body, knowledge of menstrual cycles and periods of fertility. They would know how to please their mates sexually, be aware of methods of birth control and, above all, how to become conscientious and responsible husbands and fathers.

I must admit that I found it difficult to accept the austere circumstances in which they were expected to survive, especially with the onset of winter. Denied any items of comfort—not even a bed or a chair—they were permitted the use of only basic utensils such as hunting *assegais* (spears), knives, sticks, wooden spoons and grass matting on which they would sleep on the cold dirt floor of the lodge. I guess it was very much like boot camp in many ways. But this was boot camp ratcheted up many levels. The underlying principle behind it all was discipline. Respect for ancestors and elders was very much part of the learning process too. Taushile and his three colleagues would come out of this arduous period and go out into the world holding parents and elderly members of the tribe in high esteem. This was a trait shared among young people in all tribal areas. It never failed to impress me. I often thought that white kids could learn a lot from their tribal counterparts with regard to respect for parents and elders. During the day Taushile and the two other *kwethas* spent a lot of time basking in the sun outside their makeshift hut reapplying the white clay as they received instruction from the overseer. It was a constant struggle to keep every inch of their bodies covered by the irritating clay. Every week the *sangoma* would send over a new supply, ensuring that the boys never ran out of it.

Geoff, Thomas, Viv, Ernest and I returned to the lodge periodically to film the boys. We were privileged to be welcomed back every time we came trundling through the reeds and grass bearing cameras, tripods and sound recording equipment.

"Molwe, madoda!" ("Hello, gentlemen!") they would shout out when they saw us coming.

They accepted our presence without reservation, totally ignoring the inconvenience of having lenses and microphones thrust into their faces or into the middle of whatever they were doing. During their isolation period I managed to get Peter Becker down from Johannesburg to appear in a few scenes with them. Because he spoke fluent Xhosa he was especially welcomed. We spent many memorable days shooting at the lodge, in the veld, during hunts and along the riverbank. The scenes remain some of my favorite in the entire series, with Peter intermingling with the *kwethas* while he performed as on-camera host, often improvising and describing events unscripted and unrehearsed. It was a challenge for him but he always did a terrific job encapsulating the essence of everything, delving into the purpose and deeper spiritual meaning of their activities.

A month after their *ulwaluko* or circumcision it was time for the *kwethas* to reenter society, to be officially proclaimed as adults. I was at the studio in Johannesburg when the call came through from Viv White in Umtata telling me that we had 48 hours to get down there or we would miss the crucial 'coming out' ceremony. Armed with permits and the necessary documents to carry extra fuel Geoff, Thomas and I rushed down from the Transvaal, through Natal, down the south coast and across the Umtamvuna river into the Transkei. After picking up Viv in Umtata we turned left off the national highway and headed down narrow winding dirt tracks to Mpame. Arriving late at night we caught a couple of hours of sleep and then, long before dawn the following frosty morning, we set up our equipment on a desolate beach not far from the *AbaKwetha* lodge for the 'coming out' ritual. We were soon joined by the boys' fathers and senior male relatives, all of them wrapped in thick warm blankets or overcoats against the sharp winter temperature. Each of them carried two long, heavy sticks carved from local trees. Then, still covered in white clay, Taushile and the other two *kwethas* emerged from the darkness. The gathered crowd started to beat their sticks and sing songs, praising the boys for having successfully endured their experience. Under instructions from the overseer the boys dropped their blankets, their teeth chattering from cold, and waded into a lagoon. There they waited patiently as a dozen cattle were herded onto the beach. Then, on a signal from their fathers, the *kwethas* walked out into the freezing surf, the waves crashing over them. And there, as a new sun crept above the distant horizon of the Indian Ocean behind them, they washed off every trace of the white clay. In the scarlet light of dawn I could see how pleased they were to finally rid themselves of the annoying caked white skin covering. From here on it was going to be handheld shooting for me for much of the day, with Thomas running after me carrying extra film magazines and a tripod just in case I needed it. Geoff did his best to keep out of camera range with his equipment while recording the richness of sounds around us. Viv and Ernest kept close to me, telling me what was going on and what important events I should watch for. The two of them were marvelous. Their experience on *The Tribal Identity* would have made them fabulous assistant directors on any Hollywood movie set.

Leaving the ocean and returning to the beach the *kwethas* were immediately surrounded by their fathers, adult male relatives and the cattle. Then, stooping with their heads bowed while the men stretched a blanket above them to serve as a canopy the boys slowly headed back towards their initiation lodge about a mile away. The beating of the sticks, the songs from the chorus of male voices and the bellowing cattle created an incredible aural dimension to it all. It was hauntingly beautiful. We knew we were witnessing something very ancient and truly remarkable. The sun rose higher, heralding a cloudless and perfect day. Way up on the distant hillsides women from surrounding villages and *kraals* began to gather. They sang, ululated, clapped their hands and shouted welcoming messages down to the *kwethas* as they approached the initiation hut. Huddled beneath their canopy and surrounded by the men and animals, Taushile and his naked companions could still not be seen by any females. But, judging by the joyful shrieks and calls coming from the women, it was very obvious that the boys were eagerly awaited by mothers and sisters who wanted to welcome them back into the tribe. Once they reached the hut the *kwethas'* bodies were smeared with thick coatings of animal fat to relieve the itchy dryness caused by weeks of wearing the white clay. The singing and clanking of sticks intensified as the boys' fathers presented them with the first of a slew of gifts, brand-new ochre blankets, a color signifying their transition from adolescence to maturity and manhood.

The overseer and male relatives now threw the boys' old grey blankets, tins of white clay, sticks, hunting equipment and all the utensils they used during their stay at the lodge into the hut. Then the entire place was set alight. Everything had to be burnt. The thatched hut was soon burning fiercely. The boys were not permitted to watch any of this. Just one glimpse of the fire was regarded as a bad omen, boding misfortune in years to come. As the hut collapsed in smoke and crackling flame Taushile and his companions, now proudly clad in their new blankets and accompanied by their fathers, were marched off to the local headman's village at the top of a hill. Here they were finally greeted by their jubilant mothers and female relatives. Gifts of coins, pocketknives, pipes and clothing were bestowed on them. As the young men sat on their haunches bedecked in the greasy fat and new blankets they graciously accepted these offerings, as well as being made to listen to a great deal of advice from their mothers and the elder women of the village. I didn't understand a word of it but by the way Viv and Ernest were laughing I could tell that they were also being lectured on how to become good lovers, spouses and future sons-in-law. Among those present were a couple of matchmakers, eager to introduce Taushile and his friends to young girls of marriageable age. It was a very joyous and happy occasion.

Canisters of home-brewed millet beer appeared and soon everyone was partaking of it, with the exception of the *kwethas* themselves. Their ordeal was not quite over. After receiving their gifts they were shown into a hut where they had to strip yet again. Now their bodies were smeared with red ochre. This was the final symbol of their transition to adulthood. They had to spend the rest of the day and that night secluded in the hut while their families and villagers partied outside, well past midnight. For the first time in four weeks the boys were permitted to sleep on mattresses and enjoy some of the comforts denied them during their initiation. Next morning the *kwethas* were awakened by their fathers and given one final gift—a new name. Taushile was renamed Fudumele. Loosely translated it meant 'warm.' This would be the adult name by which he would be known for the rest of his life. In the eyes of the tribe, he was now no longer an adolescent but a man.

The last I saw of Fudumele was later that day when one of his uncles rode into the *kraal*, bringing him a young brown steed as a gift. There was much trilling, singing and dancing as Fudumele, now dressed in brand-new Western clothes and shoes, mounted his new horse and rode off with his father, uncle and other relatives to the little town of Elliotdale for more celebrating. My thoughts often turn to him. As I write this, he would now be a man of 60. I wonder what has become of him. But wherever he is, part of his life is now an integral part of my own, for I shared an ancient and sacred tradition with him as he transcended from youth to adulthood. Without any doubt, it profoundly altered us both.

Eleven

Fortunately, genital alteration or mutilation as an act of ritual was not practiced on females among any of the tribes in South Africa. The cutting or tying off of the clitoris was common among many tribes on the continent at that time, especially in the northern and western regions. The excision of this extremely sensitive organ at the anterior end of the vulva deprived a woman of sexual stimulus and pleasure. It was carried out in predominantly patriarchal societies to supposedly ward off desire for extramarital sex and to assure that a wife would remain faithful to her husband. But in South Africa other forms of female initiation into adulthood were widespread, none of them physically invasive or designed to limit her enjoyment of the sexual act.

While *en route* to film craftsmen making pipes and musical instruments in Thembuland one crispy morning we came across a *kraal* where a girl had just experienced her first menstruation. She was now regarded as an *Intonjane* or female initiate. According to custom, she had to go into seclusion in one of the family's huts. Confined in it she had to wear a mask and was not allowed show her face for two weeks. She was not alone during this period of isolation but was accompanied by a couple of young post-menstrual relatives who saw to her needs. If she ever emerged from the hut to go into the surrounding bushes to relieve herself they had to cover her with a blanket so that she could not be seen, especially by males. The beginning of a girl's menstrual cycle was regarded as a blessing and a time to celebrate. Sexual maturity heralded the prospect of marriage and children. New additions to the tribe were regarded as gifts from both the ancestors and a supreme being. This omnipotent entity went by many names but was seldom contacted directly. The pathway to Him, Her or It went by way of the ancestors.

On the day the *Intonjane* ceremony began the girl's father invited relatives and friends from the surrounding district to his *kraal*. A goat was slaughtered, home-brewed beer was brought out, and dancing, drinking and festivities went on all day. The only person absent from the party was the *Intonjane* herself. Remaining in the gloom of the hut she was brought beer and meat by her young female aides, but never permitted to go outside. Much of the entertainment consisted of mock stick fighting. The Xhosas were exceptionally keen on sparring with sticks and, after a couple of beers, even older women happily joined in this sport. On occasion it got a little out of hand and sometimes drew blood. But it was a wonderful day and I was especially happy because we had our host Peter Becker with us. In his khaki bush outfit, his trio of trusty Leica, Pentax and Nikon cameras slung around his neck, we were able to get footage of him in the midst of the festivities, interfacing with the *Intonjane's* family and explaining the proceedings directly to our camera in his charming style.

On the fourteenth day of the *Intonjane's* confinement preparations were made for her 'coming out' ceremony. This was to be a major celebration. Apart from marriage and the birth of her first child it was to be the most important event in her life. On the appointed day people from all over the district arrived in droves bedecked in traditional dress. The women wore ornately decorated blankets and shawls, their heads covered in woven turbans. Cosmetics included yellow, white and ochre clay smeared all over the face, or tiny elaborate designs etched on the cheeks, nose and forehead with a dark red henna-like substance. Speckles, swirls, lines, circles, diamonds, the designs were endless with the younger women looking especially beautiful. An ox was taken into the cattle *kraal* and ritually sacrificed to the ancestors.

It is amazing what one can look at while peering through the viewfinder of a camera. Psychologically, that instrument intimately binds you to your subject or, on the other hand, it can act as a barrier between you and what you are seeing. It all depends on the scene or on your frame of mind. Whenever I shot anything disturbing I tended to make the camera a barrier, distancing me from what was going on in front of the lens. That is what I had to resort to during the sacrifice of that poor ox. I do not want to give the impression that I'm criticizing a culture that is age-old and has consistently bonded the Xhosa-speaking people to their heritage but that sacrifice truly nauseated me. The animal's rear feet were bound together, followed by the binding of its front legs. Lying on the ground it was unable to move. Two young men then held on to the bound feet as the girl's father took a long *assegai* (spear), thrust it into the ox's belly and then dug around inside the abdomen trying to find the aorta to sever it. The bellows of pain were deafening. The animal was in agony. Finally, a pocketknife was pulled out from somewhere and one of the male relatives scooped out a hole behind the animal's skull, cutting into the spinal cord. Slowly the ox bled to death. Once this gruesome episode was over I could get back into the more positive mood of the proceedings. When I asked Peter to find out why an *assegai* had to be thrust into the animal's stomach and then twisted around inside it the explanation we received was that it had something to do with the girl's ancestors and the release of the animal's life force to appease them.

Next to his own offspring and family a tribal man's cattle were his most prized and valued possessions. As a result, animals were rarely slaughtered for meat. Animal flesh was reserved for special occasions and not consumed every day. When this did happen it was invariably a communal affair and part of a process of celebration. Whenever I came across a slaughter ritual in the bush I could not help comparing it to the widespread industrialized killing of animals in Western societies where meat usually forms an integral part of every meal. Westernized societies suffer from what many now refer to as 'The Big Disconnect.' We are so far removed from animals that are eaten that we see them merely as commodities wrapped in plastic trays in supermarket freezers or as patties drenched in mustard and ketchup sandwiched in-between bread buns. Not so in the world of tribal Africa in the days that I worked on the *Tribal Identity*. At that time there was a value and a face to everything that was killed and eaten.

Following a feast of meat, boiled onions and tomatoes and the ubiquitous stiff corn flour porridge during the *Intonjane* ceremony there was traditional music and dancing for the guests. A crucial moment was when the young girl was finally allowed to emerge from the darkness of her hut. Covered in a blanket she was brought out and then revealed for everyone to see. As the people cheered she was taken down to a nearby river, ceremoniously washed and brought back to the *kraal* where she was officially welcomed back into the tribe. There was much merriment and offerings of gifts, including a brand-new red blanket which was a symbol of menstruation, fertility and her eligibility to marry. Her greatest gift was from her father—a brand-new name. As with the male *kwethas*, in Xhosa tradition you have not shed your childhood until you have given up your original name and been elevated to the level of an adult with a new one. I thought that this was the end of the festivities but just before sundown there were wild shrieks and a thundering sound from the other side of the hill. As I stared in that direction wondering what was going on everyone associated with the party made a quick dive for the nearest hut. Something was coming. Then, over the crest of the hill appeared a herd of 50 or 60 cattle, all running wildly and heading straight towards us. They were being driven by a group of *kwedinis* (young boys) on the instructions, I was told, of the local headman. The crew and I scrambled to set up the camera on the roof of our production vehicle. There we would be out of harm's way. And just in time too. Within seconds we were surrounded by cattle racing through the settlement as though this were the running of the bulls at Pamplona or the stampede of the buffalo in the movie, *How the West Was Won*. The ground shook violently as the animals surged past us, thrusting aside everything. The fireplace, cooking pots, stools, calabashes and containers of beer went flying in every direction. As the dust settled and the cattle disappeared down the road I saw how much damage had been caused to the goat pen, the granary and even to some of the huts. But, no matter. Mirth and merriment quickly returned. The father of the *Intonjane* was especially delighted as he had been honored by the headman. Apparently the act of chasing a herd of cattle through the *kraal* where an *Intonjane* ceremony was taking place symbolized the arrival of a girl's adulthood and the passing away of her childhood. It seemed like a wonderfully symbolic gesture but I wasn't quite sure about all that damage that had been caused. Was it worth it? By the way the party was going it obviously was. When the mock stick fighting began as the sun sank below the horizon we packed it up and headed back to Mpame.

Way up in the north of the country in what is today Limpopo province lies a magnificent tract of bushveld and mountains that has long been the traditional home of the Venda people. In 1975 it was known as Vendaland. That was another of the *Bantustans* earmarked for independence. Covered in baobab trees, thick grass and dazzling wildflowers it was a pristine subtropical paradise. Purple-crested Lourie birds and guinea fowl filled the forests. Beetles and francolins buzzed and chirped everywhere. Lakes and streams provided water for the villages and *kraals*. Homes were constructed of mud bricks, stone, thatching grass and stockades made from local lumber. When I first went there its principal town was Sibasa, then little more than a few trading stores, a post office, a police station, a bank, an Afrikaans Dutch Reformed church, a gas station, the regional offices of the Department of Bantu Administration and an open-air market. Today a modern town has risen there. It is named after the legendary Venda chief, Thohoyandou, meaning 'Head of the Elephant.' He ruled there around eight centuries ago. Thohoyandou now caters to a burgeoning tourist trade replete with a casino and luxury hotel but back in the seventies there was no facility whatsoever for visitors or anything remotely resembling guest accommodation. Thanks to Mr. Meintjies at the Department of Bantu Administration in Pretoria we were able to rent a comfortable, recently-built house intended for white bureaucrats and other officials and their families from the local Vendaland administrative offices. It was a large unfurnished home but we had brought stretchers and camping equipment with us. Peter, Geoff and I each had our own bedroom. The house reminded me a lot of my parents' place in Zambia, with its large cool rooms, high ceilings, tiled roof and back garden filled with the fragrant scent of orange, lemon, mango, banana, papaya, avocado and guava trees. Our local fixer, Mishack Madavha, lived in the 'native location' close to town and David Muthondi, our Venda-born camera assistant, was quite happy to board with relatives in a village on the outskirts slightly further away. As Vendaland had not yet been officially granted its independence apartheid was still in force and he would not have been permitted to stay in the house with us anyway.

The Vendas are unique among all the tribes of Southern Africa. Tall, dark-skinned and Semitic-looking they speak a language unrelated to any other. If anything, it has more in common with the dialects of northeastern Africa, thousands of miles away. There is a depth and a mystery to the spiritual beliefs of the Venda unequalled anywhere in Southern Africa with the exception of the Shangaan in Mozambique. Vendaland was a very special place. There were many sacred places where few people were allowed to go. Diviners, *sangomas* and herbalists who practiced their ancient craft there were renowned for their powers, with much of what they did shrouded in secrecy.

Initiation of the young was practiced there too. With the help of Mishack Madavha it didn't take us long to find out where an unusual rite of passage was taking place.

High in the mountains in a grove of marula trees we came across what was known as a *murundu,* an initiation school for boys. It was held once every four years. To mark their transition to sexual maturity, circumcision was once again fundamental to the ritual. In contrast to the customs of the Xhosa, here the circumcision lodge was huge, with dozens of makeshift grass huts. The initiates accommodated there were much younger than those in the Transkei. I counted well over thirty boys, most of them between the ages of around eight to twelve. Also, as opposed to the preparation that goes into the Xhosa initiation process and the brave face that must be shown during the actual act of circumcision, these youngsters had no idea what they were in for when their fathers brought them to the lodge. When the boys saw the medicine man, the sharp *assegai* blade glinting in the sun and the blood-stained stone where those in line ahead of them had just sat and had the tips of their foreskins removed, they panicked. To help them survive this frightening and painful ordeal a hundred or so *midabe,* or past initiates—older boys, teenagers and young men—were summoned from various villages to spend the next four weeks here too. One of their purposes was to drum and sing as loudly as possible during the actual circumcision procedure, drowning out the little fellows' anguished cries of pain and terror as the medicine man went about his business. They then remained at the lodge to placate and care for the youngsters during their month of healing and seclusion.

Like the *kwethas* in the Transkei the Venda initiates we filmed were daubed in white clay from head to foot. They too had to reapply the clay every day but apart from this aggravating skin covering they did not have to be nude and were permitted to wear a pair of tattered shorts and a shirt or T-shirt. Music and singing accompanied most of the ceremonies and rituals that we witnessed in Vendaland. The *Murundu* lodge was no exception. All day long the initiates and their accompanying *midabes* sang a repertoire of truly haunting and beautiful songs. A senior tribal elder by the name of Sandanu acted as *ramalia* or 'father' of the lodge. Middle aged and very serious about his important role as superintendent of the young children in his care, he wore a khaki shirt and trousers with a leopard skin cloak draped over his shoulders. On his head was an elaborate headdress made of porcupine and antelope hide. Tshikororo, a handsome mid-thirties-year-old *sangoma* and medicine man who did the actual cutting—once again using little more than a sharpened *assegai* blade without the aid of anesthetic or antiseptic—was smartly dressed in Western clothing. He also wore a leopard skin cape and a tall headdress of animal hide sewn into a crown-like hat. Tshikororo had come here from the nearby town of Louis Trichardt (modern-day Makhado) and spoke perfect English. Although he carried out the circumcision procedure in accordance with ancient Venda tradition and was an ordained herbalist, he had some knowledge of Western medicine. If an infection did set in he was able to treat it with both traditional herbs and Western pharmaceuticals. I was astounded to learn that during the month-long course of the *Murundu* lodge over 500 boys had been circumcised by him.

Because of their young age no instruction or guidance regarding sexual intercourse were provided to the boys during their stay but they were steeped in Venda folklore, customs and cultural history. It was more like a very strict summer camp with a program of daily community singing and menial work, centered around the telling of tribal myths and ancient stories around the campfire. Once a day food was brought to the perimeter of the lodge by the boys' mothers and sisters. However, although they could see them the women were not permitted to make direct contact with any of the males. The staple diet was grain and corn flour-based *putu* or *pap* served cold and hard. The women arrived around noon, left baskets and wooden dishes of food nearby and then a group of male past-initiates collected the food and took it into the lodge. During mealtimes a group of about 60 young girls from nearby villages—all prepubescent and dressed in little more than traditional aprons made of beads and cloth, just enough to cover the frontal area with the buttocks bare—arrived with *marimba* drums and traditional musical instruments. With their beautiful voices and a superb sense of rhythm they drummed and sang loudly while the little boys consumed the unappetizing-looking food.

We were happily filming the proceedings when the girls were suddenly startled by something. Panic-stricken, they dropped their drums and instruments, screamed hysterically and collapsed face down in the grass. What was going on? Then I saw the terrifying sight that had scared them. Six white devil-like figures came leaping out of the surrounding bush. They were male past-initiates covered from head to foot in white clay, their faces concealed behind frightening reed masks. They were barefooted and wore only grass skirts around their waists. Each one brandished a long wooden trident-like weapon. Though they uttered not a sound they behaved as though they had gone crazy, sprinting at high speed past the girls, encircling the lodge and then running back into the bush again. Mishack Madavha explained that they were called *Muwhiras*. Their purpose was to drive out any evil spirits from the area as well as scare the girls, just for the fun of it. With all the activity and excitement going on I had no idea what to expect. Propping the Arriflex camera on my shoulder I had difficulty shooting all the action while getting enough cutaway coverage so that the editor could construct a decent sequence out of this extraordinary material. Even Peter Becker was caught unawares, fumbling frantically with his own cameras, desperately trying to shoot stills of all the action. The *muwhiras* appeared every so often, totally without warning.

No one ever knew when to expect them. Sandanu the overseer told us afterwards that it would be pointless to announce their coming in advance because that would give evil spirits and negative forces an opportunity to hide and then return. No, they had to be caught unawares and thoroughly scared away because *Murundu* lodges, he told us, had to be kept constantly pure and spiritually clean.

Once the skirted *muwhiras* vanished into the surrounding bush an even stranger sight appeared. What looked like miniature five- or six-feet high grass huts with feet sticking out beneath them came stumbling out of the trees. There were about a half-dozen of them. Each one was accompanied by a young man wearing a pair of short trousers and carrying a whip which he used to lash out at the strange, mobile grass mound. What on earth was this, I wondered? Our assistant, David Muthondi, quickly found out these were the mystical *madagalanes*. Huddled inside the mobile grass huts were young men drawn from the best dancers from previous *Murundu* lodges. Swirling and swishing their way around the lodge the *madagalanes* had the function of 'sweeping' the place clean of any remaining bad spirits or negative energies. Rather comical, they also managed to relieve the tension among the girls caused by the terrifying *muwhiras*. The presence of *madagalanes* also meant that the impending closure of the *Murundu* lodge was near. Within days it would be destroyed, all huts and utensils set alight. Then the little initiates would be allowed to return to their homes. We returned to Sibasa that evening totally exhausted but elated. It had been a thrilling experience. According to Peter, he was unaware of a *Murundu* lodge ever having been filmed before. What we had in those film cans was pure gold. Navigating our way out of the forest was a dangerous ordeal. We nearly overturned the production vehicle a couple of times as we inched our way on dirt tracks that wound along steeply-inclined mountainsides. Groups of villagers helped us keep the trusty old Volkswagen

Kombi upright by pushing up against its side as we slowly made our way back to the main dirt road to town.

A couple of days earlier we had stopped off at the open-air market in Sibasa and stocked up on a variety of fresh fruit, vegetables and other foods. This included loaves of delicious whole wheat bread. There were all sorts of exotic things on sale in that bustling marketplace: bulbs, leaves and barks for grinding into *muti*, bottles of pickled serpents, mounds of tobacco snuff, live chickens, goats, calabashes of sour milk, home-brewed sorghum beer, jars of grasshoppers. David Muthondi had bought a few pounds of dried and salted caterpillars, a popular delicacy in that part of the world. Despite my strict vegetarian diet I nibbled on one of them to find out what it tasted like and I must confess that it had a not too unpleasant crunchy texture and nutty flavor. Peter Becker insisted on getting a few cans of precooked steak and kidney pies from the local trading store. These only needed heating in the oven back at the house. The night following the filming of the Murundu lodge after a hot shower we were lounging around the kitchen discussing the day's events. Pots of leeks, potatoes, cabbage, corn and squash were on the boil. As we sipped our chilled beers I thrust one of the canned steak and kidney pies into the oven for Peter's dinner, forgetting to pierce a hole into the lid. Stupidly, it skipped my mind that I had to allow for expansion of the can's contents. Twenty minutes later the oven exploded; the door ripped from its hinges and flew across the room like a missile, followed by shrapnel of bits of can and steak and kidney pie whizzing in all directions. Even the ceiling was covered in sticky gravy and shards of tin. Fortunately, the oven door had missed Peter by mere inches. If it had hit him I would have had the unenviable task of losing our series host and having to explain how I had put an end to one of South Africa's most respected anthropologists and authors with little more than an exploding steak and kidney pie.

One day we went looking for an initiation lodge for young girls. Known as a *Vhusha* we were told it was on the land of Chief Tshivahse. As we drove through a vine-encrusted valley we saw a palisade of intricate ancient rock walls and a cluster of huts clinging to a hillside that served as the hereditary chief's home. Soon we spotted the chief in sports jacket, flannels and dark glasses riding his bicycle. As he passed his subjects on the roadside they fell humbly to the ground, hands clasped and outstretched before them as they uttered the traditional Venda greeting, *"Ndau!"* Once again Mishack had done his pre-production work well. The chief was expecting us and was delighted to meet with us, especially Peter Becker who was well known in these parts. After a brief formality to secure permission to cross his land and on the suggestion of Mishack we presented him with an offering of a bottle of brandy and a carton of cigarettes as a token of our gratitude. Apparently, he had a fondness for both. Then we set off in a northerly direction. It wasn't long before the dirt track petered out and we had to walk another twenty minutes or so on foot.

We could hear the girls at their lodge long before we saw them. Vigorous drumbeats and a lovely chorus of young female voices filled the air. Finally, in a clearing in the midst of a great forest was a walled settlement. This was the *Vhusha* lodge. There were about twenty young girls in the encampment, bare breasted and dressed in nothing more than a thin strip of white linen cloth tied around their waist and a beaded apron covering their genitalia. They were all in their early teens. All of them had just experienced their first menstruation. With folded arms and swaying bodies they shuffled in synchronized steps around a group of drummers, singing loudly. The drummers themselves—all girls—were slightly older and wore decorated blankets, shawls and beaded necklaces. Watching over this entire group were the caretakers of the lodge, two elderly women, bare breasted and clad in the traditional long white cotton skirts worn by most married Venda women. Sullen and serious, they watched every movement of the initiates, monitoring each drumbeat and step. The purpose behind the *Vhusha* was to guide the girls through their early adolescence and to help them understand the physical changes taking place in their bodies. Once again, it was all about sex. In Venda tradition the girls had now 'seen the moon,' a phrase indicating that their menstrual cycles had begun. Although they were only here for about ten days they would be exposed to a great deal of advice and instruction. Once again—as we so often found in tribal society at that time—the emphasis was on austerity and abject humility. As a girl entered adulthood it was regarded as an indication of good character if she was humble, quiet and withdrawn. A strict code of behavior at the Vhusha lodge instilled those attitudes, together with a respect for elders that was constantly enforced. Lectures were given between hours of drumming, dancing and singing, beginning at sunrise and ending at nightfall. Much of their instruction focused on their awakening femininity, but one thing was held sacrosanct—strict sexual abstinence. The value of retaining virginity before marriage was emphasized throughout their stay. But this was only the first phase in a long initiation process that these young ladies were about to undergo. Detailed instructions and guidance regarding marriage, sexual practices and motherhood would come later, at an initiation school one step above the *Vhusha*. It was held only once every four or five years and, as luck would have it, there was one in progress near another chief's *kraal* deeper in central Vendaland. Our trusty fixer Mishack Madavha had already arranged our visit.

The sacred *Domba* initiation school marked the final phase in a young Venda girl's preparation for marriage. It traditionally began in mid-winter and went on for about two months. The one we filmed was located near the chief's *khorro* or tribal meeting place. It was in a large secluded clearing amidst a grove of trees high in the mountains, far from any villages or huts.

It was July 1975 and it was cold. When I first saw the girls—about 50 of them, all between the ages of 16 and 18—I could not believe that they were able to endure the winter weather wearing nothing more than the flimsiest *shedu* or thin leather waistband, a beaded apron covering the vagina in front and a narrow flap of beaded cloth dangling over the buttocks. They ate, slept, danced and were trained in this simple attire during their entire grueling period at the Domba lodge. Venda females have beautiful features. The girls looked magnificent with their fine bone structures, ripening breasts and slim smooth-skinned bodies. They were under the control of a middle-aged male overseer who was known as the *nyamatei*. He was also a *sangoma*, a medicine man and musical instructor. He was the only male permitted at the lodge. He went about draped in animal skins, carrying a *sjambok* or rhinoceros hide whip which he did not hesitate to use on any girl who fell out of line. Much of the time he also walked around carrying a folding trellis-like device called a *makonyana*. It was constructed of a series of sticks woven together with hyena sinew. It could be unfolded to create a long wavy gate-like contraption with a red feather sewn onto the stick at the furthest end. When this was done it was said that the red feather could 'smell out' any girls who had been misbehaving. We did not witness it performing this strange feat but any girl singled out was punished for whatever misdeed she had been guilty of committing. The *nyamatei* was assisted by a handful of the local chief's wives who oversaw meals and looked after the girls' hygienic needs. Through Mishack's negotiating skills we had been given special dispensation by the chief and by the *nyamatei* to attend and film the event. Once again I felt especially privileged. Once again Africa was letting me in on another of its myriad secrets.

A variety of drums were in the center of the *khorro*, the largest one being a huge bass drum called the *ngoma*. Cylindrical in shape, it had a diameter of about three or four feet and a length of two feet. Extremely heavy, it had been carved from the solid trunk of a marula tree. Stretched cowhide covered the top and bottom openings of the drum. These were held in place by sturdy wooden pegs. The whole thing was suspended by strips of leather tied to a beam resting across two carved upright poles. The *ngoma* was regarded to be sacred and was never permitted to touch the ground. There was a small hole on one side of it. This opening was surrounded by a series of elaborate handles and symbols carved around the drum's entire circumference. The exterior surface was daubed with a mixture of animal fat and red ochre. The hide was beaten by a heavy wooden mallet, emitting a deep, evocative, booming sound that resonated across the landscape. It was a sound that came from another time, another place, another world. The belief was that the drumbeats echoed the voice of a supernatural and unknowable supreme being. I have never heard an instrument that has made my bones and soul reverberate quite like that. There were other smaller drums, including a few funnel-shaped *marimbas*. Their tones were higher in pitch and were played either by hand or with sticks while clasped between the players' legs. Close to the drums was a roaring fire that was kept constantly alight. It had deep spiritual connotations, symbolizing the presence of ancestral spirits.

When not receiving instructions about sex and how to satisfy their future husbands the girls were informed about pregnancy, birth, motherhood and how to take care of a child. They spent much of their time dancing around the fire to the beat of those wonderful drums. A group of half a dozen girls were randomly chosen as musicians. For hours on end they beat those drums in precise rhythms, never showing a hint of exhaustion as the initiates danced. Everything was done according to tightly prescribed rules. The girls first formed a long line, the tallest in front and the shortest at the back. With their elbows bent, each one had to hold the wrists of the girl in front of her. Close physical contact was essential. With the breasts of the girl behind tightly pressed against the shoulder blades of the girl in front they slowly encircled the fire and the drums, their arms gracefully weaving in an undulating motion, their feet shuffling in coordinated synchronization, imitating the slithering movement of a python. The dance has long since become known as the 'python dance' but nothing here was what it seemed to be. Everything was shrouded in symbolism. Through our fixer Mishack we learned that the snake-like movement originated in centuries past and was believed to be closely linked to something similar to the *kundalini* force associated with ancient Hinduism. It was also symbolic of the awakening fertility within a woman's womb. The *ngoma* drum itself was also symbolic with strong sexual connotations. The upright poles from which it was suspended symbolized the male penis and virility, the hole in its side the female vagina, and the tightly stretched animal hide skin represented the fontanel of a newborn baby's head. The fire also had its meaning. The red flames depicted a woman's menstrual blood and the white ash represented male semen. Dancing began at dawn and went on until after midnight. Clutching each other tightly the girls must have been freezing in the winter weather yet they managed to keep themselves warm because of their constant movement and their proximity to each other and to the fire. Fortunately we were equipped with battery-powered lights to shoot images at night, backlighting the dancers and the musicians with the fire in the foreground. They were some of the most spectacular scenes we caught on film. I was very grateful to my crew Geoff Collins and David Muthondi for rigging the lighting setup. Those two guys displayed unremitting devotion to duty under extremely trying and difficult circumstances. What made the scenes so special was that they were *real*. Nothing was planned or rehearsed.

In addition to making *The Tribal Identity*, I would come back to a similar Domba initiation lodge four years later with a different crew to shoot another anthropological documentary.

On that occasion my sound recordist Alan Seleznick captured one of the most haunting renderings of the primary Domba melody that I have ever heard. Beginning with a solemn "Boom, boom, boom… boom, boom, boom" from the *ngoma* drum, then joined in by the marimbas, the girls' voices slowly flowed into the rendering, beginning very low and finally breaking out into a heart-rending lament to the ancestral spirits. The song was a call for guidance, blessings and health in the years to come. As far as I was concerned few things equaled the impact of hearing that music on a moonless night, surrounded by darkness and the wonderful smell of the African bush.

Because its culture was so spiritually rich Vendaland offered many opportunities to encounter the strange and the inexplicable. One occasion was the rare and seldom-seen offering to the python god and to the tribal ancestors who, as legend and tradition had it, inhabited the waters of the sacred and much-feared Lake Fundudzi. This ceremony usually took place once every five years. Its purpose was to appease the ancestors and to ask for rain, good crops, health, fertility and general well-being. In ancient times live maidens from the tribe were sacrificed to the waters. When we filmed there the offerings took the form of home-brewed beer and a variety of fruits and leaves. An old priest, deeply versed in the legends, lore, mythology and mysteries of the tribe, was to officiate.

Mishack had arranged that Peter Becker, the crew and I would rendezvous with local headman Netshiavu at his village early in the morning for the long trek down to the lake at the bottom of a steeply ravined valley. It was impossible to drive there so Netshiavu had provided a dozen young women from his village to help us carry our equipment. In tribal Africa women do most of the manual labor, not men. It was hard work, with thorn bushes, dense clumps of trees, slippery slopes and tall sharp grass making the trip especially difficult. It reminded me of William Holden, Jack Hawkins and their detonation party trekking through the jungles and rainforest of Burma in quest of their objective in *The Bridge on the River Kwai*. I searched my memory banks for some appropriate movie tune to help me along the way but could only come up with Irving Berlin's *There's No Business Like Show Business* which I promptly proceeded to whistle. I guess it seemed totally out of place under the circumstances so both Peter and Geoff thought me crazy and chuckled all the way down to the lake. But long before we had slipped, skidded and slid all the way down the sloping crevices surrounding the lake, ripping our clothes and skin on cacti and *Hak en Steek* (Catch and Stick) thorn bushes, the two of them had joined me in my Broadway renderings and were whistling loudly too. Show business was alive and well; sacred lake or not, the show had to go on.

Once we reached the shores of Fundudzi we were all politely asked to remove our shoes as a token of respect towards the ancestral spirits. We duly did so, setting up our camera and sound recording equipment while we waited for the ceremonies to begin. The headman, his helpers and musicians—about a dozen young men and women—undressed and then girded themselves with skirts of leaves and various other regalia, including shell necklaces, deer antlers, rattles and body paint. They looked fabulous, especially in the clear, crisp light of morning against the background panorama of the shimmering lake. It was an ethereal and very beautiful scene, the atmosphere charged with something strange and indefinable. Mishack whispered to me that he felt sure the tribal spirits were present and watching us. After an hour of waiting I began to worry because there was still no sign of the priest. According to headman Netshiavu he was to have been fetched from his secret home deep in the surrounding hills by a couple of Netshiavu's senior male relatives. At last the party arrived. The mere sight of the priest was spellbinding. A hush fell over the entire assembly as a thin, wrinkled, wiry, ancient, grey-haired, hunched-over little man, hardly able to walk, hobbled through the bushes, supported on either side by one of the headman's assistants. His eyes were glazed over. Surely, I thought, he must be blind. It must have been a very long time since those eyes had witnessed anything. Mishack came over and told me that the old man was also virtually deaf. Headman Netshiavu, dressed in a girdle of fresh leaves and a grass skirt, fell to the ground, clapped his hands and greeted the priest respectfully with the traditional, *"Ndau."* Then, through a translator who had to shout loudly into his left ear, the old priest was introduced to Peter Becker, to the crew and then to me. Peter was fascinated by the old man. His eyes filled with tears as he shook his hand. As I said earlier, Peter was a very spiritual man. He was deeply tuned in to the metaphysical realm. He was sensitive to the ritualistic beliefs and religious practices of all the tribal people he encountered but I had never before seen him become so emotionally moved as he did when he met that old Venda priest. Here was a man beyond a name and an identity. Here was someone who had stepped out of the pages of Africa's ancient past; a mysterious, unknowable individual who was acquainted with things that we ordinary mortals were unable to even contemplate. As Peter chatted to him through the interpreter we were astonished to learn that he was over a hundred years old. He remembered seeing the old Transvaal Republic's President Paul Kruger in his horse-drawn carriage during a parade in Pretoria when he was a youngster. This, he told us, was "before the war started with the English." It was easy to figure that one out. If it had happened before the Anglo-Boer War the man must definitely have been well over a century old.

We were told that we had to observe strict silence during the proceedings. The only person other than the priest who was allowed to speak was Peter. The plan was to have him on camera for part of the time, describing the action and its significance. I positioned him near the camera about thirty feet or so from the old priest. This would allow me to focus on the ritual then zoom back to include Peter in the scene. As I was showing Peter where to stand he inadvertently stubbed his big toe against a sharp rock and winced in pain. Meanwhile, the ceremonies began to get under way. In the background, musicians were blowing on antler horns and pounding on drums as the old priest held his hands high, faced the lake and wailed softly. Then he picked up one of the calabashes of home-brewed beer which he proceeded to pour slowly into the waters, all the while chanting to the spirits. Camera and sound recorder were rolling and capturing it all but off-screen Peter was pulling all sorts of faces because of the pain in his toe. Just like watching someone who had just slipped on a banana peel our assistant David Muthondi began to giggle. He had an infectious sense of humor and it wasn't long before Geoff, his ears covered by headphones, also began to stifle a chuckle. And then I started too. You know how it is. Suppressed laughter spreads like wildfire. Even Peter's face turned red as his pain quickly gave way to snickering.

Headman Netshiavu and one of his aides beckoned to us to keep silent but it was hopeless. Soon we were gasping in a futile attempt to conceal our mirth. It was awful but we couldn't help it. Then, suddenly, the old priest put down the calabash of beer he was holding and held up his hand signaling that the music should cease. He turned around to face us. He was well over thirty feet away from us. He certainly could not see through those glazed eyes and it was impossible for him to have heard our laughter. Yet, there he was, staring at us, his hands still held high as if to say, "Quiet!" But he said nothing. He merely glared at us for a second or two and then, in unison, both the camera and the tape recorder suddenly stopped working. They simply died as though someone had ripped them from their power sources. Instantly all laughter and merriment on our parts disappeared. What was going on? Geoff and I panicked. We furiously fiddled with cables and batteries and checked fuses, and then realized that everyone's eyes were upon us. Could *we* have caused this? Mishack was summoned by the old priest who whispered something into his ear. Clearly perturbed, Mishack went over to Peter and quietly told him that our disrespectful behavior had angered the ancestors and the spirits of the lake. They were upset. We would not be permitted to continue filming the ceremony. On hearing this a cold shiver went rippling down my spine. Geoff's face went white.

While Peter and David profusely apologized to Mishack for our misconduct, Geoff and I feverishly tried to trace the technical faults in the camera and the Nagra tape deck but there were none to be found. We changed batteries, cables, fuses, even film magazines and tape reels. But the equipment was as dead as a dodo. Amazingly, the voltage meter from Geoff's tool kit showed that full power was coursing through the circuits of both machines. But they would not run. It was uncanny. We had never seen anything like it. Meanwhile, the old priest had turned his back on us and continued to chant and pour offerings into the lake. The headman, his aides, the musicians and everyone else connected with the ceremony concentrated their attention on the ritual and were now ignoring us. They proceeded as if we weren't there. As Geoff and David fiddled with the equipment Peter and I huddled together and desperately tried to figure out what we should do. Peter called Mishack over again and requested that he please ask the old priest to hold up the proceedings and wait until we had rectified our technical problems. Not looking very hopeful, Mishack approached the priest, shouted something into his ear and the old man whispered something back to him. Mishack came back shaking his head, telling us that our gear was not broken but had been "blocked by the ancestors." Nothing would work again until the entire ritual was over. The problem was simply that the spirits were not happy with our disrespectful behavior and would not allow us the privilege of recording any more of the sacred event.

I could not believe this was happening. All I knew is that we weren't getting the sequence on film and I didn't know what to do. As Peter and I were deeply upset we pleaded one more time with Mishack, begging him to ask the priest to offer our apologies to the spirits. Once again he ambled over to the old priest, waited for an appropriate moment and again conveyed our request. The old man turned to the lake and stared at it silently for a minute or so while everyone waited and watched. Mishack came back to us and shrugged.

"Who knows?" he said softly. "Perhaps the ancestors will be forgiving. Let's wait and see."

The old priest continued to silently gaze out over the lake, then slowly raised his withered and bony arms and chanted for a few seconds. Then he stopped, turned around, and stared at us. Without having realized it Geoff had left the Nagra tape recorder switch in the 'on' position because suddenly the machine started whirring again, the two tape spindles turning normally. Geoff caught his breath and looked up at me, wide-eyed. Instinctively I reached out and turned on the camera. Sure enough, it began running flawlessly as though nothing had ever happened. But Peter and I both knew that something profound had indeed occurred; something totally beyond our understanding. Peter was so taken aback by all this that for the following ten minutes he couldn't perform on camera. However, by day's end all was well. We had got what we came for, capturing the ceremony on film and on tape with no further technical hitches. What had happened? We will never know. It was eerie and totally beyond explanation. That night, back in Sibasa, Geoff and I meticulously went through the equipment again and found absolutely nothing out of place. Peter had experienced many strange things during his years of research among tribal people but this one eclipsed them all. It defied logic. In my own mind I have absolutely no doubt at all that powerful supernatural forces had been at work that day.

82

83

84

85

86

87

88

89

90

91

92

93

94

95

96

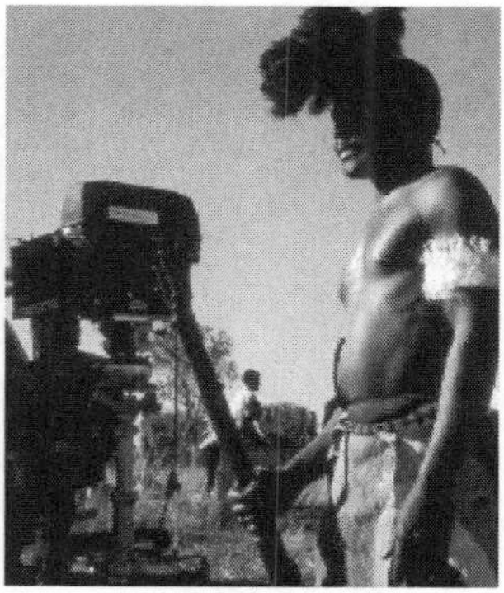
97

98

99

100

101

102

103

104

105

106

107

108

109

110

111

ne Star

MESSAGE IS

Professor turns actor

cus on
rs of

112

Film focus on 2m. years of South Africa

TWO MILLION YEARS of history—a fascinating story told by stone and bone implements found at Makapansgat near Potgietersrust—is being squeezed into a one-hour colour documentary film being made by a Pretoria film company.

Central figure in the film is Professor Raymond Dart, the 78-year-old professor of palaeontology at the University of the Witwatersrand.

On Friday Professor Dart spent long hours before the camera at the Makapansgat Caves, going back into the past to bring to life Australopithecinae — man's apelike ancestors.

The film will be shown to millions in Europe, Britain and America. It is a tribute to Professor Dart's work.

In the eerie amphitheatre surrounded by caves there was a stillness where every sound is magnified and Professor Dart's voice rang out to a background of winging bats and rock doves.

"Kenya has its sites which tell the story of the evolution of stone implements," Professor Dart said for the film script.

"At Makapansgat South Africa has a story of a far more primitive man who was introduced to the use of stone tools through his use of bone, and here his prolific use of bone tools is unparalleled."

As he spoke he exhibited implements fashioned from the bones of giraffe, warthog and hyena.

FIRST TOOLS

He was throwing light on the past, going as far back as two million years. He told the future film audiences that bone tools shaped the economy and way of life of these early hunters.

"These tools speak volumes of man's first glimmerings of intelligence and of how these man-like creatures faced their future problems," he said.

The film is directed by Mr. L. Friedberg, of Panorama Films, and will be completed in May this year.

Mr. Friedberg is also planning a film with Prof. Phillip Tobias, head of the department of anatomy at the University of the Witwatersrand, which will go back 23-million years.

113

114

115

116

117

118

119

120

121

122

123

124

125

126

127

128

129

130

131

132

133

134

135

136

137

138

139

140

141

142

143

144

145

146

147

148

149

150

151

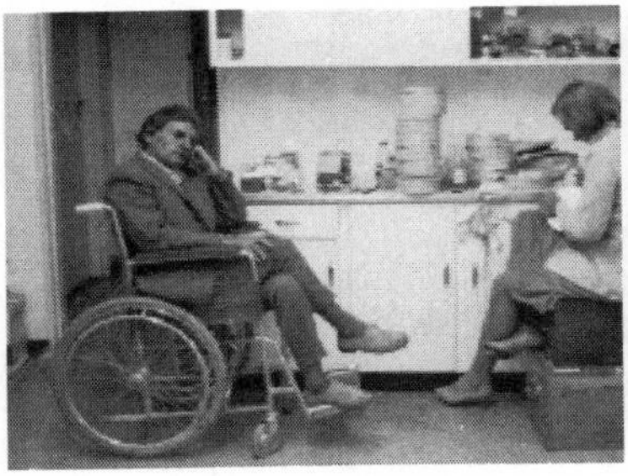
152

153

154

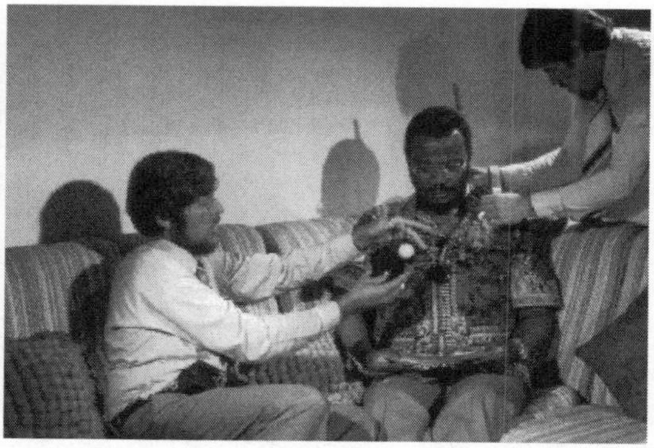
155

156

157

158

159

160

161

162

163

164

165

166

167

168

169

170

171

172

173

174

175

176

177

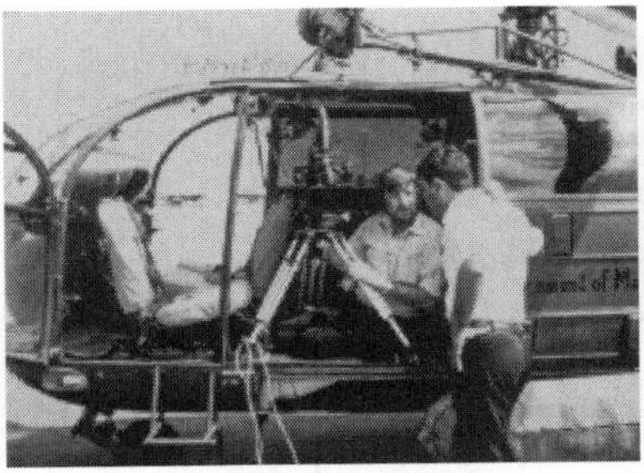

178

179

180

181

182

183

82 Farm worker at the 'Pioneer Column' memorial to white settlers who colonized Rhodesia (modern-day Zimbabwe) for the British Empire in the 19th century. Photo taken in Matopos mountains, Matabeleland during the production of the motion picture *Shangani Patrol*, 1970.
The film was about the conflict between British troops led by Major Allan Wilson against warriors of Matabele King Lobengula.

83 'Granny Rosenfels,' matriarch of the extensive Rosenfels farming family at the graves of her ancestors who settled in Rhodesia (modern-day Zimbabwe) during the 19th century. Photo taken near her farm in the Plumtree district of the Matopos mountains during the filming of *Shangani Patrol*, 1970.

84 Strange rock formations, Matopos mountains, Matabeleland. Many of these oddly balanced boulders—some weighing many tons—emit a strange hollow ringing sound when struck by a stone, stick or hammer. Geologists have determined that the geological features were the result of weathering and wind but local tribes claim the rocks embody an eerie, otherworldly nature under the influence of tribal ancestors and spirits.

85 The hill I fell in love with and the one local farmers referred to as *'Lionel's Kopje'* in the Matopos mountain range, 1970.

86 With *Shangani Patrol* director David Millin (left) and assistant cameraman Michael Sandler at the grave of Cecil John Rhodes, 19th century British Imperialist, colonialist, mining magnate and founder of Rhodesia, the territory named after him. Contemporary university Rhodes Scholarships still bear his name. Photo taken at World's View in the Matopos mountains during a break in filming.

87 On location in Matabeleland, Rhodesia for the production of the feature film, *Shangani Patrol,* 1970.

88 Filming *Shangani Patrol.* In the foreground are actors portraying Major Allan Wilson and his patrol. 3,000 local extras played Matabele warriors.

89 I set up a shot for *Shangani Patrol.*

90 Camera operator Ivo Pellegrini lines up shot on lead actor Brian O'Shaughnessy who played Major Allan Wilson.

91 Camera crew and grips doing tracking shot for *Shangani Patrol*

92 Filming *Shangani Patrol*

93 Yours truly with a group of extras playing Matabele warriors on set of *Shangani Patrol*

94 Working on *Shangani Patrol*

95 Working on *Shangani Patrol*

96 With stills photographer Sid Yankelowitz and 1st unit assistant cameraman Michael Sandler on *Shangani Patrol*

97 Matabele warrior waits for his call on *Shangani Patrol*

98 Authentically attired Matabele warriors

99 Matabele warriors rest between takes during filming of *Shangani Patrol*

100 Matabele warriors

101 Matabele warriors

102 Scene depicting Matabele warriors digging for water in dry river bed, *Shangani Patrol*

103 Matabele warrior prepares to attack with *assegai* (spear) and cowhide shield, his only weapons against the guns of British troops, *Shangani Patrol.*

104 Matabele warrior and one of his wives as featured in *Shangani Patrol*

105 Matabele children as featured in *Shangani Patrol*

106 Final onslaught of Matabele warriors on Major Allan Wilson's patrol in *Shangani Patrol*

107 The last members of the British patrol defend themselves against the Matabele

108 Carnage. The final battle in *Shangani Patrol.*

109 Dr. Charles Kimberlin 'Bobby' Brain, Director of the Transvaal Museum, Pretoria, South Africa, points out features of a two-and-a-half-million-year-old *Australopithecus africanus* hominid fossil skull at Swartkrans excavation site for the documentary on the history of Early Man in Africa, *The Turning Point*, 1970.

110 Filming ancient hominid fossils at Kroomdraai excavation site for *The Turning Point*

111 With Prof. Raymond Arthur Dart, discoverer of the first hominid fossil found in Africa, the so-called *Taung Baby,* at the world premiere of *The Turning Point* at the Institute for the Achievement of Human Potential in Philadelphia, USA, 1971.

112 – 113 On the front page of South Africa's largest daily newspaper, *The Star,* Johannesburg, during production of *The Turning Point,* 1970

114 – 115 Iconic images of the magnificence of the African bush

116 Elephant on the banks of the Zambezi River, Zambia, 1973

117 Shooting feature film *Lelik Is My Offer* in Natal, South Africa, 1974. Camera crew in background.

118 Lining up crane shot in vineyards of Cape Province, South Africa for horror film, *House of the Living Dead,* 1973

119 With camera operator Russell Seabourne, director Joe Stewardson and assistant cameraman Ivor Pringle on production of *Lelik Is My Offer,* 1974

120 Shooting musical comedy *Die Spook van Donkergat,* Langebaan, Cape, South Africa, 1972

121 With director Diana Ginsberg (who became my second wife), art director Ian Haselau and assistant cameraman Roger Martin, shooting *Die Spook van Donkergat,* Cape Town, 1972.

122 British director Ray Austin directing actor Mark Burns in the horror film *House of the Living Dead* in Cape Town, 1973. Production designer Anita Berman—my first wife—in background.

123 Lining up shot for *House of the Living Dead,* 1973.

124 With camera operator Russell Seabourne on yet another major historical epic, *Die Voortrekkers* (The Pathfinders), South Africa, 1973.

125 A member of *Die Voortrekkers* camera crew, assistant grip Jerry Mpobole.

126 *Die Voortrekkers* was an Afrikaans-language film set during The Great Trek in the 19th century when descendants of Dutch colonizers—known as Boers—trekked by ox wagon from the British-controlled Cape of Good Hope into the hinterland of South Africa to set up their own independent republics. Along the way they clashed with indigenous tribes. One of the Voortrekker leaders was Piet Retief. He and his party met their deaths at the hands of warriors led by Zulu King Dingane at *KwaMatiwane* near *Umgungundlovu* (the royal kraal) in what was later known as Natal, now called KwaZulu in South Africa on February 6, 1838. This film featured many thousands of extras. To keep production costs as low as possible crowd scenes were shot in what was then still known as Rhodesia. Like *Shangani Patrol* three years earlier local tribes and locations in the Matopos mountains near Bulawayo were used as extras in the movie.

127 Set of the interior of King Dingane's royal kraal, *Umgungundlovu.*

128 Scene in *Die Voortrekkers* depicting Voortrekker leader Piet Retief and his party negotiating with Zulu King Dingane. The king was played by South African actor Bingo Mbonjeni and Piet Retief by Patrick Mynhardt. Also in the scene is Lance Lockhart-Ross who played a member of the Retief negotiating party.

129 The massacre of Piet Retief and his party by Zulu warriors in *Die Voortrekkers.*

130 A scene from one of the many feature films I shot during my early years as a Director of Photography. This one depicts a British soldier in the second Anglo-Boer War in South Africa during 1899–1902.

131 Author, historian, anthropologist Dr. Peter Becker, host of the TV documentary series, *The Tribal Identity.* South Africa, 1975.

132 Headman Netshiavu of the Venda tribe and Peter Becker prepare to descend to sacred Lake Fundudzi (in background) to meet shaman and priest for ancient ritual of offering to the ancestors in Vendaland, South Africa, 1975.

133 Venda headman Nethsiavu prepares ground corn, millet, fresh fruit and homemade sorghum beer for offering to the tribal ancestors.

134 Peter Becker, shoes removed out of respect to the ancestral spirits and 'Ancient Ones,' arrives on shore of sacred Lake Fundudzi, Vendaland.

135 Arrival of shaman, tribal elder and priest at Lake Fundudzi to officiate at offering to the ancestral spirits and 'Ancient Ones' of the Venda tribe.

136 On questioning the half-blind shaman before the ceremony at Lake Fundudzi got underway it was determined that he was well in excess of a hundred years old. Although he spoke no English and could neither read nor write he vividly recalled witnessing incidents as a child in South African history that proved his age. Extremely powerful and spiritually advanced, after our motion picture camera and sound recording equipment mysteriously stopped functioning halfway through the ceremony the old man appealed to the ancestors to 'unblock' whatever it was that was preventing us from filming the ritual. The equipment inexplicably began working again after his request. The incident defied all rational explanation.

137 Overseer—the only male permitted to be present at *Domba* initiation school located in isolation deep in the mountains for pubescent Venda girls who have reached sexual maturity—holds a *makonyane* 'smelling out' trellis stick during traditional daily 'Python Dance.' Vendaland, South Africa, 1975.

138 Male overseer uses *makonyane* to determine if any girls are not up to standard during the very grueling and disciplined *Domba* initiation school. Those girls 'smelled out' by the *makonyane* will be singled out for scolding or discipline.

139 Discipline, humility and respect are some of the most essential aspects of instruction during the Domba initiation school for pubescent Venda girls. Here the girls crouch in submission to their male overseer and senior

female instructors.

140 Discussing filming the Venda drummer girls with anthropologist, Peter Becker. Together with our small crew and the overseer we were the only males allowed at the Domba school.

141 Preparing to film the Domba drummers.

142 The only clothing worn by the Venda initiates is a small embroidered patch covering the buttocks and genitals, even in the midst of the cold of winter.

143 The Domba 'Python Dance.' The girls cling to each other and emulate the movement of a snake during the dance. This signifies sexual awakening, maturity and is in many ways similar to the rising of the Kundalini spirit and female procreative energy from the base of the spine practiced during yoga in Hinduism.

144 With the male overseer and shaman watching, adult female guides teach the young Domba girls secrets of tribal lore, traditions, customs and how to become adept in sexual behavior as future wives.

145 Centerpiece of the Domba initiation lodge is the *Ngoma* drum. It has deep spiritual, sexual and metaphysical significance.

146 Peter Becker preparing to do an on-camera presentation with the young Domba drummers.

147 Filming Taushile Debeza and two other *AbaKwetha* young male initiates who have emerged from their long period of isolation in the bush. The day begins at dawn when they wash all traces of white clay from their bodies in the surf of the Indian Ocean near Mpame, Transkei, 1975. With me is assistant Thomas Makhubela who was by my side during much of our filming in Xhosa and Zulu tribal areas for *The Tribal Identity* television series.

148 Essential rite of passage for young Xhosa males, Transkei, 1975. These three *AbaKwetha* initiates will spend a grueling winter in the bush following circumcision. As their wounds heal they will live frugally, have strictly limited diets, not be permitted to wear any clothing and spend much of the time learning about discipline and the rites and rituals of the tribe, as well as receiving important lessons in sex education, health and future marriage from their overseer. This was one of the few occasions

when their entire bodies were not daubed in pure white clay to ward off evil spirits. Our featured *Kwetha* initiate Taushile Debeza is on the right. After his initiation is complete his name will be changed to indicate his transition to maturity and adulthood.

149 Local villager 'Ernest' and our assistant and translator Thomas Makhubela in Transkei, 1975. We could not have accomplished our filming in Xhosa areas without the help of these two men.

150 'Ernest' and Viv White, our two essential 'fixers' during all the filming done in Transkei territories for *The Tribal Identity*. Viv was born, grew up and lived in Transkei until the South African government forced him and his family to leave when 'independence' was foisted on the region under prevailing apartheid policies at the time, 1975.

151 Our 'fixer' Mishack Madavha in Vendaland with tribal headman and a public affairs officer appointed by white-controlled South African government, 1975, planning our shooting schedule in the Venda tribal territory.

152 After an exhausting day's shooting anthropologist Peter Becker waits while assistant cameraman/sound recordist Geoffrey Collins cans up the day's exposed negative film for later processing. This is the kitchen in a rented house in Sibasa, Vendaland where—that same evening—Peter Becker was almost killed by an exploding oven door when I forgot to pierce holes in a can of steak and kidney pie that I was heating up for him. The wheelchair was used as a camera platform to shoot mobile scenes in local marketplaces and tribal villages.

153 Tswana chiefs, headmen, elders and senior tribal representatives meet near Seshego in the white-controlled South African government-invented 'homeland' of Lebowa to discuss our request to film rituals, sangomas and scenes in the area for *The Tribal Identity*, 1975.

154 Zulu Paramount Chief Prince Mangosuthu Gatsha Buthelezi, Ulundi, KwaZulu, 1975.

155 Preparing to interview Zulu Paramount Chief Prince Mangosuthu Gatsha Buthelezi. Sound recordist Alan Seleznick attaching microphone to Buthelezi.

156 Women gathering near Seshego for public ceremony, 1975.

157 Tswana woman grinding maize (corn) for making *putu* or *pap*, a staple among all tribes in South Africa, 1975.

158 With crew and young Venda women, 1977. Back row from left: Alan Seleznick (sound recordist), Clive de Klerk (assistant cameraman), Mishack Madavha (fixer/assistant director), yours truly (director/cinematographer), David Muthondi (technical assistant/translator).

159 Crowd gathers for meeting of *Kgotla* (tribal court) in Tswana village near Seshego, 1975.

160 Lovely landscape south of Pietersburg (modern-day Polokwane), South Africa.

161 Our production base camp at Mpame, Thembuland, Wild Coast, Transkei. From here we shot many sequences in Xhosa, Thembu and Pondo territories for *The Tribal Identity*, 1974–1976. Indian Ocean in background.

162 Typical Venda domestic mud-brick hut.

163 Venda thatched *kraal* or village, 1975.

164 Cattle, the measure of a tribal man's wealth, 1975.

165 Geoff Collins placing microphones among a group of Sotho women

166 Traditionally attired male Pondo *sangoma* or medicine man, Transkei, 1975.

167 Male Venda *sangoma* using *makonyane* 'smelling out' stick trellis to diagnose illness, malady or source of misfortune.

168 Powerful Tswana *sangoma, 'Shabalala,'* who successfully carried out exorcism of invasive evil spirit on patient.

169 Female Tswana *sangoma* interprets patient's problems by using her bone set and beaded water divination totem doll. (Seen on grass mat next to set of bones.)

170 Female Tswana *sangoma.*

171 Shooting on sand dunes of Namib Desert, South West Africa (modern-day Namibia), 1977.

172 Filming South African Defense Force's surface-to-air missile battery exercise during Cuban occupation of Angola, 1978.

173 Accompanying South African troops to border between South West Africa (Namibia) and Angola during South West African war of independence and Cuban occupation of Angola, 1978.

174 Boarding South African Air Force Mirage IIICZ fighter jet at Swartkops

Air Force Base, Pretoria, South Africa to film aerial sequence of simulated enemy aircraft interception above Mozambique during that country's civil war, 1978.

175 Preparing to film sequence from South African Air Force naval helicopter, 1978.

176 Strapped in and ready to go!

177 Emergency Naval 'casavac' (casualty evacuation) by South African Air Force helicopter of crew from stricken Japanese fishing vessel on Atlantic coastline, 1978.

178 Preparing to shoot from Mauritian government helicopter for documentary about island of Mauritius, Indian Ocean, 1977.

179 Scene in preparation for interview with Commanding Officer of South African Air Force Maritime Patrol Command's 35 Squadron at D.F. Malan Airport, Cape Town, 1977.

180 South African Air Force Maritime Patrol Command's 35 Squadron Avro Shackleton aircraft patrols South Atlantic Ocean for Soviet Navy vessels and submarines, 1977. Note extended radar dome beneath fuselage.

181 Rigging camera gear for shooting on board South African Navy's Daphne class submarine, 1978.

182 Preparing to film on board submarine. On left is Navy Liaison Officer Lt. Paul van der Bijl and on right is sound recordist Philip Key. Simonstown Naval Dockyards, Cape Town, South Africa, 1978.

183 South African Navy Daphne class submarine at sea. Atlantic Ocean, 1978.

Twelve

In addition to Vendaland other homelands in South Africa were also earmarked for independence during the 1970s. These were places with strange-sounding names like Bophuthatswana, Gazankulu and Lebowa. Many tribes speaking different languages lived in these designated areas, including the North Sotho, Ndebele, Pedi, Karanga, Tsonga and Tswana. As we roamed the territories with their diverse landscapes and culture for the shooting of *The Tribal Identity* we came across many remarkable ceremonies and rituals. A large proportion of them seemed alien and otherworldly. *Sangomas,* diviners and herbalists abounded everywhere. There was no shortage of fascinating material to film, all of it giving insight into a wonderful array of customs denied to most whites because of the alienation caused by apartheid. The more we traveled in those areas the more I realized how we had all been divided into neatly separated cultural compartments. We were totally cut off from one another, losing out on much that could have enriched our lives and the country as a whole.

One day we were *en route* to meet a chief in Seshego, Lebowa, not too far from the city of Pietersburg (modern-day Polokwane). Along the way we came across a village which our local guide told us was the home of a highly respected male *sangoma*. He specialized in divination and 'smelling out' ceremonies. We stopped to film a bone throwing session during which a patient complained of having bad dreams and excruciating headaches. He was diagnosed with a malady caused by ancestors who were angry with him for the way he was treating one of his wives. The prognosis was that a cure was possible provided he wear a magical amulet on his left wrist to control his temper and then take a powder that would help him return to a normal sleep pattern.

After filming the session and the dispensation of *muti* Geoff and I decided that we would like to have the bones thrown for us too. Eager to please and happy to accept the small fee required for the reading the diviner agreed. I sat down for my reading. Once again, the very first thing that came up was the presence of a *ndlovu* or elephant spirit. He said it was around me all the time. This alleviated any lingering doubts that I might have had about the matter since my bones were read months earlier by that remarkable *sangoma* in KwaZulu and, indeed, by the albino *nganga* in Zambia years earlier. The spirit must surely have belonged to the elephant that died in front of me in Mozambique. After my session was over I sat in a corner of the *ndumba* hut to puff on a cigarette and think about the matter while Geoff took his turn. He was told that he had "a bad illness in his chest." This was quite true. He was a chronic asthma sufferer. He was also told that "dark energy" sometimes surrounded him and that he should get *muti* to protect himself against it.

"What kind of *muti*?" Geoff wanted to know.

"*Paba Shimani*," the diviner told him. "But I do not have any here for you. You must ask around for it."

We had no idea what he was talking about, thanked him and went on our way. But for weeks afterwards Geoff kept bringing up the topic of the mysterious *'Paba Shimani,'* wondering where he could obtain it.

A month or so after that we met a gentleman whose name I can only recall as Mr. Molepo. He had some sort of position with the Lebowa Department of Cultural Affairs and he took Geoff, Thomas and I to a room containing glass showcases near his office where he wanted to put together a display of various items which had historical and cultural significance. Pointing to a nondescript dried plant about a foot long in one of the cases he said it was used by local diviners for combating hardships and even for eliminating competition for a lady's attention. He said that if a child was going to write an important exam at school his mother could sew one of the plants into his jacket and that would ensure that he got good grades. You can imagine our surprise when he told us that its name was *'Paba Shimani.'* Geoff could hardly contain himself but, try as he might, Mr. Molepo was not going to part with any of his precious *Paba Shimani*.

A few days after this incident we were in a rural area filming a magnificent panoramic landscape when a small pickup truck drove by and stopped. As so often happened the driver knew our guide. The two men excitedly exchanged greetings and started chatting. Our guide introduced Geoff, Thomas and myself to the driver and we learned that he had a reputation for being a very powerful *sangoma*. On learning this Geoff immediately asked him if he could get him some *Paba Shimani*. Needless to say he didn't have any but went back to his pickup, fumbled around in the cab and came back carrying a very small dried and shrunken turnip-like plant. It was white, had no skin on it and was pitted with multiple bite marks. Its texture looked something like that of a golf ball. The *sangoma* gave it to Geoff and told him that it was far more powerful than *Paba Shimani*. He went on to say that if there was anything he feared, did not like or thought was dangerous and approaching him he should bite a tiny piece out of it and spit it out in the direction of the oncoming problem. It must have previously been used many times because of all the pit marks on it.

From that day onwards Geoff kept this strange piece of vegetable matter with him at all times. He eventually had it sewn up into a small yellow chamois leather bag and transferred it from the back pocket of his jeans to a clean pair whenever he changed. Nothing more was said of the object until many weeks later when we arrived at the home of a healer who was going to perform a ceremony that we were hoping to film. The event was to take place on a Sunday and on the Friday before that we visited him to negotiate for the necessary permission. But before discussions began he said that he would like to check and make sure "we were alright from his ancestors' point of view."

He showed us into a tiny corrugated iron shed. As our eyes grew accustomed to the gloomy interior thin beams of daylight from tiny holes in the metal walls and ceiling of the shed revealed the *sangoma* perching on his haunches in a corner. He was making strange incantations under his breath. After a short while he got up and told us that something was wrong. He asked Geoff and Thomas to leave and then as he continued to utter his incantation he waved his arms around me and patted me down from head to foot. After this little vetting process he let me go and asked me to send Thomas in to see him. Minutes later Thomas emerged from the shed and said that he too was clear. Now it was Geoff's turn. Ten minutes later both Geoff and the *sangoma* came out of the shed but Geoff was looking decidedly worried. The *sangoma* reported that there was a problem with him. He said that after consulting with his ancestral spirits he had been warned that Geoff had "a tiny white ball of *muti* in his pocket and should get rid of it and not bring it back on Sunday." Dumbstruck by this discovery Geoff dug into his back pocket, pulled out the little yellow bag containing his vegetable amulet and went to lock it in the glove compartment of our van. As soon as this was done the *sangoma* asked the three of us to go back into the shed with him. Closing his eyes and making a few more utterances he declared us clear. All was well and the man happily agreed to let us return on Sunday. And that was that. But as Alice would have said in the fable about her adventures through the looking glass, when it came to matters of the paranormal things got even "curiouser and curiouser."

On another occasion a *sangoma* that we came across was using water to determine a client's problem. A wooden bowl held about an inch or two of specially sanctified water in it. The *sangoma* picked up a small dried calabash that had been beaded and painted to look like a human figure and put it on top of the patient's head. Then he placed the calabash in the dish of water.

Unbelievably, the calabash started to vibrate, causing ripples in the water. The pattern and frequency of the ripples were all the diviner needed to find out what was ailing the man. According to his diagnosis someone had put a spell on him that had caused him to have worms. He was told to drink the water from the bowl and was then handed a small package of foul-smelling ground-herbs mixed with some kind of fatty substance. The patient was told to go away, tell no one what was wrong with him, boil the mixture in a deep saucepan for five minutes, drink a cupful of it, then throw the rest of it in a bath of water and soak in it for twenty minutes. Did it work? I have no idea. But my hunch is that it did.

At another village we found a male *sangoma* who was being consulted by a woman whose husband had left her. She wanted to know where he was and she also wanted to find out what he had done with the money that she had saved up and kept in an empty marmalade jar inside their hut. With his client sitting on a low wooden stool in front of him the *sangoma* stripped off his shirt, then put on a headband of beads and feathers and perched on the ground. He handed his client a *makonyana,* a trellis-like instrument similar to the one that we had filmed being used by the male *nyamatei* overseer at the Domba initiation school in Vendaland. Lighting a small fire the *sangoma* asked the woman to unravel the instrument and extend the trellis about two or three feet in front of her with the red feather that had been attached to the furthest stick facing away from her. She was instructed to hold the contraption with both hands. He asked her to address the *makonyana* directly with her question. When she inquired about the whereabouts of her husband the entire trellis began to tremble. The woman began to look frightened but the diviner told her not to worry and to just keep holding tight. The sticks began to clatter and then, almost like a gate swinging in a breeze, the structure swayed to her left, ending at a 90-degree angle away from her. As if this were not enough, the red feather at the end of the trellis bent over and began quivering in that direction. Speaking in Sotho the *sangoma* told her that it was pointing towards Pietersburg. Yes, he told her, that is where her husband was. He had absconded to that city.

"And what about my money?" she asked.

Once again the *makonyana* wavered around as though it was being attracted and then repelled by some invisible magnetic force. This way, then that. Finally, it ended up facing in exactly the same direction as it had before, with the red feather pointing the way. No question. Her husband had taken the money with him to Pietersburg. The poor woman started to sob. Without showing any emotion whatsoever the diviner asked her whether her husband had any siblings here in the area where she lived. Perhaps they might take pity on her and help her. In between sobs and sniffles the woman replied that her husband had a brother but he had moved away recently and she was not sure where he was.

"Well, ask *makonyana*," the diviner suggested matter-of-factly.

The woman uttered a few stilted words and instantly the instrument swept around in the opposite direction, pointing 90 degrees to her right. The feather was quivering and shaking so much that I thought it would break free from the stick.

"That is the direction of Makotopong village," the diviner said satisfactorily. "Seek him there. That is where you will find your husband's brother. He will help you."

Then he reached out, grabbed the *makonyana* from her and folded it up. The session was over. Deeply upset at what she had learned the woman left but she seemed determined to heed the *sangoma's* advice and find her brother-in-law in Makotopong, about thirty miles away. Incredibly, about a week later we learned the outcome of the story. We left our hotel in Pietersburg one morning and drove out to the township on the outskirts of town to pick up our guide. He was thrilled to tell us that he had heard the result of the woman's quest. The woman had walked all the way to Makotopong, made a few inquiries and actually managed to find her brother-in-law there. He had taken pity on her and agreed to help her financially by giving her the same amount of money that his brother had stolen from her. As Winston Churchill would have said, it was just another riddle wrapped in a mystery inside an enigma.

One of the oddest places we ever visited in Lebowa was the village of a man who went by the name of Shabalala. His reputation as a healer, diviner, herbalist and powerful worker of wonders spread far and wide. It had taken us all of a month of bargaining and negotiating to get him to agree to be filmed. On the appointed day we arrived at his *kraal* and it was obvious that something very important was going on. Drums were beating loudly and a lively chorus of male and female voices drifted from a central circular arena-like space under a corrugated iron roof. This was situated in the middle of a conglomerate of huts, outbuildings and animal paddocks. There were people everywhere, some in tribal attire, but most in Western clothes. Shabalala must have had at least six or seven wives as all the huts were inhabited and dozens of little kids were running around in a bewildering assortment of dressed and semi-dressed states. The smallest ones were completely naked with nothing more than a strand of beads tied around their waists. The veld in the vicinity was littered with the wrecks of old cars, ploughs, water tanks and even an ancient-looking metal bedstead. Rusted chassis and greasy automobile engines lay here and there, all of them covered in weeds and grass. Colorful flags of infinite designs fluttered from poles. I have seldom seen a place of such contrasts. We found Shabalala in the arena, surrounded by drummers, singers and an enthusiastic audience. He was a large man of at least 250 lbs. It was difficult to tell his age but I guessed him to be somewhere in his mid-forties. He wore an extravagant headgear of porcupine quills and feathers. Around his waist was a bright skirt of multicolored cloth and leather strips, yet he sported a conventional Western-style blue striped shirt and tie. Beads were everywhere: around his waist, neck and ankles. His wrists were covered in bangles. Strips of white fur and feathers were tied around his knees. He looked amazing. More picturesque was the fact that he was lying flat on his back on the concrete floor in the middle of the arena. A heavy wooden grain container had been perched on his stomach and two women with sticks were pounding it, as though they were crushing corn. Violent energy was beating down on Shabalala's stomach and rib cage. If it had been any other mortal every bone in his body would have been broken by the sheer weight and pounding yet Shabalala seemed totally immune to the discomfort. Lying there under that excessive weight he was singing loudly in harmony with the choir and drums. It was a bizarre, spectacular scene.

We were informed that this performance was merely to demonstrate his strength. He was doing it for his disciples and the audience around him. I wanted to know why and was told that a young woman who had been possessed by an unknown evil entity had been brought in that morning and Shabalala was going to exorcise it. To do that he needed the support of all his assistants as well as the encouragement of all the visitors who had come to witness the exorcism. He also needed to prove his powers to the possessing spirit, hence this display of physical endurance. I was all over the place with my camera but not a soul showed the slightest interest in me. Their eyes were only on Shabalala and his patient. She was a very forlorn-looking young woman who sat in the corner of the arena. She looked dazed and confused, her eyes rolling up into her head as she swayed from side to side. She was surrounded by a number of Shabalala's young female assistants who held her hands and daubed her forehead with cold water. Suddenly Shabalala threw off the heavy wooden load, shouted, stood up, eyes flaring. He called out to a group of four young male attendants who were standing among the crowd, each brandishing a long stick. The ends had been wrapped in cloth and soaked in gasoline. The attendants immediately lit them with matches and ran over to Shabalala, swinging the fiercely burning torches around him. As they swished and hissed in streaking flame and smoke I thought he was going to be seriously hurt but he always managed to dodge the fire, laughing loudly and singing at the top of his voice. They aimed for his body, head, feet, arms, but he eluded harm. I have no idea how he did it. The heat from the flames was so intense and the direction of the swinging torches so unpredictable that I sank back into the crowds, shooting everything from a safe distance. Ten minutes of this and Shabalala screamed again. He rushed over to the possessed woman and began to run circles around her. All the attendants including the torch-bearers rapidly withdrew from the arena. Spitting on the poor woman, then yelling curses at her, Shabalala was demanding that the spirit identify itself and leave her body. This went on for half an hour. I don't know how he kept up that incredible level of energy. I have no idea where he summoned the means to keep shouting and dancing. The singing had now stopped but the drums were still rat-a-tatting throughout the proceedings. Suddenly, just as if she had been injected with a powerful dose of anesthetic the young girl keeled over. Shabalala called for his female aides. They rushed over, carrying a bucket of water and a pile of towels. These were plunged into the water and wrapped around the girl. After about ten minutes she came to. She was bewildered, that much was obvious, but I could clearly see that her awful daze and confused state of mind had gone. Shabalala leaned down beside her, asking her name and a lot of other questions. As she answered he began to beam. The exorcism had worked. He announced to the crowd that the evil possessing spirit had left her. There were shouts of joy everywhere. Then the singing and drumming commenced again. But now it was more like a party than a ritual. The young girl, wrapped in the wet towels, was led into one of the huts to rest and sleep.

But the day had not yet ended. Shabalala had another client waiting to see him. We followed him to his *ndumba* or consulting hut where a sickly-looking middle-aged man sat on the doorstep. One of the aides explained that the man was feeling ill and had a high fever. Shabalala said nothing. He merely pried open the poor fellow's mouth, peered inside and poked around under his tongue. Then he felt around at the back of the man's neck. He called out to one of his assistants and a strange object was brought out of the hut. It was a cork top from a champagne or wine bottle. It had two long porcupine quills stuck into it at a sloping angle, one on either side, in a 'V' pattern. At the bottom of the cork was a blunt needle. Shabalala mumbled something to one of his assistants and the patient was instructed to strip to the waist. Then Shabalala gently placed the weird device on the man's right shoulder with the blunt end of the needle touching the skin. Letting go of it, Shabalala watched how the cork miraculously balanced itself, the two quills acting as counterweights. It seemed to lean in the direction of one of the quills and that was all Shabalala needed to know. He immediately decided on a cure and told his aides to prepare for it. Our guide came over to me and told me I was going to witness what was known as *siduwe*, a rare form of treatment very seldom performed. Shabalala was going to transfer the man's fever from his body into that of an animal. In this case it was to be a rather scrawny brown goat. As much as I abhor any form of animal cruelty or sacrifice in the name of a god, religion, ancestor or even to cure an illness, I was curious to see how this would be done. What happened next was unbelievable.

The bleating goat, tethered to a rope, was brought to a clearing outside the hut. Shabalala walked over to it, crouched down and gently cupped his hands around the animal's head. No pressure was applied. In fact, Shabalala was being especially gentle with the creature. It continued to bleat for a few moments and then there was silence. Its breathing slowed. As I watched all this through the viewfinder of my camera my heart was pounding. I was truly fearful that this little animal was going to be subjected to something awful. Then, amazingly, its eyes closed. It had been hypnotized! The goat had gone to sleep!

One of the aides untied the rope and lay the animal on its side in the dust. Then Shabalala beckoned for the patient to come over and lie down next to the goat. As Shabalala oversaw the procedure one of the aides instructed the man to lie very close to the animal and exhale his breath into its nostrils. As he carried out this instruction aides covered both man and animal with a light red blanket. At no time at all did the goat show any sign of waking up. In fact, it never moved. After about ten minutes the blanket was lifted and the patient was told to get up and go and rest in the shade under the porch of the *ndumba* hut. Next thing I knew Shabalala was holding a long, sharp, steel-bladed knife. An aide brought an enamel bowl which was placed close to the goat's throat. The knife flashed in the sunlight. There was a short squeal from the goat and then a fountain of blood spurted into the bowl. In less than a minute the creature was dead. I was trembling. Then I remembered to get a photographic cutaway of the patient sitting there all by himself in the shade. When I looked at him I couldn't believe the difference. He was a changed man. He seemed physically different. Meanwhile, the bowl of blood was poured into a couple of jars. One of them was handed over to the patient to take home. An aide told him to pour it into a bath and soak in it for an hour. By tomorrow, he said, not a trace of fever would remain. And I did not doubt that for one moment. As for Shabalala, I never saw him again. The sun was sinking and he had already wandered off, finished with the procedure, with the patient and, obviously, with us. Drumming and singing continued as we packed away our gear. The last thing I noticed as darkness fell and as we drove away from the village was the young girl who had been exorcised. She was sitting amidst a group of women outside one of the huts, happily sharing a canister of home-brewed sorghum beer, laughing merrily, just as if nothing had ever happened.

If *The Tribal Identity* taught me anything it was an inescapable awareness of how much the people of South Africa were living on two entirely disparate planes. When I came back to Johannesburg from trips to the tribal homelands I crossed the threshold from one world to another. Dirt tracks gave way to freeways. Mud huts were replaced by skyscrapers. Margins were sharply defined. You left a road of dust and mud, then turned onto another road that suddenly became a four-lane highway and in no time at all you had gone through a wormhole in time. You left one universe, instantly to emerge in another.

Of course, some homelands were more developed than others, but most people were in a state of paucity and depravity. In later years Bophuthatswana would have its massive Sun City casino complex, hotels, resort and Superbowl entertainment center—the latter officially opened in 1980 with a series of live performances by Frank Sinatra—but all of this stood just a stone's throw away from unspeakable poverty. Slot machines jangled and fortunes were won and lost in huge casinos not far from shanty towns. An array of fancy restaurants overlooking pools and tennis courts beneath the shadow of a monorail lay just beyond a bend in the road where, over the next hill, people in rags stood in line waiting to fill buckets with water from the one single faucet that served an entire village. While Sun City glittered and dazzled like a jewel—a miniature version of Las Vegas—the villages and huts of the local black people were pitch dark at night. Electricity was still a dream for them. And past them whizzed luxury coaches and expensive limousines carrying visitors from nearby Johannesburg and Pretoria to a wonderland where everything could be had that was illegal in white South Africa. Did Sun City's visitors ever look out of their vehicles or stare down from their aircraft windows as they approached this place of endless forbidden fruits and fun-filled titillation as they eagerly anticipated the gambling tables or the nudie reviews and soft porn movies that lay in store for them? Did anyone *notice* the appalling poverty, pollution, starving kids and lame donkeys that lined the way to paradise? But then of course no one ever experienced the wonderful ceremonies celebrating the installation of a chief or a ritual for the dead or the traditional naming of a baby or the warm kinship between people that underscored life deep in the tribal areas where no white visitor ever set foot. Perhaps they caught some of it on Sunday evenings when the eight episodes of *The Tribal Identity* went on the air. The fan mail to Peter Becker and viewer feedback to the SABC exceeded everyone's expectations. It was just as we suspected. Whites knew *nothing* about their black neighbors. On the whole they relished the opportunity to learn more about them.

Peter Becker and I saw much of each other socially after the series was finished. Through my close association with his family I had become particularly friendly with his son Harold, daughter-in-law Natalie and their two children, Simon and Samantha. I was delighted when they moved from Johannesburg to Cape Town in the early eighties because my wife and I also decided to move to the Cape with our children in 1982. This was to be a staging point in a slow process that would culminate in our move to the United States in 1986 because at no time did I lose sight of my dream of one day settling in Hollywood. I mention all this because one Sunday morning in early May 1984 there was a knock at the front door of our home overlooking the Atlantic Ocean at Bantry Bay in Cape Town. We weren't expecting anyone and I was both surprised and delighted to see a smiling Peter Becker standing there, puffing away at his corncob pipe. He had arrived completely unannounced. This struck me as very odd. It was unlike him. We sat down to tea and Peter told me of his plans to go to Arizona to do some field research work. He loved that state and had been there many times, tracing the history of its Native American inhabitants. As we talked I sensed that there was something he wanted to tell me but he was holding back. Eventually I just said, "Peter, what's bothering you? Why have you really come here today?"

He put down his cup, stuffed a clump of cherry blossom-scented tobacco into his pipe, thought for a moment and said, "I have a strange feeling about this trip. I felt I had to fly down this weekend before I left for the States. For some odd reason I knew I had to see you, Harold, Natalie and the kids before I left."

"Do you have any idea why?" I asked.

I was pushing. Peter didn't act on hunches. He either knew a thing or he didn't. There was little place for guesswork in his life. He stared out of the big picture window of our living room at the Atlantic. Dapples of light reflected on his face. He was carefully considering his response.

"I don't think I'll be coming back," he said, almost matter-of-factly. "Not this time."

"What are you talking about?" I asked. "What do you mean you won't be coming back?"

"There's something about this trip. I don't know what it is but I know something is going to happen."

A coldness slithered up my spine. I didn't know what to say. But one thing was for sure. Peter had genuine insight into things. He was a deeply spiritual man. In addition to his close connection to African tribal shamanism and through his ability to use a *sangoma's* set of bones as instruments of divination, he also firmly believed that ancestors played a direct role in one's life. But there was more. To him, reincarnation was an unequivocal reality. Few knew that he was also a follower of Hinduism and a devotee of a guru, the spiritual teacher Sai Baba in India.

"Have you told Harold?" I asked.

"No, not yet," he replied. "I'm going to have lunch with him, Natalie and the kids today. I'll tell them then before I fly back up to Jo'burg this evening."

He stared out of the window at something I couldn't see or

even guess at. I didn't want to press him further on the matter. He finished his tea and then came over and gave me a hug. When we saw him out of the front door he hugged my wife Diana and then shook my hand African-style, grasping the palm, then the thumb, and then the palm again.

He looked at me and smiled.

"*Sallah Kahle,*" he said in Zulu. ("Stay well.")

I never saw him again.

Later that month he was standing on the side of a little-used dirt road near the town of Florence in Arizona taking a photograph of the landscape. As he stepped back to get a slightly better angle of the view the only car that had come by in the past hour rounded a curve in the road and hit him. He was killed instantly. When I heard about the tragedy I called his son Harold immediately.

"He knew it was going to happen," Harold said. "He told us he wasn't coming back."

Later that month I was in Johannesburg on business and I bumped into an old friend, a travel agent. She had been responsible for making all of Peter's travel arrangements over the years. She verified what Harold and I already knew.

"It was so odd," she said. "Just before he left for New York Peter called and thanked me for always being so considerate and helpful when booking his flights, hotels and rental cars. The next day a beautiful bouquet of flowers arrived at the office with a simple note from him saying, 'Thanks again. Goodbye. Love, Peter B.' I didn't know what to make of it. But now I do."

Had Peter foreseen his own death?

Absolutely. This was Africa. Anything was possible.

Thirteen

From the mid-seventies to the early eighties I worked on a wide range of productions. They introduced me to subject matter and places I had never imagined. Fortunately I had a very good friend who helped facilitate things. Barney Joffe was one of the country's top film editors. With a bubbling sense of humor, always ready to tell a joke and with an enviable capacity to look on the bright side of life, Barney worked his way up in the industry from editing newsreels to becoming head of the English documentary department at SABC Television. Were it not for him I certainly would not have managed to get the range of contracts from the SABC that I did. These included fictional dramas, children's programming and documentaries. Barney was one of those people with whom I had a great personal and professional relationship, and to whom I will always be indebted. Shows that I worked on during the late seventies to mid-eighties included an examination of the Soviet military threat to the Gulf oil supply route around the Cape of Good Hope, NGO programs to develop rural agriculture, the performing arts, medical research, tertiary education, family planning, commercial aviation, a history of the country's Indian community, Hinduism, Islam, economics, retail marketing, profiles of local artists, the steel industry, greenhouse gases and acid rain, architecture, the gold mining industry and too many others to name. I also produced a series that looked at the workings of the navy, army and air force. War was raging in Angola at the time. Backed by the Soviet Union Cuban troops had flooded into Angola, much to the consternation of London, Washington and Pretoria. In Mozambique conflict raged between the opposing FRELIMO and Renamo political parties. Directly to the north the bloody Rhodesian 'bush war' still festered between white and black. In South West Africa resistance fighters were battling for that territory's independence from South Africa.

They were troubling times. The military needed as much public support as it could get and the state-owned TV network obliged by commissioning a series of documentaries about it. With my camera I got to streak through the skies above Mozambique in a Mirage IIICZ fighter aircraft flying at a speed of Mach 2.3. I pulled five Gs doing loops and barrel rolls in Aermacchi MB-326 trainer jets. I traveled in an armed personnel carrier along the Kunene River deep into Angola in search of Cuban military positions. I dived under the Atlantic Ocean in a Daphne class submarine, hung out of a Shackleton maritime patrol aircraft filming Soviet Kiev-class tactical cruisers including the formidable *Minsk,* flew on missions in Lockheed C-130 and Transall C-160 transports to supply troops in South West Africa and Angola, holding on as we avoided surface-to-air missiles. I got horribly seasick on board a Gabriel missile-equipped Reshef class strike craft as it sliced through Indian Ocean waters at 34 knots per hour, and almost passed out when the helicopter I was traveling in lost a bolt on a rotor blade and plunged twenty feet down onto the deck of the naval survey vessel, *SAS Protea*. So, turbulent though they may have been they were also undeniably exciting times. I don't think I ever experienced so many thrills as I did working on those military shows.

One day we were filming a naval exercise at sea. There were five ships involved. We were on board a frigate. A target was being towed by one of the other vessels. Our frigate's crew was practicing firing skills. The air force had laid on fighters to strafe us from above. There was frenzied activity at all battle stations. From the big 115mm cannons to the 40mm antiaircraft guns young guys in uniform were running around feverishly as commands were barked from the ship's PA system. The noise was deafening. Booming explosions and the clang of empty cartridges falling into bins proved to be a nightmare for our sound recordist but the visuals were terrific. Most of the young men on board were national servicemen doing their compulsory two-year military training. Once a guy had been 'called up' for service he could indicate his preference to join the army, the navy or the air force. Most of them ended up in one of the divisions of the army but the lucky ones got into the navy and a select few were drafted into the air force. Of course, this applied to whites only. While some Colored men were taken in as permanent members of the navy no blacks were ever accepted for military service at that time. In the midst of all the chaos and noise that day on the frigate a conscript of about 17 or 18 years old came running over to me, his face covered in black ash and an anti-flash mask with just his eyes showing. Surrounded by smoke and panting crazily he pulled off his mask, looked me straight in the eye and accusingly yelled: "Y'know, you guys are a bunch of fucking bullshitters!"

"Why?" I asked.

Without hesitating he said: "I volunteered to join the navy because of all those movies they showed us in high school and I thought life at sea would be fun but what happens? I bust my fucking balls doing basic training and then I come aboard only to find that I have to sleep in a bloody hammock, have no privacy, get seasick every day and nothing is like those stupid damn movies you guys make. There isn't even any background music. I mean, for chrissake, *where's the fucking music?!*"

Another explosion ripped through the air as a jet fighter screamed overhead. And then the guy was gone, a nameless blue uniformed young serviceman swallowed up in noise and clouds of black smoke back to his battle station. He was right. Where indeed was the music? I couldn't help but roar with laughter.

The last big project I did during my tenure at the Independent Film Center (IFC) before I set up my own production company in Cape Town was *Then Came the English*, a very ambitious—and expensive—series on the history of the British presence on the subcontinent. It was a saga that began in 1795 and was what lay behind the story of the country's English-speaking white community. Part of it was filmed in the UK. When I was over there doing preparatory work I met a number of people in government plus peers, authors, historians and authorities from all walks of life. Getting permits to work at Windsor Castle included taking a meeting with the Keeper of the Privy Purse Major Sir Rennie Maudsley in Buckingham Palace. That was quite an experience. Tea at the palace. Fortunately I had brought a dark pinstripe suit with me to London. I think one of the most special of all the very enjoyable experiences we had in England during the production was filming with the Duke and Duchess of Beaufort at their marvelous country home Badminton House in Gloucestershire. The vast estate was the birthplace of Lord Charles Somerset, first British Governor at the Cape of Good Hope back in 1814. We interviewed many interesting people on camera including Earl Kitchener of Khartoum, authors Malcolm Muggeridge and Thomas Pakenham, broadcaster Anthony Lejeune, Member of Parliament Julian Amery and Member of Parliament and grandson of his namesake, Winston Spencer Churchill. One of the most articulate of them all was South African-born author Sir Laurens van der Post. But perhaps two of the most compelling were survivors of the Anglo-Boer War that Britain had fought against South Africa at the turn of the 19th century.

Lieutenant Colonel Eric Liddell, OBE was well into his nineties when we filmed him at his home in Barnes, just a block or two from where the Thames curls its way through the greater London metropolitan area. Archibald Bowers was close to 100 when we interviewed him at his daughter's house in Dartford, Kent. His memory was astonishing. When he was sent out to South Africa as a young man to serve queen and country he was placed in charge of his regiment's horses. It was his duty to ensure that 'fresh' horses were always available and that injured, tired or unfit animals were efficiently disposed of. Accounts vary but most sources list the British Army as having supplied

520,000 horses and 150,000 mules for use in the two phases of the war between 1899 and 1902. Many perished during the ocean voyage from England but the war itself accounted for the deaths of some 350,000 horses and 50,000 mules. The losses by the Boers are difficult to estimate but some experts place that figure at around 150,000 animals. With tears in his eyes Bowers told us how he prided himself at being able to bring down a sick or injured animal with just one bullet. After a battle he would take his rifle and shoot severely injured horses from the saddle as he galloped among them. He spoke of the horrendous treatment of the horses by men who possessed few skills in horsemanship. Stirrups would pierce horses' flanks until blood flowed. Heavy-handed use of the reins would tear open the sides of their mouths. Legs would be broken as animals labored to haul Maxim guns into place. These memories haunted the quiet, unassuming and seemingly very gentle man for the rest of his life. Following the interview in the tiny living room of his daughter's humble home they would continue to haunt me too. Interestingly, South Africa has one of the world's few war memorials dedicated to animals lost in battle. It stands in the city of Port Elizabeth (contemporary iBhayi). The inscription on it reads, *"In recognition of the services of the gallant animals which perished in the South African War, 1899-1902."* It also bears the words by John Ruskin based on his *A Crown of Wild Olives* which states, *"The greatness of a nation consists not so much in the number of its people or the extent of its territory as in the extent and justice of its compassion."*

In 1982 my family and I had settled in Cape Town as part of our plans to move to the United States. There was still no sign of apartheid coming undone. The new president Pieter W. Botha was as adamant as ever to ensure that white Afrikanerdom remain firmly in control. While some laws were eased against the black population it was not much more than cosmetic window dressing. In most large metropolitan areas blacks were now being allowed the use of hotels, theaters and restaurants alongside whites but the ruling National Party was still in charge and blacks were persistently denied the vote. As far as my wife and I were concerned the writing was on the wall. We no longer wanted our children exposed to racism. It was time to leave. While plans were hatched and arrangements made for our move to California I remained as busy as ever. One of the series I made was called *A Delicate Balance*. In the early eighties gloomy forecasts predicted that Africa's population was growing at a staggering rate of 81% per decade. This was in contrast to Europe's which was increasing at an average six percent. Human numbers were in an out-of-control upward spiral.

Africa was a continent in crisis. Then, as now, water resources in many regions were being stretched to the limit. Industrial effluent was poisoning rivers, dams and seashores. Estuaries had become clogged. Agricultural use of pesticides, herbicides and fertilizers were destroying species diversity. Excessive run-off of nitrates and phosphates into streams and lakes were encouraging unwanted growth of hyacinth and algae. At sea, the anchovy and pilchard industries were collapsing due to overfishing. Poor land use had turned pastures into deserts. Aluminum cans and plastic bags littered once pristine rural landscapes. Where poaching had not brought many species to the brink of extinction in Southern African conservation areas the 'carrying capacity' of the land had been exceeded and wild animals were having to be 'culled'—shot or machine-gunned from the air—in huge numbers. It was Dr. Bernhard and Michael Grzimek's nightmarish vision of the 1956 film *No Place For Wild Animals* coming true. What had horrified me as a child in that movie theater so long ago had become a real and tangible thing. But it wasn't only Africa that was at stake. The rest of the world had no room for complacency. Natural resources were being consumed at an alarming rate everywhere. Greenhouse gases were on the increase. European and Asian cities were being eroded by acid rain. Social decay was nibbling away at civilization as unemployment and crime rose. Worldwide, between ten and 25 million people were dying due to unsanitary water supplies.

A Delicate Balance concentrated on Africa but major sequences for it were shot all over the globe. The series covered a broad spectrum of issues, from unregulated toxic traffic fumes in Taipei in the Republic of Taiwan to congestion and overcrowding in Toledo, Spain. From Houston to Hong Kong we searched for stories that highlighted the human impact on the environment. But none of this would have meant anything without a sense of balance in the programs. I wanted to find an example of some place—*any* place—where the environment had not been upset by the presence of man. I wanted to use this is a springboard into the series. I wanted to say, "See, this is how things *could* be if we stopped overbreeding and screwing things up."

But where to find such an example? And then my trusty researcher Esme Jacobson came up with a brilliant idea. Why not travel to an out-of-the-way island; an island inhabited by humans and where the ecological integrity of the place remained untarnished? Fortunately, such a place did exist. Marion Island is situated 46 degrees 52 minutes South, and 37 degrees 51 minutes East some 1,600 miles southeast of Cape Town. Because it is so remote it is virtually a self-contained ecosystem. I saw it as a time machine, like a miniature world captured in a bottle, unaffected and unimpaired by anything from the outside. Strictly speaking, of course, nowhere on Earth is like that. Everything is part of a greater whole. But Marion came very close to being a uniquely intact and self-sustaining sanctuary.

And so it was that in August 1982 my assistant Derrick Louw and I watched Table Bay recede into the distance as we headed towards the chilly Southern Atlantic on board the icebreaker and scientific research and supply vessel, *SA Agulhas*. Built mainly to ferry scientists and replenishments to *Sanae,* South Africa's research station on the northern shore of Antarctica, the 7,000-ton 368-feet long vessel was built for the South African Department of Transport by Mitsubishi Heavy Industries in Japan. She was launched in 1977. With her white superstructure and bright red hull—essential for spotting her in the ice—she carried every amenity on board including a helicopter flight deck and hangar containing a French-built Aerospatiale Puma SA 330 all-weather heavy lift helicopter. She carried a doctor and was fitted out with a fully equipped operating room. Her seven decks included a gymnasium, library, dining rooms, lounges and extensive 'wet' and 'dry' research laboratories. In addition to comfortable officer and crew quarters she had excellent accommodation for a hundred scientists and passengers. Her commander was Captain Bill Leith. A clean-cut, slightly aloof and withdrawn man in his late forties, he ran a tight ship. He was a strict disciplinarian. Everything on board had to be spick and span, and all systems had to run like clockwork. One night he invited me up to his private cabin for a drink. When I asked him if he was ever scared of the sea he thought for a moment and then said, "You know, I respect the elements enormously. We plow merrily through the water and cut our way through ice and think we're masters of the environment but we're not. We're neither infallible nor impervious to nature. I know full well that there are just a few inches of steel between me and a fate I dare not even contemplate. So, afraid? No. Respectful? Very."

He poured me another scotch and I changed the subject.

I used to enjoy the occasional evening sitting on a stool in a corner of the bridge as a volunteer assistant to the Officer of the Watch. Passengers were encouraged to participate in this all-important task. We had to be on a constant lookout for 'growlers.' Though rare these were small chunks of ice that had broken off from icebergs and sometimes drifted northwards from the frozen regions around Antarctica. I liked spending a few hours up there in the warm silence of the bridge, peering through the big windshields into the darkness ahead. Very little was said among the three or four people always on watch. Captain Leith frowned upon idle chatter. Concentration levels had to be kept high. Apart from a green glow from the radar screen, a slightly golden incandescence from the illuminated compass and a couple of red lights winking on instrument panels, the wide, spacious bridge was purposely kept dark, allowing human vision to adjust to the blackness outside. There were few sounds up there other than the rhythmic ticking of a big electric chronometer on the rear bulkhead and a sort of whirring sound coming from the autopilot. It sent signals to the hydraulics deep within the ship, making constant corrections to ensure that the big vessel remained precisely on course. Traveling at an average of 12.5 knots an hour it would take just under a week to reach Marion Island. As we headed southwards it got colder by the day. The decks became slippery as a thin film of ice formed on them. Along the way we filmed the hydrographic mapping of the ocean floor by sonar equipment which bounced signals off the seabed. This region of the South Atlantic was still relatively unknown and uncharted. We also captured glimpses of life aboard the ship. The *Agulhas* was carrying two new members who would join Team Marion 39, the 39th group of men already stationed on the island. Working for the Department of Transport's Meteorological Service, island-based teams included meteorologists, mechanical engineers, radio technicians and a medic, usually twelve in all. The teams spent a full year on the island. Also on board were the helicopter pilots and their supporting ground crew, plus a team of scientists who would spend a few weeks on Marion while the *Agulhas* was anchored offshore unloading fresh supplies and loading waste for transport back to the mainland. There were marine biologists, mammalian specialists, ichthyologists, ornithologists, entomologists, atmospheric scientists, geologists and even a *dominee* or priest from the Afrikaans Dutch Reformed Church. A short, feisty, friendly young man by the name of Louw Bouwer, the *dominee* was actually an army chaplain assigned to the voyage by the Department of Defense to cater to the moral and spiritual needs of the group. He was a terrific guy and played a mean game of pool. He could gently tap a cue and sink a ball with almost divinely-inspired accuracy. Nobody could ever beat him. The scientists on board were going to study plant ecology, biology, wildlife breeding habits, atmospheric physics and geomagnetism. Because it was such an enclosed ecosystem, Marion was a vast living laboratory, ideal for examining the way all living things interacted with each other, as well as with the ocean, the weather and the physical conditions of the island. It was a perfect place for our purposes. The senior scientist among the group was Professor George Branch, an expert in limpets and seaweed. He was a professor in the Zoology Department at the University of Cape Town, world renowned for its marine research. I decided to focus the story on him, using him as our central science character. An amenable and likable man in his late thirties or early forties he looked the part of a marine biologist. He had a crop of dark unkempt hair and facial stubble well on its way to becoming a healthy thick beard. We would concentrate on his work yet carefully weave it around the activities of the other scientists.

It was a grey and dismal dawn when I stood on the poop deck of the *Agulhas* as Marion was sighted off the port bow. Squalls of rain and bitter cold winds made the disembarkation process extremely difficult. There was no dock to speak of so the ship had to anchor about a quarter mile offshore. Some of the men made the journey to land by large inflatable Zodiacs powered by outboard engines while most of us were ferried to base camp by helicopter. Cargo was strung in nylon nets beneath the Puma. This included all our filming equipment and it was with bated breath that I watched our trunks and cases swing through pelting rain and high wind, to be gently deposited on a large wooden deck close to the buildings of the base. Most of the structures were built on stilts above the marshy ground.

High winds made it necessary to anchor them into the rock with steel cables. Hostile though it was, Marion was a fascinating place. It is a volcanic island twelve miles long by seven-and-a-half miles wide. Geologically, it is relatively young. It dates back some 400,000 years when a volcano rose from the ocean floor and spewed lava that cooled to form basaltic rock. Marion's volcano was still classified as active. For the scientists the place was particularly interesting as there was relatively little time for animals to colonize the land. Few organisms lived there so evolution and interaction between species and plants could easily be studied.

There was a strong link between land and sea. Birds fed at sea, came to the island to roost and breed, fed their chicks and deposited their guano there. The guano in turn washed ashore, affecting the growth of marine plants. Limpets then thrived on the seaweed and other birds subsequently ate the limpets. It was a cycle of interdependency, with one organism relying on another. There was rich material to make our point that a self-sustaining ecosystem functioned beautifully when unimpeded by human activity. To preserve this integrity all human waste—from plastic bags to tin cans to excrement—was scrupulously controlled, contained and then sent back to the mainland in South Africa for disposal. As a proclaimed nature sanctuary Marion's elephant seal population was slowly reestablished after earlier brutal exploitation by whalers and hunters. Conditions on the island were unique in that the wildlife was unafraid of humans, allowing researchers to approach colonies of seals, penguins and birds at very close range.

There was little vegetation besides lichen, ferns and grasses. Due to the persistently strong westerly winds known as the 'Roaring Forties' there were no trees. The terrain was very boggy and wet. Sunshine was uncommon and rainfall was high. Getting around was difficult. At the base it was easy enough as wooden and metal pathways connected all the buildings, but going out into the field was exhausting. Wherever Derrick and I carried camera, tripod and recording equipment we sank to our knees in mud and bog. I discovered muscles I never knew I had. I was totally out of shape and unprepared for the grueling environment. Wrapped up in confining and uncomfortable rain gear and wearing heavy boots I was often out of breath, having to stop every twenty or thirty feet to rest. But it was well worth the effort. We captured wonderful scenes on film. Penguin species included Kings, Rockhopper, Macaroni and Gentoos. Bird life was abundant. There were Skuas, Giant Petrels and King Cormorants. But the one that caught my imagination and inspired me the most was that most regal of birds, a creature of legend and mythology, the Wandering Albatross. For me, the close encounters we enjoyed with that remarkable creature were the highlights of the making of the series.

Ornithologists Steve Fugler and Ian Newton from the Cape Town-based Percy FitzPatrick Institute of Ornithology led us across a soggy landscape of moss and bog studded with craggy basaltic rocks. A cold brisk wind brought an occasional light drizzle. The sky was grey. It was a typical day on Marion Island. This was one of the few breeding grounds of one of the world's most beautiful creatures, and we were headed for an encounter with it. About a mile from base camp Steve stopped and handed me his binoculars.

"Up there," he said, pointing to a ridge on the next hill.

I took the glasses and saw a juvenile wandering albatross sitting on its exposed nest in the middle of a mound of mud and grass. It was magnificent. The bird would spend the first nine months of its life up there in the cold and rain, never venturing from the nest. Buffeted by wind, its legs folded beneath its enormous body, it was covered in snowy white down. A short slender neck connected the body to a magnificently regal face with dark, glossy eyes and a yellowish hooked bill. It just sat there, looking around waiting. But for what? I asked Ian and he told me that it was anticipating the arrival of one of its parents who would bring it food. This would only happen occasionally as its diet consisted of squid and fish which the male and female adults gathered far out to sea, sometimes as far as a hundred miles away. A young chick of this size—about 26 lbs.—needed at least four to five pounds of food as often as possible to survive. Because feeding was such a demanding affair mating pairs bred only once every alternative year. Fifty percent of chicks usually starved before gaining maturity.

We approached the nest with the big bird showing no sign of fear. It allowed us to come right up to it and even touch it. As I filmed the gorgeous creature from every angle Ian explained that albatross adults are monogamous and mate for life, returning to the same breeding site for a full life span, in some cases as long as a staggering 70 years. Mating usually begins when the bird is eight years old. A single white egg is laid with the chick hatching after two months and then remaining in the nest for about nine months. During the early stages of its development the parents take turns to sit on the nest while one searches for food. This particular youngster was in the later phase of growth and was therefore left alone much of the time. It was at least six pounds heavier than an adult, requiring the extra body weight to survive the harsh weather conditions of these cold southerly regions. Once the down is shed and the bird grows feathers the young albatross fasts for up to 50 days, reaching an adult body weight of around twenty pounds before flying out to sea. An adult's wingspan reaches up to eleven or twelve feet, making it the world's largest oceanic bird. In windy conditions it merely spreads its wings and takes off, but on windless days it requires lots of space to run before soaring skywards. This is why their nests are built on ridges and hillsides making things easier for the young adults' first take-off. Wandering albatrosses have been known to fly as far as 600 miles in one day, seldom making much effort to remain aloft. They use their great wingspans to glide, even at night, traveling at speeds of up to 50 miles per hour. They cover enormous distances. Some have been recorded to fly over 10,000 miles from their breeding grounds. They remain in the air for exceptionally long periods of time, alighting on the water only to feed before returning to land to breed.

Steve and Ian wanted to demonstrate that the youngster had an effective method of protecting itself while its parents are out to sea. If provoked by another animal or bird it will regurgitate the contents of its stomach over its attacker. The acidic juices and pungent oils clog other birds' feathers, impairing flight. Reluctantly I agreed to let Steve crawl up to the chick and make menacing though harmless movements in front of it. Suddenly there was a loud gurgling sound and the bird stood up, vomit spewing from the creature's mouth all over Steve. After he retreated the bird simply settled down quietly again as though nothing had happened, there to continue its patient wait for the return of its parent.

The ornithologists regularly weighed selected young albatrosses from a dozen nest sites to monitor their growth rate. This was necessary to determine whether the birds were growing at the correct average recorded rate for the species, a direct indication of whether they were getting enough to eat. The process of weighing a 26 lb. albatross is no easy matter. Scientists had to slug it out through muck and mire to reach the bird, physically pick it up, and bring it back to base camp where it could be placed in a special sling and then hooked up to a scale. Steve was tall and lanky and Ian much shorter. Both originally from Britain, they had colorful cockney accents and wonderfully dry senses of humor which often kept me chuckling. The day eventually came for the weighing of one of the selected birds sitting on its nest about 500 yards from the laboratory buildings. Steve was the stronger of the two men. He approached the nest and, wearing his rain gear and a pair of heavy-duty gloves in case that beautiful hooked beak decided to take a bite at him, he scooped up the animal and stumbled back to base through the bog with the creature in his arms. Ian fussed around them, muttering and cackling like a mother hen, slurping through the mud making sure that both Steve and the albatross were alright. Just then Steve let out an almighty shriek.

"Ouch! Jesus!" he yelled. "The bleedin' thing's got me by the friggin' knackers!"

The young bird's head had somehow reached down and it had firmly clamped its beak around the most sensitive and painful region of Steve's lower abdomen. The thick plastic rain gear had proved to be no barrier. My assistant Derrick ran to try and help Ian dislodge the beak while Steve stood there helplessly, sinking ever deeper into the mud, holding on to the precious living cargo that was attacking his most private of private parts. I should have gone to their aid but there was nowhere to put the camera down in the boggy terrain so I kept on shooting, capturing for posterity one of the most unusual and I hesitate to admit amusing natural history scenes I have ever filmed. Fortunately both Steve and the albatross escaped the incident relatively unscathed.

Evolution was the force that shaped life on Marion. Entomologists from the University of Pretoria showed us how a species of moth, identical to one found on the mainland, had adapted to conditions in this harsh environment. They no longer grew wings but had developed long rear legs for jumping around in their search for food. Wings were useless in this place of roaring winds. If they took to the air the little insects would simply have been blown out to sea. Like their cousins in similar environments in the cold southern regions, petrel birds burrowed underground, making nests where their eggs could hatch safely out of the path of the brutal winds.

All too soon it was time for us to depart Marion. The plan was that Derrick and I would join the brand-new Sea Fisheries Research Institute vessel *RS Africana* which was *en route* to the island after having completed her sea trials in the Indian Ocean.

She was to call briefly at Marion, proceed to a latitude as far as 50 degrees south and then head west for about a thousand miles. Her task was to sample the water at various depths and assess the extent of pelagic and deep-water fisheries in this far-flung Southern Ocean region. After ten days she would head northeast again, back to Africa. Team 39's leader arranged with Captain Bill Leith of the *Agulhas* that when the next helicopter flight took place to pick up another load of trash from the island Derrick and I would hitch a ride. We would be flown to the *Agulhas* and then transfer to the *Africana* with all our gear as soon as that ship arrived. The scheduled day for returning to the *Agulhas* came but heavy rain and high winds prevented the chopper from taking off. Days went by and the ghastly weather didn't let up. Meanwhile, the *Africana* had materialized out of the squalls and clouds one morning and had anchored about a mile away from the *Agulhas*, awaiting our arrival. Her master, Captain Derek Krige, said he could only wait another two to three days at the most and then he would have to raise anchor and continue with his mission. I was getting extremely jittery about the whole affair. I felt guilty about delaying the *Africana*, nervous about missing her if she had to depart before we could board her, uncomfortable about having to rely on Bill Leith's chopper and embarrassed about overstaying our welcome on the island. But everyone was extremely accommodating and nice about it. On my birthday, September 3, they threw a little party for me in the recreation room at the base. I even challenged Rev. Louw Bouwer to a game of pool and lost.

Derrick and I had been assigned warm, spacious sleeping quarters in a laboratory building on a small hill about a hundred yards away from the main buildings. One morning I was in our room working on my notes when the phone rang. It was the base commander, Chris Grove. The weather was lifting, the winds subsiding, and the helicopter from the *Agulhas* would be landing within twenty minutes. Derrick and I had to be on the pad with all our gear packed and ready to go by then, failing which we would miss the flight. Heaven knew when we'd be able to get away as even worse weather was expected. Besides, Captain Derek Krige had decided to up anchor the following day and we might then completely miss out on doing a story about the *Africana*. Panic stations. Where was Derrick? I called the recreation room. Was he down there playing pool? No. In the met office? No. In the kitchen helping to prepare lunch? Nope. Where then? All alone, I borrowed a four-wheeled cart from the storage warehouse, rattled my way back up to our hut, loaded our heavy bags and equipment onto it and with great difficulty began to make my way down to the helipad. The slatted wood and metal walkway made it extremely difficult to push the unwieldy load. Before I got halfway to my destination I saw the helicopter lift off from the rear deck of the *Agulhas*. A big, black cloud streaked with lightning was not far behind it and the wind was already picking up again. It was going to be a desperate race against time. Men from the base had already reached the pad, their canisters of sealed trash already snugly tied up inside the nylon mesh net ready for attaching to the Puma's hook and pulley. I wasn't going to make it.

With my thick parka, plastic rain gear and heavy boots I was sweating profusely and my heart was pounding. Where the hell was Derrick? And then I saw him, a red figure racing through snow and bog. He had not known about our impending departure and had decided to go on a little photographic safari to shoot some penguin chicks at a nearby rookery. Thank heavens the guys waiting for the Puma's arrival saw that I needed help and came charging over to assist me. We all reached the pad just as the helicopter landed. I don't know who was more out of breath, Derrick, the other men or me. Last minute thanks and good-byes were said and soon we were thud-thud-thudding our way above grey water to the *Agulhas*. The rain began just as we landed and the chopper was safely secured to the deck. But even if the weather did clear we couldn't be airlifted from the *Agulhas* to the *Africana* as she had no deck space for a helicopter to land. We would have to transfer by Zodiac. But when? I spent the rest of the morning in the radio room talking to Captain Krige on the *Africana*. He was sorry, he understood our predicament, but if we weren't aboard his ship by 11am the following morning he was departing for the south. Nothing that Captain Bill Leith of the *Agulhas* or I could say was going to change his mind. He had his orders and that was that. Glumly I watched the heavens open as thunder, lightning and torrents of rain engulfed the ship. The windows frosted up. The decks turned to glass as sleet became ice. It was terribly disheartening.

At around 4pm the world suddenly went silent. The elements retreated, leaving us with a brief window of opportunity to transfer to the other ship. A crane swung over the side of the *Agulhas*, dropping a large Zodiac into the water. Our equipment and luggage was bundled into a net and lowered into the inflatable craft. Then Derrick was hoisted into it, followed by me. The guy on the outboard fired up the engine and we were on our way to the *Africana* which was riding the swells about a mile away. About halfway to our goal the rain and wind suddenly whipped up again. Within seconds we could hardly see the white-hulled ship through the grey sheets of rain. The water became turbulent. Then violent. Swells turned into mountains. We were heaving and crashing our way through a tempest. I thought of the trawler *Atlantic Endeavor* all those years ago. But this was worse. That vessel was at least solid and sturdy. But this inflatable craft was pliable. She writhed, contorted and changed her shape as we rose and fell. I was terrified of losing our equipment overboard. Though tightly sealed in waterproofing all our gear was swamped with foamy water. It seemed to take forever before the soaring hull of the *Africana* loomed in front of us. Somebody shouted at us from above and then a hook suddenly appeared out of nowhere. It was attached to a cable dangling from a winch that had been slung over the side. The Zodiac's pilot helped Derrick and me secure the big yellow nylon net containing our gear to the hook, then he looked up, called out, made a circular motion with his hand and instantly our things disappeared into the grey mist.

And then the rain started again. I wasn't sure what was making us wetter: the pelting rain or the waves crashing into the Zodiac as we heaved and slammed against the *Africana's* hull. There was more shouting and indistinguishable words when suddenly a rope ladder tumbled over the side of the *Africana*, flaying out and slamming against the hull. Our pilot pointed at it and made a motion indicating that that was the way up.

"What about the crane? Can't they lift us up?" I yelled.

"Too rough," he shouted back over the sound of the banging of the ladder and the crashing of the waves.

This was becoming a very perilous affair. The Zodiac could not remain in such close proximity to the heaving steel hull of the ship. I looked at Derrick. He looked at me. We were very scared. I gave him the honor of scuttling up that absurdly dangerous thread of knotted rope first. He reached out, grabbed it and somehow pulled himself all the way to the top. Then I heard shouting from above.

"Come on!" someone yelled. "Quickly!"

I nodded a thank you to our Zodiac pilot, reached out into space, caught the rope ladder that was swinging wildly against the *Africana's* hull and started pulling myself up. In an instant the Zodiac's engine revved up and the craft was gone. It was now just me, a flimsy ladder made of rope, a steel wall that was pulling itself away from me one moment then slamming back at me the next, with an angry, crashing, freezing ocean barely three feet below me.

"Come on!" someone yelled again from above.

I managed to climb four or five rungs. But it was impossible. I was numb from cold and fear. My heart was pounding and my hands were being hammered every time the rope ladder slammed against the ship's hull.

"Come on!"

But I couldn't go on. Panting for breath, every muscle rebelling against what I was asking my body to do, I decided to stop—just stop, and stay there forever if need be. I would just dangle there in limbo until the sea or the wind or the rain or the terrible swinging and banging against that hard ice-cold hull claimed me.

"Come on!"

I looked up. A bearded face stared down at me and a hand was extended. But they were an eternity away.

"Come on!" the man shouted. "You can do it!"

And somewhere in the din and chaos of it all I heard Derrick's voice. My arms were breaking. I was going to black out.

Bang! Another collision with the hull, crushing my fingers. I was blinded with pain. The rain intensified. The pathway to hell and damnation was not down to a fiery inferno but swinging on a rope ladder dangling above lashing seas. And then I summoned a surge of hope. I *had* to get out of this predicament or I knew I would die if I didn't get myself aboard the *Africana*. Step by step, pull by pull, inch by painful, agonizing inch I climbed up that ladder until half a dozen hands reached out, grabbed me and pulled me over the side. I landed on the deck with a thud, staring into boots and galoshes and shimmering wet planking. I just wanted to lie there forever. But then a bearded face wearing a big, broad smile appeared upside down in front of me and said: "The captain will see you on the bridge."

And then I think I passed out.

Half an hour later after a mug of steaming hot coffee and a change into dry clothing I was shown onto the bridge and welcomed by Captain Derek Krige, his First Officer, Chief Engineer and medic. Kevin Dunning, the second mate who had come to my rescue, smiled from ear to ear as he introduced

Derrick and me. It was almost as though he was proudly showing off something that he had caught in the vessel's fishing nets, two examples of a weird new species, dredged from the depths. The bridge was warm, the welcoming friendly. We were shown below to a comfortable two-berth cabin amidships and given a separate cabin for stowing our equipment and for charging batteries. It was all very civilized. As we were arranging ourselves the ship shuddered slightly. The engines had started and we were underway. Krige had obviously decided to leave immediately to get ahead of the storm. It soon became evident that the *Africana* was no *Agulhas*. The ship was pitching and rolling wildly. At just under 3,000 tons gross weight and 255-feet in length she was a lot smaller and lighter than the big icebreaker. But she was brand-new and boasted every bell and whistle for a vessel of her type. Built in Durban as a fisheries research ship she was equipped with a rear slipway, trawling gear, nets, fishing lines and enough laboratories, computers and scientific equipment to undertake any fact-finding task for the Sea Fisheries Research Institute. Her engine room and main machinery were built in an acoustically dampened shell on a spring-mounted 'raft' within the hull, making minimal contact with the main structure of the vessel. This was to avoid interfering with all her sensitive electronic equipment, especially the acoustic devices used for finding fish and for bouncing signals off the ocean floor. She could travel at 14 knots, had a complement of 52 officers and crew, and accommodation for 17 scientists. The food was good, the library well stocked, but the weather was terrible.

What should have taken about a week turned into almost two weeks of unmitigated misery. The seas were worse than anything I had ever seen or could imagine. After dropping steel cables connected to a device known as a 'rosette sampler' as deep as 15,000 feet in the water column to collect specimens for measuring salinity, phytoplankton, zooplankton, larvae and fish eggs, Captain Krige had hoped to turn around and head back to

Cape Town. But it was impossible. He had to keep the bow of the ship pointing directly into the wind and stormy seas, riding over the gigantic swells constantly coming at us. I had never seen anything like it. These were monstrous mountains of water often over a hundred feet high. We had to sail over the tops of them, falling over the other side into deep valleys of icy Southern Ocean. If we tried to turn around in these seas we would have been swamped or simply capsized. As it was, we were often listing dangerously to port and starboard. The rolling of the ship frequently exceeded the builders' specifications. I would spend hours on the bridge with my eyes glued to the inclinometer, the instrument that showed how many degrees to port or starboard the ship was listing. At times it felt as though we had rolled 90 degrees from the vertical, even though the meter indicated only about 30. It was impossible to stand up without clutching onto something solid and perpendicular. Thank heavens for anti-sea sickness patches. I always had one stuck behind one of my ears and they really did work. Not once did I even feel queasy.

Filming on board was a logistics challenge. We had to assemble the tripod first, brace it down securely, then mount the camera on it. The footage we got was spectacular. One of the tricks of shooting in a ship at sea to capture the sheer violence of the tossing, heaving, yawing, pitching and rolling motion during a storm is to frame the shot on something solid like the bow or mast or the window frames on the bridge. This gives the audience a reference point. Then you lock the pan and tilt head, making sure that the solid object always remains stationary within the frame. Then you step back, turn on the camera, and let nature and the elements do the rest. Because you have composed the frame to create an impression of it being an integral part of the ship, the seas and skies will thrash around crazily, giving the audience a feeling of actually being on board the vessel. I shot hundreds of feet of film through the main windows of the bridge. The camera was pointed towards the front of the ship as bow and forecastle crashed into walls of ocean which thundered over the foredeck, then swirled around the foot of the foremast before the *Africana* groaned, creaked and roller-coastered her way over the top of the swell. It was spectacular stuff but scary as all hell. Many a time I was sure the hull was going to snap in half. Every time we crashed down into a cavernous hole in the ocean the floorboards shook and a deep thud echoed through the ship. How she took all that pounding I shall never know. It certainly said something about the standard of South African shipbuilding. The nights were the worst. It was too terrifying to try to see what we were heading into. It was better to curl up with a book in one's berth than to try to come to grips with the reality of what was happening. Fortunately, the library contained many of South African author Wilbur Smith's novels and I read every single one of them, often going without sleep for days. Mealtimes were straight out of a Mack Sennett comedy. Dishes went slipping and sliding all over the tables, with soups, spaghetti and salads ending up in people's laps or spilling across the floor. The chef and galley staff eventually resorted to solids only. With the exception of urns of black coffee tightly secured to the bulkhead on a self-serve table in the dining room anything liquid was out of the question. One night at around midnight there was a particularly frightening roll to starboard. I was sure we were about to capsize. Suddenly an almighty crashing of plates and pots and cutlery echoed from the galley on the floor above us. Next morning we were eating off cardboard picnic plates and drinking from Styrofoam cups as not a single piece of crockery or glassware had survived.

I developed a close friendship with the *Africana's* 'sparks,' or radio operator. Originally from Manchester, England, Stan Garnett was a short, white-haired old timer from way back. He was in his late sixties and had seen service as a crewman on destroyers during World War II and then spent years on whaling ships. Close to retirement age he had an absolutely marvelous sense of humor and was an endless supply of wonderful yarns from his very full and fascinating life. He was also versant with all the latest technology coming out at that time, including things like domestic PCs. This was 1982 and the personal computer industry was still in its infancy. As it was, I was totally enthralled by radically new equipment like the facsimile transceivers—or faxes—and the global positioning system (GPS) on board the ship. Stan took great delight in explaining them all to me. But despite his up-to-date knowledge, old habits die slowly. He insisted on receiving the nightly weather report in archaic Morse code from Cape Town Radio. His radio room—or 'shack' as he called it—was situated directly behind the bridge on the uppermost deck of the ship. This was customary in the maritime world. If a vessel ever found herself in trouble or began sinking the last place that would become submerged was the highest deck in the superstructure so the radio shack was always situated up there, allowing distress signals to be transmitted for as long as possible. But there was a disadvantage to this arrangement. Being so high up accentuated the ship's rolling movement. I would go up and spend an hour or two with Stan after dinner. The signal from ZSC—the call sign of Cape Town Radio—came in at around 7pm. Stan was so short that when seated his feet didn't touch the floor. His chair was on wheels. Every time the ship lurched or rolled he would go careening across the uncarpeted floor, crashing into desk and bulkhead, a cigarette dangling from his mouth and ash spilling all over him as he sat scribbling the weather forecast in a spiral notebook. How he made sense of all those heavily distorted dits, dots, dashes and tweet-tweet-tweets as he was flung about with the furious sound of waves crashing and steel creaking, completely drowning out the radio signals, I have no idea. But after fifteen or twenty minutes he would wedge a pencil above his ear, light up another cigarette and nonchalantly announce, "No change for tomorrow."

Then he would wheel himself back to his beloved transceiver, twirl a few dials to silence the thing, clutch the metal handle on the bulkhead and proceed to tell me another wartime or whaling story. I don't know what I would have done without Stan's company on that tempestuous voyage.

One morning after breakfast Captain Krige announced that we were all to don lifejackets, assemble inside one of the two interior passageways on the boat deck, brace ourselves near an exit where we could speedily reach a lifeboat and hold on tight. He said that a prayer from each of us would be in order too. We had traveled well over a thousand nautical miles beyond the point where we should have turned around and headed back to Cape Town. If we kept on going on our present course we would hit the Falkland Islands before we knew it. And that wasn't a good idea as the war between Britain and Argentina was in full swing at the time. No, he was going to risk turning the vessel around. It was time to go home. But we all had to be fully aware of the dangers involved. It was going to be tricky. He would try to wait for a break in the onrushing swells then come around as quickly as possible. We would know when it was happening and we were to maintain our places until given the all-clear. Colored crewmen had already been sent outside to man the winches and davits at the lifeboats. Krige would give a short blast on the ship's horn before he attempted the turn. I wondered about those poor young Coloreds in that turmoil outside. Would they be OK? No one else seemed concerned so I kept the matter to myself. God help them, I prayed. Derrick and I were beyond being scared. With the scientists and everybody else who were not required on the bridge or in the engine room we assembled to await our fate. I held on to the guard rail that ran the length of the passageway so tightly that my knuckles turned white. We seemed to wait forever. And then it happened. There was a terse blast on the horn and then the ship began to lean perilously over to the port side. The leaning got more and more acute. I was certain we were about to roll 180 degrees, going bottoms up like the stricken vessel in *The Poseidon Adventure*. Things creaked and groaned as we clutched the railing, falling over, over, over…

And then, a miracle. Just as I expected to see cold green Southern Ocean water come crashing through the doorway from the boat deck the ship slowly righted herself, leaning dangerously in the opposite direction, and then stabilized. Krige had done it. A loud cheering burst forth as we all rushed up to the bridge. If the faces of those of us down below had gone white, Krige's face was surely a thousand times more ghost-like. It was also covered in sweat. His eyes were still wide with fear, his hands tightly gripping the wheel. The three or four other officers on the bridge were all equally scared but they had clustered around their captain, slapping him on the back and congratulating him in Afrikaans. It was time to party. That night a jubilant celebration took place in the cabin of the chief scientist, marine biologist Denzil Miller. Relieved and soaked to the bone by a trifle too much alcohol after having survived the perilous turn nobody seemed particularly interested in what I had to say but I told them the story about the many *sangomas* who had predicted that one day my life would be threatened by the 'big water.' I couldn't help thinking about how uncannily accurate all those soothsayers had been but no one seemed to care. And I guess I couldn't blame them. We had survived a potentially terrible death at sea.

By dawn the next morning the storm had subsided slightly. By the second day it was like a duck pond outside and we were visited by a large pod of huge southern right whales. There were about a half dozen of them on either side of us, their blowholes emitting whooshing fountains of spray and air every time the leviathans exhaled. They stayed with us for the better part of a day before veering off to some mysterious destination. The rest of the journey back to Africa was uneventful. Table Mountain had never looked so welcoming as we glided into harbor. It was good to set foot on solid ground again.

A Delicate Balance was slotted for weekly transmission on Sundays. It got good reviews in the press and even picked up a few honors including an Eastman Kodak *Visible Spectrum Award* from the South African Society of Cinematographers. But its time slot was awful. It aired on Sunday afternoons. Did its environmental message get through to those to whom it was aimed? I doubt it. In summertime South Africa everyone was barbecuing at the beach or splashing around in swimming pools, not watching TV.

C'est la vie.

Fourteen

As a result of the programs I had made for TV about indigenous tribes, the Indian community and English-speaking South Africans in the seventies and early eighties I was asked to produce two one-hour shows on the history of the 'Colored' people. These were the descendants of Malay slaves first brought to the country during the 17th century by the Dutch, as well as those born later of mixed racial parentage. I didn't want to take a conventional historical narrative route so I chose to weave the story around the fact that the Coloreds were the first people in the country to regularly perform operas for the public. Predominantly Cape Town-based and speaking only Afrikaans they learned Italian and German phonetically. This allowed them to sing works by the likes of Puccini, Verdi, Rossini, Mozart and Wagner in front of white audiences. But the shows were strictly segregated. It was okay for them to appear in operas on stage but under apartheid laws Colored people were not permitted to sit among white audiences in the Cape Town City Hall.

Our on-camera host was a man by the name of Cedric Adamson. He was director of an amateur performing arts organization called the Eoan Group. It was this organization that originally began staging operas for white audiences in the 1950s. As a Colored himself—born of a white mother and a father of Javanese extraction—Cedric had personally witnessed the government's appalling treatment of his people. The film opened with him standing in a field of rubble on the slopes of Table Mountain. He had lived there as a child. The site had once been called District Six. It had been a sprawling suburb of winding roads and densely packed houses where the Colored people had lived for generations. But under the laws of apartheid the entire place was bulldozed and its inhabitants forced to move to areas far beyond the city. This had caused traumatic consequences for Cedric, his family and the Colored community as a whole. They were simply ejected from their homes and dumped in undeveloped areas far beyond the precincts of white residential areas. Without any bitterness he told us the story of his people and then took us into a history of the country's performing arts. The production was a very moving experience for me. It provided insight into the indignities suffered by the Colored people under the iniquities of apartheid. I had seen what it had done to the Africans and to the Indians and now what it had wrought upon the Coloreds.

But I was already familiar with much of their plight. Evidence of this was rammed home whenever I took the family on weekends away in the farmland and vineyards of the Cape province. Some of the farms were still paying their Colored workers according to what was called the *dop* system. Half of a male or female laborer's weekly salary was paid out in the form of cheap wine. This was the *dop* or 'tot' system. Every Friday workers lined up at the farm paymaster's office and received half their wage in cash and the rest of it in an equivalent value of cheap wine. The result was that thousands of workers were in poor health, chronically addicted to alcohol and so dependent on their employers that few were motivated to better their positions in life. Their children suffered horrendously. Parents were often so inebriated or financially destitute that many did not bother to send their offspring to school or to health clinics. We sometimes spent weekends on a big wine estate in the Cedarberg mountains near Clanwilliam about a hundred miles north of Cape Town. The ambling Cape Dutch style mansion and surroundings were picture-postcard material. In the evening we sat on the lawn at the back of the house overlooking valleys of fruit orchards and tall pine trees. On all sides vineyards stretched as far as the eye could see. We would light a fire and stare up at the stars in a sky as wondrous as a dome in a planetarium. As darkness enfolded us the embers of the fire were the only form of illumination. On our first visit my children got the fright of their lives one night when out of the surrounding blackness ghost-like apparitions slowly emerged. As my eyes adjusted to the low light I could see that they were small Colored children, their clothes torn and tattered. There must have been about a dozen of them, all without shoes. Some were no older than ten. They were carrying even younger ones on their backs. We invited them closer and as they stepped up to the fire they told us that they lived on the farm where their parents were laborers. We offered them cookies and marshmallows which they gracefully accepted. Many of them had rotten teeth. I asked them where their parents' quarters were and next morning I went to find it. It was appalling. All the adults were out working in the fields but the kids we had met the night before were lolling around sitting under the shade of trees and playing in the dust or doing nothing at all. Their living quarters were a disgrace. Filth and squalor were everywhere. The whole place screamed of poverty. I wasn't surprised. What could you expect to find when half these people's salaries were being paid in the form of alcohol? And all of this on one of the country's biggest, wealthiest and most respected wine estates with its mansion brimful of antique furniture and imported European art.

During those years the population of the country was officially divided into four main groups, Whites, Blacks, Asians and Coloreds. Based on figures of the 1980 census the Coloreds numbered 2.5 million out of a total of 24 million. They were the shadow people of society. Because they were the offspring of parents coming from one of the other three racial groups they fell into a sort of no-man's land. Neither white nor black nor brown they were simply referred to as Colored.

Following that project I got a contract to produce two TV documentary programs about the history of the world's monetary systems and on the development of coins and banknotes. Then I made a series examining creativity among children and on how young people could benefit from being involved in the arts as part of their primary education. This was followed by a series documenting the history of South Africa's small Jewish community. At the same time I was also assigned a number of films about the history of South African Airways (SAA). This was to commemorate the airline's upcoming 50th anniversary. I had grown up with SAA in my backyard, just across the fence from my home during the years that I lived in Germiston and Kempton Park. Germiston was the home of SAA when I was a kid and Kempton Park was where the country's big new international airport—now called Oliver Tambo International—was constructed after the war. Airplanes and air crews were always around me as a child and as a teenager. SAA was the largest airline on the African continent. It had the most modern equipment and a safety record, route network and customer approval rating second to none. Over the years its name frequently appeared in independent travel polls abroad listing it as one of the world's best carriers. In those apartheid days the color scheme was orange, white and blue, which also just so happened to be the colors of the Afrikaners' ruling National Party. The airline's logo was a winged springbok—a local species of antelope—leaping against a painted orange background on the tail of the aircraft. So I called the series *Springbok in the Sky*.

The airline came into being in 1934. To expand its fleet a number of Junkers JU52 aircraft were ordered from the factory in Germany. Faster and more spacious than anything in the fleet at the time the big three-engine all-metal machines could seat up to 14 passengers. On November 1, 1934 the first of the gleaming new silver Junkers JU52 aircraft droned across the sky above Johannesburg, bound for Rand Airport located just outside the nearby city of Germiston. I was anxious to track down footage that might have been filmed of one of the delivery flights or to find any surviving German pilots who had flown any of the new airplanes to Africa from Europe. Fifteen of the machines had originally been delivered. With my buddy Barney Joffe's help at the SABC a search through the vaults at the National Film Archives in Pretoria turned up a delightful black and white trilogy of documentaries entitled *The Blue & Silver Way*. Made just before the outbreak of World War II these films chronicled the heydays of the Junkers fleet with SAA. But there was nothing about their epic danger-ridden flight from the factory in Germany and then down the length of Africa. With the assistance of SAA's public relations department in Johannesburg and the airline's Frankfurt office we eventually found out that a documentary had indeed been shot of the delivery of one of the aircraft in 1937. Not only that, but a clean unscratched 16mm copy of the film had been tracked down to a vault in Germany. Even more remarkable, the film was shot in color by the pilot. This was astonishing. Color film was only rarely used on major Hollywood movies those days, let alone on documentaries shot on an aircraft traveling across the wilds of Africa. Even more exciting was the discovery that the pilot who had been in command of the flight was still very much alive. He was happy to give us an interview. I was overjoyed.

Filming *Springbok in the Sky* took us all over the world. When we got around to shooting the German sequences I was most anxious to view the footage of that 1937 delivery flight, and I especially wanted to meet and interview the surviving pilot. I knew that he was 86 years old and living in retirement in a quiet little village just southwest of Munich. His name was Hans Baur. That's all I knew about him. One morning in 1983 I marched into SAA's Frankfurt offices with my crew. With us was a small contingent from SAA's public relations office in Johannesburg. We were met by SAA's manager for Germany, Reinhard Zeisner, Sales and Marketing Officer Eric Eichberger and, oddly, a representative from the Department of Foreign Affairs in Bonn. Those were the days before the unification of West and East Germany. The West German capital was still in the city of Bonn, not Berlin. I didn't quite understand the reason for his presence and thought the German government was merely being courteous by welcoming a foreign film crew to the country in recognition of SAA's long association with the country. Throughout the apartheid era relations between South Africa and Germany had been cordial, though very much downplayed by both sides.

The first thing we did was to go over to the film vault and view the 1937 footage. It was amazing. Scenes showed the shiny new Junkers flying above the Rhine, the Nile, over the pyramids at Giza and over the Serengeti Plains. There were scenes shot from the ground and of the aircraft in flight. There were shots of the aircraft landing at dusty airstrips in Cairo, Tripoli and Juba, on green fields in Mbeya, Tanganyika and at Salisbury, Southern Rhodesia. There were hilarious scenes of wild animals being shooed off airfields and landing strips and of local tribesmen swarming around the aircraft. Half-naked black men formed bucket brigades as they passed big cans of petroleum from stockpiles to technicians perched on the wings who then poured the fuel into the aircraft's tanks. The logistics behind the delivery flight must have taken months of preparation. Luckily for us it had all been beautifully captured on film by Hans Baur, the man who had piloted the aircraft. I selected the sections I wanted duplicated for the TV series and then we all went to a fancy Frankfurt restaurant for dinner.

The plan was to depart for Munich by autobahn the next morning to interview the long-retired Hans Baur. As we seated ourselves at the dinner table the tall well-dressed official from Bonn ordered some good Rhineland wine and then proposed a toast to the success of our mission. Reinhard Zeisner, an extremely warm, friendly and easy-going man who had run the SAA's operations out of Frankfurt for a number of years, then tinkled his glass with a fork, stood up, and reiterated the good wishes for a successful shoot. It was, he told us, an honor and a pleasure for him to be so closely connected with an airline that was about to celebrate its fiftieth anniversary. Altogether there were about nine or ten of us around the table and we tucked into an evening of good food, fine wine and stimulating conversation. At around 11pm Zeisner, Eichberger and the emissary from Bonn isolated me from the crowd and pulled their chairs up as yet another bottle of expensive Rhine wine was ordered from the cellar. All three of them spoke a very good English even though I was trying my best to practice my rather pathetic German. While we were all having a good time and perhaps a trifle too much to drink Zeisner's relaxed and friendly disposition changed to one a little more serious. I sensed something interesting coming. He pulled his chair closer to mine and said, "The people at the Foreign Office are only too pleased that we're interviewing Hans Baur but they ask that we confine the questions only to matters concerning the Junkers delivery flight. There must be no other questions."

I looked at the government man from Bonn who was staring at me.

"Sure," I responded. "Why? Is there something I should be aware of?"

Zeisner and the Foreign Office man leaned close together and exchanged a few quick words in German that I couldn't catch. Then Zeisner turned to me and said, "How much do you know about Flugkapitan Generalleutnant Hans Baur?"

"Well," I said, "from what I was told he was a pilot with the Junkers Company and of course I know he was in charge of the delivery flight. Why, is there more?"

Zeisner, the government man and Erich Eichberger exchanged glances. Then Zeisner looked at me, nodded and sighed.

"We thought you knew."

"Knew what?" I responded, now feeling a little uneasy about where this was all going.

"Well," said Zeisner, "Hans Baur was a prisoner of the Soviet Union for ten years after the war. He still has war injuries and was only released in 1955. He does not like to talk about his wartime experiences."

And then it dawned on me. If Baur was a pilot he must surely have served in the military during World War II. He must have been a pilot with the Luftwaffe. Well, if so, that was fine with me.

"So?" I said. "He saw military service. Was he shot down?"

"No, he was not shot down," replied Zeisner.

He waited for my reaction. I shrugged. A new bottle of wine arrived and we held back on our conversation while the waiter uncorked it and filled our glasses. Then Zeisner clinked his glass against mine, looked me straight in the eye and said, "Flugkapitan Generalleutnant Baur was the personal pilot of Adolf Hitler."

You could have knocked me over with a feather.

I tossed and turned in bed all night, not sleeping a wink. I sat smoking, staring out of my hotel window at the Frankfurt skyline. I was about to meet and interview a man who had been one of the closest associates of Adolf Hitler. Could this possibly be true? Talk about six degrees of separation. This was going to be an unbelievable *one* degree of separation from a man who has gone down in history as one of the most vilified individuals who ever lived. Hitler was the man behind World War II. Hitler was the man responsible for the deaths of over 60 million people, more than three percent of the entire planet's population at the time. Hitler was the mastermind behind the Holocaust, the intended genocide of Europe's Jews. Hitler was responsible for the destruction of my very own father's family in Latvia. Hitler created more havoc and suffering than any man in history. I realized that when the time came for me to shake Hans Baur's hand I would be only one handshake away from Adolf Hitler himself. How do you deal with that? The thought overwhelmed me. I wasn't sure whether I felt sick deep down inside or merely terrified. How would I handle the situation?

Next morning Eichberger was at the wheel of our Volkswagen

Kombi minivan as we hurtled down the autobahn to Munich. With us was an SAA public relations team from Johannesburg and my crew. Before I knew it we were approaching Munich from the northwest. About twenty miles from the city a sign flashed by. It said, "Dachau." A chill went through me. Dachau was a concentration camp established by the Nazis just after Hitler came to power in 1933. Over 40,000 people died there, at least 90% of them Jews. I had visited Germany many times prior to this trip and I liked the place enormously. It was efficient, clean, tidy. I could swear that even the weeds in the forests grew in neat little rows. The people for the most part were always friendly, always helpful and especially appreciative if you spoke to them in German.

I had worked on a German TV drama series shot on location in South Africa in the sixties and so I was fairly proficient in the language. I loved visiting the country. But whenever I had traveled across Germany by train on previous occasions I had not been able keep the dark Nazi past at bay. I could not help being deeply conscious of the clickety-clack of steel wheels on rails, particularly at night. Normally, it was a rhythmic sound that lulled me to sleep. But in Germany it had always conjured up ghosts and images of a terrible time that I had miraculously not experienced. Pressing my face to the train window I had often stared out as light from the carriages splashed out onto vacant sidings, empty platforms, fences, factories, fields. Who had once been lined up alongside those very tracks that I was traveling on, waiting to be bullied and forced aboard waiting cattle trucks and then ferried to horrible fates? How many Jews, gypsies, sick, infirm, mentally retarded, homosexuals, political prisoners and other 'undesirables' had once heard the very same clickety-clack of the rails that I was hearing? It was always sobering. Had my own father's very own family once traveled on those rails, never to return from wherever they were being taken? I looked over at Eric at the wheel of the Kombi. He was a quiet sort of a guy, mostly keeping his thoughts to himself. He spent much of the time chewing on pungent slices of garlic bologna. I was sipping a can of Coke Light as we passed Dachau. Then we turned south and headed towards a beautiful lake called Ammersee. It was alongside its banks where geese and ducks preened their feathers in the little village of Herrsching that we would find 86-year-old retired Flugkapitan Generalleutnant Hans Baur, Adolf Hitler's personal pilot.

We rendezvoused with SAA's German operations manager Reinhard Zeisner, with Werner Kraft, manager of the airline's Munich office, and also the man from the Department of Foreign Affairs at our small but comfortable hotel in Herrsching late that afternoon. There we spent the night. The next morning nine of us were sprucely attired in jacket and tie. We boarded our two vans and headed out along the lakeshore after breakfast in search of Hans Baur's residence. It didn't take long to find it. The charming double story house looked more like a Swiss chalet than a Bavarian house. It could have been a photograph on a fancy box of chocolates. It was on a quiet side street, set against a tall forest filled with birdsong behind it. In front of it was a freshly painted light brown wooden fence. A glorious array of scented purple blossoms skirted the front door. The upstairs floor had wooden shutters on either side of cute lace-curtained windows. An array of TV aerials sprouted from the sharply angled roof. The place could not have looked more peaceful. With Zeisner taking the lead we lined up outside the buffed and polished front door. Seconds after the bell was rung the door flung open and an elderly smiling grey-haired woman stood there in a bright red outfit. She wore just a hint of makeup and had a short string of pearls around her neck. It was Frau Crescentia Baur, wife of the famous aviator.

"Willkommen! Willkommen!" she beamed, bidding us to enter.

We trooped inside and were invited to sit down in the

spacious living room. Frau Baur called to her husband who was pottering around somewhere upstairs. I heard the stairs groan and creak as he slowly began to make his way down. At 86 years of age and with a leg wound from his war injuries affecting his ability to walk it took him a few minutes to descend the staircase with the use of a cane.

I glanced around the room. My head began to spin. Evidence of the Third Reich was everywhere. I thought it was illegal to display that sort of stuff anymore. Well, obviously you could in the privacy of your own home. Breaking Reinhard Zeisner's rules of conduct I got up and examined some of it. There were framed portraits of Baur dressed in his flying uniform with Hitler beside him. One photograph depicted him with Hitler in front of one of the special Luftwaffe JU52 aircraft assigned to the Führer after he became Chancellor. Another showed Baur with Hitler during his 1932 election campaign. There were others with Hitler and Martin Bormann, Heinrich Himmler, Ernst Roehm, Albert Speer. One showed Baur in his SS—Secret State Police or *Gestapo*—uniform with Hitler and Rudolf Hess. When Baur entered the living room I suddenly felt frightened. I thought my legs were going to buckle. It was as if I was in the presence of Adolf Hitler himself. I couldn't believe this was happening.

Everyone rose. Here was a living, breathing remnant of the innermost sanctum of Hitler's and the Nazis' Thousand-Year Reich. I stared long and hard at him. The man from the ministry in Bonn was the first to shake his hand. Then he introduced Baur to the rest of the group. I purposely hung back. I didn't only want to shake the man's hand, I wanted to hold it, to feel it, to sense his essence, his vibration, his soul, his history. Few if any had been as close to Hitler as this man. When I did shake it I knew that I was only one handshake—a single layer of human skin, a thin layer of tissue and cells—away from Adolf Hitler himself. My flesh tingled. My head spun. How many times had Hitler grasped and shaken that very same hand? But when I looked into Baur's sparkling blue eyes I sensed no coldness, no harshness, no hostility, no threat. I quickly realized that instead of a representative of a time of unspeakable tyranny and war and suffering, the five-feet tall man who stood before me was really a very nice guy, a quietly spoken, meek, gentle, elderly man living in the twilight of his life. I reminded myself that we were not in this room because of Adolf Hitler or a horrifying period in human history or even an ideology that had sent millions to their deaths but simply because of aviation. This man had been a pioneer at a time when flying down the spine of Africa was still a dangerous and difficult feat. We would confine ourselves to that. We sat down. We had important business here.

After coffee and light banter we set up our lights and equipment and soon we were ready to roll. With Zeisner by my side as interpreter the interview began. Baur talked about the delivery flight of the Junkers as if it were yesterday. He remembered the route vividly. From Munich the plane flew to Rome, then to Tripoli, Benghazi and Cairo. Then it followed the course of the Nile down to Juba in the Sudan and then on to Mbeya, Tanganyika. There was only enough fuel on board for a four-and-a-half hour flight so each leg had to be carefully planned. The craft was equipped with a Morse code radio. Language was a problem. The air crew spoke no English and with the exception of the once-German colony of Tanganyika few radio operators along the way could understand German. Baur's greatest challenge was obtaining reliable weather reports. After taking off from Tanganyika for Southern Rhodesia he got caught in a violent storm. Rain pelted the aircraft's windshield. The maps on board showed no elevation or mountains along the route so Baur trusted his compass and his instincts. Flying blind he maintained a flight level of 10,000 feet, hoping that there was nothing that tall along the way. The rain came down continuously. When he reached what he believed was the city of Salisbury he descended below the clouds and, expert aviator that he was, the airfield lay directly beneath him. The aircraft landed safely but caused quite a commotion.

"Do you realize that you aren't permitted to fly in bad weather, my good fellow?" the very British airfield manager demanded of Baur as he stepped from the Junkers.

Baur and his crew could not understand a word of English and were marched off to the local police station for questioning. Eventually an interpreter was found and Baur was informed that he was liable for imprisonment as the entire Salisbury area had just been quarantined because of sleeping sickness caused by the tsetse fly. Although he tried to explain that he had been flying for almost ten days and knew nothing of the quarantine the aerodrome manager was adamant that Baur and his crew be locked up. Further questioning revealed that Baur had been a pilot during World War I. This really piqued the interest of his interrogator who had been a pilot with the Royal Flying Corps.

"What kind of aircraft did you fly?" Baur was asked.

"Many different machines but in the closing phases I was flying a Hannover CL fighter," Baur answered through the interpreter.

"Fancy that!" said his questioner. "I was flying a Sparrow."

"Ah!" Baur blurted out in German. "A 'Spatz!' I shot down six of them!"

A strange camaraderie suddenly sprang into being, bonding the two men. Once on opposite sides of a war they now had stories to share and wounds to compare. They had become instant bosom buddies. The case against him was dropped. The following morning Baur took off for Johannesburg, landing at Rand Airport in Germiston on January 13, 1938. The flight from Munich had taken two weeks.

I asked Baur why he had been chosen for the delivery flight. He told me that he had joined the Munich-based airline, Bayerischer Luft-Lloyd, in 1921. In 1923 the airline was incorporated into the Junkers Luftverkehr, owned by the Junkers Aircraft Company.

In 1925 that company amalgamated with Deutscher Aero Lloyd, becoming the Deutsche Luft Hansa, later renamed Lufthansa. As the company's top pilot with an excellent track record of flying the difficult alpine passenger and mail route Baur was chosen to ferry the leader of the increasingly popular National Socialist (Nazi) Party around the country on his campaign to become elected as head of the Reich. After his very first flight with Baur, Adolf Hitler insisted that Baur be assigned to him as his personal pilot. And so began a friendship and a professional relationship that was to last until Hitler's final days in the bunker beneath the Chancellery in Berlin in 1945.

Without a trace of embarrassment Baur took pride in telling me that as Chief Pilot to the Führer he would only fly to South Africa on Hitler's orders or with his permission. When the Junkers Aircraft Company sought out the best man for the job of delivering the JU52 to Johannesburg they approached Hitler and asked whether they could 'borrow' Baur for a few weeks. Baur expressed his enthusiasm about the invitation to Hitler. He had never been to Africa. The assignment appealed to him. But Hitler would have none of it. One evening over a private dinner with Hitler Baur pleaded with him to let him go.

"Absolutely not," said Hitler. "What will happen if you get eaten by animals or cannibals?"

"Ag, mein Führer," Baur implored his boss, "that will not happen."

"Well you had better be right," Hitler retorted. "I require your services for some time yet."

"And you will have it, I promise," said Baur.

Hitler brought the discussion to an end by reluctantly agreeing to let him go, on condition that he report his position by radio to Berlin every day.

"That way at least we will know where to look for you if you go down," the Führer concluded.

And that was that. In November 1937 Baur took to the air,

Africa-bound. His only complaint about the assignment was that the return trip from Cape Town to Bremen took 28 days by sea, twice as long as his flight out.

With the interview in the can I called a wrap and shook Baur's hand. Yes, *that* hand, the one that been gripped by his Fuhrer's hand uncountable times. He beamed, rose to his feet and called out: "Centa! *Schnapps, bitte*!"

Apparently he always called his wife Centa. Soon she appeared carrying a silver tray laden with glasses and bottles of kirshwasser, slivovitz, scotch and beer. The couple showered us with typical Bavarian hospitality. Drinks were followed by a lunch of cold cuts and salads served buffet style in the dining room. The meal included the best potato salad I had ever tasted. After a couple of tots of good strong slivovitz I broke the rules by asking Baur to tell me about the memorabilia in the house. The man from Bonn looked at me in horror. I was not supposed to venture there. But Baur was game. Softened by the schnapps and with a wave of his hand he dismissed my question and said he had far better things to show me.

"Centa!" he called. *"Meine fotoalben, bitte!"* ("Centa, my photograph albums, please!")

Frau Baur disappeared and came back moments later carrying a pile of heavy leather-bound albums and scrapbooks. She plopped them down on a low table in the living room. Baur seated himself in front of them and invited me to draw up a chair beside him. The rest of the day was a journey into an era and a time that I don't think I will ever forget. In the pages of those albums were behind-the-scenes images of festive occasions, functions and events depicting Baur with the Führer inside the Reichstag, with Eva Braun at Berchtesgaden, dining in restaurants and in front of airplanes. Others showed Baur and Hitler with Reichsmarschall Hermann Goering, Dr. Josef Goebbels, Italian dictator Benito Mussolini, and him and Hitler in the Wolfsschanze bunker complex in the Goerlitz Forest. Everywhere the Führer was near him, shaking his hand, standing close to him, smiling and happy and proud of the only man I think he ever really trusted. There were pictures of Baur's weddings. Crescentia was his third wife. When he married his second wife Maria on May 13, 1936 Adolf Hitler was his best man. The private ceremony took place in Hitler's personal Munich apartment. There in front of me were the photographs to prove it. Once the war began Baur had been given the command of his own squadron of VIP transport aircraft. He personally knew every single member of Hitler's military associates, government and staff. Throughout the day he kept referring to Hitler as *"Meine freund, der Führer"* (My friend, the Führer) and he told glowing stories of the good times they had together. He was very fond of the man. I think I saw a glint of a tear in his pale blue eyes as he spoke of him. He said that whenever Hitler attended an official dinner he always ensured that there was a place for him at his table. He was treated more like a family member than as a subordinate military officer.

Baur enthralled us by telling us an amazing story that I'm certain few people knew. Apparently one of Hitler's favorite possessions was an oil painting by the artist Anton Graf of King Frederick the Great of Prussia. Wherever he was it always hung in his office. Baur was personally responsible for transporting the large, gold-framed work in a heavy crate whenever Hitler traveled or changed his headquarters. Hitler even had it with him in his bunker during his final days in Berlin. On April 30, 1945 Baur was summoned to Hitler's office in the bunker beneath the Reich's Chancellery. Grabbing Baur's hands as he entered the room Hitler told him that the end was nigh. He thanked Baur for his long years of faithful service, for being so loyal and trustworthy and for being one of the few friends he ever had. As a parting gift he presented Baur with his most precious possession, the painting of King Frederick. Baur was deeply touched but begged his Führer to please escape with him to an airfield and to allow him to fly him to safety in Japan, Latin America or an

Arab country. But Hitler's mind was made up. The war was lost. There was no point in prolonging the agony. He intended to take his own life in the bunker that day. Baur's protestations fell on deaf ears. Before they parted Hitler gave his Chief Pilot one final instruction. He was to deliver his deputy Martin Bormann with important documents to the navy's Grand Admiral Karl Doenitz in Schleswig-Holstein. This was because Doenitz was to become the new leader of the Nazi Party and of Germany after Hitler's death. Agreeing to carry out his Führer's orders Baur bowed, then left the room. Realizing that the Red Army was only blocks away from the Chancellery Baur changed from his uniform into camouflage clothes. Fear struck deep into the hearts of those still in the bunker. Many turned to Baur, begging him to shoot them. Refusing to oblige, Baur removed the painting of Frederick the Great from its frame, rolled it up and stashed it in a backpack. At about midnight on May 1, Baur, Bormann and 13 others made a run for it. Somewhere in the chaos of the burning and battered ruins of Berlin the group became separated. Baur never saw Bormann again. Hours later both Adolf Hitler and his mistress Eva Braun would be dead in the bunker.

In the early light of dawn on May 2 Baur was strafed by Russian machine gunfire. Badly wounded in the left leg he was taken prisoner and his backpack with the painting in it was confiscated. His leg injury was so bad that amputation had to be carried out by a Soviet military doctor. In November he was shipped out by freight train to the Soviet Union and locked up in the infamous Butyrka prison. When interrogation revealed that Baur had been Hitler's personal pilot his life became a misery. The Soviets did not believe that Hitler was dead and were convinced that Baur knew of his whereabouts. Months of agonizing torture and solitary confinement followed. Josef Stalin took a personal interest in him and insisted that he be forced to give up any information he may have had on any surviving members of the Nazi leadership. But Baur knew nothing more than he had repeatedly told them about Hitler's intended suicide in the Berlin bunker. In May 1950 Baur was accused of helping to plan the war against the Russian people. Dragging himself around on a crude artificial left leg he was sentenced to a hard labor camp. The following years saw him transferred from one gulag to another, ending in the Woikova camp near Moscow in 1954. He was finally released in October 1955 after normal diplomatic relations had been established between the Soviet Union and West Germany.

As we packed up our gear after an utterly fascinating day I felt as though I had personally experienced World War II from a totally new perspective. I felt strangely moved and fascinated, yet I was also drained from the sheer emotional weight of it all. Did my meeting with Baur tell me anything about racial hatred and the roots of genocide? Not really. Baur seemed oblivious to all that. To him, World War II was about champagne and flight plans and dinners with the Führer. It was about flying and about transporting Hitler safely around the battle-scarred skies of Europe. I never broached the subject of concentration camps and gas chambers and Jews and the Holocaust, and even if I had how much would Baur have known or spoken of them? Being so close to all the Nazi leaders he probably would have known plenty. But none of that was really part of his world. His was a detached and distant dimension to the war and the Holocaust. He had little direct connection with it. Or did he? I found it all rather bewildering but I could not bring myself to feel any animosity towards him. Just before we left the house Baur brought out a copy of the German edition of his biography, *Mit Machtigen zwischen Himmel und Erde* (With Might Between Heaven and Earth). He sat down and inscribed it to me with a message of how much he had enjoyed our meeting. Then he signed the book as well as a photograph of Adolf Hitler and himself in his SS uniform—replete with the skull and crossbones motif on his cap—happily shaking hands outside the Berlin Chancellery in

1938. With genuine warmth and pride he presented me with those two remarkable gifts. Very mixed feelings surged through me as we drove off. I glanced back to see him and Frau Baur waving goodbye to us from their doorstep. They were just a little old couple seeing off their guests, quite innocent and tiny in the overall scheme of things. We rounded a bend and they disappeared from view.

The next morning as we drove northwards on the autobahn to Frankfurt via Augsburg I sat hunched up with my thoughts. My mind went back twenty years to the day that I consulted that little old lady the albino *nganga* in faraway Ndola, Zambia. Her words and David Phiri's translation of them would not stop bouncing around like phantom voices in my head. She had foreseen what had now become real. She had predicted that I would come face to face with "someone close to the most evil man who ever lived." Those were her exact words. I could only stare out at the beautiful passing Bavarian countryside.

How on earth could she have foreseen what had just come to pass?

Fifteen

On August 15, 1985 South African President Pieter Willem Botha stood up in front of a packed audience of loyal supporters in the Durban City Hall and made a speech. The occasion was the Natal Congress of his ruling National Party. But it was not only the people in the beautiful Victorian-style building who listened. The eyes and ears of the world were upon him. Audiences around the globe were expecting him to sound the death knell of apartheid. Botha had promised major reforms. As early as the mid-seventies he had warned Afrikaners to "adapt or die." The status quo could not be maintained. The political order had to change. His leadership was already being challenged by the far right, especially by the Conservative Party and the *Herstigte Nasionale Party* (Reformed Nationalist Party). Botha had inched closer to racial reconciliation than any Afrikaner prime minister before him, proclaiming that he would end the divisive system in force in the country since the National Party came to power in 1948. Perhaps he would spell out the details as he stood at the dais, sultry and unsmiling, speaking in his heavily Afrikaans-accented English.

His speech was delivered against the context of a dramatically changing political landscape. The black 'homelands' had become economic and political disasters. Many of their leaders who had accepted quasi-independence from their white masters had turned out to be corrupt and ineffectual. The primary purpose of those out-of-the-way 'independent republics' had become little more than sources of cheap black labor for South Africa's white urban and industrial areas. Times were unsettling. South Africa's economy was in recession. The country's Portuguese-ruled neighboring territories—Mozambique and Angola—had come under black rule ten years earlier and white-dominated Rhodesia had lost its war with black freedom fighters, metamorphosing into Zimbabwe in 1980 under a black majority government. South Africa was now the last bastion of white supremacy on the entire continent. It stubbornly refused to yield to local and foreign pressure to embrace the indigenous people in the political process. It had become the focus of increasing global anger and condemnation.

Though some things had changed for the better, much still remained to be done. Admittedly, bans on interracial sex and marriage had been repealed. Many places of entertainment and even public transportation had become multiracial. The Group Areas act had been slightly amended and the detested pass laws had disappeared. Job reservation—where the color of a person's skin decreed what he or she could or could not do—was gone. Strikes by blacks for better labor conditions were no longer illegal. A new constitution provided for a 'tricameral parliament' made up of white, Indian and Colored representatives. However, the white parliamentary chamber still held sway over the Indian and Colored chambers and, most significantly, blacks—the majority of the population—still had no representation. They had the vote in their various ethnic homelands but not in 'white' South Africa itself. Residential segregation was slowly being eradicated but, by and large, blacks were still not being allowed to live in white neighborhoods. Education, health and welfare services for blacks, Indians, and Coloreds were still strictly separated and were generally inferior to those for whites. South Africa's military might was continuously used against neighboring countries to prevent them from harboring members of the still-banned African National Congress (ANC) and for speaking out against South Africa's racial policies. In 1984 local peace activist Bishop—later Archbishop—Desmond Tutu was awarded the Nobel Prize for Peace, something which really riled the government. Tutu repeatedly called for the release of detained political prisoner Nelson Mandela. But to no avail. Botha's heavy hand still extended over South West Africa—later to be renamed Namibia—as he was adamant to keep the territory under South African domination in violation of repeated UN resolutions. Under his orders military raids were sent in to many sub-Saharan nations to destabilize the region. Despite a 1984 peace accord signed with President Samora Machel of Mozambique to end hostilities between the two countries South African militia were still clandestinely assisting antigovernment rebels in Mozambique and in Angola.

Frightened at the prospects of where the country was heading and exasperated at their inability to bring about political reforms, white liberals and intellectuals began a slow exodus from the country. A relentless brain drain was underway. Those who remained behind were prepared to clench their teeth and bear it or to fight. But there was no way South Africa's powerful military machine could be defeated. Abolishing apartheid would be a slow, tedious process. Black and white community groups, unions and social organizations galvanized to form the United Democratic Front, spearheading widespread strikes, boycotts and attacks on police and government installations. World opinion was behind them. British and American administrations under Margaret Thatcher and Ronald Reagan faced mounting pressure to apply sanctions against the country, especially when military units went into black townships to quell riots and uprisings. Scores were detained or killed in skirmishes. TV screens around the world showed gruesome scenes of dead and dying schoolchildren who were shot while waving placards or throwing stones at police and militia patrolling the townships. Acts of sabotage began to weaken the economy. GDP started falling while inflation steadily climbed. In July 1985 Botha declared a state of emergency in many parts of the country. And now, at the National Party meeting in Durban, the world expected him to announce sweeping changes that would finally be more accommodating towards the black population. Perhaps peace could be restored. The SABC estimated that approximately

500 million people around the world watched the live or taped telecast of the speech. And what did they hear?

"Today we are crossing the Rubicon in South Africa," Botha declared. "There can be no turning back. We have outgrown the outdated colonial system of paternalism as well as the outmoded concept of apartheid."

There was mild applause in the City Hall. After all, these were his people, his supporters, his disciples. What concessions was their beloved President about to make to foreign dis-investors and local black troublemakers? Then there was a shift in Botha's mood.

"I have been patient," he continued. In his usual old-fashioned schoolteacher manner he waved his forefinger at the TV cameras and said: "Don't push us too far. Decisions about South Africa's future will be made by South Africans, not by foreigners."

Botha was warning the world to back off, to leave the future of the country to him and his henchmen. At the same time he was sending a very clear message to local black activists to lay down their stones, rocks and placards and do as they were told. He wasn't going to budge on African enfranchisement. Power sharing with blacks was out of the question. You could sit next to a black person in a restaurant or a theater and you could sleep with one if you so desired but share power and the ballot box with them? Never. South Africa would remain a white-ruled society, whether the world at large liked it or not. Following Botha's speech the next day the foreign exchange rate of the country's currency dropped dramatically. The stock market plummeted. Bad times clearly lay ahead. In 1986 American public dissatisfaction with South Africa's stubborn racist policies reached such heights that it caused the US Congress to pass the Anti-Apartheid Act despite Ronald Reagan's personal veto. This would bring about the banning of new investments and loans to South Africa, the termination of commercial air links between the two countries and the prohibition to import many South African commodities into the United States, including the popular gold Kruger Rand. Many other governments would follow suit. The world was turning its back on the place. Doing business with South Africa was seen as something dirty.

For me it seemed pointless to even think of remaining in the country any longer. With the state-owned SABC as the only outlet for TV programs and the film industry firmly in the hands of Afrikaner-controlled corporations, what could I do? During the previous two years I had done a lot of freelance directing of dramatic programming for the SABC's Channel Two. Much of it was for Xhosa-speaking black audiences. I did not speak the language so we had an SABC-appointed black language expert on every show to help with interpretation. This was not only for my convenience but to protect what the SABC called *"taal suiwerheid"* (language purity). Under the laws of apartheid heaven forbid if a word of English, Afrikaans or one of the ten other major indigenous languages slipped in to 'spoil' the purity of the language of the show. One of the productions I directed for a Cape Town-based Afrikaner-owned company was a two-hour drama called *Isihogo Sisemhlabeni* which roughly translated as 'Hell on Earth.'

It was the story of a black fireman who was part of Cape Town's large firefighting service. According to the script—written by two young English-speaking women but translated into Xhosa—the firefighter gets called out to help put out a roaring blaze on the slopes of Table Mountain. In the midst of the inferno he gets engulfed by flames and is severely burnt. His colleagues cannot find him and in the ensuing chaos he is left for dead in the charred forest. A couple of days later he is found by what was colloquially called a *bergie,* or a homeless Colored person who wanders the slopes of the mountain. The *bergie* carries the severely injured fireman to his secret hideout in a cave on one of the hidden beaches of the peninsula and nurses him back to health over a period of months. At first the firefighter suffers not only terrible physical disfigurement but also from memory loss. As he regains scattered bursts of memory of his past life with his wife and family in one of Cape Town's black townships the *bergie* tries to help him reconnect with them. It was a poignant tale of suffering and determination.

The black cast all gave terrific performances. My white and black crew was wonderful. The show was well received by critics and audiences and at the SABC's annual gala awards ceremony—a South African version of the Emmy Awards, if you like—it scooped honors for Best Drama, Best Actor, Best Actress, Best Supporting Actor, Best Screenplay and Best Cinematography. I was totally overlooked. As far as the SABC was concerned the show had no director. It was a blatant example of the kind of anti-Semitic sentiment that pervaded the top echelon of the government-run television network. If I had not been an English-speaking Jew things would have been very different.

In addition to that kind of dismissive treatment everything produced in the country at that time still came under the watchful eye of the Censorship Board. I saw myself with no option. It was time to pack up and leave. Besides, I was getting worried about the future safety of my children if civil war broke out. I envisioned the Afrikaners and the Africans soon going at each other's throats, battling it out in armed conflict. War does not make distinctions as to whose side you're on if you're caught in the crossfire. Victims would far outnumber the perpetrators. Fortunately my first wife and her husband were planning on emigrating to London so my eldest son Simon and my daughter Jessica were going to be out of harm's way. But what about David and Amanda, my children from my second marriage to Diana? I had to get them out to a place of peace and security, free of the curse of racism. With the assistance of very expensive and disappointingly inefficient American lawyers in New York and Los Angeles we began to lay our plans for moving to California.

I did so with very mixed feelings. As much as I ached to realize my American dream I knew I would miss Africa very much.

In 1986 my family and I settled in Los Angeles where I established an independent production company. Under my arm I carried an anti-apartheid documentary called *Across the Rubicon*. I had made it before I left South Africa, knowing that it might serve as a calling card when I began to seek work in Tinseltown. I also carried a copy of the environmental series *A Delicate Balance*. These were my showreels and they got noticed. Our new life in America got underway. After dabbling in various small productions I secured a gig as writer/producer on a blue chip documentary series for the Public Broadcasting System (PBS) called *The Infinite Voyage*. It was a prestigious, high-budget series with the accent on science. Underwritten by Digital Equipment Corporation of Massachusetts it was made in conjunction with the National Academy of Sciences in Washington DC. The first show I did was about dinosaurs. Called *The Great Dinosaur Hunt* it was great fun to work on, featured some remarkable scientists and brought dinosaurs to the attention of audiences long before *Jurassic Park* and its many sequels came along. I could not believe my good fortune because, among others, it won the American Association for the Advancement of Science's Westinghouse Award for Science Programming on Television. The second show I did for the series was about global warming and climate change. It featured two Nobel Prize-winning scientists and many others involved in the comparatively new science of understanding how man-made gases were adversely affecting the health of the planet. It premiered before Congress in Washington DC. A relatively little-known Senator from Tennessee by the name of Al Gore was in attendance. At the conclusion of the hour-long screening he sauntered over to me and said: "Lionel, that was inspiring. You've got me thinking. We really should do more to bring the problem of global warming to the attention of the world."

And the rest, as they say, is history.

But the third show was and still remains one of my all-time favorites. Without hesitation I can say that if there was one topic that I could have chosen to make my move to America worthwhile it was that one. I have always loved space, astronautics, astronomy, science and the quest to unlock the secrets of worlds beyond our own. I had tried to catch a glimpse of the Russian *Sputnik* spacecraft through my cheap little telescope when I was a teenager in South Africa in October 1957. I was entranced by the accomplishments of NASA during the *Mercury* and *Gemini* programs, especially as I watched footage of early missions when I worked in television in Zambia. Just like that self-proclaimed head of Zambia's 'Space Academy' who we interviewed in the studio with his young retinue of 'astronauts-in-training' I too dreamed of the day when I would witness humankind go to the moon. I was consumed by the *Apollo* missions. In the absence of television in South Africa when the first moon landings occurred my ears were constantly tuned to *The Voice of America* on shortwave radio, monitoring every mission. *Apollo 11* will forever remain seared into my consciousness. So nothing can describe my sense of good fortune when my third show for *The Infinite Voyage* series was all about the *Voyager* spacecraft mission to the outer planets.

Two robotic spacecraft were launched from Cape Kennedy in 1977. *Voyager 1* would visit Jupiter and Saturn while its twin, *Voyager 2*, would follow the same itinerary and then, if the little craft was up to it and if Congress approved the budget, *Voyager 2* would go on an even more daring mission, traveling all the way to explore Uranus and Neptune. The double mission was dubbed the 'Grand Tour.' It turned out to be a resounding success, with the two spacecraft returning more data than had been accumulated in any previous mission or indeed in all the centuries that humans have stared up at the sky and wondered what was up there.

The list of scientists and engineers who appeared in the show represented some of the finest minds of our species. At the time of this writing the two *Voyager* spacecraft had traveled in opposite directions over 14 billion miles (22 billion kilometers) from Earth, making them the most distant man-made objects to have left our solar system. *Voyager 1*, cruising at 35,000 miles an hour, will reach our nearest star Alpha Centauri in approximately 40,000 years. That star lies at a distance about two light years away. Unlike other robotic explorers that have either smashed into planets or their moons or gone into perpetual orbits around our own solar system, the two *Voyagers* will never cease journeying. They could continue on their wanderings for an eternity. Or perhaps one of them might be intercepted by an alien intelligence. In preparation for such an eventuality one of the scientists involved with the planning of the mission, Carl Sagan, chaired a committee responsible for selecting pictures, sounds, music and verbal messages from our planet that were recorded on a 12-inch gold-plated copper disk that was attached to the side of each *Voyager*. As far as I was concerned those two disks embraced the very essence and best of the human spirit. They are, surely, humanity's most sublime and sophisticated calling cards. When I questioned Sagan about them he eloquently referred to them as, "Messages in a bottle cast into the cosmic sea."

At the conclusion of filming I wracked my brain to find an appropriate ending for *Sail On, Voyager!* I kept thinking of those gold-plated records bolted to the side of the spacecraft. That is how we must end, I told the executive producers. John Allison our talented head of special effects said he could create a visual with our *Voyager* spacecraft model and computer-controlled motion-control rig. *Voyager* would fly past the camera with the camera following it and then, with a slight twist in orientation, the craft would pass a distant star whose light would be reflected on the gold surface of the record. That became our final shot. With the last few sentences of the voice-over narration beautifully delivered by actor Frank Langella we see *Voyager* sweep into frame and then we follow it just long enough to see the record and then—as Jack Tillar's beautiful music score soars to a loud and noble phrase—we slow down to allow *Voyager* to pull away from us and continue its journey alone, receding into the far distance of space against a background of stars. Over this we hear greetings in five of the 55 languages recorded on the disk, ending with the voice of a child saying, in English, "Hello from the children of planet Earth."

But I had to put my own subtle stamp on the scene. I knew I would never work on a show like that again. I had to do something special with it. We were obliged to end with the English greeting of course but without revealing too much of my motives to anyone at the studio or the network I selected two other languages immediately preceding the English greeting. They were Nguni (Zulu) and Sotho, two of the languages spoken by the indigenous black people of South Africa. This gave me the opportunity to tie the *Voyager* spacecraft, the movie, the message and my own African roots together. It was like the closing of a circle in a long-held dream for me. There went the sounds of Africa… headed for the stars.

Sail On, Voyager! was a profound and ambitious film, one of which I knew I would always be proud. Had it been my swansong, my final film, I would have been happy. In my value system things just don't get bigger or better than that. Making sure that copies were sent to each one of them through the National Academy of Sciences the show was lauded by all my heroes, from Arthur C. Clarke (author of *2001: A Space Odyssey*) to Isaac Asimov, Ray Bradbury and Neil Armstrong. We even received a congratulatory note from President George HW Bush's Office of Science and Technology at the White House. I was very happy about the whole project, especially about being able to include those indigenous African voices from my homeland.

Other great projects followed, including a six-week shoot in

Antarctica. The purpose was to put a barometer into the earth and test its health for climate and environmental change. On the journey down to Palmer Station, one of the United States' two research stations on the frozen continent, I once again came face to face with the raw, savage power of the ocean. Yet again it reminded me of the warning I had received from the amazing old albino *nganga* in Zambia many years earlier that 'the big water will try to destroy me.' The surroundings around Palmer were indescribably beautiful. A large snow-clad cliff swept up behind the base. The view from up there of the soaring mountains, ocean and ice pack was enough to make anyone stop, stare and simply get sucked into the mystical magnificence of the place. As soon as you were out of sight of the base and away from the stench of the electrical generator's diesel fumes you were enfolded by a wide, wonderful wilderness untouched by humans. During the summer down there the sun never set. Depending on the weather I was fond of trudging through snow and crackling ice up to the summit of the cliff at midnight to gaze at the sun peeking at me from just above the horizon, looking as though it was attached to the blood-red ocean in quivering mirage-like waves. It was then that the world became eerily silent. A large colony of elephant seals that occupied a flat rocky outcrop nearby ceased their constant bickering and grumbling, and all penguin and bird activity stopped. Despite the ambient daylight the animals' internal biological clocks told them it was time to sleep. Every now and then you would hear a distant thunderous crash as a gigantic chunk of ice broke off the end of a glacier and plunged into the sea. I quickly realized what an enormous privilege it was to be down here at the bottom of the planet in an environment so alien and so pristine. Wars, revolutions, rebellions, religious squabbles, strife, pestilence and the petty foibles of nations all seemed so far away. The place cleansed one's soul, purging it of unwanted garbage. It was refreshing in a unique and wonderful way. I increasingly found it difficult to find the right words to enter into the diary that I jotted in every day.

In addition to the elephant seals—one or two of which occasionally came over to the base and awkwardly lumbered around the buildings, growling loudly whenever you approached their big, blubbery mass—there were also leopard seals whose favorite diet was penguin. Their open jaws revealed exceptionally long canines and sharply pointed incisors. Once they had caught one of the penguins in the water they thrashed their heads from side to side, shredding the penguin's skin before swallowing the remaining fleshy mass whole. The leopard seals were in turn preyed upon by orca or 'killer' whales. Like it or not, nature can be cruel. As in Africa, I often saw Antarctica's version of the harsh brutality that sometimes defines life in the wild. I think what surprised me most about the Antarctic was the abundance of living organisms down there. In addition to seals and whales we filmed birds such as albatrosses, petrels and skuas. There were various species of penguin including kings, gentoos, rockhoppers and adelies. Most of the scientists at Palmer were engaged in research about the marine ecosystem. We often went along with them on inflatable Zodiac outboards to visit bird nests, and seal and penguin breeding colonies. For safety reasons there was a boating limit restricting travel to a maximum two-mile radius from base.

We spent a few days filming with Mark Chappell—a biologist from the University of California, Riverside—on Torgersen Island, about a mile from Palmer Station. Mark and his team were studying an enormous adelie penguin rookery. Adelies grow to a height of just over two feet, with adults weighing in at around eight pounds. With their white bellies and black wings and backs they looked just like someone in a tuxedo or a symphony orchestra conductor, or a formally attired 19th century English butler in coat and tails. With short beaks and tiny white rings around each black eye adelies are an exceptionally cute yet dignified bird. But the commotion and noise at the site was hard to believe. They bickered and argued over little stones and pebbles which they often stole from one another to build little round nests on the rocks after the snow and ice had melted. Two eggs were laid during the breeding season which was well in progress while we were there. The adults formed pairs and took turns to incubate the eggs which they daintily pushed between their webbed feet with their beaks. Once the eggs had hatched the parents guarded the chicks for about two weeks before the brownish down-covered youngsters banded together in large groups. This allowed the adults to leave the nest and dive for fish and krill. When they returned it was incredible to see how the little penguins could instantly detect their parents by their calls, maneuvering their way to them past thousands and thousands of other birds. To my ear they all sounded exactly the same but, clearly, every single one of those creatures had its own distinctive voice. Although there was safety in numbers in the 'creches' formed by the babies I watched many of them being preyed upon by marauding skua birds. The skuas also attacked unhatched eggs, smashing the little shells and pecking at the developing embryos inside. Whenever this happened the shrieking and screaming of the penguins was completely deafening. I was told that roughly twenty percent of the eggs were lost to predation by skuas. Nine weeks after hatching the young adelies took to the water, diving to great depths and swimming at breakneck speeds underwater in their search for food. These were birds that flew not in the air but in the water. It was instinctive to them and it never failed to enthrall me as I watched them.

One day we went out with ornithologists Craig and Deborah Strong who were observing and counting populations of gulls, cormorants, giant petrels and skuas. Traveling by Zodiac we visited two distant locations, one more spectacular than the other. The air was so clear that far out to sea you could easily make out a profusion of floating shapes. Deep into infinity—

brilliantly clean and sharply defined with incredible clarity—icebergs of all sizes glistened and shone. There were blue castles and buttresses and towering crystalline structures that you could almost see through. There were sparkling diamonds and tinkling golden needles of ice floating, drifting, like a panorama from some surreal Salvador Dalí dream. Sitting low on the water as we zoomed around in the Zodiac the spray from the bow was sharp, cold and tingling as it hit exposed areas of your face. The experience was exhilarating. Little fragments of ice, drifting like shards of broken glass from a shattered chandelier, shot up and could easily cut your skin. But it was sheer magic hurtling through those sculpted fields of ice. Everywhere was ice; so much of it that it blinded and hypnotized as you whizzed by. Occasionally we were dive-bombed by skuas and screamed at by gulls. Once we reached our destinations we had to drag the little boat ashore and make our way to various breeding colonies through deep snow. Instantly you sank to your knees in the stuff and every step was a superhuman effort. You fought, battled and ached your way to the rookeries and nests. Often we had to bypass groups of huge, blubbery, asthma-wheezing elephant seals who barked, growled and grunted at us. Incredibly, they weren't scared of us. They needn't have been. Humans in Antarctica are forbidden to harm any wildlife and the animals' collective conscience of the early grisly sealing and whaling days seems to have faded from the survivors' memories.

Another interesting study program that was taking place was headed by biologist Farooq Azam from the Scripps Institute in San Diego. He and his team were investigating the complexity of the Antarctic food web, with special concentration on marine phytoplankton. These tiny, microscopic plants lie at the base of the food chain. As phytoplankton grew and multiplied small fish, krill and other animals consumed them. Larger animals then ate these smaller ones. Depending on their proliferation and abundance, phytoplankton showed the presence of pollutants in the ocean or where changes in the climate had created warmer or colder water. Phytoplankton required sunlight, carbon dioxide and nutrients such as iron for growth. Because sunlight was most abundant near the ocean surface, that is where we found most of this important food source. But with increasing ultraviolet exposure due to the ozone hole Farooq wanted to find out what this was doing to the phytoplankton. And there was something else he needed to know. What was global warming doing to the entire marine environment? Most nutrients essential to the survival of phytoplankton came from far below the ocean depths. When surface waters were cold these nutrients rose to the top where they were absorbed by the phytoplankton. However, increasing worldwide temperatures due to the greenhouse effect was warming the oceans, preventing the life-sustaining nutrients from reaching the surface. In effect the phytoplankton were beginning to starve, robbing the delicate marine food chain of its most essential commodity. Clearly, Antarctica was being adversely affected by rising global temperatures. Talking to Farooq—a reserved, quietly spoken but warm and patient man—sometimes made my head spin. His brilliant mind and fascinating discussions exposed me to a bewildering complex of topics embracing protozoa, zooplankton, bacteria, sediment fluxing, nucleic acids, proteins, amino acids and other mysterious wonders. But I was learning fast. I had to. By the time I got back to the US mainland I had to know what it was that this movie had to say about what was happening to our planet.

Day by day, Palmer Station turned out to be increasingly fascinating. It takes a special sort of individual to want to spend any length of time in a place like that. I noticed that everyone had their own little peculiarities and idiosyncrasies. Some people were obvious loners, others blatantly extroverted. Many had strange habits. The base's radio operator—a guy in his late thirties—sported a foot-long beard and long locks that fell to his shoulders. He never ventured from the radio shack except to sleep or go to the bathroom and he wore only a knee-length embroidered woolen tunic, socks and sandals every day. He was a gem; a total eccentric who cared naught about what others thought of him. Richard the chef was a great drinking buddy to be around during the short opening times at the bar after dinner. The biologists were typical of many biologists I had come across during my career. There was a subtly noticeable arrogance about some of them, especially among the students and assistants who were there. It was as if knowledge of the workings of life provided them with the right to feel slightly superior to the rest of us mortals. I came to the conclusion that, on the whole, people are pretty much the same everywhere. The scientists reminded me of those on Marion Island or on the *Africana* research cruise years earlier. The technical, maintenance and engineering types were carbon copies of those on Marion Island and countless similar remote places I had been to. The ship's officers and crew were duplicates of some of the men and women aboard other research and naval ships on which I had sailed. It was uncanny, but as I spent time in close proximity to this little community thousands of miles from anywhere I became more and more convinced that there may really be no more than about a dozen or so different human 'types.' I began to believe that everyone was merely a version or a derivative of one of these basic groups. I might be utterly wrong about the matter but if Palmer was a microcosm of the world at large I sure felt that way at the time.

Early one morning at about 2am I couldn't sleep in our quarters in the basement of one of the buildings at Palmer. I was also suffering the pain of severely cracked lips caused by the high levels of ultraviolet radiation outside. The rest of the base was quiet. Everyone else was asleep so I made my way up to the video viewing room and pulled a couple of videotapes off the shelf. One was an episode of the terrific early seventies' BBC documentary series, *The Search for the Nile*. Entitled *Find Livingstone!* it recounted the epic journey of Henry Morton

Stanley in his quest to find the great missionary-explorer David Livingstone in Africa in 1871. Wonderfully narrated by the late James Mason it took me back to the continent that I increasingly realized how very deeply I loved and missed. It was strange glancing out at the white world lit by a weak sun outside as I sat folded up in a comfortable lounge chair in the warm room. What was I doing here? Shouldn't I be back in Africa making films? I was suddenly seized by doubt and confusion, not quite grasping where life's mysterious trail was leading me. Here I was, in Antarctica, watching a film about Africa. Equally strange yet exhilarating was the next video I picked from the shelf. It was John Carpenter's scary 1982 remake of the original 1951 sci-fi thriller, *The Thing*. All about a remote Polar outpost that was terrorized by an extraterrestrial discovered in a spaceship under the ice it gave me pleasant shudders as I watched it. I looked outside. Yes, the story could easily have been set right here at Palmer Station. What if there *was* an ET buried under the ice waiting to be discovered and revived? What if it annihilated us all? How would the outside world ever find out about our fate? It was disturbing but a lot of fun to let thoughts like that run through my mind as I watched the cast battle the alien entity hell-bent on their destruction.

During mid-December a shipload of 24 VIPs arrived at the base. Representing the United Nations as well as a variety of governments and research organizations from around the world they had just attended an annual meeting in Chile to discuss what was known as the Antarctic Treaty. The treaty was formulated to *"insure in the interests of all mankind that Antarctica shall continue forever to be used for peaceful purposes and shall not become the scene or object of international discord."* The treaty also provided for harmonious scientific cooperation between all nations and was aimed at preventing any one single country from laying claim to the frozen continent. The delegation was headed by Peter Wilkniss, Director of the Division of Polar Programs at the

National Science Foundation in Washington DC. A jovial kind of a guy, I pulled him aside as soon as he stepped ashore and arranged to take him up to the top of the ice-covered hill behind the base to interview him on camera that same evening while the sun was low on the horizon behind him. As we trudged through snow and sludge in our heavy boots and cold weather gear, our exhaled breaths palpable in the crisp air, he turned to me and said rather jokingly: "Isn't this awful? Damned awful. I can't stand the place."

I found this hilarious coming from the man in charge of the US's official polar research program and I somehow felt that he really meant it. But Peter was a good sport, laughed all the way to the top, did exactly as I asked and gave us one of the best interviews for inclusion in the show. Despite his obvious discomfort he cared very much for this "damned awful" place and was determined to ensure that Antarctica remain free of the political wrangling and exploitation of its natural resources that plagued every other corner of the globe.

The visiting delegation included dignitaries from the then-Soviet Union, China, Finland, Canada, Italy, Germany, the United Kingdom, Chile, Argentina and a few other countries. I especially enjoyed interviewing Professor Sun Lin who was Director of the Department of Treaty and Law at the Ministry of Foreign Affairs in Beijing, China, and Professor Vladimir Bardin, a world-renowned glaciologist based in what was then still called Leningrad in the USSR. Palmer Station rolled out the red carpet for these people and on their final night at the base a sumptuous banquet was held in their honor. A slide show, speeches and presentations followed the dinner. It was a fascinating evening indeed. The cafeteria, dining area and bar had been decked out with flags representing all the nationalities that made up the VIP party. The food was superb, wonderful Chilean and Californian wines were served in sparkling crystal glasses, and if you didn't know where you were you could have sworn that you were in some fancy hotel or convention center somewhere in a big American city. The VIPs duly departed on the *Erebus* after being shown around the base, and on December 16 the icebreaker *RV Polar Duke* tied up at Palmer Station's dock. We boarded her the following day and set sail for even more southerly regions of Antarctica.

The 1,831-ton, 219-feet-long *Polar Duke* was a very comfortable ship with accommodation for 14 officers and crew and 23 passengers. She was a sturdy, no-nonsense sort of a vessel, created for the hostile environment of the polar seas. Her white superstructure, green decks, yellow masts, brightly painted deck cranes and red hull identified her as a sophisticated floating laboratory. Like the *SA Agulhas* that I had sailed on years earlier her hull was crimson so that she could be easily spotted in the ice. Built in 1983, in the Vaagen Verft shipyard in Kyrksaeterora, Norway, she was owned by the Carino Company Limited of St. John's, Newfoundland, Canada, and operated by Rieber Shipping in Bergen, Norway. She was under charter to the National Science Foundation as one of the vessels involved in the US Antarctic Research Program. She could travel at a maximum speed of fifteen knots and with her ice-strengthened hull she could force her way through seven-feet thick pack ice. Although this ostensibly made her an icebreaker, when she encountered denser floes or bergs she had to slow down and carefully maneuver her way around these potentially lethal destroyers of ships.

Her officers were Norwegian, her crew Chilean, all under the command of Captain Karl Sanden, an early-forties, tall, dark-haired, ruggedly handsome man with piercing blue eyes and well-trimmed beard and moustache. Calm and softly spoken he gently rattled away in Norwegian to his officers but spoke an excellent English. Though amiable towards his passengers—the scientists, their support staff and my own film crew—when we boarded the ship at Palmer Station I instantly sensed hostility from him and his First Officer, Steinar Jakobsen. Once again, the stigma of South Africa's apartheid policies had caught up with me. Scandinavian countries, led primarily by Sweden and Norway, were aggressively anti-South African during the apartheid years. Many major corporations, especially Swedish, had already withdrawn their investments and ceased operations in South Africa. All Volvo and Saab automobile dealerships, for example, had long closed down there. Scandinavian governments were donating large sums of money to black resistance movements such as the ANC and had become increasingly belligerent towards 'white' South Africa. Through trade sanctions they were intent on isolating the country from the rest of the world. At international bodies such as the United Nations they were very vociferous about eradicating apartheid. As we boarded the *Polar Duke* we all had to turn our passports over to Karl who was required to keep them in the ship's safe until we disembarked. I was not yet a naturalized American citizen and even though I was a legally registered green card-carrying resident of the United States I still carried a South African passport. The minute I handed it over I got a very nasty look from both Karl and Steinar.

"South African, eh?" Karl said as he thumbed through the document, handing it over to Steinar for registration, then subconsciously running his hands down the side of his corduroy trousers as if he had just handled something dirty. I nodded a little sheepishly as both men stared at me. I had no idea what to say. I suddenly felt distinctly uneasy and even though that first uncomfortable introduction would soon be replaced by a normal regimen of work and life aboard the *Polar Duke* there was always a lingering feeling that the Norwegians would rather not have had me on their vessel. After all, I was a white South African and therefore automatically a racist, a persecutor of innocent, indigenous black people. From their perspective, no matter who I really was or what I may have done—including emigrating from

South Africa in order to escape the ugliness of its policies—in their eyes I was guilty. Nothing would have made any difference to them. I had been branded, even here, at the very edge of the world. And how could I blame them?

Routine quickly took over and within a few days of sailing the continental landmass of Antarctica lay not far off the port side of the *Polar Duke*. But you wouldn't have known it because it was totally indistinguishable from the thick, jagged layer of ice that totally covered the sea around us. It was impossible to discern where the ocean ended and the continent began. We were completely surrounded by pack ice from horizon to horizon. Everything was a radiant white, below, above, everywhere. It was like being inside a gigantic shimmering translucent egg, the light of a thousand suns outside the shell radiating inwards. It was impossible to see anything because of the intense glare. Heavy-duty sunglasses coated with special filters for reducing the intense levels of ultraviolet radiation in these latitudes were essential, especially with the ozone hole directly above us. Gazing around I felt as if I was floating in some kind of ethereal-like ride in a clever theme park attraction or visiting a science fiction set conjured up by Hollywood special effects wizards. There were no ups, no downs. Everything was the same, a bright, blinding, all-encompassing white emptiness; a world without beginning or end, a chasm in space and time. The only sense of anything real or recognizable came from the cold steel deck and the bright red hull of the ship beneath my feet. What struck me also was that the old albino *nganga* in Zambia had foreseen all this.

"You will see a world where everything is white," she had told me. "No color. Only white. White everywhere."

Her visions had been astonishing, her predictions uncannily accurate. It was totally beyond my understanding. I longed to talk to others about that remarkable old woman and her clairvoyant powers but I never did. I knew it would have only opened me to ridicule, especially among a community made up largely of scientists.

Better to keep quiet than to be labeled a crackpot.

Our position was now 67° 42′ south, 72° 3′ west, deep within what the navigational charts refer to as the 'Antarctic Circle.' I had never been this far south before. Seldom had I felt more remote, more cut off from everything familiar. We were at the lowest extremities of the Earth. Compass points had no meaning down here but when I studied the charts on the bridge or consulted the numbers on the satellite navigational readouts on the flickering monitors I realized that my adopted home California lay over 10,000 miles to the northwest. South Africa, land of my birth, was some 6,000 miles to the northeast. For all I knew I could have been on another planet.

The *Polar Duke* was on an important mission. Although we were surrounded by things gargantuan—a vast ocean, endless ice packs, towering icebergs, empty horizons, immeasurable skies, a gigantic continent totally shrouded in ice—we were after something infinitesimally small. The primary objective of our search was a tiny marine creature called *Euphausia superba,* a shrimp-like crustacean more commonly known as krill. When fully grown it attains a length of about two inches and weighs less than a third of an ounce. But this little animal's role in the well-being of Antarctica and the world's oceans was crucial, out of all proportion to its miniscule size. Krill was the keystone of the marine food chain, the creature upon which all other animals depended. It was preyed upon by fish, squid, sea birds, penguins and seals, even the great whales. Remove the krill and you break a vital link in the food web. The result? The entire ecosystem collapses. Global warming, climate change and the presence of humans were threatening to do just that.

Marine biologist Langdon Quetin and his team of scientists and students were on board the *Polar Duke* to carry out an intensive study of these incredibly abundant yet elusive little creatures. Krill fed on the microscopic plants called phytoplankton that were being studied by Farooq Azam and his team from the Scripps Institute. But exactly how did krill find the phytoplankton and convert it into energy? What were the krill's breeding habits? It had been estimated that females each produced almost 10,000 eggs every summer, but how did the juveniles survive? What would rising sea temperatures and potentially reduced krill populations do to the overall Antarctic ecosystem? Many nations, including Japan and the then-Soviet Union, were already harvesting krill in enormous quantities for commercial purposes, using it for human consumption as well as for animal feed and fertilizer. They were virtually sucking the animals out of the ocean *en masse,* then freezing them aboard huge factory ships. What would a depletion of krill do to the worldwide marine food web? Answers to questions like these were what Langdon was here to find out so this sector of the *Polar Duke's* voyage had been dedicated to his work. My crew and I were along for the ride to cover the story on film.

Every lab, working space, nook and cranny of the ship was filled with holding tanks, instruments and equipment to service the krill investigation program. One of the principal tools in Langdon's formidable bag of tricks was a submersible remotely operated vehicle, or 'ROV.' Armed with powerful lights and video cameras it was tethered to the *Duke* via a long cable, just like the robotic machine that helped explorer Robert Ballard locate and examine the wreck of the *Titanic* in 1985. Langdon planned to use this device to probe beneath the ice and search for the enormous swarms of krill that were known to inhabit these parts. But Langdon was more of a hands-on guy than a manipulator of a remotely controlled machine. He wanted to get up close and personal to the krill and that meant diving beneath the ice. No one knew what the exact population numbers were. At that time it was estimated that there were at least 150 million tons of the tiny creatures in Antarctic waters. Two divers, Tom Frazer and Mike Conway, were included in Langdon's team.

They waited patiently for a break in the ice pack. When the time came they would join Langdon in the daunting task of donning heavily insulated thermal wet suits, loading their gear, underwater cameras and other devices aboard an inflatable Zodiac, then going overboard to dive beneath the ice and examine the krill population themselves. They would gather data on how the creatures fed on the phytoplankton that had grown just beneath the crust of ice, take photographs and collect samples of eggs and adults for study back on board the *Polar Duke*. I thought those folks were insane to brave those freezing depths. Things don't get much riskier or more dangerous than that, but everyone including Langdon himself was very gung-ho about it all. The team spent much time on the bridge staring at instruments and depth finders, eagerly awaiting the captain's word that conditions were right for them to plunge into the subzero depths of the Bellingshausen Sea in the region known as Ellsworth Land on Antarctica's western flank.

We had inched our way around a minefield of breathtaking icebergs in the open sea for the first few days after leaving Palmer Station, then entered the thick pack ice. We were now dead in the water. Or, more accurately, dead in the ice. We hadn't found any krill yet, so the ship's crew and the scientists were bouncing acoustic signals off the ocean floor and using an array of other state-of-the art equipment to search for the little animals that we knew were down there somewhere. Krill populations were often so numerous and densely packed that they could extend for miles in all directions. Once the ship was stationary the ice accumulated very quickly around the hull. Precautions had to be taken to ensure that we could get out before we became snared in the ice's vise-like grip. As a safeguard the *Polar Duke's* propeller never stopped turning but its blades had been 'feathered' into a neutral position so that it provided no thrust, or 'bite.' The prop or 'screw' always spun at precisely 600 revolutions per minute. If it did stop there was always the danger of the ice freezing solid around it, trapping us with little hope of escape. Chief Engineer Terje Fjelle took great pride in explaining the ship's propulsion system to me. I was fascinated to learn that motive power and speed depended on the angle of the blades, not on the propeller's rate of rotation as in normal vessels. It was all part of the ingenious methods that humans had come up with in order to penetrate and survive these treacherous realms.

But scary as it was, stuck in the middle of nowhere surrounded by a frozen icescape or slowly sailing through open seas littered with icebergs, Antarctica was astonishingly beautiful. It never failed to move me, especially as it was way beyond anything that I had ever imagined. Fears often evaporated as I gazed out at this magnificently alien place. The menu in the ship's mess was a mixture of Norwegian and Chilean dishes, most of it very meaty or fishy. Steinar also kept a large leg of dried and salted lamb in his cabin. He often brought it down to mealtimes and people were invited to slice slivers off it which they could munch on like jerky. It emitted the most revolting stench and made my stomach turn. Nevertheless, I always found something to eat and never went hungry. However, after a while I began to start looking like the cold potato salad and the rather unappetizing boiled carrots and peas medley that formed the bulk of my vegetarian diet. I shared my cabin with one of the members of the krill team, though we hardly saw one another. Once the krill had been located Langdon put his team on a round-the-clock schedule, sometimes diving to collect specimens but most often throwing nets over the side while the ship was underway to dredge up thousands of pounds of the little creatures. This generated a great deal of work on board. Innumerable holding tanks in the main 'wet lab' on the ship's stern had to be maintained; people were endlessly peering through microscopes, dissecting the little crustaceans, making copious notes, updating logbooks, manning measuring equipment and entering data into computers. Everyone was constantly running around with determined looks on their faces carrying bottles, jars and buckets, or slopping around drenched decks and laboratory floors, forever relocating specimens from place to place. Langdon's team of students were kept especially busy doing the bulk of the fetching and carrying, but they also ran much of the electronic equipment in the labs. The wet lab was the focal point of all activities, a throbbing hive of activity. Krill, their eggs and their larvae in all shapes and sizes were stored everywhere as tanks fizzled with foamy seawater that was pumped in from the outside. Ted, my roommate, was on night shift. His work would start after dinner at 8pm and he would only stumble into our cabin at around nine the following morning, rip off his damp clothes that reeked of fish, then collapse, utterly exhausted, into the bunk above mine. After pulling the privacy curtains on the side of his bunk tightly shut, he slumbered through the day. Whoever was asleep when the other came in, we always tried not to disturb one another. Light was always a problem. We had to keep the cabin dark but as there was constant daylight outside the slatted wooden blind over the porthole was always kept closed.

There were other scientists on board the *Polar Duke*, some of whom had completed their research, others still awaiting their turn. Geologist Eugene Domack and his team from Hamilton College in Clinton, New York had devoted the previous few weeks to drilling for cores in the sediment of the ocean floor to help them understand climate change. Now they spent much of their time in labs amidships analyzing those cores. The process was fascinating. Glaciers relentlessly moving towards the sea from the mainland at an imperceptible snail's pace collect material such as rocks, pebbles, dust particles, even gases and air bubbles trapped in ice which are then deposited into the ocean by the icebergs that calve off the glacier. Over time, as the icebergs melt, this material sinks to the ocean bottom, adding layers of atmospheric and geological history to the muddy seabed. This could then be drilled, cored, brought aboard and studied. The samples provided telltale clues about the geology and health of Antarctica. Atmospheric particles accumulated since the beginning of the Industrial Revolution clearly showed how wind currents had brought gases produced by human activity 10,000 or more miles away down to these southerly zones. Gene's task was analogous to the study of tree rings. Each ring or, in this case, layer of sediment on the ocean floor spoke volumes about the climatic conditions of every year in the distant past. But, unlike tree rings, sedimentary samples pushed the story back thousands or even tens of thousands of years. Geologist Charlie McClennen, of Colgate University in Hamilton, New York, was also involved in this exacting field. He had equipment that sent sonar waves to the sediment bed below. The signals penetrated the ocean floor, showing what sort of material lay down there. The human imprint on the planet was evident everywhere, from the stratosphere above us to the muddy depths of the ocean below. It made for disturbing findings. Carbon dioxide, methane and a variety of chemicals had been deposited in huge quantities in and around Antarctica. Human impact on the health of the planet was beyond dispute. Add to this the mass exploitation of krill from commercial harvesting and it became abundantly clear that even the ocean—as evidenced by what was happening in Antarctica—was in deep trouble.

As the krill program continued the ship moved from pack ice to open sea and back again, following a precise grid pattern previously mapped out by Langdon Quetin in conjunction with Captain Karl Sanden. The *Duke's* speed increased in open waters but it was always disconcerting to hear and feel the occasional deep thud as she brushed against a growler or a berg, often larger than the ship itself. Everything would judder violently during these collisions but I knew that Karl wasn't taking any chances. He knew exactly how much the ship could take and how hard he could allow her to graze against a big berg. Nevertheless, those encounters were always unnerving, especially during times when you lay in your bunk and the inner bowels of the *Duke* resonated loudly with the impact. When the ship traveled more slowly in pack ice—usually moving at no more than two or three knots an hour—you often heard a frightening metallic screech as she rode up onto the ice sheet and then cracked it with her sheer weight. Huge chunks of ice then slithered beneath the keel, scraping underneath us with a terrifying grinding sound. Often it felt as if we were driving over a gravel road in a vehicle without any suspension. Groaning as she moved over gigantic chunks of broken ice the *Duke* shook every bone in your body, the noise of ice shattering against steel utterly deafening. Just as well there were 24 hours of daylight. I would have hated to be plowing through those conditions in the dark.

Whenever the opportunity allowed I would don my heavy cold weather gear and position myself in the v-shaped steel triangle that is the ship's bow, lean over the edge and gaze ahead as we cut through the pack ice. It was always a spectacular show. The frozen white landscape seemed interminable—a place without end. As the *Duke* slowly moved forward gigantic cracks raced through the ice in front of us. Like long thin tendrils the cracks zigzagged ahead, forcing the ice to part open slightly, beckoning us to follow. Then, as the ship's weight mounted the ice it caused it to splinter even wider, thrusting enormous walls of the stuff high up on either side of us. They hung there momentarily before shattering and then came crashing down into the grey-green water with an almighty splash. It was spectacular.

The cold was always biting and merciless. Unless people had work to do topside the decks were usually deserted. After a heavy blizzard or even a light snowfall they were slippery and very dangerous. One misplaced step and you could be overboard and no one would know about it. Icicles often hung from railings and sharp-edged corners. They sprouted from rigging, wires, davits, cables and masts. Despite the cold, the wind and the discomfort, there were long periods of feverish activity on the midship deck areas of the ship. We spent many hours filming Langdon's team casting large 'bongo' nets over the sides. These specially designed nets with their ultra-fine nylon mesh tapered from a wide circular opening to a tightly sealed lower end to which a container was attached. Their shape made the nets look just like bongo drums, hence their name. Apart from capturing vast quantities of krill the nets yielded up many weird and wonderful creatures of the deep. Some were like sideshow freaks or from scenes out of a cheap mid-fifties horror movie. There were transparent worms, creatures that looked like inflated balloons and thin living ribbons of yellow ooze trapped in translucent gas bags. There were long jelly-like threads of life, little red bulldozers with bulging eyes, tiny orange-colored tick-like animals. The ocean forever threw up its mysteries and the weirdly wonderful members of its varied cast of characters. It was astonishing. These tiny creatures were straight out of *Star Wars*. There was a multitude of life—infinitely rich, diverse and strange. I had never imagined anything like the organisms we were finding. Even Langdon and the marine biologists were often stymied by what came out of those nets.

One evening after dinner during a lull in the topside krill work I decided to spend some time alone with my thoughts and soak up a little of the powerful ambience of this extraordinary place. The ship was slowly traveling ever more southward through a broken patchwork of pack ice. I knew that the chances of me ever coming down again to this desolate place were highly unlikely so I had to absorb as much as I could of its many moods. I slipped on a couple of extra sweaters, bundled up in my parka, turned up the hood, donned my UV sunglasses and pulled on my gloves and boots and went above. But I took a couple of extra things with me—lightweight headphones, a Walkman tape deck and a recording of British composer Ralph Vaughan Williams' marvelous score for the 1948 film, *Scott of the Antarctic*. A magnificent piece of music, he later reworked it as his seventh symphony, calling it *Sinfonia Antarctica*. The film starred John Mills as British explorer Robert Falcon Scott who undertook two expeditions to the frozen continent, one in 1901 and a second in 1910. On that expedition Scott traveled on foot and by dog and pony sled across the continent, hoping to be the first person to reach the South Pole. On January 18, 1912 he and four of his men attained their objective, only to find a small tent supported by a single bamboo pole flying a Norwegian flag. Inside the tent was a document containing the name of Norwegian explorer Roald Amundsen and four others. They had beaten Scott to it by four weeks. Bitterly disappointed, Scott headed back towards his ship hundreds of miles away, only to become bogged down by blizzards, fatigue and diminishing supplies. His last diary entry was dated March 29, 1912 and ended with the words, *"I do not think I can write anymore."* The five men all succumbed to Antarctica's brutal weather, their frozen bodies discovered by a search party eight months later.

I wanted to pay homage to those brave souls, to a very fine film that told Scott's amazing story, to Vaughan Williams' marvelous music, and to offer my respects to all of the early explorers who faced this deadly white world, so I made my way through hatches and stairways to the poop deck on the stern where the wind was blowing a gale. Once again it was snowing. It was so bitterly cold that I could hardly breathe, the air stinging my nostrils as I inhaled. Nevertheless, I planted myself on a large crate of scientific paraphernalia that had been lashed down on the deck, then held on tightly to a nearby ice-encrusted deck support beam and let my mind drift with the music. It was an amazing experience, almost hallucinogenic. The last time I heard Vaughan Williams' score was in the warm comfort of a theater in South Africa many years ago. Now, here I was, living the music and the movie. And this wasn't a soundstage at Ealing Studios in London either. This was the real thing, the actual location where the story took place. As I sat there, shivering but mesmerized, something caught my eye. I pulled off my headphones and stuffed the Walkman into my parka pocket. Over on the starboard beam there was definitely something moving—something small and dark. The ship was sailing at about eight or nine knots through choppy waters studded with uncountable small platforms of broken ice. I searched the area where I thought I saw the object or animal. And suddenly, there they were—three little black and white adelie penguins excitedly pacing the ship. They jumped and scampered from one floating ice block to another, running around cackling and chatting among themselves, staring at us. This went on for at least ten minutes or more. Then, inquisitively, they hopped and hobbled right up to the hull itself, inspecting the huge noisy steel giant that had invaded their domain. They were so occupied trying to find out what this great big thing was that one of the three little guys got lost. He drifted off on a big chunk of ice, desperately calling out to the other two. But they didn't hear one another and the single bird became hopelessly separated, only to disappear into swirling flakes of snow.

The remaining two continued to pace us, following the red hull, running wildly around the pack ice, cocking their heads, calling out to the metal monster for a response and listening attentively to the throb of its engines. They frequently jumped off the ice into the water, becoming streamlined rocket-propelled submarines, darting beneath us like sleek torpedoes, traveling at unimaginable speeds just below the surface to the next large piece of ice before the ship reached it. Then, like spring-loaded jack-in-the-boxes, they leaped out of the water to land on the ice, feet first, in a stand-to-attention soldier's pose, to await us. It was fantastic. I'd never seen such a display of athleticism. But as the pack ice dissipated the ship picked up speed and changed course. The two little penguins, in a miscalculated move, took a wrong turn and were soon left behind. The last I saw and heard them was as they ran around a large chunk of ice calling out excitedly to us and to one another, chirping, shrieking, their little flippers feverishly trying to stop us like a cop trying to wave down traffic. And then… they were gone. It was enchanting.

The ice was thinning out, the snow had stopped falling and the wind had almost died down. Now the ship was moving at a faster clip. Obviously, Langdon and Karl were eager to get to their next plotted position. I decided to go inside and stop by the passengers' lounge to get a Coke, of which there was a never-ending supply on board this well-stocked ship. Then, as I glanced out of the lounge's large windows, off the port bow there was what appeared to be a fountain of spray followed by an almighty wheezing sound. Whales!

I rushed outside, ran along decking and platforms, dodging machinery and winches, breathlessly reaching the bow to find half the people aboard the *Duke* already there with binoculars and cameras. It was a pod of at least a dozen humpbacks, some of the largest creatures in the sea. Arching their backs as they dived—the very maneuver that gives them their name—these warm-blooded denizens of the deep often reach a length of 50 to 60 feet and can weigh anywhere from thirty to 50 tons. Black or grey-white in color, they had two large blowholes on the top of their heads, situated high above their eyes. Their exhaled breaths sounded and looked like gigantic plumes of steam shooting from the boiler of a gigantic old steam locomotive. Often they would porpoise and dive, then suddenly soar high out of the water, their two enormous flippers looking like aircraft wings, then fall back with an explosive splash. Each time I caught sight of their eyes I knew I was looking at an incredibly sentient being. Brief as those moments were, those eyes were windows into souls. I suddenly longed to dive next to them, to get to know them. Surely, these leviathans could share many secrets about themselves and of life on the planet. The whales seemed playful and unafraid, and were obviously feeding on a vast swarm of krill. Humpbacks have no teeth. Instead they have hundreds of 'baleen' plates hanging from their jaws. Often incorrectly referred to as 'whalebone,' these plates are made of keratin—the same protein substance that forms hair and nails in humans—and are covered in coarse grey bristles that act as filters for food intake. Each of the giant animals consumes anywhere from 2,000 to 10,000 pounds of fish or krill *per day*. Most of us were speechless as we watched them. They frolicked around the *Duke* for over an hour before taking off in an easterly direction. Fortunately, this was a spectacle that would be repeated many times over the next few days.

One evening over dinner some of Langdon Quetin's students were chatting about the whales and the conversation turned to the environmental protection organization, *Greenpeace*, of which they were all openly critical. The mere mention of the name *Greenpeace* opened up a hornet's nest among the Norwegian officers sitting at their own table nearby. This quickly led to a heated discussion about the pros and cons of whaling. I sat there taking it all in as the Norwegians and the young American students debated the issue. Many of the kids were in favor of the International Whaling Commission's (IWC) moratorium in force at that time but it turned out that nearly every single one of the Norwegian officers was, at some point in their career, involved with either sealing or whaling. They were clearly frustrated about IWC policy. To them those were not gentle giants that had paid a courtesy call on the *Duke* but lucrative sources of blubber, oil, meat and baleen, all of which fetched handsome prices in many parts of the world, especially in their own country and in Asia. Norway has consistently defied the IWC and resumed whaling, much to the chagrin of other nations and environmental and animal rights groups worldwide.

It was the day before Christmas, 1990. The krill research work had been put on hold. The ship had stopped and would continue on to the next location on the grid after the holiday. Two makeshift Christmas trees had been set up in the passenger lounge and in the mess. They brought a lovely splash of color and festive touch to this otherwise austere environment. There wasn't much for us to film so I went up to my favorite thinking spot on the stern and stared out at the world of solid ice that had once again engulfed us. And an extraordinary thing happened. A Weddell seal suddenly crawled out of a hole in the ice, plunked herself no more than ten or twelve feet away from me, her blue-black coat glistening as she just lay there staring at me, her oily-dark eyes locked with mine. She seemed so innocent. She rolled over on her back, not taking her eyes off me, then rolled onto her stomach again. I could swear that she was trying to communicate with me, not with words or sounds but with those incredibly captivating eyes. And why did I instinctively feel that she was a 'she' and not a 'he'? Every once in a while she would softly bite into the ice, gobbling up little chunks of it, for what purpose I have absolutely no idea. Her mouth and tongue were a lovely shade of pink, in sharp contrast to her dark coat. She was beautiful; her face friendly and warm and, was I imagining it, but was that a *smile*? It was just her and myself. In the most distant place on Earth. We could have been alone in the stars, far from anything even vaguely terrestrial. We stared at one another for at least a half-hour and then, with a slither and a splash, she was gone. I knew I would never see her again but by some strange, inexplicable means I felt that we had bonded in some mysterious way. An overwhelming sense of respect for Antarctica swept over me. It wasn't only the seal but the mere fact that the place was so distant and so different from anything I had known. This was nature in the raw. It was vast. It looked empty, but I knew it wasn't. Life in myriad forms teemed down there. And everything was so clean, so unblemished. Humans had not yet crowded, cluttered and tarnished it. The place was pristine and, yes, pure.

After the seal disappeared I just sat there. I looked around the deck area and found only ugliness. Everything was metal and iron. There were hooks and hatches and stairways. There was the stench of grease and oil, of cleaning rags, of paint. Toolboxes and nylon ropes nestled between crates and boxes. Everywhere was the pounding thud of diesel engines and generators and pumps. Right next to where I sat was a large, damp wooden container, about five square feet in size. Stenciled in red across its side was the word: 'BIOLOGICAL.' I had no idea what was inside it but it obviously belonged to one of the science teams on board. That's all it said: 'BIOLOGICAL.'

I pondered on it. What was inside the box? What did it matter? What did it represent? That *did* matter; it embodied the very symbolism of our presence here. It was just a box sitting on a deck of a ship with the word 'BIOLOGICAL' on its side but it screamed out the fact that man was here, with all of his instruments and his test tubes and machines and Petri dishes, probing, measuring, mapping, peering into the heart of nature, trying to comprehend, fathom, classify, categorize and label things. With chemistry and physics and the full spectrum of his sciences man comes to Antarctica to plunge in and shape and modify the inner heartbeat of the natural world.

I felt that the creatures down there didn't stand a snowball's hope in hell. This was the last frontier on Earth. Despite international treaties and conferences man would make inroads here. This great continent was part of the world on which humans lived and therefore vulnerable. It was already under siege. From man-made chemicals in the atmosphere. From global warming. From tourism. From study. From exploitation of its resources. Surely, like Africa and all other places before it, greed would bring others. Apart from krill and whales, who knew what else lay beneath the ice? Minerals? Coal? Oil? Fresh water for an increasingly thirsty world where dams and rivers had already been polluted beyond redemption? I sensed a dreadful depth of guilt and sadness as I realized that Antarctica would inevitably go the way of all places to which man had found his way. And now, we were here. First come the explorers, then the scientists and, soon, the exploiters. Sadly, science will open the way to the commercialization, industrialization and rape of this great virginal continent. 'BIOLOGICAL.' That mute label on the damp crate said it all.

I was suddenly awakened from my mental meanderings as Bing Crosby began to belt out, "I'm dreaming of a white Christmas," over the PA system. It was one of the ship's officers' idea of a joke but an appropriate one nevertheless. We were surrounded by a white world and just as the song came out of the tinny-sounding loudspeakers all over the ship it began to snow. I couldn't help chuckling. I pulled myself out of my reverie and went inside. A party was already in full swing in the lounge and mess area. Chief Steward Oddbjorn Holm had cooked up a really lavish Christmas dinner, though with little fare for a vegetarian. But there were candles and Christmas crackers and wine and adequate quantities of potent Aqua Vita to drink. On the notice board in the mess were a number of faxes containing Christmas greetings. One was from our production offices in Los Angeles, one from the National Science Foundation and another which contained this message:

> Our best wishes to all. Studying the Antarctic will reveal the earth's secrets for the benefit of all mankind. Merry Christmas and Happy Holidays. Regards, The Bush Family, Washington DC.

This was George Herbert Walker Bush talking, of course, not his son George W., who came to office 11 years later. I thought it was nice of the First Family to remember us.

Mood music and the Bing Crosby songs soon became Christmas carols which became noisy sing-alongs and, as the evening progressed—the world still as bright as day outside—naughty nautical ditties in Norwegian and English eventually took over. It was the strangest Christmas I had ever had and a very good time was had by all. Most exciting of all was the fact that in two more days we would—in the words of Langdon and Karl—go 'off station' and set course for Chile. After a brief stop at Palmer Station to offload Langdon, his team and their swirling tanks of krill specimens for further research work in Palmer's well-equipped labs, the *Duke's* final destination would be the little town of Punta Arenas at the tip of the South American continent. When we docked at Punta Arenas on January 4, 1991 all talk was of war in the Persian Gulf. Eight days later Congress voted and approved the use of US forces to oust Iraqi invaders from Kuwait. Although I looked forward to boarding my Lan Chile flight to Santiago, and then a Pan American Airways flight that would take me over the heart of South America to Sao Paulo in Brazil, then to Rio de Janeiro, and finally on to Miami, Florida, the impending Gulf War played havoc with flight schedules to and from the United States. I shrugged it off and welcomed the opportunity to explore the little remote, wet, windswept harbor town of Punta Arenas. Walking the streets the day after we disembarked from the *Polar Duke* I realized how much I had missed greenery during the past few weeks—leaves, plants, grass, trees, anything that grew in the ground. I relished the gardens, parks and tree-lined thoroughfares of the town, even admiring the weeds that grew from cracks in the concrete of the sidewalks. My eyes drank in the restful hues of any vegetation around me, all of which had been totally absent in Antarctica. It gave me a new appreciation for the flora of our world, all too often taken so much for granted.

What was it that the old Zambian *nganga* had said?
"White. Only white. Everything white. No color."
Uncanny.

Sixteen

The Antarctic movie was followed by a one-hour Special for the National Geographic Society. It was called *Mysteries Underground* and was all about caves and caving around the world. In addition to writing and directing the show I also acted as one of two cinematographers on it. You can imagine my surprise when I received a 1993 National Primetime Emmy Award for my work. That pretty much wrapped it up for me as a cinematographer. I saw the award as a buttoning up of more than thirty years behind the lens. After that token of recognition I was quite happy to give up the camera in favor of concentrating on writing, directing and producing.

Next was a stint as Supervising Writer for four seasons of shows called *Mysteries of the Bible* for the A&E cable network, plus two series called *Ancient Mysteries with Leonard Nimoy* and *History's Mysteries* for The History Channel. As a freelance writer I worked on shows for the Discovery Channel, Bravo, American Movie Classics and The Learning Channel, dealing with topics such as the famous de Mille family dynasty. That show highlighted the work of legendary director Cecil B. DeMille (*The Ten Commandments, Samson and Delilah, The Greatest Show on Earth*), his brother William C. de Mille who founded the country's first theater school, and his niece Agnes de Mille who became one of the nation's greatest choreographers (*Rodeo, Oklahoma!, Brigadoon, Carousel, Paint Your Wagon*). The show was hosted by a consummately gifted actor whose work I had always admired ever since my childhood, Charlton Heston. Other productions covered future weapons, the history of firearms, early railroads in America, the museums of Southern California, vigilantes and the treatment of blacks in the Deep South following the Civil War. The latter was an absolute eye-opener for me. I had no idea about the extent and brutality of racism that had existed in America. Crimes committed by members of the Ku Klux Klan and the staggering quantity of lynching and murders perpetrated by whites upon blacks were far beyond anything that had occurred during the worst years of apartheid in South Africa. If ever there was an exposé of double standards and hypocrisy when it came to how people abroad viewed government policies in South Africa that show rammed it forcefully home for me. Even though racism had never been signed into law in the United States the country's divisive racial history was far more violent and bloodstained than South Africa's had ever been. Between the 1880s and the 1930s more than 5,000 blacks were brutally murdered or lynched in the Deep South for trivial offenses, often for the lamest of reasons. An excuse was always found to victimize 'niggers.' The most popular of all was that they were 'interfering' with white women. Thousands were accused of cases of molestation and rape that they never committed. But any good reason for a lynching was enough to bring out the crowds. Local police were often in cahoots with frenzied white mobs who dragged blacks to their deaths. The form of murder was exceptionally gruesome. The victim was often savagely kicked and beaten, and body parts—fingers, ears, genitals—were sometimes cut off and sold to spectators as 'souvenirs.' People were even burnt to death but the most popular spectator sport was lynching by hanging from a tree. It was an unbelievably gory period in American history. As I uncovered facts and conducted interviews with historians I was stunned by what I learned. Washington DC, the Federal government and the world at large had stood silently by as alcohol-crazed white mobs, church groups and even youngsters committed the most unspeakable acts of violence against innocent, defenseless people. Notices of executions were nailed up in prominent places, and families arrived with kids and picnic baskets to enjoy a weekend 'lynch party.' Smiling groups had their photographs taken with smoldering corpses in the background dangling from branches.

Racism in America endured well into the late sixties. It was an everyday accepted thing, even long after that perverse racist South African prime minister Dr. Hendrik Verwoerd had been assassinated in parliament in Cape Town. America had not begun to change until Malcolm X and Dr. Martin Luther King Jr. ushered in the Civil Rights movement and prodded the nation's consciousness. For decades the United States government had ranted and raved about apartheid while tolerating extreme racism at home. In response to segregation, oppression and the wide scale maiming and murdering of blacks the National Association for the Advancement of Colored People (NAACP) was founded on February 12, 1909. Its first office was in a room of the *New York Post* building above the streets of Manhattan. Every day that a lynching was reported a flag flew from the window of the NAACP. It carried the simple wording: "A Black Man was Lynched Today." Despite its high-profile presence in New York City few noticed. And the killings went on.

One of the most memorable moments during the production of that show was meeting a white-haired black man who was then 84 years old. He was Dr. James Cameron. I met him in his office in Milwaukee, Wisconsin. He was a gently spoken individual who touched my life deeply. Not only did he remember the racist days of the Deep South but he was the only living survivor of an attempted lynching. Cameron had seen the impressive multi-million-dollar Museum of the Holocaust being constructed in Washington DC and thought: Why is there no museum to the victims of white oppression in this country? And so he scrounged up the funding, found premises and in 1988 opened America's Black Holocaust Museum in Milwaukee. Containing grisly exhibits of slavery, black oppression and lynching, this little-known and under-funded museum deserved far more recognition than it received. Today, of course, it has been superseded by the National Museum of African American

History but when I met him his was the only museum of its type in the nation.

Visiting it was a haunting experience. As I listened in spellbound horror Cameron told me that on the balmy evening of August 6, 1930 in Marion, Indiana his life changed forever. He was just 16 years old and was persuaded by two friends, Tommy Shipp (18) and Abraham Smith (19), to join them in committing a robbery. All three young men were desperately short of cash. They planned to hold up a car on the outskirts of town and rob the driver of his wallet. Cameron agreed to participate in the plot but he was not aware that his two friends were armed. On the way to the hold-up point—a curve on a lonely road in the forest outside town—Cameron had second thoughts. He backed out and made for home. Just then a car came down the road and he heard it screeching to a stop at the bend in the road behind him. He knew that Tommy and Abe had held it up. Then his heart almost stopped as he heard gunshots. Running as fast as he could he headed for home, dashed through the sparsely furnished parlor saying goodnight to his parents and dived under the covers of his bed. He was terrified of what might have happened. It wasn't long before he found out. At midnight there was a pounding at the front door. It was the cops. Cameron had been seen with Shipp and Smith by eyewitnesses prior to the hold-up. He was taken into custody. It was only after he was thrown into a small cell on the second floor of the jailhouse that he learned that Tommy Shipp and Abe Smith had killed the male white driver of the car, leaving the man's female companion untouched. Now Cameron was implicated in the murder. His two friends were incarcerated on the ground floor of the jail and in the early light of dawn a mob of angry residents carrying torches and ropes surrounded the building, demanding "release of the niggers so that justice can be done." Law enforcement officers tried to keep the crazed crowd at bay but they broke through, got hold of the keys, unlocked Shipp and Smith from their cells, dragged them outside and beat Smith to death. Shipp was gruesomely kicked and then hauled off into the woods. Cameron could see all this happening from the small window of his cell upstairs. He was paralyzed with fear, knowing that he would be next. A half-hour later the frenzied mob returned, yelling, "We want Cameron! We want Cameron!"

The police officers tried to prevent the crowd from entering the building but within minutes Cameron's cell door was thrown open and he was hauled off into the woods. All along the way residents of the town including women and children shouted abuses at him, spat on him and beat him with shovels, pickaxes and rifle butts. He was punched until he was almost unconscious. Then, just as he thought he was going to pass out the mob threw him to the ground at the base of a tree. He looked up and through the tears, blood and sweat that stung his eyes he saw the body of his friend Abe Smith dangling from a rope above him. As Cameron put it to me, "I bowed my head, shivering like a babe, and prayed to the good Lord above. I'm innocent, dear God, I'm innocent. Please save me."

And then a noose was roughly thrust around his neck. He was expecting death to claim him but he continued to pray, begging for a miracle, and then someone from the crowd shouted, "Let the damn nigger go so that he can be jailed for life and always remember what he did."

All Cameron could remember after that was the noose being pulled from his head, a lot of manhandling and more kicking, beating and yelling and then he passed out. When he came to he was back in his cell, bruised, beaten and bleeding but alive. The miracle had been granted. James Cameron languished in jail for four years before the female occupant of the car that was held up came forward and stated that Cameron had not been involved in the crime. He subsequently received an official pardon from Indiana Governor Evan Bayh and was released on parole.

In the ensuing years he moved to Milwaukee, wrote his

autobiography, *A Time of Terror*, took several jobs which included being a table waiter, laborer, construction worker, laundryman, janitor, ditch digger, shop owner, newspaper reporter, shoe-shiner and factory worker. In between all this he had also formed the Madison County Branch of the NAACP. I was humbled by the presence of this articulate and gentle old man. We ended the show with his interview, a powerful indictment on the kind of bigotry and hatred that still bedevils society, perhaps more so today than ever before.

It was not until June 13, 2005 that the United States Senate officially apologized for previous government inaction on lynchings. One of the resolution's chief sponsors, Senator Mary Landrieu, a Democrat from Louisiana, admitted that the public nature of many of the lynchings had been exceptionally ugly.

"This was a community spectacle and the Senate of the United States knew it," Landrieu said. "There may be no other injustice in American history for which the Senate so uniquely bears responsibility."

Fortunately, someone was there to witness her historical admission. Confined to a wheelchair and smartly attired in a dark suit, James Cameron, aged 91, shook hands with Senators and accepted their apology on behalf of all the victims of those most heinous of days.

Meantime, in South Africa the racist story had taken a dramatic turn. On February 11, 1990 political prisoner number 46664 had been released from detention by President Frederik Willem de Klerk. When Nelson Mandela finally walked into the sunlight and into freedom after 27 years of incarceration the ANC was unbanned and the final strokes of bringing down apartheid swung into action. On April 26, 1994, I stood lost in thought on the sidewalk outside the South African Consulate General's offices in Beverly Hills. I was still a South African citizen at the time and was one of scores of others waiting in line to cast my ballot in the country's first multiracial democratic election. I had already been watching news bulletins depicting lines of thousands who queued up for miles at polling stations all over South Africa. There they were, people arriving by bus, car, train, ox wagon, donkey cart, on horseback, by bicycle or on foot. They were rural farmers, city dwellers, soccer moms, fishermen, shepherds, clerks, tribal chiefs, engineers, lawyers, herdsmen, taxi drivers, women balancing clay pots on their heads. It was heart-wrenchingly wonderful. People of every color—for the very first time—were casting their votes in South Africa. Secretly I yearned to be standing in one of those lines in South Africa, preferably in the heartland of Zulu or Xhosa territory, smelling the grass, hearing the bellowing of cattle, watching clouds cluster in the intense blue sky, listening to the babble of accents and dialects. But it was amazing to be voting in the very same election right here in America. In line ahead of me was a black man who was working in the music industry. Behind me was an Indian, a computer science professor. But most of us were whites, all émigrés to the Land of Opportunity, to the Golden State from our motherland in Africa. Anyone who had any proof of South African birth or citizenship could vote. As we waited we chatted. And we beamed. The feeling of joy was overwhelming. This is what we had all dreamed of. This is what we had fought for, ached for, longed for. Over twenty million people were voting for 18 political parties competing for 400 seats in the National Assembly that day. The result was that Nelson Mandela's ANC won by a wide margin, gaining 252 seats in parliament.

May 10, 1994 was a day I shall never forget. I sat mesmerized in front of the TV in our living room as I watched dignitaries from around the world gather in the flag-bedecked amphitheater of the Union Buildings in Pretoria. I so much wanted to be there, filming it all, just as I had photographed so many other ceremonial occasions in South Africa in previous years. But none was like this, none so important, so extensively covered by the world's media. When Nelson Mandela stepped from his gleaming limousine to take his oath of office I could hardly believe it as the white Chiefs of Staff of the armed services, bedecked in their uniforms and sporting their medals, lined up at the curbside to greet him with a firm salute followed by a friendly, "Good morning, sir!"

Was this actually happening? Were these the same people I had known during apartheid's heyday, now welcoming their new black president? Fighter jets flew overhead—aircraft I knew well from my days of making films with the South African Air Force—leaving smoke trails in the country's new colors. They were followed by three helicopters slowly carrying the newly-designed national flag slung beneath their bellies. The crowd on the lawns that stretched in front of the nation's administrative buildings roared their approval. I watched as 76-year-old Nelson Rolihlahla Mandela accompanied by his daughter Zinzi climbed the carpeted stairs to the dais. Within an hour he was sworn in as President of the Republic of South Africa. A 21-gun-salute boomed out, scattering flocks of doves into the brisk air above the country's capital city. On May 24, 1994—after 33 years of being an outcast—South Africa was readmitted to the Commonwealth. On June 16 the United Nations lifted its arms embargo against the country and eight days later South Africa reclaimed its seat in the United Nations General assembly.

And so died the terrible thing called apartheid.

But 1994 held other things in store for me. That was the year I was diagnosed with my autoimmune-induced kidney disease, as described at the beginning of this book. The onset of the disease turned my life upside down. The only solution to the dilemma was to suppress my natural protection system against foreign bodies or disease. I began by taking a heavy daily oral dose of an immunosuppressant called chlorambucil. The drug was similar to what was given to cancer patients suffering from lymphocytic leukemia or to those who had organ transplants. It blocked the formation of DNA and RNA, and helped to avoid the body rejecting a transplant. In addition, three times a week I was infused with Prednisone, administered directly into my veins. It wasn't long before my immune system was so suppressed that if anyone with a cold or a sore throat came near me I picked up their ailment immediately. Also, the drugs were making me feel as though my insides were on fire. My head pounded. My heart palpitated. At the same time I had to start wearing tight waist-high compression stockings that squeezed my legs all the way from the toes and feet up to the groin to force the build-up of fluid in my lower extremities back into the bloodstream. This condition—commonly known as edema—was not only unsightly and dangerous but extremely uncomfortable. I had to wear suspenders under my shirt to prevent the stockings from slipping down. The suspenders cut into my shoulder blades, requiring padding on each shoulder. The stockings were hot, scratchy and cut into my skin. I was swallowing heavy doses of diuretics to counteract the edema by increasing urine flow so that fluid retention could be minimized. But the diuretics—often referred to as 'water pills'—were causing my leg muscles to go into the most excruciating bouts of spasm. It was a miserable state of affairs.

One morning as I sat in a chair in the infusion room at Cedars-Sinai hospital in Beverly Hills with a tube dripping Prednisone into my veins, I thought back to that old albino *nganga* in Ndola all those years ago. Once again she had proven herself right. She had predicted this illness. Speaking in Bemba she had told David Phiri to inform me that I would suffer a very serious sickness that would bring me close to death's door. Everything that the amazing woman had foretold had come to pass, from my two marriages to the number of children I had to moving across the oceans and settling in a foreign land. She had predicted my encounter with the elephant, the storms at sea, the unfolding of my career, my meeting with Adolf Hitler's personal pilot, and now this. It was unbelievable.

My condition deteriorated fast. I started losing so much protein that it began causing muscle decay. Even worse, the lack of protein was sapping me of energy. I felt constantly exhausted. By noon I was usually slumped over my desk like a narcoleptic, half-asleep. Despite getting the best treatment that modern allopathic medicine and my excellent doctors could provide I needed to start doing more to try to stop my kidneys from failing so I began including alternative healing methods. First came Chinese medicine. That seemed to offer some relief from the discomfort and the nausea but it was expensive and the constantly boiling herbs and powders on the kitchen stove caused an unbelievable stench to permeate every corner of the house, not to mention the foul taste of drinking the thick brown gunk that it produced. The queasiness that followed the consumption of these concoctions was awful. I know that many Chinese remedial treatments do work but Dr. Jiang the sweet little elderly Chinese lady who practiced her ancient craft in a fancy Wilshire Boulevard office suite couldn't speak much English and communication with her was difficult. But of real concern was the fact that the treatment was designed to take place over a long period of time and my two kidneys weren't going to give me the luxury of time. They were atrophying. Fast.

I had to try something else, so next came Ayurvedic medicine. I found Dr. Patel, a Hindu doctor. He had a subdued, reflective manner and prescribed a combination of powders and a very strict diet that left with me a very narrow range of virtually tasteless food. I was constantly hungry. And I never seemed to be able to leave his consulting room after my biweekly sessions without paying hundreds of dollars for a handful of multicolored powders that he scooped from a few dozen bottles and jars into a little brown paper bag. As pleasant and honest as this man was communication was once again minimal. Granted, the first time I visited him he stared into my eyes, examined my tongue, peered up my nostrils, held my hand for a minute or so and asked me a lot of questions. But ensuing sessions involved little more than a cursory glance at my legs to check on the edema. The colorful powders he dispensed were very pretty to look at but utterly disgusting to drink. The mixture made me feel so ill that the biliousness it caused was worse than the discomfort from the edema. And it did not quell the inner burning sensation from the chlorambucil and my overall lack of energy and stamina. I believe in the Ayurvedic system but this too was a long-term treatment and time was not on my side.

As the next few months went by my proteinuria levels—the presence of protein in the urine—continued to soar. Healthy kidneys don't allow significant amounts of protein to pass through their filters. However, when filters are damaged kidneys tend to let proteins such as albumin leak from the bloodstream into the urine. My energy levels continued to plummet and the edema stubbornly refused to disappear. I was up against a war raging within my body. What had I done to bring this on? I felt I had little alternative but to continue dabbling in every form of alternative healing I could find. I stood on my head, chanted naked incantations to the moon, recited mantras, meditated, prayed. I tried acupuncture, aromatherapy, hands-on healing, homeopathy, kinesiology, yoga, faith healing and Native American shamanism by drumming in the nearby Mojave Desert. I was told to eat large fresh radishes, Japanese mushroom stew and steamed asparagus. However, after a few months I could barely take it anymore. I was constantly nauseous, weak, unable to concentrate, my weight ballooned and I started suffering from what some support groups on the web called a 'moon face' condition caused by the Prednisone. I was incessantly short of breath and constantly dizzy. Then the bone marrow in the area of my left knee began to deteriorate. The heavy chlorambucil dosage was destroying blood cells and the knee was the first area where it began to show up. While the edema had been somewhat reduced, now I could hardly walk because of bone marrow loss. An MRI revealed just how serious the problem was. Was I ever going to survive this battle?

In March 1997 at the height of my illness my wife and I went on a road trip to Mexico. An indefatigable collector, Diana wanted to buy some rare handmade ceramic pots from a renowned local artist in the popular coastal town of Ensenada. However, my interests did not lie in ceramics during this stressful period. My real motive for taking the trip was to visit the set of the filming of James Cameron's production, *Titanic,* which was taking place at the new Fox Baja Studios at Rosarito, just across the border from California. I had arranged special VIP visitors' passes to the set from the 20th Century Fox studios' publicity offices in Los Angeles. As a *Titanic* buff I was very eager to see the 90% scale replica of the giant liner that had been constructed in a huge tank right on the beachfront. I was excited as we crested a hill while heading southwards and suddenly saw the ship looming above the tank at the edge of the shoreline with smoke spewing from her funnels. What a sight! The *Titanic* had been reborn.

We pulled up in the parking lot of the studios and a guide showed us around. He took us into soundstages where the elaborate interior sets had been constructed and then to the towering reconstruction of the ship itself. But as fascinating as it all was the visit was agony for me. I could hardly limp around the sprawling lot. I was nauseous, short of breath, and my knee felt like someone had run a white-hot spear through it. As I admired the sheer scale of the production one predominant thought kept surfacing in my mind. I was convinced that I had to get off the medication. It was killing me. If I was going to perish I'd rather succumb to the disease itself than to the cure. But I plodded on with my life and my career, visiting doctors for intensive tests every two weeks. Many other side effects were beginning to show up, including blinding headaches, bleeding gums, excessively high blood pressure, heart palpitations and elevated cholesterol levels.

But I never stopped working throughout this period. Difficult as it was I had to keep my mind occupied. Besides, I couldn't afford to stay at home and lick my wounds. My son was in college and my daughter in high school. My wife's income as a film editor couldn't support all our needs so I had to persevere. Fortunately, I was allowed to spend much of my time writing at home, attending meetings and screenings at production offices only when absolutely necessary. Then, in May 1997, I developed an agonizing case of shingles down my back, right down to the groin, along the perineum and up to the testicular area. It was awful. Shingles are caused by the chickenpox virus. I had contracted the illness as a child and the virus had obviously lain dormant for about 40 years. Now, with my weakened immune system it reawakened in full force and attacked a nerve that traced a path down my back and under my abdomen to my crotch. I have seldom experienced such discomfort. Causing blisters to break out on the surface of the skin it lasted for a nearly a month. During that time I could neither sit nor lie down without squirming in agony.

As 1998 dawned I thought my days were numbered so I decided to visit my two older kids from my previous marriage in London. Simon was 28 and Jessica 26. It would give me a little quality time with them. Without admitting it to them I saw it as an opportunity to see them for perhaps one last time before the illness got the better of me. After a very emotional farewell to them at the airport one morning I flew back to Los Angeles for the most uncomfortable eleven-and-a-half hour journey of my life. My legs were so swollen that even with the compression stockings if I so much as bumped them against the seat in front of me they began to leak fluid.

Enough is enough, I thought. A few weeks later I stomped into my nephrologist's office and said I couldn't go on with the treatment. I was taking myself off the medication. He was sympathetic and understanding but he persuaded me to try one other form of drug before I threw in the towel.

"It's called cyclosporine," he said. "It's also an immunosuppressant but it's not quite as aggressive as the Prednisone and chlorambucil. We haven't had much success rate with it in cases like yours but would you like to give it a try?"

When I learned that cyclosporine was produced from a fungus rather than from a mixture of chemicals I agreed. I'd try it for a couple of months to see what happens.

Despite the illness I was still just another gun for hire in the cutthroat Hollywood freelance system. I was willing to take on any assignment that came my way. Shows I worked on included an examination of the evidence regarding who was really behind the killing of President John F. Kennedy, a story of the discovery of ancient Thracian gold treasure found near the Black Sea, life in the tidal region of a tropical rainforest, a biography of General Phineas Banning who helped develop Long Beach, San Pedro and the Port of Los Angeles. Then an interesting job offer came along for a two-hour TV special to investigate the nature of death. It was intended as a serious scientific quest for possible answers as to what happens to human consciousness after the demise of the physical body. In other words, does consciousness or 'soul' or 'spirit' survive death?

"There are more things in heaven and earth, Horatio, than are dreamt of in your philosophy," said Hamlet in Act One of Shakespeare's play. Perhaps the Bard knew something that we did not. It certainly prods us into contemplating the question: Does the spirit survive after death? That was what the two-hour TV special, *Beyond Death,* set out to explore.

"Don't forget, this is about whether there *is* such a thing as a soul, and whether it can be contacted after death," one of the production executives said emphatically. "What we *don't* want is any New Age mumbo-jumbo horseshit."

"Or about spooks and haunted houses either," snapped

another as they gave me my marching orders before production began.

We had sat around a table for days trying to define exactly where the show should go, what subjects it should contain, and what the 'throughline' narrative should address. The A&E cable network wanted a thought-provoking, scholarly investigation, and not a piece of run-of-the-mill sensationalism simply designed to entertain couch potatoes about zombies and things that go bump in the night. The program had to be based on hard scientific research.

"No hocus-pocus Houdini crap," I was told. "No poltergeists. No spooks. Science. We want *science!*"

And that is what we set out to get.

Some societies—like America—are pretty much in denial about death. It is not something to be talked about. You've got to keep it at arm's length, pretending that it doesn't really happen except in movies or on TV. When it does smash its way into your own world when a loved one passes away all you have are the comforting support of others and the compassionate words of a priest or religious leader to help instill within you a belief that it is only the body that has gone, and that the essence of the person continues in some form of altered state. Many turn to religious faith, hoping or believing that the one who has died will be restored to another level of existence. Many cultures easily embrace death not as something temporal but transitional. Although the Judeo-Christian and Islamic tradition says that the 'soul' of an individual survives the demise of the physical body and may end up in 'heaven' or in 'hell,' other cultures—particularly in the Orient—see death as a stepping stone to another chance at life here on Earth; in other words, a natural process in a cycle of births and rebirths in which the soul reincarnates, learning lessons, acquiring experiences, rising above past mistakes, eventually returning... where? To the source of its creation? Whatever our convictions or beliefs, few of us are ever going to win any arguments over the matter. But doubtless all of us think about it from time to time.

If, as some serious investigators say, the soul is just another word for our consciousness how can we prove that it exists? Other than measuring brainwave activity or natural electrical impulses that are present in the body, consciousness is not something that you can place in a Petri dish, put under a microscope or hold in the palm of your hand. So, when the body dies, what happens to consciousness? This is what *Beyond Death* set out to probe. It was an enormous challenge. For 'editorial balance' and to avoid criticism of being biased we had to include the views of people on both sides of the fence—the believers and the non-believers. The topic was fraught with complexity and controversy. As one of the skeptics in the show put it: "When you're dead, you're dead. End of story."

But is that really the case?

We filmed seances, covered public 'spiritual readings' and 'sittings' in the homes of mediums, interviewed people who had undergone 'near death experiences' or NDEs following surgeries or accidents, questioned doctors and neuroscientists and spent time with a pediatrician who had devoted fifteen years documenting the experiences of very young children who had survived NDEs. Amazingly, just about all of the children—and we questioned a dozen of them and their parents—were revived from brief periods of clinical death and all had similar stories about 'tunnels of light,' 'angels' and 'people in white robes' who coerced them into 'returning home to mom and dad' from a place all of them referred to as 'heaven.' None of the children were related or knew one other. They were all under the care of Dr. Melvin Morse, Associate Professor of Pediatrics at the University of Washington in Seattle, who asked them to draw pictures of their experiences. We were dumbfounded when Morse pointed out inexplicable similarities in the images of the drawings showing white-coated figures, large rooms, control panels with blinking lights and the ubiquitous 'tunnels leading back home.'

At one of the group séance-like sittings in Reseda, Los Angeles medium Brian Hurst explained that the dead were—as he put it—"bioelectrical beings." It was merely the body that was gone. The personality, the experiences, the presence of the individual prevailed. As a medium, he 'felt' them trying to contact him through a sensation in his solar plexus.

"It's not about being clairvoyant," he told me. "It's more a matter of being clairsentient and clairaudient. I am not only aware of these beings but I can clearly hear them." He also had a spirit guide whom he referred to as 'Dr. Grant' who helped him in his work. Seeing Brian in action was unbelievable. It looked like he had a private hotline to the spirit realm as messages from the deceased poured in for various members of the audience. One night a Chinese woman and her adult daughter were not only given a message from their late son and brother but it came in the form of Chinese words. Brian struggled with the pronunciation and then added: "I'm told that I'm speaking in something called *Tir'Chu*."

He looked at the two women who were clearly in a state of shock.

"Does that make any sense?" he asked.

With tears pouring down her cheeks the younger woman said: "Of course. That is the name of the local dialect of our village in China."

Considering the innumerable dialects spoken in that sprawling land of over a billion people it was remarkable. There was no way Brian could have known anything about it, let alone speak it. And he certainly could not have known of the circumstances of the death of the late young man which the message discussed, nor of the very personal memories of childhood conveyed to his mother and sister. Brian added that he was imploring them not to worry about him, assuring them that he was fine in the spirit world. Not only that but that he "had important work to do and was happy." Another message came for a woman whose deceased Turkish father profusely apologized to her for being so uncaring and detached from her prior to his death. On and on they came, messages of past experiences, of love, of reassurance. A consistent theme in all of them was that everything was well in the spirit domain, even after traumatic deaths following tragedy, illness and accident. Pain and suffering had been vanquished. Though there were many tears that night there was also something very warm and uplifting about it all.

We filmed at the Human Energy Systems Laboratory at the University of Arizona in Tucson where researchers Doctors Gary Schwartz and Linda Russek were trying to determine whether mediumship was in any way related to the phenomenon of telepathy. The mysteries and potential of the human mind were also being explored at the Monroe Institute in Virginia. Visiting the facility was a compelling experience. The Institute was isolated in a magnificent landscape high above the Blue Ridge Mountains. The Institute's Research Director at the time was F. Holmes 'Skip' Atwater who explained to me that when former broadcasting executive Robert Monroe founded the Institute in the early seventies it was due to a series of spontaneous experiences that had drastically altered his life, beginning in 1958. Unpredictably and without willing it he found himself leaving his physical body, exploring places far beyond conventional concepts of time and space. Wanting to tap into the forces creating this state of affairs Monroe began experimenting with sound. His work brought him to the conclusion that artificially generated audio tones could stimulate the brain sufficiently to create a modified state of mind. But more importantly, it could create an elevated state of consciousness, and through that, an altered state of being. It was a remarkable breakthrough. Ever since, the Monroe Institute has been a unique mental rejuvenation center as well as a place where groundbreaking research into human consciousness has been carried out.

After lunch one day I toured the facility with Dr. Darlene Miller, the Institute's quietly spoken Clinical Psychologist and Program Director. With us was a man I shall refer to only by his first name, Dick. He was a middle-aged retired engineer from Falls Church, Virginia. Dick had specially driven down to be interviewed for our show. During his long professional career in the aerospace industry he had often attended programs at the Institute. I was told that over a period of time visitors could advance through various degrees of altered consciousness called 'Focus Levels.' Dick was one of the few who had reached 'Focus 34,' one of the highest levels attainable. As we sat outside a large soundproof chamber before filming Dick undergoing one of the profound awareness-inducing states, he told me that over the years his consciousness had expanded so much that he had experienced 'astral travel' and that he had even encountered many deceased family ancestors, including his own father who had died when he was just six years old. Dick was a scientist, a realist and not a publicity seeker or a prankster. His comments, I instinctively knew, were based on truth, not nonsense. In fact, he was extremely reticent to speak about them and only did so because of my consistent coercion. Darlene Miller told me that her work at the Institute led her to the conclusion that there is no death, only the termination of one's physical being. Vast numbers of people who had undergone programs at the Institute left the place free of any fear of dying. It certainly lent credence to what so many have been saying for so long, that we're not physical beings having a spiritual experience while on the Earth plane, but spiritual beings having a temporary physical experience.

Of all the facilities investigating the nature of consciousness and the power of the mind few impressed me as much as that most exemplary of academic institutions, Princeton University. Once the home turf of Albert Einstein this Ivy League establishment in New Jersey is not easily dismissed when it comes to serious scientific research. At the time the university was carrying out investigations into psychokinesis or the ability of the mind to influence or move physical objects. This played into our theme because we wanted to know whether thought—or consciousness—was confined to the brain or able to transcend the domain of the physical or the physiological. The faculty entrusted to undertake the program was none other than the Department of Engineering. The man who headed the program was Dr. Robert Jahn, Professor of Aerospace, Dean Emeritus, School of Engineering and Applied Science. He had taught and been published in fields as diverse as advanced space propulsion systems, plasma dynamics, fluid mechanics, quantum mechanics and engineering anomalies. The name of his investigative unit was called the PEAR Lab, an acronym for Princeton Engineering Anomalies Research Laboratory.

In a warren of rooms and laboratories in the basement of the engineering block in one of Princeton's imposing white stone buildings Jahn and his team went about their business. They were tabulating how many times subjects or 'operators' partaking in the experiments and using nothing more than a concentration of pure thought could affect or, for example, influence the height of a jet of water spurting from a fountain or the swing of a pendulum or a sequence of numbers produced by what they called a 'random event generator' or even the movements of small electrically-powered robot-like toys scooting around on a table top. In the case of the latter the operator would mentally decide to make the little robotic toys turn left or right or move in a straight line or even travel in a reverse direction. The results of these experiments were startling. Over a period of years, time and time again the overwhelming majority of operators sitting in the same room as the experiment or across the hallway or even on the opposite side of the world as far away as Brisbane, Australia could influence the instruments, fountains, pendulums and toys by thought alone. Jahn told me that he had been conducting these experiments for over twenty years with hundreds of different operators and the 'anomalies' were repeatedly replicable. In a riveting on-camera interview he went on to claim: "The inescapable inference from our experimental results is that consciousness can access other parts of space and time than that in which it is physically immersed, and that consciousness is not restricted to the human physiology but that it can expand itself into other worlds and other times, even beyond bodily death."

He went on to tell me that he implicitly believed that the human consciousness or 'soul' is here for some kind of learning experience. That was quite a statement from a man like Jahn. He was an engineer, not an evangelist, priest or showman.

Making *Beyond Death* was a process that never failed to induce amazement. It constantly brought back thoughts of those healers and diviners, the *ngangas* and *sangomas*, in distant Africa. Were they perhaps already ahead of the mainstream scientific community in understanding the mysteries of death and what lies beyond the boundaries of the physical?

My own view is that they are.

184

185

186

187

188

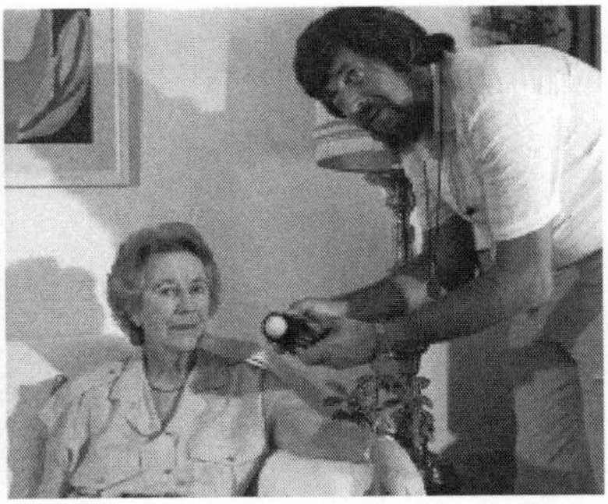

189

190

191

192

193

194

195

196

197

198

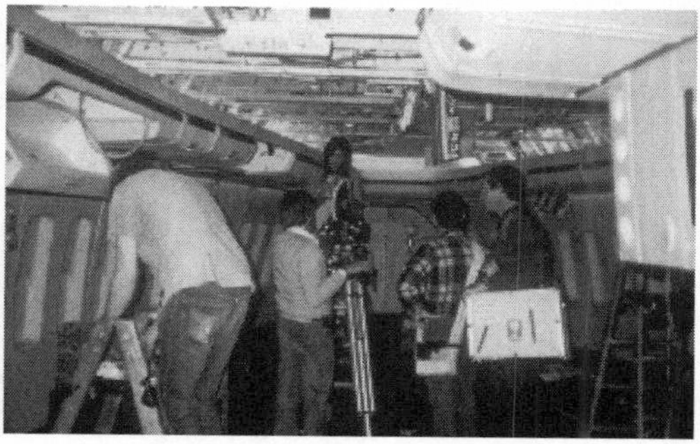

199

200

201

202

203

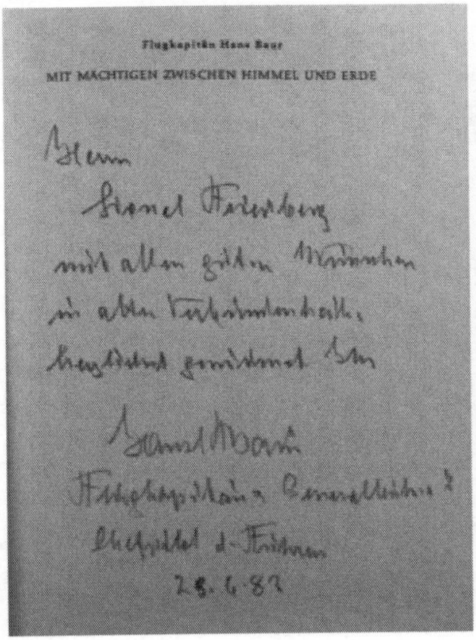

Flugkapitän Hans Baur

MIT MÄCHTIGEN ZWISCHEN HIMMEL UND ERDE

204

205

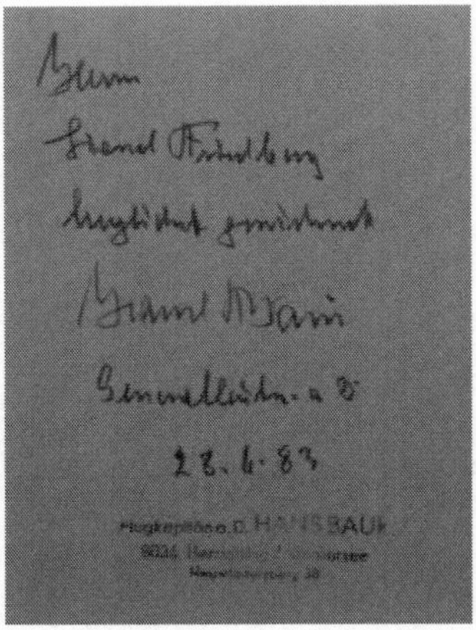

206

207

208

209

210

211

212

213

214

215

216

217

218

219

220

221

222

223

224

225

226

227

228

229

230

231

232

233

234

235

236

237

238

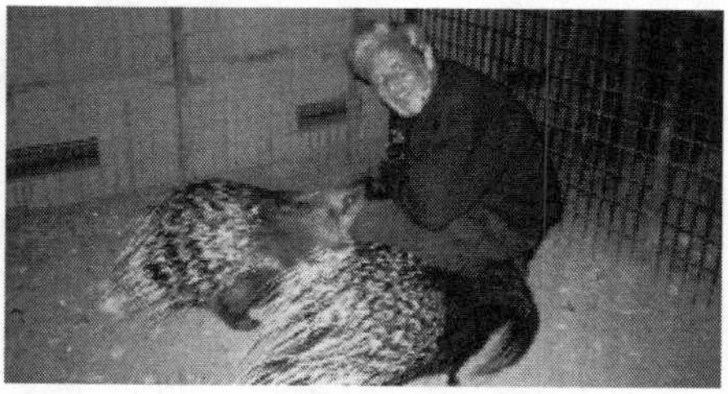

239

240

241

242

243

244

245

246

247

248

249

250

251

252

253

254

255

256

257

258

259

260

261

262

263

264

265

266

267

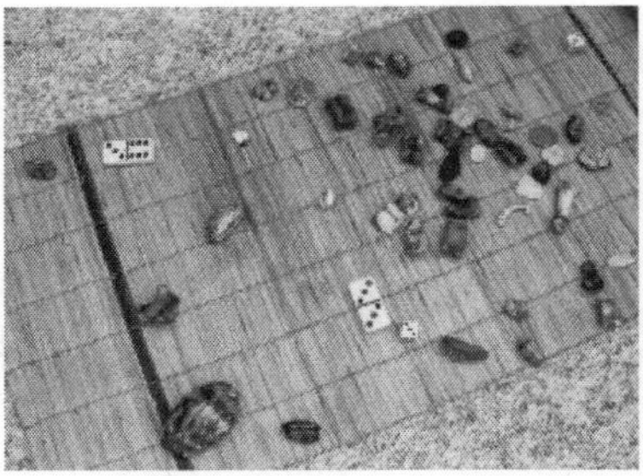

268

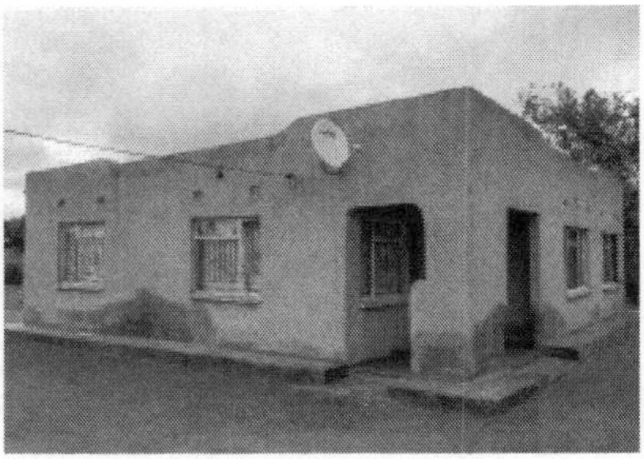

269

270

271

272

273

274

184 Filming Hindu fire-walking ceremony, Durban, Natal, South Africa, 1978. Sound recordist Bruce McFarlane with microphone.

185 Devout Hindu pierced with pins and needles. Amazingly, he suffered no bleeding, pain or discomfort due to the strength of his faith. Durban, Natal, 1978.

186 Going over lines with series presenter Dewar McCormack, host of *Then Came the English,* a major series on the history of British colonialism and the introduction of English as a major language and culture in Southern Africa, 1980.

187 Preparing to film an interview with Bishop (later Archbishop) Desmond Tutu, 1985.

188 His Grace, the Duke of Beaufort, Master of the Queen's Horse, at his family's estate, Badminton House, Gloucestershire, England. He is about to be interviewed for *Then Came the English,* 1980. His home has been the principal seat of the Dukes of Beaufort since the 17th century.

189 Lighting South African Member of Parliament Helen Suzman for the TV docudrama *Across the Rubicon,* 1985. She served as the most vociferous representative of the anti-apartheid movement for nearly 40 years. At the height of the apartheid era she was the sole voice against racist legislation in the whites-only Afrikaner-dominated parliament.

190 Lighting anti-apartheid activist and author Alan Paton in 1981 for an interview for *Then Came the English.* He wrote the iconic anti-apartheid novel *Cry, the Beloved Country* in 1948.

191 Lighting Chief Minister Cedric Phatudi of the pseudo-independent 'homeland' or *Bantustan* Lebowa with anthropologist Dr. Peter Becker for *The Tribal Identity* in Seshego, South Africa, 1975.

192 British journalist, satirist, broadcaster and spy, Malcolm Muggeridge, Robertsbridge, UK, 1980.

193 96-year-old Lt. Col. Eric Liddell, OBE, British soldier and survivor of the Anglo-Boer War in South Africa. At his home in London, 1980.

194 97-year-old Archibald Bowers, British soldier and survivor of the Anglo-Boer War in South Africa. At home in Kent, UK, 1980. It was his duty to take care of his regiment's horses.

195 Memorial to the half-million war horses who died serving British and Boer

forces during the Anglo-Boer War in South Africa between 1899 and 1902. Port Elizabeth, South Africa.

196 Inscription on the war horse memorial.

197 – 199 Filming at Boeing Commercial Airplane plant in Seattle during construction of new fleet of Boeing 747-300 jetliners for *Springbok in the Sky*, documentary series about the history of South African Airways, 1982.

200 Interviewing Joe Sutter, legendary 'Father of the 747 Jumbo Jet' at the Boeing plant in Seattle, 1983.

201 With Boeing technicians and South African Airways crew during delivery flight of the last of a batch of new Boeing 737-300 medium-range airliners en route from the Boeing factory in Seattle to South African Airways' base in Johannesburg. Photographed during a two-day technical stopover at Las Palmas, Canary Islands, 1983.

202 Interviewing Adolf Hitler's personal pilot, Flugkapitan Generalleutnant Hans Baur, at his home in Herrsching am Ammersee, Bavaria, Germany, 1983. Incredibly, the meeting was foreseen by female albino *nganga* in Ndola, Zambia, Africa twenty years before the event took place.

203 – 204 Hans Baur's autobiography (translation: *With Might Between Heaven and Earth*) presented and inscribed to me after filming his interview in Bavaria, Germany, 1983.

205 Photograph of Adolf Hitler and his personal pilot Flugkapitan Generalleutnant Hans Baur taken during World War Two. Presented to me by Baur after interviewing him on film at his home in Bavaria, 1983.

206 Inscription and autograph from Hans Baur to me, 1983

207 Shot taken by me during filming of the construction of the ill-fated World Trade Center Towers from a helicopter, New York City, 1971

208 Filming with documentary crew at World Trade Center Towers, New York City, 1983

209 Filming supersonic jetliner, Concorde, with documentary crew at Kennedy Airport, New York, 1983

210 Filming from the top of the Empire State Building, New York City, 1983

211 Filming in San Diego with world-renowned paleontologist and dinosaur expert Dr. Robert Bakker for *The Great Dinosaur Hunt* for PBS television, 1988. The documentary won the Washington DC-based American

Association for the Advancement of *Science's Westinghouse Award for Best Science Program on National Television.*

212 With Academy Award-winning actor Charlton Heston during filming of *The DeMille Family Dynasty* for American Movie Classics (AMC) cable TV channel, Hollywood, 1997.

213 Asteroid and comet hunter Carolyn Shoemaker and her husband planetary scientist and geologist Dr. Eugene Shoemaker searching for asteroids at Mount Palomar Observatory, California, 1990.

214 Directing planetary scientist and geologist Dr. Eugene Shoemaker at Meteor Crater, Arizona for the PBS documentary, *Sail On, Voyager!* for the science series, *The Infinite Voyage*, 1990. Sound recordist Ken King on left, cameraman Peter Pilafian on right. Shoemaker had trained astronauts how to search for intriguing lunar rock samples during NASA's *Apollo* program during the sixties.

215 With astronomer Carl Sagan, filming *Sail On, Voyager!*, 1990.

216 Filming *Sail On, Voyager!* at Hemet-Ryan Airport, Hemet, California, 1990. Standing from left, Assistant Cameraman Murray Van Dyke, Sound Recordist Ken King, Director Lionel Friedberg, NASA/JPL Engineer Harris 'Bud' Schurmeier, Production Assistant and Researcher Peter Koeppen, Associate Producer Jolie Ancel, Technical Assistant Art Martin. Squatting, foreground, Cameraman Kevin McKnight. In addition to being a brilliant engineer who designed the two famed *Voyager* spacecraft that visited Jupiter, Saturn, Uranus and Neptune and that have now left the Solar System en route to the stars and the most distant regions of the Milky Way galaxy Bud Schurmeier was also an excellent glider pilot. We introduced him in the movie in a sequence depicting him flying his glider in the thermals above Southern California.

217 Filming with Ray Heacock, the engineer in charge of the team that built the *Voyager* interplanetary spacecraft at the Jet Propulsion Laboratory (JPL) in Pasadena, California for NASA. Full-scale mock-up of *Voyager* in the background.

218 With film crew and Ray Heacock at full-scale replica of Voyager at JPL, Pasadena, California, 1990.

219 Filming with Dr. Edward C. Stone, Director of the Jet Propulsion Laboratory

(JPL) and Project Scientist for NASA's *Voyager* interplanetary mission. Model of *Voyager* behind us. Director of Special Effects, John Allison, on extreme right. WQED Special Effects Studios, Glendale, California, 1990.

220 Working with Special Effects Director John Allison and JPL's Dr. Edward C. Stone in 1990 on construction of a three-dimensional model of the surface of Jupiter's moon Io. It was there in 1979 where the first evidence of volcanic activity on a celestial body beyond the Earth was found by the Voyager spacecraft.

221 Examining a model of the Voyager spacecraft for *Sail On, Voyager!* with Dr. Edward C. Stone at WQED Special Effects Studios, Glendale, California, 1990.

222 Filming the largest dish at the Goldstone Deep Space Communications Complex in the Mojave Desert, California, for *Sail On, Voyager!*, 1990. Dishes of the Deep Space Network (DSN) in the US, Spain and Australia have been communicating with the two Voyager spacecraft ever since they were launched from Cape Kennedy in 1977. The Voyagers are now the two most distant man-made objects from the Earth, having traveled in excess of 14 billion miles. They will reach Alpha Centauri, the nearest star in our galaxy, approximately 40,000 years from now, provided they are not intercepted by an alien intelligence.

223 With Neil Armstrong, the first human to set foot on the moon, during the shooting of a documentary on the history of flight. Mojave Airport, California, 1994.

224 In Antarctica for *Secrets from a Frozen World* for PBS, 1991. This incredible white wilderness was clearly foreseen by the *nganga* in Zambia decades earlier. All her predictions and visions came true.

225 "There is no color," the *nganga* had told me years ago. "There is white, only white… everywhere."

226 – 230 Filming in Antarctica for *Secrets from a Frozen World*, 1991.

231 Filming members of the United Nations and a delegation from the Antarctic Treaty organization visiting US scientific research base, Palmer Station, Antarctica, 1991.

232 On set for TV series *Harts of the West*, Hollywood, 1994.

233 Bringing home my Primetime Emmy Award for Cinematography for

Mysteries Underground (National Geographic/PBS), 1993.

234 – 245 Working on *Growing Up* series for Animal Planet, 2003–2005.

246 With wildlife conservationist, Rita Miljo, at Center for Animal Rehabilitation and Education, Phalaborwa, South Africa, 2004. Miljo made a unique contribution towards conservation by rescuing and rehabilitating baby baboons whose parents were killed because they are generally regarded as 'vermin' by local farmers.

247 Louise Joubert, Director of SanWild Wildlife Trust, Gravelotte, Limpopo Province, South Africa, 2004. Here she displays killing devices and wire snares found on the wildlife sanctuary's lands that were used by poachers. The destruction of Africa's wildlife is a pandemic problem of unimaginable proportions and requires immediate world attention and assistance.

248 Surrounded by clusters of 'ant hills' or ancient termite mounds at SanWild Sanctuary, Gravelotte, Limpopo Province, South Africa, 2004.

249 – 250 General surgeon and urological specialist Dr. David Cumes MD lives and works in two very different worlds—Western allopathic medicine and ancient forms of traditional African healing. Here he interprets patterns formed by his personal set of divination bones and other oracular objects in his *ndumba* hut at his home in Santa Barbara, California. After extensively studying traditional African tribal healing methods, herbal medicines and shamanic divination systems and then becoming ordained as a *sangoma* in Africa Cumes frequently consults the bones prior to or after surgery for his American hospital patients.

251 – 253 Comprising bones from various wild African animals such as lion, giraffe, wild pig, baboon, hyena, antelope, anteater and crocodile the divination set also includes seashells, pebbles, stones, seed pods, animal teeth, man-made metal amulets, coins, dice and other objects, each one having a specific meaning to the owner of the set. The way the objects fall in proximity to one another, their angle, the direction they face and whether they are 'right side up' or 'upside down' influences the reading or interpretation. By carefully analyzing the pattern of these objects a *sangoma* such as Dave Cumes can diagnose an illness, foretell events that will come to pass or gain insight into the prospects, aspirations, misfortunes, maladies or problems concerning a patient.

254 – 255 Typical collection of herbs, plants, instruments and accoutrements of a *sangoma*. These objects—primarily of African origin—are in the *ndumba* healing hut of Dr. David Cumes in Santa Barbara, California. Jars, tins, bottles and calabashes containing a variety of liquids, ointments and powders are scattered amidst rattles, drums and antelope horns for summoning ancestral spirits or for dissipating negative energies that may accompany a patient who has come for a consultation. These objects are used for analyzing illnesses, foretelling the future, connecting with departed loved ones, inspiring dreams or for cleansing dark forces. A *sangoma's* function embraces many regimens and operates on many levels, transcending the physical and the metaphysical. It bridges the worlds of the living and the dead. *Sangomas* in Africa have been practicing their craft since time immemorial. The work is as relevant today as it was in ancient times.

256 – 257 Dr. David Cumes with fellow white *thwasa* students—those undergoing training to become *sangomas*—at their 'teacher' P.H. Mntshauli's *kraal* in Swaziland (modern-day Eswatini), Southern Africa, 2000. Whether white or black, it takes many years for a *thwasa* student to become a fully ordained and practicing *sangoma*.

258 Swazi *sangoma* and traditional African healing teacher P.H. Mntshauli in his *ndumba* hut at his *kraal* near Manzini, Swaziland, 2000. He is surrounded by herbs, powders, liquids and potions that are used as *muti* or medicine for physical, spiritual and metaphysical healing.

259 Typical *sangoma* practice and traditional *muti* (medicine) store in a suburb of Johannesburg, South Africa, 2005.

260 *Sangoma* named 'Queen' with her divining bones set inside her place of practice and *muti* store, Johannesburg. She holds a wildebeest fly whisk for 'pointing out' the bones.

261 'Queen' the *sangoma*

262 Interior of a typical and traditional African *muti* (medicine) store in Newtown, Johannesburg, South Africa, 2005. Note racks of herbs, powders, canes, beads, animal skins, tail whisks and other *sangoma* items for sale. My friend, author Alexandra Levine (on right), a devout believer in traditional African healing systems, poses behind the counter with the

shop staff.

263 With *ngoma* Moses Shado Mahlabisane Dludlu—a practitioner even more powerfully attuned to the metaphysical and spirit realm than the average sangoma—in his *ndumba* healing hut in Barberton, Mpumalanga Province, South Africa, 2005. With him is a male *sangoma* assistant and a female *thwasa* student.

264 Having bones read for me by Moses Shado Mahlabisane Dludlu's male *sangoma* assistant in Barberton, Mpumalanga Province, South Africa, 2005.

265 Moses Shado Mahlabisane Dludlu comes to visit us at our home in Los Angeles, 2006.

266 Moses Shado Mahlabisane Dludlu casts his set of divination bones for me on the patio of our home in Los Angeles, 2006.

267 Moses Shado Mahlabisane Dludlu studies and interprets the bones for me in Los Angeles. It was during this reading that he decided I needed an immediate ritual to seek out and 'bring home' the spirits of my ancestors.

268 Detail of the way in which the bones had fallen.

269 The simple home of *sangoma,* medicine man and 'prophet' Johannes Mohlwane. Seshego, near Polokwane, South Africa.

270 My first visit to the *sangoma,* medicine man, healer and 'prophet' Johannes Mohlwane in 2007. On the left is my friend Peter Tsheola, tour guide and official from the South African Department of Environmental Affairs. Mr. Mohlwane is in the coat with one of his grandchildren. On the right is one of his assistants.

271 My last visit to Mr. Mohlwane in Seshego, Polokwane, South Africa in 2014. By then he had become extremely ill and totally blind. Although I had not been to see him for seven years he recalled our first meeting in intricate detail. Once again he prescribed *muti* (medicine) for me to take back to the United States for my own serious health issues. He 'blessed' and 'energized' the items after going into a trance state and babbling in an unknown language. He was an extraordinarily gentle, caring man and one I shall treasure knowing. He passed away not long after this meeting.

272 By 2014 South Africa had become a totally different country compared to the years of my childhood. This magnificent bronze statue of anti-apartheid activist, political leader and the country's first black President

Nelson Mandela by sculptors Andre Prinsloo and Ruhan Janse van Vuuren towers in the grounds of the Union Buildings, the nation's legislative capital, in Tshwane (Pretoria).

273 On a visit to the Apartheid Museum in Johannesburg to relive memories of a sadder, darker time in South Africa's history, 2004.

274 With a talented new breed of young South African filmmakers, Johannesburg, 2014. Sound recordist Wandile Mnguni, on left, and writer/director Sibusiso 'Sibs' Shongwe on right.

Seventeen

By 1999 I was slowly learning to live with my illness. My hair had turned grey due to the medications I was taking but, fortunately, the lingering nausea and tiredness were subsiding so I continued working. One of my next projects was a major science series for the National Geographic Society called *The Shape of Life*. It was about the evolution and development of the various phyla or 'body plans' that determined all the species that live on Earth today. For a year I was based at a studio in Cannery Row on Monterey Bay in Central California working with a team of film makers and experts from all over the world. It was a high-definition series designed to make biology and paleontology palatable to general audiences. The aim was to explain how and why organisms follow eight basic biological designs—or body plans—to create the enormous range of animal life on our planet, including ourselves. It was a challenging gig. The science was heavy-going. The research and learning phase was intensive. But as it all came together the visuals were spectacular.

We were working with some of the best natural history and computer graphics houses in the business. Viewers of the shows were able to travel through the amazing innards of a sponge, the basal animal to all creatures on Earth. We brought the mysterious 'Cambrian Explosion' to life. This was an event when unexpectedly, in what seems like a sudden flashpoint in time 540 million years ago, thousands of new organisms appeared as if out of nowhere in the planet's oceans. This little-understood phenomenon sparked the dawn of all animal life as we know it today. A particularly memorable sequence was the recreation of a weird creature called *Anomalocaris*, one of the Cambrian Period's most prevalent and fearsome predators. I seldom enjoyed a project as much as that. But I had a difficult time staying on top of my illness while I was in Monterey. At one stage it got so bad that I could not accompany the crew on a major shoot to Sulawesi in Indonesia. Once more my thoughts turned to how I might bring matters under control. I called up a friend in Santa Barbara, just north of LA. He was usually a good touchstone for me to run things by.

David Cumes is a special guy. And a very unusual one. We met in LA in 1986. He is a fellow South African, just three weeks older than me. He studied medicine at the University of the Witwatersrand in Johannesburg. In 1975 he emigrated to the United States to take up a urology residency at Stanford Medical Center. After teaching at Stanford and practicing as a urologist in Seattle he set up a private practice in Santa Barbara in 1981. Trained in classical medicine Dave's mindset and modus operandi were firmly rooted in traditional allopathic practices. Nothing could be further from his mind than the series of strange events that would eventually happen to him. After going through a deteriorating marriage that ended in divorce, Dave turned his attention to the great outdoors. He liked nothing more than hiking, camping and the joys of spending time in wilderness areas. Recognizing the power that nature has to heal he formed a company called Inward Bound and began taking small groups of people on what he called 'healing journeys' into remote wilderness areas. Trips to Peru exposed him to *curanderos* or traditional shamans who convinced him that despite his medical training there were many other methods of alternative healing being practiced by ethnic groups around the world. His curiosity piqued, on trips back to South Africa he began to visit *sangomas* to determine what sort of healing methods they were practicing. Consultations with them always involved the throwing of bones and, to Dave's surprise, the *sangomas* began telling him things like, "The bones say you should be doing work like ours. The bones are calling you. They say you are a doctor but you should be doing African medicine. Your grandmother is telling you to be initiated in African healing. Your ancestors want you to learn the healing ways of the continent of your birth."

Time after time, from one *sangoma* after the other, the messages kept coming. But Dave's left-brained outlook on the world kept convincing him that those messages were misleading, that there was no way he could possibly become a practitioner of African medicine. And that's when the headaches began. Even the most potent anti-migraine medications would not alleviate them. After consulting a renowned and especially powerful *sangoma* in the sprawling apartheid era-built black township of Soweto outside Johannesburg he was told that unless he listened to the messages of the bones and began training as a *sangoma* his headaches would not go away. In fact, they would get worse. The headaches, he was told, were due to 'ancestor sickness.' They were being caused by ancestral spirits and other entities calling for his attention. Amazingly, as soon as he left South Africa to return to the United States the headaches stopped. But the minute he set foot on African soil on his next trip a few months later they returned. Visits to *sangomas* revealed that they would not stop until he was initiated as a *sangoma* himself. He decided to look more deeply into the matter.

"Learn the healing ways of Africa," he was told. "Heed the call of the spirit world."

Dave now felt he had little option. He decided to seek out a teacher. One of the names that often came up as he made enquiries was that of an elderly Zulu *sangoma* by the name of P.H. Mntshauli who lived and practiced in a settlement outside Manzini in the neighboring country of Swaziland (modern-day eSwatini). Undaunted but not quite sure where his search would take him Dave rented a car, crossed the border into Swaziland and set out to find 'P.H.' When he finally located him P.H. said that he had been expecting the visit. And so, Dave's *thwasa* or education period in the ways of the *sangoma* began. But the process would take years. Without giving up his urology and surgery practice in California he returned to Africa two or three times a year to spend a few weeks or even a month with P.H. to absorb what had to be learned at the foot of the master.

It was about this time in his *thwasa* studies that I contacted him to discuss my illness. As always he was sympathetic and understanding but he told me that the doctors I was seeing at Cedars-Sinai Medical Center in LA had an unquestionable reputation and were among the best in the world. I could not be in better hands. I knew that Dave was undergoing training as a *sangoma,* and he went on to say that he would be returning to South Africa in a few months to take a small group of Americans into wilderness areas there for an Inward Bound experience. But prior to that he would be spending a couple of weeks with his teacher in Swaziland. The idea of spending time in the African bush suddenly seemed extremely attractive to me.

"Wow, wish I could go with you," I said.

"Well," he responded, "why don't you?"

I couldn't see my way clear to go, especially with my health issues so I made a couple of excuses. But Dave was adamant.

"Tell you what," he said. "Why don't you come out to Africa with me, make a movie for me about my studies with P.H. and about the *thwasa* process and then you can join me for the group tour. I plan to take the folks to meet a number of *sangomas* as part of their African wilderness experience. Perhaps the *sangomas* and herbalists can help you with your glomerulonephritis. Who knows? And what's to lose?"

It didn't take me long to agree to the proposal.

And so began one of the most remarkable experiences of my life.

The year was 2000. I had not been back to Africa since I emigrated to the United States with my family in 1986. The changes that had taken place there since my departure exceeded all expectations. Apartheid was gone. A black government was in power. Economic development following the restoration of normal diplomatic relations with the rest of the world were phenomenal. Foreign investment was at an all-time high. Johannesburg had grown in every direction of the compass. I hardly recognized the place. It was difficult to navigate the plethora of new roadways, freeways and suburbs that had sprung up. People were smiling. They were happy. There was a lilt to everyone's walk, especially among the crowds of black shoppers thronging the sidewalks and shopping malls. A new black middle class had developed where none had existed before. It was amazing.

The first thing Dave and I did when we arrived in Johannesburg was to rent a car and visit a female *sangoma* by the name of Nomsa Lizzie Dlamini in Soweto on the city's outskirts. Dave had consulted her a year or so previously and wanted to find out whether his *thwasa* studies were going according to plan. We met Nomsa at her small, impeccably maintained home on a side street in Orlando West, part of the greater Soweto area. A very congenial woman probably in her early forties she wore Western-style clothing but she was draped in beads and cloths of various colors and patterns. These were the standard accoutrements of most urban female *sangomas*. They provided spiritual protection and fostered psychic and metaphysical powers. We removed our shoes, sat down on the concrete floor of the main room of her home. Nomsa lit a couple of candles and threw the bones. She reminded Dave that during his previous consultation with her she had told him that his ancestors were anxious for him to start training in the ways of the *sangoma*. Now that he had agreed to that, had found his teacher and was continuing to engage in all the daily rituals associated with his *thwasa* regimen the ancestors were happy. They approved of his progress. She predicted that he would one day make a very fine *sangoma* indeed and that he would bring the wisdom of ancient Africa to the New World. I filmed the bone reading for the documentary and we left in high spirits.

The next day we met a *sangoma* friend of Dave's by the name of Moses Shado Mahlabisane Dludlu. He was an extremely articulate, tall, handsome man in his mid-thirties. His very demeanor exuded strength, confidence, virility. A Zulu by birth he was a social anthropology honors degree graduate from the University of the Witwatersrand. He had not completed his PhD as he too was 'called by his ancestors' to practice traditional healing. In fact, his expertise was such that he had gone beyond the capabilities of a *sangoma*. He referred to himself as a *ngoma*, a healer even more deeply attuned to the restorative powers of nature. Chatting to Shado about the role of traditional healers and diviners in contemporary South Africa was fascinating. Opportunities for them had certainly changed since I made *The Tribal Identity* three decades earlier. Shado made his home in Barberton, about 200 miles to the east of Johannesburg, but business and professional reasons often brought him to the city. We filmed an interview with him at the University of the Witwatersrand about the importance of the *sangoma* in the 'new' South Africa and then set off by road for Barberton. The plan was to spend a couple of days with him before traveling to meet with Dave's teacher P.H. in Swaziland. The drive through the province of Mpumalanga was spectacular. As we traversed forests and rivers and made our way through magnificent mountain passes I realized how much I had missed the sheer magic of this enticing landscape. That little ceremony of burying something personal in the soil on the outskirts of Ndola that I had undertaken years ago on the instructions of the albino *nganga* in Zambia had worked its magic. The essence of Africa still ran deeply within my veins. It had defined me. It had helped make me who I was. What made the drive all the more exciting that day was the fact that I was traveling in a vehicle with two *sangomas*, one white and one black. Granted, Dave still had a long way to go before he was officially ordained as a full-fledged healer in the African tradition, but these two guys were following the same path, an unbroken one that led from the ways of ancient Africa into the modern world. It was exhilarating.

The moment we arrived at Shado's humble cluster of huts in a township outside Barberton we were descended upon by neighbors and friends. A few were either *sangomas* themselves or studying to become one. Clearly, traditional African medicine had taken on big time. It was no longer spoken of in secret or rendered to the shadows as it had been during the days of apartheid. It was in the open now. And it was being embraced in both urban and rural environments. People kept arriving all afternoon. As they knew Dave was coming to visit many of them bore gifts: bottles of beer, cans of soda, home-brewed sorghum beer in a variety of different containers, fruit, loaves of bread, sacks of potatoes, bags of white flour, cuts of meat in metal plates and basins that were covered in plastic wrap. Clearly, a feast was planned for that night.

By nightfall Shado's healing hut, his *ndumba*—where he stowed his divining bones, cloths, herbs and medicines—was filled to capacity with guests. Intended to accommodate no more than a dozen people it was now bursting with at least three times that many. It was early spring. The month was October. The weather was pleasant but the interior of the hut was stiflingly hot. A couple of Shado's assistants and *thwasa* students started a fire outside beneath barbecue grills onto which fresh husks of corn had been stacked. There is nothing more delicious than corn on the cob roasted over an open fire. When those were cooked they were piled into metal basins and taken into the hut for distribution among the crowd. Next came a number of large three-legged iron cooking pots in which the staple maize meal porridge known as *putu* or *pap* was prepared over the fire. When this was ready T-bone steaks, lamb chops, goat meat and sausages were laid out on the grill and roasted.

Inside the *ndumba* the party was in full swing. Groups of women were clustered against the walls, some of them carrying infants. But the little ones were invariably fast asleep and completely impervious to the heat, the cramped space and the noise. Most of the women held a portable hand drum. These were carved out of lightweight wood about ten or twelve inches in diameter and about two to three inches deep. They were open at one end and covered by synthetic material or goatskin tightly stretched over the other end. When beaten they emitted a loud, high-pitched sound that bounced off the rafters. People were trilling and swaying vigorously from side to side as they beat the instruments, all in perfect unison. This created an infectious sense of rhythm among the crowd. Everyone—men, boys, girls, children—sang or clapped loudly. It was wonderful. Food and drink were constantly being passed around, and by about 10pm the place felt like one big raving buzz.

By midnight some of the women and younger folk began disappearing into the darkness outside and it was then that joints of potent *dagga* (marijuana) began being passed around. Fortified by the beer and alcohol the effects of the weed created a spirit of unbridled *joie de vivre,* the likes of which I had seldom seen. Through a smoky haze I caught occasional glimpses of Dave and Shado among the crowd. Dave did not partake of the weed but both of them were engaged in feverish conversation or laughing. He also spoke no vernacular languages but somehow or another he was managing to talk with the partygoers, even though not everyone there could speak English. The evening had turned into a marvelously rambunctious affair but at no time did it get rowdy or out of hand. At about two in the morning things began winding down. Many people had had too much to drink to walk home so Dave volunteered to drive them to their respective huts in the township in our rental car. The vehicle quickly filled up, bursting with at least twice as many passengers than it was designed to hold. The last half dozen to hitch a ride could not be accommodated within it so they climbed onto the roof or clambered onto the front and rear fenders, clinging on to whatever they could as the car slowly lurched down the unpaved road into the night, everyone singing at the tops of their voices. Shado, his assistants and I cleared away most of the party things, and when Dave returned an hour later we tossed sleeping bags onto the floor of the *ndumba*. Shado wrapped himself up in a few bright cloths, huddled up in a corner, and Dave and I curled up in our sleeping bags and slept the sleep of the dead.

Next morning we awoke a couple of hours after sunrise. A goat bleated somewhere outside. In the distance roosters were crowing. Smoke drifted from doorways and chimneys of neighboring huts. Children were laughing down the road. We stumbled outside, washed ourselves at the outdoor water pump in Shado's yard and then brewed some coffee. Amazingly, none of us were in the least bit hung over. Shado had planned to take Dave and I to a river on the outskirts of town as he wanted Dave to experience something essential to his progress as a *thwasa*. But before we set out for that he threw the bones for Dave in the *ndumba* and did a reading to ensure that all would be well for what was to come. When the session was over he invited me to sit down for a reading too. Neither Dave nor I had mentioned it to him but the very first thing that came up in the pattern in which the bones had fallen were my health issues. After studying the bones Shado took a deep breath, leaned back and looked at me.

"I'm sorry, my friend," he said. "I see that you are not well."

He went on to say that I was suffering from something affecting my blood and two of my vital organs. He was right, of course. The immune system resides in the blood and it was both my kidneys that were ailing.

"I think you need help," Shado said. "This condition of yours is serious. At some point you need to get strong *muti* for it."

Later that morning we arrived at a lovely stream on the outskirts of town. It was surrounded by weeping willows. The water was crystal clear and looked very inviting in the cool shade. Birds called from above and a couple of butterflies darted just above the surface. Shado had stripped down and put on his traditional *sangoma* loincloth and beads. He perched down in the reeds on the bank of the stream. Inviting Dave and I to sit close by he explained that one of the essential steps in the educational process of a *thwasa* is to confront what is known as the *nzunzu*, a mysterious water spirit that lurks within rivers, streams and lakes throughout Africa. As he talked I immediately thought of the legendary *Nyaminyami* that is said to live in the waters of the Zambezi river that divides Zimbabwe from Zambia. I also thought of the ageless water spirit that was said to exist at the bottom of Lake Fundudzi in Venda, the one that anthropologist Peter Becker, my film crew and I offended when we burst into laughter during the sacred ceremony that we had filmed there in the mid-seventies. Shado explained that one day Dave would have to confront the *nzunzu* as part of his *thwasa* education. This particular morning, however, he should enter the water to sense the existence of an equally important but far less powerful water spirit than the one he would eventually have to meet before he could become a recognized *sangoma*. He clapped his hands and chanted a Zulu intonation to the water. Then, switching to English, he said, "Please help my friend Dr. Cumes with his *thwasa* studies. Help him to become the *sangoma* and healer that he is capable of being. *Thokoza*."

The Zulu word *'thokoza'* means rejoice or be happy. Shado often used it after a bone reading or ceremony to thank his ancestors for their assistance. Then Shado looked at me, clapped his hands twice to summon the ancestors again and said: "And here is my friend Lionel. Please help him too. May his ancestors come to his side and protect him. His illness is debilitating him and he needs healing. *Thokoza*."

I was deeply moved by this request. For Shado to be invoking something so profound without being asked to do so by either Dave or me was a clear indication that his heart was in the right place, that he sought nothing to gain for himself from any potential healing I might receive. A feeling of goodwill and positivity spiraled up within me. I turned to the water, clapped my hands twice and softly uttered, "*Thokoza*."

Shado then instructed Dave to enter the water. He stripped down to his briefs and slipped into the pool. Shado and I watched as he immersed himself completely, spending up to twenty seconds at a time underwater and swimming from one bank to the other. When he finally emerged he looked as though he had had some kind of revelation or encounter within the watery depths. We felt it unnecessary to question him. Something had happened down there. Words were pointless and we drove back to Shado's place in silence.

The next morning Shado fired up a faded old beige-colored Volkswagen minivan that was parked behind one of his huts. It coughed and sputtered before the engine settled down into a rattle. Dave and I followed in our rental car as he led us to an old trading store just outside the township. This was owned by an Indian family and it seemed as though everyone—grandpa, grandma, ma, pop, kids, cousins, aunts, everyone—worked in the store. Inside was a wild variety of everyday essentials from zinc bathtubs to blankets, mattresses, candles, kerosene lamps, sacks of sugar, bags of flour, tobacco, canned goods, paraffin, soap, rice, flashlights, batteries and spare bicycle parts. Hanging from the shadowy rafters above this vast display of merchandise were dozens of different cloths in an amazing assortment of styles and colors. About five feet long and two or three feet wide some of them were in plain colors but many sported prints of bright patterns or images. These included the new South African coat of arms and flag, portraits of Nelson Mandela, prominent members of the ruling African National Congress, historic tribal chiefs, Zulu kings, crocodiles, snakes, lions, elephants, *assegais* and shields. They were used by women as wraps, for turban-like head dressings or for tying babies onto backs and very often as loincloths for men. The purpose of our visit to the store was to procure some of the cloths. Dave already had a selection of them for draping around his body or hanging around his neck when he performed his *sangoma* rituals, but he wanted to add a few more to his selection for use back in California. Shado had recommended I get some cloths too. He said I should use them draped over my shoulders during meditation or whenever I felt that I needed metaphysical protection. A half-hour later Dave had bought a couple of plain white and red ones while I had selected a dozen depicting wildlife, historic African personalities and traditional tribal patterns. I felt very pleased with myself as I stuffed them into my travel bag. I was determined to use them during my twice-daily meditation sessions. Then it was time to say goodbye to Shado, and Dave and I headed for P.H.'s *kraal* some 75 miles away.

After crossing the border between South Africa and Swaziland we continued on the busy main highway towards Manzini. An hour later we turned off onto a dirt road, bumped along for about twenty or thirty minutes, segued onto a potholed track and eventually reached a gate. We stopped, honked the horn and a wiry grey-haired old man about five feet tall emerged from a distant cluster of huts. It was P.H. Once he had opened the gate he and Dave embraced warmly. The student from faraway California had come back to his teacher. We parked the car, unloaded our bags and settled ourselves in a spartan room in P.H.'s compound. It had a small window but no beds or any furnishing. Dave claimed his side of the room, laid out his sleeping bag and I took my side. We would be here for about ten days before traveling northwards to meet up with the Inward Bound tour group from the States.

When P.H. wasn't in his *ndumba* practicing his craft, dispensing *muti* or monitoring Dave in his *thwasa* studies he went about casually dressed in an old pair of slacks. He was always barefoot, often wore a thick patched-up old grey sweater that seemed far too hot for the climate and on his head he wore a tubular black leather headband, similar to those worn by traditional leaders of

King Shaka's military regiments in times gone by. When he was in his *ndumba* throwing bones or teaching Dave how to interpret them he wore his traditional *sangoma* outfit of loincloths or animal skins and beads. He had a snow white beard with sideburns and his face was lined with wrinkles. These became accentuated every time he smiled, which was often. It was hard to gauge his age but he was probably somewhere in his late sixties or early seventies. His teeth were the whitest and most perfect I had ever seen in a man of his years. His eyes sparkled every time he held you in his gaze. He spoke an excellent English and was the quintessential wise old teacher at whose feet any student would have been only too happy to sit. His *kraal* and compound were large. His rotund wife Miriam sometimes assisted him in his work by gathering herbs, barks and leaves in the surrounding countryside for preparation as *muti*. She also helped to make fires for boiling water for his small sweat lodge and even occasionally saw patients herself. He had two teenage sons, Ndoda and Nduna. They took care of the compound and the animals. There were cows, goats and chickens and, wandering among the huts, a couple of cats and two or three rather forlorn, hungry-looking but friendly medium-size mixed-breed black dogs. Surrounding the huts were open fields, some of which had been planted with corn, others with potatoes, pumpkins and spinach. The nights were as quiet as can be, with only the odd hooting of an owl to break the silence. All in all, it was a sublimely peaceful place. Throughout our stay I slept like a log in my sleeping bag on that hard, unforgiving floor. Dreams were vivid and intense.

Dave's *thwasa* studies included a number of daily routines. These included bouts of drumming and practice sessions with P.H. in the *ndumba* during which he was tested on the interpretation of the bones. Very importantly, twice a day he had to add water to a small black clay pot containing a mixture of herbs and other mysterious ingredients, stir it and then briskly beat it with a straw-like stick to create a foam. Using his fingers he had to daub some of the foam on his forehead, chest and in-between the shoulder blades. The strange concoction was intended to provide 'food' for his ancestral spirits or for any other *amandawus* or benevolent spiritual entities who were working on the metaphysical plane to help him become a *sangoma*. After applying the foam to his body he had to slurp from the edge of the clay pot, drinking as much of the remaining foam as he could. What was left was smeared on his face. The whole process had to take place while he was kneeling on a goatskin mat. When he practiced this ritual in the morning he had to face the east and in the evening to the west. Rites and rituals filled the day, but there was always time to walk, to explore the surroundings, to sit in the shade and chat.

Two other white *thwasa* students were also staying at P.H.'s *kraal* while we were there. Both were undergoing training with P.H. They were from South Africa and I shall refer to them only as Kobus, a twenty-something-year-old Afrikaans guy from Johannesburg, and Isolde, an effervescent and pretty late-thirties-year-old woman from Durban in the province of Kwa Zulu-Natal. I was glad she was there because she, like me, was vegetarian. We cooked and shared our evening meals together. On the first day P.H. offered to read the bones for me. It was during the late afternoon as a gentle breeze blew in from the west, cooling everything after another day of scorching heat. Dave sat by my side in the *ndumba* as P.H. passed me his antelope hide bag containing the divination bones and other items, had me drop a pinch of snuff into the bag as an offering to the ancestors, then asked me to state my name and blow into it. After I did that I turned the bag upside down and spilt its contents onto the grass mat on the floor in front of P.H. He sat there stern and cross-legged as he stared at the items lying on the mat. Dave leaned in to listen as P.H. began interpreting what he saw. Using a stick to point at the bones and other items with one hand while fingering the string of cowry shells draped around his neck with the other, P.H. deciphered the objects as though he were reading an exact account of the last few years of my life.

He told me that I was indeed a very sick man. Without divine help I might easily succumb to my illness. I had "bad blood." Organs located on either side of my mid-torso region were being severely impacted by the "badness in the blood." He could help me. He had special *muti* for me. Treatment would start the very next day. But I needed a really strong cleansing procedure in addition to what he could offer. I needed to have a "*femba*."

"A what?" I asked as Dave looked at me with concern and pity written all over his face when he heard the word. He knew what it was.

"*Femba*," P.H. repeated. "It's like an exorcism."

My heart skipped a beat. I thought of the actress Linda Blair playing the young girl Regan in William Friedkin's terrifying 1973 film *The Exorcist* and the horrifying experience the character underwent as her body was taken over by a demon. But in his explicit and articulate way P.H. explained that exorcism may not be the right description for what I needed. It was not that I had to purge myself of malevolent spirits who had taken possession of me but that I needed help to rid myself of the negative energies that were interfering with my psyche. This was what was causing the illness. However, no matter what I was told, I was very reticent to undergo the procedure. In fact, I was downright scared. After lengthy discussion it was explained that the *femba* ritual was too specialized, too exacting for P.H. to perform it himself. There was another man, a very powerful *sangoma*, who would do it. Finally we agreed that P.H., Dave and I would go into Manzini two days later to meet that man and arrange the place, date and time for the *femba*.

I did not sleep that night. There was a constant knot in my stomach. Was this all nonsense? Was it mumbo-jumbo lunacy or what? Dave assured me that I should take it very seriously. I kept thinking back to the old albino *nganga* in Ndola many years earlier and her prediction that I would one day face a very serious health condition. I thought also of the *sangomas* I had encountered with anthropologist Peter Becker during the making of *The Tribal Identity* TV documentary series in the seventies. I had had more than enough evidence to prove that the mysterious ways of the African traditional healer were based on principles way beyond my understanding but which were all rooted in something very real, very tangible. I had only to remain patient and open-minded.

Next morning just as I awakened P.H. called out my name from outside. I got dressed, put on a pair of sandals and went over to his *ndumba*. It was going to be another scorching day. With folded arms P.H. was patiently leaning against the doorway waiting for me. As soon as he saw me he shook his head and barked, "Get rid of those silly shoes, man. Walk barefoot. Feel the Earth beneath your feet. Expose yourself to nature. Connect with the Earth's energy. Never put barriers between yourself and the healing forces of the natural world."

I wasn't going to argue and did as he commanded. Wincing as my feet encountered pebbles and stones I followed P.H. into his *ndumba*. He told me to sit down and listen carefully.

"Your treatment starts today," he said. "What you will do is the preparatory phase for the *femba*. You must do this willingly and do exactly as I say. Do you understand?"

I nodded. He handed me a rolled up length of faded crimson-colored rubber tubing. It was about a half-inch in diameter and four or five feet long. Then he gave me a dirty-looking plastic nozzle that he said should be connected to one end of the tube. Handing me another plastic connection he said that it should be attached to the other end of the tube. Then he passed me an old metal bucket that had a handle on top and a spout soldered to the bottom. It looked as though it had been rigged together from an old metal paint can as I could discern some faded artwork or writing still visible on the outside.

"You connect the tube to this bucket," he instructed.

After setting down a large brown jug containing a smelly, murky brown liquid at my feet he said that I was to pour its contents into the bucket.

"There is too much for only one use," he said. "It will take about three pours for you to use it all up."

I was beginning to get the chills as I began to realize what all this was about and sheepishly asked, "And where does the nozzle go?"

P.H. smiled and handed me a half-full jar of Vaseline petroleum jelly.

"Where do you think? Into your backside, of course," he said. "Go to the bathroom and undress. Make sure you are properly greased up. After the first application of the *muti* you hold it in. Wait for half an hour. Then evacuate. Pass as much as you can. After that reinsert the pipe. You can go outside if you like but you must keep the pipe inside you. You can walk around but you must use the *muti* until all of it has been absorbed. And do not eat or drink anything until tonight."

And that was it. I had my instructions. This was going to be the mother of all enemas.

Before starting the ritual P.H. told me that the liquid he had given me was a special mixture of herbs to cleanse my internal organs, especially the ones that had the 'bad energy' in them. It would help to get rid of negativity and to fortify them. Clearly, from his reading of the bones he had honed right in on my failing kidneys. It took a couple of trips for me to carry all the paraphernalia to the communal bathroom. But a couple of hours later I had administered most of the pungent brown liquid into my rear end. To achieve that I first had to fill the bucket with the *muti*. In the absence of a faucet or tap on the bucket I had to pinch the rubber piping with the fingers of one hand, then hang the bucket on the shower outlet above the bathtub, crouch down in the tub with my bare butt in the air, insert the nozzle and let go of the pipe. Within minutes the bucket's contents drained into my innards. I felt like I was going to burst. The sludge within me quickly did its job. I held it in for as long as I could. And then just as it seemed that I was about to explode I leaped out of the bathtub and planted myself on the toilet for the inevitable to happen. As instructed, I repeated the process. An hour later I desperately needed some fresh air. When I felt that I could not possibly evacuate anything more from my colon I administered the last few dregs from the jug. Naked as the day that I was born I kept the rubber piping plugged into my butt and then wrapped a towel around my waist. Then I unhooked the bucket from the shower outlet, held it above my head and stumbled out into the sunlight. Only to be greeted by the stares and mortified reactions of Dave, Kobus, Isolde and P.H.'s wife and kids. Gasps and giggles erupted into laughter. But I cared not one iota what anybody thought. I was going to remain outside with that pipe inside me until I absolutely had to make a dash back inside to the toilet again.

Later that afternoon after a shower I collapsed onto my sleeping bag and slept soundly until sunset. When we all met for dinner that evening there were amused looks all around the room. P.H. was the only one to retain a serious composure and wanted to know how I felt. I had to admit that I felt strangely cleansed from within. I sensed that something truly cathartic had happened. P.H. nodded. Yes, that was good. He declared that the first phase of my treatment was over. Amazingly, that night I slept until dawn without the need to go to the bathroom at all. For the past few years I had been getting up at least four or five times a night to relieve my bladder because of the heavy doses of diuretics that I had been taking. There was a burning sensation in my bladder and my kidneys throbbed. I would be lying if I said it wasn't painful but something strangely positive was definitely going on inside me. I wondered how the kidneys and bladder were being affected by what I had siphoned into my butt but I wasn't going to question anything.

Two days after the enema Dave, Kobus and I drove into town in Kobus' Land Rover. We were going to buy supplies and to meet the man who would be performing my *femba*. I wandered into the general trading store to browse around and pick up some items that would satisfy Isolde's and my vegetarian dietary needs. While examining the shelves and vegetable section I noticed P.H. and Dave chatting to a short, thin black man in a drab brown suit and red tie on the sidewalk outside. Carrying my purchases with me I wandered outside to join them. P.H. introduced the man to me as Mr. Mazia. I was very surprised to note that his attitude towards Dave, Kobus and I was similar to the way a black servant used to act in the presence of a white employer during the days of apartheid in South Africa. He seemed unduly respectful, even meek and shy. He spoke in very low tones, barely above a whisper. He also found it difficult to make eye account. He preferred to gaze at the ground instead of looking directly at you. Black servants and employees were once expected to do that out of respect for their white superiors. This struck me as extremely odd. Swaziland had never been subservient to the laws of apartheid and had been independent from British rule for decades.

I leaned over to Dave and whispered, "Who is he exactly? Do you know him?"

"I met him here when I started my *thwasa* education," Dave whispered back. "Don't be deluded. He is a very powerful healer. He is the one who will perform the *femba* on you. He did mine."

I couldn't believe it. I was expecting that the person who would do the ritual that I was dreading would be strong and assertive, perhaps even overbearing. But this guy? He seemed like such an unlikely candidate. Nevertheless, P.H. arranged that my *femba* would take place in two days' time at Mazia's own *kraal* in the mountains far to the east. A price was set for the procedure, I handed Mazia the money and we shook hands.

His handshake was very limp, making me doubt his capabilities even more.

That night at P.H.'s *kraal* Isolde and I noticed that one of the small black mongrels that lived on the property was whining pitifully. On examining her we were shocked to see that half of her uterus was hanging outside her body. We called Dave over and after careful scrutiny he pronounced that she was suffering from advanced vulval cancer. The poor creature was in agony. We debated what to do about it. Dave was a urologist and general surgeon. Isolde had extensive veterinary experience. Both agreed that the most humane solution would be to put her down. We found P.H. and informed him about the situation. Amazingly, he did not seem as concerned as I expected him to be. Sadly, this was something I found time and again in many rural and tribal societies. There just did not seem to be an abundance of empathy or compassion for the suffering of animals. When he was told that we thought it best to euthanize the dog P.H. merely shrugged it off and walked away saying, "If that's what you think is best."

While Dave went to fetch his medical bag Kobus, Isolde, P.H.'s son Ndoda and I subdued the dog and held her down. She showed little resistance and seemed to know that we were trying to help her. When Dave arrived he filled a syringe with a mixture of morphine, valium and *Phenergan* (promethazine hydrochloride). As we held the poor creature down he deftly injected the needle directly into her heart and emptied the syringe. There was just a quiet whimper from the dog. The cocktail should have stopped her heart immediately. But the hapless animal continued to breathe and tried to get up. We were all horrified. Refilling the syringe Dave injected her again. But death did not come. None of us had ever seen anything like it. By now Isolde and I were both sobbing but still we held the little animal down. Time passed interminably but that incredible dog desperately held on to life. A third attempt slowed her breathing but by then Dave and Kobus had little option and suffocated her. When her body finally went limp Ndoda picked her up and we asked him to please dig a grave in the field for her. That night neither Dave nor I could sleep. It had been an extremely upsetting experience for everyone. The next morning Dave and Kobus buried the little animal in the grave. Dave then washed himself off with a garden hose. We were grateful that the traumatic experience was behind us. But in actual fact it was far from over. We had not heard the last of that pitiful little creature as we would later discover.

On the appointed day of my *femba* Dave, Kobus, Isolde and I bounced and bone-rattled in Kobus' Land Rover as he drove us on the hour-long journey to Mazia's *kraal*, high in the mountains overlooking the Mozambique border. Kobus had been given detailed driving directions by P.H. and Dave was more or less familiar with the dirt road, having been to Mazia's settlement for his own *femba* a couple of years earlier. The road wound back on itself many times as we climbed higher and higher. The further we drove the worse conditions became. But the view was stunning. Great big folds of mighty landscape spread away in all directions. Farms and *kraals* were few in this remote region. Much of the countryside was still pristine. Vast fields of gently billowing grass covered the hills.

As night began to fall we reached Mazia's place. We pulled up alongside a few other vehicles. One of them was fitted with South African license plates. Beyond the cars a cluster of huts was surrounded by a wire fence. Some of the huts were round, others square. One or two were constructed of brick but most consisted of walls made of mud or knotted-together sticks and branches. In the center of the compound was a large circular mud hut with a tall thatched roof. A wisp of smoke curled from an opening at the top. This structure dominated everything. People were drifting in and out of it. Many were women holding drums or carrying babies. Near the vehicles a group of laughing teenagers and small children were congregated around a pole with a small platform at the top of it. Then I heard clanging sounds. A young male baboon clambered up the pole and perched on the platform. It was chained to the pole and clearly very distraught. It was being kept there by the youngsters as a pet or totem of some sort. My heart went out to it especially when I saw that it was carrying what remained of a lit cigarette. This was what was amusing the kids so much. To me this was blatant animal cruelty but I could not interfere. It would not be appropriate. We were there as guests. Willingly or not, I was there as a patient.

We were greeted by two very polite young men who spoke perfect English. They told us they were Mazia's assistants and ushered us into the big circular hut. It was crammed with people. There were a few men and adolescent boys seated around the sides of the structure but most of those present were women and children. I guess there must have been about thirty or forty people altogether. Most of the women held drums similar to the ones used at Shado's get-together in Barberton. The majority of them also had small children or babies. Two or three were breast-feeding. Hardly anyone took any notice of us as we entered. A support pole in the center of the floor was decorated with strings of beads, small deer antlers and a dried python skin that was twirled around it. One half of what had once been a large oil barrel was placed next to the pole. It held burning embers of coal or charcoal. This supplied warmth and was also the only form of illumination. There was a small cleared area around the pole, and to my complete bewilderment I saw that a young white woman was sitting there. She was probably in her early twenties. I figured that the car with the South African plates parked outside must have belonged to her. Except for a pair of skimpy white panties she was completely nude. She sat with her legs outstretched, feet towards the fire. She smiled at us as we entered. One of the young men quietly asked me whether I was wearing any underwear or whether I would like a loincloth because I too had to strip off all my clothes. I removed my shorts, shirt and sandals and, wearing only my blue jockey briefs, I was instructed to sit down next to the young bare-breasted woman. Amazingly, there was no sense of embarrassment between the two of us. We introduced ourselves. It seemed like the most perfectly normal thing to do; simply two half-naked white adults meeting as total strangers around an open fire in the center of a mud hut surrounded by dozens of tribal folk in the highlands of Africa. What could possibly be more normal than that?

She told me that she was from Johannesburg, was an advertising executive and that she was starting her training as a *thwasa*. She had been told by her *sangoma* teacher to come here for a *femba* in order to get rid of any disincarnate entities, ghosts, ill-intentioned supernatural forces or malevolent beings that may be clinging to her or that may impede her spiritual progress. A couple of rows behind me sat Dave, Isolde and Kobus. I couldn't see them but I could feel them watching me. Directly opposite the young woman and I was a second doorway. But no one was using it. People entered or left the hut only from the main doorway behind us. A pathway had been kept clear to the doorway in front of us. Then I noticed the two young male assistants who had met us walk briskly down the cleared pathway and stealthily disappear into the darkness outside.

Now the drumming started. One by one and in isolated groups the women began beating their instruments. Within minutes everyone in the hut was either singing, trilling, ululating or beating their drums. Even though it was becoming excessively loud the cacophony created what felt like an ethereal shield of protection around me. It wasn't long before I wasn't even aware of the naked young lady sitting with outstretched legs beside me. My senses seemed to be focused only on myself, on the vibrational rhythm of the drums pounding my bones, within my marrow and in my thoughts. I felt the heat of the fire on my toes and a strange feeling of something indefinable coursing from my feet up through my legs and then creeping up into my spine.

Was this the *kundalini* spirit that I had sought so often during my metaphysical searches, meditations and yoga practices? I had never felt a sensation like that before.

Suddenly there was a terrifying scream from outside. Instantly the drumming and singing ceased. The hut went utterly silent. Other than a muffled cough from a child here and there, no one made a sound. I was startled as two figures appeared in the doorway in front of us and entered the hut. Wearing animal skins, loincloths and strings of beads they revealed themselves to be the two young male assistants who were now in full tribal regalia. They struck a formidable and splendid pose. They waited on either side of the doorway inside the hut. For a minute or two they just stood there, solemn and silent. No one said anything. There was only the sound of the metal brazier quietly clicking and pinging as it contracted and expanded from the heat of the fire.

And then Mazia entered the doorway. But the man who stood there framed by the dark archway of night behind him was not the man that I had met at the trading store in Manzini. He was wearing a black loincloth and a leather belt from which hung a variety of strips of animal hides. I recognized them as lion, zebra, buffalo and antelope. There were also thin strips of animal skins tied around his ankles and wrists. But this was definitely not the Mazia I had been introduced to. This was a man transformed, someone else, a person far more powerful and fearsome. This was someone from a distant, mysterious, ancient time. All signs of meekness and humility were gone. I could sense his strength, his power. His bare chest rose and fell with heavy breathing. His arms were outstretched, his feet wide apart. Around his neck hung necklaces of bones and shells. The pieces tinkled as he breathed. Hardly blinking, he glared at the young woman and me. There was something ferocious about his stare. His eyes were wide and bloodshot. I could swear that he was possessed, that his body had been taken over by an entity of some sort. Dropping down on all fours like an animal he began making his way towards the young woman next to me. As he prowled towards her his breathing intensified. Guttural sounds were coming from his throat. He had become the incarnation of a wild beast. As he neared us I instinctively felt that he had become a hyena. His mannerism, his gait, his breathing, his eyes were more hyena-like than human. When he reached the woman she shrank back nervously. Then a black woman materialized out of the darkness behind her. She was one of Mazia's wives or assistants. She knelt down to provide back support for the young woman who was now recoiling in terror. Glancing askew at her I could see that she had shut her eyes and was wincing. Mazia began to sniff and smell her, beginning at her feet and moving slowly all the way up her legs and torso. Breathing deeply when he got to her breasts he pulled his face back slightly so as not to brush against them.

When he reached the top of the young woman's head the smelling and deep breathing stopped. He slowly stood up and called out to his male assistants. One of them came running over carrying a calabash. He bowed and handed it to Mazia. Holding it above the young woman's head he uttered some incantations and then slowly poured a clear liquid onto the crown of her head. I had no idea what it was. As there was no odor it was probably just water. When he had emptied the contents of the calabash he handed it back to his assistant, then stood above the woman and in a very normal tone of voice addressed her directly. He was speaking either Zulu or Swazi. The black female assistant who was still crouching behind the young woman spoke softly into her ear, translating everything into English for her. It was difficult for me to hear what she was saying but I assumed it was a message from either Mazia's or the young lady's ancestors. The discourse was apparently about the pathway of *thwasa* that she had chosen to follow. I got the feeling that the pronouncements were positive, that all would be well with her training. From the way she responded with a reticent nod of her head I guessed that Mazia had declared her clear of negative forces, that she was ready for the next phase of her *thwasa* training.

When Mazia had finished addressing her he turned his attention to me. He strode over to my feet, dropped down on all fours again and began the heavy breathing routine once more. I felt my palms growing sweaty. To say that I was nervous would be an understatement. A visible transformation came over him again. Once more he was becoming another entity, a wild animal, a hyena. With his nose barely inches from my skin he began to smell me. He sniffed at my toes, then my feet. Moving upwards he smelt my legs, my body, my groin. I began to feel very frightened. I could hear a chortling sound in Mazia's throat, then a rumbling in his chest as he took deep inhalations. His intake of air was so strong that it was tugging at my body hair. I could feel his hot breath on my skin. I wanted to jump up and run. But I was paralyzed. When his nose reached the area of my left kidney he hesitated, then stopped. He pulled his head back and grimaced. Then, very slowly, his face went back to the spot where my kidney was and he inhaled even more deeply. All at once he began to make very disturbing gurgling sounds. Pulling his face back rapidly he began to burp and belch. Clearly, he was about to vomit.

I thought he was going to puke all over me but one of the assistants came rushing over carrying a small, empty wooden barrel. Mazia leaned over it and disgorged a stream of foul yellowish-brown slime into it. Then he gasped for air. The other assistant appeared carrying a calabash of water. Mazia slurped down the water. Then he heaved and regurgitated into the barrel again. This went on for about a minute. Now Mazia turned his attention to the right-hand side of my body. As soon as he inhaled the area at my right kidney the vomiting routine was repeated. Again and again he spat into the barrel. I have no idea where all that slime came from.

When he had finished regurgitating the people in the hut broke out in applause. There was loud clapping and cheering. I could even hear Dave, Isolde and Kobus' voices among them. Drumming and singing began again as Mazia turned his attention to my torso, my chest, my back, arms, hands, neck and head. But there was no more vomiting, no more sickness. It was only my kidneys that had triggered that reaction. I tried to make sense of what was happening but by this time I felt strangely light-headed. There was also a loud high-pitched whistling sound in my ears. But Mazia was not finished with me. He stood up. Looming above me like a giant he turned his face upwards to the thatched ceiling. It seemed as though someone or something was calling to him from up there. He closed his eyes and held out his hands as an indication that all drumming, singing and talking should cease. Within seconds the hut was silent. But Mazia did not move. He was listening to something but whatever it was he alone could hear it. A couple of minutes later he opened his eyes, looked down at me and began to speak in a somber tone. His composure, his voice and his manner told me that this was Mazia the man once again. The entity that had taken over his body during the smelling out session was gone. With one of the young male assistants translating into English I was given a very strange message.

He said that my paternal grandfather was there in spirit with me. He had passed into the realm of the ancestors a long time ago. Mazia said that I had never met him personally but that he was constantly watching over me. However, he was very concerned about my state of health and well-being. The illness that I had inside me was caused by actions and events that would be very difficult for me to understand. But my grandfather wanted to help. Mazia asked me whether I recognized the sign of my grandfather that I carried on my body. I was not sure what that meant so I said no, I did not. What was the sign? He pointed to my right foot. I had been born with a hammer index toe. At the middle joint the toe pointed downwards. Once as a child I had asked my mother about it and she said that it had been like that since birth. It was an insignificant physical aberration and I had never thought anything of it. It had never troubled me and I'm certain nobody else had ever paid the slightest attention to it. But Mazia said the impediment was not there by chance. It was a visible indication of my very strong connection to my grandfather. Did I not remember my father once telling me about what had happened to my grandfather's foot? It occurred a long time ago, in a country far to the north, in a very cold place.

As he spoke memories came ebbing back to me. My father was born in Riga, Latvia on the banks of the Baltic in 1905. His father Marcus was a poor peddler. There were five siblings, three brothers and a sister. There was always a shortage of money. Living as Jews under the Czar was difficult. Few people had trades or professions. Grandfather sold things, fixed things, did odd jobs. Once he had been asked to erect a brick wall at the bottom of the garden of a wealthy Riga family. Dad, then a teenager, was asked to help him. Years ago I remembered him telling me all about the incident. He was helping his father put the top layer of bricks on the wall during a snowstorm when one of the bricks dislodged and fell. It hit his father's foot on the index toe of the right foot, shattering the bone. Ever since that accident my grandfather had suffered from chronic pain in the entire foot. He developed a limp, an affliction that lasted until the day he died. As Mazia and the interpreter waited for my reaction I felt as though my father had just retold the story to me, even though it had been ages since I last heard it as a kid. I just looked at Mazia and nodded. Yes, I understood.

Mazia cleared his throat and went on. With his assistant translating he said that my grandfather wanted to strengthen the bond between us. He wanted me to help him with his walking in the spirit realm. In return, he would assist me to deal with my own illness here in the physical world. As I listened a million questions flooded my mind. How was this to be achieved? How could I create a relationship with my deceased grandfather? How was I to help him with his walking? How could he—a man I had never even met—be of assistance to me with my autoimmune-induced kidney disease? But I remained silent and Mazia continued.

You will have many doubts about the procedure, Mazia warned. But if I was serious enough about establishing a relationship with my grandfather and willing to accept healing from the world of the ancestors I was to dismiss all doubts, all skepticism. If I did that I would be able to see how the world of the living and the dead could be bridged, how healing energy could easily flow between them. As for the procedure on how to accomplish that he told me to find a cloth, a special cloth in which I could wrap myself for protection. I was to use it as a covering over my shoulders whenever I wanted to make contact with my grandfather. It had to be blue in color. Ideally, it should have some white patterns or markings on it. The cloth could not be found in stores. I would have to search for it or have it specially made. In addition, I needed to find a cane or walking stick. It should be made specifically for me and not something bought in a store. Whenever I went out of the house I should take the cane with me. But its purpose would be for my grandfather's benefit, not mine. By using it I would help him with his walking in the spirit realm. If I did that then Grandfather would accompany me on my own long path of life on the physical plane. He would assure that I was protected from the illness that was ravaging my body. I should try to obtain those two items—the cloth and the cane—without delay. Grandfather was in great need of my assistance and my illness would get progressively worse without his help. I was mesmerized by what I was hearing. Mazia stood looming over me, saying no more and waiting for his instructions to sink in. Then he turned and left the hut. The *femba* was over.

On the way back to P.H.'s place Kobus carefully negotiated

the Land Rover along the treacherous road. All of us in the vehicle could not stop talking as we analyzed the events that had just taken place. Dave was convinced that Mazia had spoken the truth, that I should procure the cane and the cloth without delay. He had been witness to incidents of a similar nature before. This good friend of mine, this Western-educated Caucasian urological surgeon from California, was of little doubt that my ancestral grandfather whom I had never met had crossed the invisible threshold between the living and the dead and had reached out to me that night in a mud hut high in the hills of Swaziland.

And I for one was not going to question that.

Eighteen

The next morning I awoke at 5.30. Dave was already in the communal kitchen making coffee. We each poured ourselves a mugful of the brew and then strode outside into the courtyard. We did not say much. We were both still processing the events of the previous evening. As we strolled past P.H.'s *ndumba* hut we heard his voice from within. He was dressed in his usual outfit of slacks and grey sweater and was pottering around with some bottles of *muti* on a shelf. He invited us in. We entered and he told us to sit down at the grass mat where he usually consulted patients. He finished what he was doing and then joined us on the floor. His face beamed with the broadest, warmest smile that I had yet seen.

"So," he said, addressing Dave. "How was last night?"

No one had told him about what happened at Mazia's *kraal*. Other than a very unreliable landline fax machine in his nearby office P.H. had neither telephone nor mobile cell phone. There wasn't any way that he could have known what transpired at Mazia's *kraal* the previous evening. Without going into details Dave expressed his approval of everything that had occurred. P.H. nodded, showing off his two rows of gleaming white teeth. Turning to me he asked, "And what about you? Was the *femba* up to your expectations?"

I sought for the right words but how could I possibly answer a question like that? P.H. saved me the challenge.

"Your grandfather has spoken to you, hasn't he?" he said with a distinct twinkle in his eye. He paused, holding me in his gaze before going on. "He instructed you to find a walking stick to help him. Yes?"

I looked at Dave. I couldn't believe this. How could he know that? But Dave merely returned my blank stare and shrugged.

Then, still seated on his haunches, P.H. twisted round and

searched among the dusty collection of bottles, containers, calabashes and other items on the musty shelves behind him. Clapping his hands to disperse a large handsome red and brown rooster that had bedded down on a pile of sacking inside a flattened cardboard box he leaned behind the shelving and pulled out a walking stick recently hewn from a local tree called Lead Wood *(combretum imberbe)*.

"For you," he said. "I carved it myself two weeks ago. I knew there was going to be a call for it."

I was stunned. He carved it *knowing* that there would be a call for it? Again I looked at Dave. He said nothing. He was as surprised as I was and there wasn't anything in his face to hint at how P.H. had any knowledge of what was revealed at the *femba* ceremony. I thanked him for the cane, dug into my wallet and pulled out a few bills of South African currency which I handed to him. Accepting them graciously he added, "And don't forget the cloth that you need for whenever you want to communicate with the ancestors."

He knew about that too. It was unbelievable. But what was the point of trying to understand it?

A couple of days before our sojourn at P.H.'s place came to an end he threw the bones for me again. This time he carefully pointed to some of the divination pieces and said, "You see here, this one symbolizes your grandfather. And here, this is you. Look how his bone is embracing you. He is happy with what you have done for him. And this is your maternal grandmother. She is close by you too because she also celebrates your commitment to your ancestors. She too is taking good care of you."

I had known my maternal grandmother well. She was a gentle, caring white-haired lady who had adored me as a child. Even when she had been confined to a wheelchair in a tiny bedroom in the back of her daughter Nelly's small farmhouse she always did whatever she could to express her love for me. During the last years of her life she was receiving a puny pension of £11 per month from the South African government. Yet, whenever we visited her when I was a kid she would secretly squash a newly-minted £1 bill into my hand. That represented nearly ten percent of her monthly income. Ouma was that kind of person. She was filled with tender warmth and abundant generosity. I loved her dearly. The last time I saw her was as a teenager before my parents and I left South Africa for Northern Rhodesia over forty years earlier.

While interpreting the other bones and items that lay on the mat P.H. suggested that I consider having a sacrifice performed in honor of my ancestors. He said that if I bathed in a ritual bath containing the blood of a sacrificial chicken I would connect myself closer to the ancestors and perhaps gain more assistance for dealing with my illness. Regrettably, I told him that I could not agree to that. Having animals killed for either my own or my ancestors' benefit would violate one of my most basic and profound beliefs.

"And what is that?" he wanted to know.

"Respect for all forms of life," I replied.

He nodded, then said, "I fully understand. But you do know of course that animals have been used for sacrifices by people in cultures all over the world for longer than we can remember."

I said that, yes, I knew. But that still did not validate the practice for me.

"That is your choice then. And you are right," he sighed. "Mercy and compassion are two of the most important things we are here to learn in our incarnation as humans."

"So you believe in reincarnation?" I asked.

"Believe?" he responded. "It is a matter of fact, not belief, my friend. Rebirth is as real as this hut in which we sit. It is as inevitable as the sun that rises above the horizon every day. If you believe in something then you are saying that you have blind faith in it. But if you *know* something that makes it different. And I *know* reincarnation to be a fact."

This was an unusual statement to hear from a rural African. In tribal societies life is influenced by the ancestors and not by the laws of karma as perceived by the followers of Eastern religious paths. But what P.H. was saying felt right. It struck a chord deep within me. He was describing how I had viewed the subject ever since my friend Bill Pullen had introduced me to the concepts of Hinduism and Karma decades earlier.

"Animals are God's pure, innocent beings," he said. "We humans have freedom of choice. They do not. When we choose to kill and maim anything it places a great burden on us, especially when we know it to be wrong or when it inflicts pain. Animals do not know this. They are innocent. And we have to learn and respect that."

"And yet you slaughter and make sacrifices of them," I said.

He nodded and then very softly said, "Yes. And we shall pay dearly for it."

In that case I asked him why he had suggested I bathe in water containing blood. He thought for a moment and then said that few things could bind us more closely than blood. Within blood is the essence of life. It contained the life force of the physical being. By immersing ourselves in it we could tap into that force.

"So how then can I get the benefit of that force if I cannot use blood?" I wanted to know. His response was unexpected.

"Look to your ancestors. Your grandfather and your father and even you yourself practiced a ritual where you honored God through the invocation of something very similar to blood. It was red. It was liquid. I can see it here in the bones. Also, your mother lit candles for you, did she not?"

I thought of the weekly Friday night candle lighting ritual that heralded the onset of the Jewish sabbath.

"There was also your father," added P.H. "Look, here he is."

He pointed at a bone on the mat that symbolized my dad.

"He took part in the ceremony too. Like his own father before him his role was to provide wine for everyone. And when the prayers were over he drank from the wine, and then he passed it around for everyone else to drink. That is the red liquid that I see. Is this not so?"

I could not believe that P.H. was visualizing all those tiny details of the ancient Friday night Hebraic ritual in a bunch of bones and amulets lying on the mat before us. Even though I could not see them myself he was describing events always practiced in our home during my childhood. Although my mother was a convert to Judaism when she married my father she was exceptionally loyal to all of the religion's many rites and rituals.

"Look to the wine," he said. "Look to its color. It is very similar to blood. Once there was life in it too. It came from a plant that grew. It's just that for us Africans blood is accessible and easily available. But red wine serves the same purpose. It is perfect for you. You can use wine in place of blood."

I thought of the Eucharist and how wine symbolized the blood of Christ. A feeling of relief surged through me. If I could replace blood with wine in my own rituals I could still be accessing the essence of many important ceremonies without having to resort to ending the life of an animal. I suddenly felt relieved.

"Relax, my friend," P.H. smiled, patting me on the knee. "No need for blood. No need to kill. Wine is fine."

I thanked P.H. for everything but before our little gathering was over he took me gently by the arm and said, "One more thing, my friend. Get yourself a ring. A man's signet ring. For the finger. Whenever you do a ritual for your grandfather wear it for him. It will bring the two of you even closer."

I made a mental note of everything that P.H. had said, and two days later Dave and I bade him farewell and left Swaziland. We set off to meet up with the members of the Inward Bound tour group in South Africa. Soon there were twelve of us. Five women and two men had flown in from the US. One young woman was from South Africa. There was also Rupert, a white tour guide based in the northern city of Polokwane and Peter Tsheola, a black man, also from Polokwane. He had taken time off from his full-time job with the Department of Environmental Affairs to act as an interpreter for us on our upcoming encounters with *sangomas*, diviners and healers. In addition there was Boet the big, burly and ever-friendly white Afrikaans tour bus driver.

Over the next twelve days we traveled extensively through the provinces of Mpumalanga and Limpopo, hiking in breathtaking countryside, meditating under the stars, visiting tribal folk in their *kraals* and consulting *sangomas*. One after the other the traditional healers demonstrated their skills by divining, providing insight into personal and business affairs, diagnosing illnesses and dispensing a variety of herbal and spiritual remedies. At one place Marilyn from California received treatment to help her with a spinal problem. After a ritual bath in tepid water mixed with herbs she declared that the pain she had been suffering from backache for years had disappeared. Chris was going through emotional and personal issues. A female Shangaan *sangoma* by the name of Vikesa hypnotized a white hen, rubbed some powder into its mouth and nostrils, perched the bird on top of Chris' head and made some loud pronouncements to it while the hen remained there, absolutely docile and motionless. She intoned Chris' ancestors for help, and after about ten minutes she gently removed the hen from his head, placed it on the floor and it peacefully strutted into the sunlight outside, clucking as though nothing had happened. This was followed by a ritual bath in which Chris immersed himself in water into which a variety of powdered *muti* had been mixed. His verdict a week later was that he had been sleeping more soundly at night than he had been for months and that vivid dreams had been coming to him, providing clear insight as to how to resolve his issues. In a remote settlement Richard was given a message by a tall, gaunt woman with very dark eyes who cast the bones and told him that he had a 'big sickness' inside him that was literally eating him up alive. She proclaimed that no potion, no medicine, no treatment could save him and that he should learn to be at peace with himself and create a closer relationship with his ancestors because he would soon be joining them. The fact is that Richard was suffering from a very aggressive form of prostate cancer. It had metastasized and was spreading rapidly throughout his internal organs. He would be dead within a year of returning to the United States. On and on the messages and insights came. It was fantastic, especially as none of the healers or diviners had known anything about any of us prior to our visit.

Perhaps the most remarkable of all the encounters during this phase of our tour was when Dave himself was subjected to a *femba* spiritual cleansing session at the home of a woman named Grace. A number of powerful *sangomas* and traditional healers sat in a room where about a dozen drummers pounded out a rhythm to assist Dave in a ritual dance. As he gyrated around the room to the beat he suddenly collapsed. I was filming the procedure and became very concerned about what was happening to him. Nevertheless, remaining true to the creed of my profession my eye stayed glued to the viewfinder and I continued filming, capturing everything that happened. As Dave fell to the floor two of the younger male *sangomas* rushed towards him from the crowd. They helped him to sit up and then stretched his legs out in front of him. One of them supported him from the back. His eyes were closed and his body began to shiver. More people came forward to help. Some held onto his feet, others grabbed him by the shoulders. The oldest of the traditional healers among them began to yell in very agitated terms.

"Hamba!" he shouted. *"Hamba!"*

Hamba is a word used by speakers of all the main indigenous linguistic groups in South Africa. Even whites often resorted to it. It meant: "Go away! Leave! Begone!"

Again and again the old man shouted this while Dave

trembled. The drumming continued unabated. As minutes went by Dave's shaking slowly subsided and he looked wide-eyed around him as two of the men shook their fists and chased an unseen apparition out of the room. It was extremely disturbing but utterly fascinating to watch. When it was all over it was explained to Dave that the disincarnate spirit of a small black dog had been found adhering to him. The spirit was not sure whether to leave him or not. But because of the intensity of the drumming and the metaphysical *muti* of the *femba* ritual it was finally dispersed. Dave had been cleansed of the entity. The dog was gone. That evening after dinner at the small resort where we were staying the members of the tour group were spellbound to hear the story of the sick dog that had to be put down at P.H.'s place. Dave had no doubt at all that it was the spirit of that self-same little animal that had been released. Now it was free to return to its own ancestral realms.

When the Inward Bound tour was over I took leave of Dave and the group and began traveling on my own. I went down memory lane to places associated with my childhood as well as visited family and friends. Once I reached the Cape of Good Hope I stayed with friends Harold and Natalie Becker in the picturesque little fishing village of Hout Bay just outside Cape Town. Harold was the son of my good friend the late anthropologist Peter Becker with whom I had made the documentary television series, *The Tribal Identity*. Peter and I had remained buddies until his tragic death in Arizona, details of which I related earlier. While Harold and Natalie's son Simon had grown up and left home, their daughter Samantha was still living with them. As a young child Samantha had been very close to her grandfather, Peter. Now in her teens she often dreamt about him. One morning at breakfast she came in, sat down at the table and dabbled with her spoon and cereal thoughtfully. When Natalie asked her what was bothering her she put down the spoon and looked at me.

"I don't understand it but I had a vivid dream of Ratsy last night," she said.

Ratsy was the nickname the family used for Peter. "He showed me a big blue cloth and told me that I should help Lionel look for one exactly like it because he needed it."

My jaw dropped. Was Samantha describing the cloth that both Mazia and P.H. had told me to get for my ritual meditation sessions? Any doubts vanished when Samantha went on by saying, "But the blue won't be enough. It will need something white on it. And Ratsy showed me exactly what it should look like."

I nearly fell off my chair. When Harold and Natalie saw how shocked I was they asked me if anything was wrong so I related the story of my *femba* ritual, the grandfather stick and the blue cloth to them. Because of so many accounts that they heard from Peter after his travels in tribal territory they weren't really surprised to hear my tale.

A couple of days later Samantha accompanied me into a small linen and haberdashery store in Hout Bay where she helped me select a length of beautiful royal blue cotton cloth. As soon as she saw it she pronounced it similar to the cloth she had seen in her dream. Then Sammy—I always called her that—selected a cut of pure white cloth which she said she needed for adding a white pattern to the blue. I paid for the two fabrics and for the next couple of days Sammy remained in her bedroom, busying herself with scissors, needles and thread. None of us were allowed to see what she was doing until she had finished. When the work was done she brought the cloth out to show me. It was dazzling. She had trimmed the edges of the blue material with a thin white stripe and in the middle of it she had sewn a starburst motif, similar to the traditional Shield of David (Magen David) pattern used in Judaism. It took my breath away. I knew that it was exactly what Mazia and P.H. had in mind. I had no doubt that it was what my grandfather had shown them. But most amazing of all was that the deceased Peter Becker had shown it to his granddaughter in a dream. I knew it was all interconnected in some strange and unfathomable way. None of it was coincidental. Via a circuitous metaphysical route a message from my long-dead ancestor had been transmitted via my dead friend Peter to his granddaughter and brought into the world for me.

But the story wasn't over yet. One morning Sammy and I were strolling through a busy cobblestone square in Cape Town on our way to have a leisurely lunch together. We spotted a few street vendors peddling their wares on the sidewalk. Sammy ran over to one of them and began examining a tray of bronze and copper rings on display. Without hesitating she picked up a chunky bronze male signet ring with the initial 'N' on it. But, oddly, the letter was not depicted upright. It was lying on its side.

"You should buy this," Sammy said.

By the smile and look on her face I could see that she was determined that I should possess it. I immediately thought of P.H.'s last words to me about getting a ring for my grandfather. I paid the seller and pocketed the ring. That evening just before I turned in I draped the cloth Sammy had made for me around my shoulders and settled down for a quiet meditation session. And then I remembered the ring we had bought. I fished it out of my pocket and slipped it onto my left ring finger. It fitted perfectly. The only puzzling thing was the 'N' initial on it. I wondered why Sammy had chosen it. As I turned my finger this way and that I suddenly realized that I had been misreading the letter. It was not an 'N' at all. Looked at in the appropriate way it was actually a letter 'Z.' But why a 'Z'? Giving up on trying to figure it out I closed my eyes, lapsed into my meditation and envisioned that I was reaching out to my grandfather in long-ago and distant Riga in Latvia. If I had been alive at the same time as him I would have referred to him as *'Zaida,'* the Yiddish word for grandfather.

And then, Bam! It hit me. Grandfather Marcus was really *Zaida* Marcus. That's what I would have called him, *Zaida* Marcus. Without her realizing it Sammy's choice of the 'Z' initial had also not been by chance. It was all too much to comprehend. But then, as I have said before, it was pointless trying to rationalize or figure any of it out.

On the day I arrived at Cape Town International Airport for my flight back to the United States I was lugging my heavy wheeled suitcase behind me, an overstuffed cabin bag containing reading matter and all my medications slung around my shoulder and, of course, my grandfather's walking stick. Check-in for the flight had not yet opened. An old friend from my childhood had come to see me off and we sat in the cafeteria sipping coffee. I was due to travel on a South African Airways flight by way of Ihla do Sal in the Atlantic to Fort Lauderdale and then to Atlanta. From there I would catch a connection to LA. The first leg was going to be a long journey, somewhere in the region of 16 hours. My friend—to whom I had previously related the story of the walking stick—said that I may not be permitted to take the stick into the cabin with me. Bear in mind that this was still ten months before 9/11 occurred and so security was nothing like it is now, but I wondered whether she was right. I was flying economy class and airline personnel may object to me trying to find a spot to stow the large cane in what would no doubt be another full cabin.

Once the check-in desks opened I took my place among the multitudes and shuffled towards the counter. I checked in my big bag but as I was about to leave the desk the white female check-in attendant spotted my stick and said that I could not take it into the cabin with me. It would have to be stowed in the aircraft's hold. Her superior, a black man who was speaking in Xhosa to another individual in the background, overheard the conversation and came over to ask whether I needed the stick as an aid for walking.

"No," I responded, not wanting to lie. It was obvious that I was able to get around perfectly adequately without the use of a cane.

"Well, then what's it for?" he asked.

I didn't know what to say, so I shrugged and said, "It's for my grandfather."

"Is he traveling with you?"

I shook my head.

"So is it a gift for him in America?" he wanted to know.

Again I shook my head.

"Where is he then?" the man asked, a hint of irritation creeping into his voice.

I looked at him for a second or two, decided that I definitely wouldn't spin any lies about the matter, leaned towards him and quietly said, "He is past."

"Past?" the man responded. "You mean he is..."

He did not finish his sentence. He was a Xhosa and he knew exactly what I was trying to say. A broad smile swept across his face.

"A-a-a-h..." he cooed.

Stepping over the weigh-in scale next to the check-in desk he came over to me, pumped my hand and said to the agent: "It's fine. Let this man through. He can take the stick with him."

A half-hour later when the flight was called I approached the departure gate with my boarding pass, shoulder bag and walking stick. Two young black agents—a man and a woman—were checking everyone's boarding stubs. As soon as the woman saw me she smiled and said, "Nice walking stick."

I nodded, handed her my boarding pass and said, "Thank you. It's for my ancestors."

Her eyes lit up. I could swear she wanted to lean forward and embrace me. Instead, she began babbling something in Xhosa to her male partner.

"*Hau*!" he said. "Your ancestors? *Hau, baba*."

'Baba' is a typical term of endearment among the peoples of Southern Africa. I could not have been given a nicer nor more meaningful farewell salutation as the two of them ushered me through for boarding. I was directed to my window seat in the mid-section of the main cabin where a friendly black female cabin attendant helped me wedge the cane on the floor between my seat and the cabin bulkhead. And there it remained for the duration of the long flight to the States.

From that day onward I resolved to incorporate elements of African healing into my daily regimen of medications and meditation to help me cope with my chronic autoimmune kidney condition. I began to do two meditations per day, one in the morning and then just before bedtime. Every time I settled into a comfortable chair for the fifteen- to twenty-minute session I draped the blue and white cloth over my shoulders. Not only did it provide a sense of bonding with my grandfather and, indeed, all of my ancestors but it also reminded me of my Jewish roots. When praying male worshippers drape a prayer shawl called a *'tallit'* around their shoulders in accordance with the precept dictated to the Israelites in the Book of Numbers.

Every weekend I began to undertake a ritual bath, again to bind me to my ancestors as well as to whatever higher forces may be accessible to me. Into the water I put my grandfather's ring. After adding a tumbler full of kosher red wine to the water—as instructed by P.H.—I took my grandfather's stick, stuck the lower end of it through the bronze ring and then swirled it around in the water to make sure the wine was fully diluted. As a student of ancient Jewish mysticism called Kabbalah I twirled the ring and the wine around exactly 18 times because, according to legend, the Hebrew number 18 is the numerical value of the word for life. Did it all make sense? I'm not sure. But it was a lovely ritual and it always gave me great comfort to practice it.

Nineteen

In 2004 I got a really nice gig. It was as producer and supervising writer on a documentary TV series for Animal Planet. Based out of a production company in Studio City my job was to find stories of very young wild animals whose mothers had either died or abandoned them. This caused humans to intervene and raise them. Called *Growing Up* the stories were as diverse as the animals themselves. The shows I was involved with were about a baby elephant, giraffe, penguin, baboon, zebra, rhino, walrus, camel, black leopard, sitka deer and lynx. Each one of these amazing animals had to be reared in either a zoo or wildlife sanctuary after they were found in the wild. I loved them all but I was particularly fond of the walrus. He was discovered swimming helplessly off the coast of Alaska. His mother had been killed after being hit by the propeller of a passing ship. He was named Nereus after the Greek god of the sea and was brought to the Indianapolis Zoo for raising. I had seldom known a cuter nor more endearing creature. He got to know me because of my regular location trips to the zoo and eventually I was allowed to feed him and interact with him. It was a heartwarming experience, as was my relationship with Kisa the baby lynx. She was reared at the San Diego Zoo. Every time I went there she too recognized me. The black leopard that was looked after at Pat Craig's amazing animal sanctuary outside Denver was another animal that remembered me whenever I turned up to film a sequence. I had so much fun on that series. It allowed me to develop an even greater respect and admiration for animals, and it also taught me a lot about what makes them so important in our quest to understand ourselves.

Stories of three of the babies, the baboon, zebra and rhino, were all set in South Africa. This required several location filming trips to Africa which, needless to say, I was thrilled about. Of equal importance was the opportunity the trips provided for me to reacquaint myself with some of the *sangomas* that I had met during the Inward Bound group tour with Dave Cumes a few years earlier. I was also able to visit with Peter Tsheola, the man who had acted as our translator. Once the *Growing Up* series was completed I undertook a private vacation trip back to South Africa with my wife, Diana. Once again I was dealing with a flare-up of my kidney disease so Peter arranged for me to visit what he called a 'healing prophet.'

I had no idea what to expect the day Diana and I met Peter at our hotel in Polokwane. We rode with him to meet the healer. Paved highways eventually gave way to a series of dirt roads in an area that was once part of the apartheid-era *Bantustan* or black 'homeland' called Lebowa. Economic development there had been minimal. Clusters of whitewashed concrete huts and the occasional brick house dotted the landscape, most of them separated by strands of aging barbed wire fences. Dogs loitered in the shade of sparse clumps of trees. Abandoned wrecks of old automobiles and trucks littered yards. Here and there children played, many of them barefoot and wearing tattered hand-me-down clothing. The place was poor and decrepit, a sad reminder of the failure of the Afrikaners' apartheid dream. Eventually we pulled up to a dilapidated gate outside an unpainted house.

"This is where Mr. Mohlwane lives," Peter announced.

Diana shot me a worried look. I could see grave doubt in her expression. Was this a safe place? Where exactly *were* we? Why were we there? Peter opened the gate and led us into a large yard in which groups of black people were sitting. They were all there to see Mr. Mohlwane. Some were elderly but most were in their prime or middle-age years. One or two of them muttered something to their neighbors when they saw Diana and I, two white folks in casual summer attire, but they soon lost interest. They were all nicely dressed, squatting or sitting in near the house. Apparently it was in there that Mr. Mohlwane consulted with his patients.

A man dressed in dark corduroy trousers and a plaid shirt appeared. He was wheeling a bicycle and came over to meet us. He shook Peter's hand and was then introduced to us. He was one of Mr. Mohlwane's assistants. He spoke no English so were it not for Peter communication would have been impossible. The man wheeled his bicycle over to the house, propped it up against the wall and then informed us that he would let Mr. Mohlwane know that we were there. He briskly walked over to the outbuilding, opened the door and let himself in. Peter suggested that we sit down. A large bare eucalyptus tree trunk lay against the fence near the gate, and so we wandered over and perched ourselves on it. Peter was wearing a light brown jacket. As we sat down he removed it and handed it to me.

"Put this on," he said. "Out of respect."

I nodded. I wished he had told me earlier to be more appropriately dressed. I was in sandals and shorts. I slipped on Peter's jacket. The temperature was stifling, especially in that empty backyard where the sun's rays bounced back in full force from the yellow dust. Twenty minutes later the door in the outbuilding opened and a thin man about five feet two inches in height appeared. He began walking towards us, followed by a deputation of three other men, one of whom was the man we had met on arrival. I assumed correctly that the thin man was the prophet healer, Mr. Mohlwane. He was wearing pale blue slacks, a brown shirt and a heavily soiled knee-length coat. On its collar was pinned a glittering silver badge that identified him as a member of the Zion Christian Church, or ZCC, the largest splinter Christian church group in the southern hemisphere. At that time its membership exceeded five million. As he approached us Peter went forward, and in a very humble and subservient manner offered him his hand in greeting. I later learned that Peter had gone to him some months earlier for help with some physical problem of his own, the nature of which he had not shared with me.

Mr. Mohlwane came over, shook my hand and then Diana's, grinned and pointed to himself and said in Afrikaans: *"Ek is Johannes. Johannes Mohlwane."* ("I am Johannes, Johannes Mohlwane.")

I turned to Peter and asked him to thank him but to please not to struggle trying to make us understand him. I was more than happy for Peter to do all the interpreting. When Peter relayed this to him Mr. Mohlwane grinned again and said, *"Dankie, dankie."* ("Thank you, thank you.")

He said something to Peter and then began pacing back towards the outbuilding. I recognized the language as Pedi, one of the dialects of the North Sotho speaking groups. Peter said that he and I should follow but that Diana should remain outside and wait.

Inside the building was a spacious room. On the wall hung a photograph of the ZCC church headquarters at a place called Moria, about thirty miles to the east of Polokwane. A bucket of foul-smelling dark liquid was boiling on a little coal stove in the corner, adding to the stifling atmosphere. On one side a number of shelves held a variety of boxes and bottles filled with *mutis*, powders, herbs and other substances. Once Mr. Mohlwane's retinue had entered the room behind Peter and myself the door was closed. In the dim light I was asked to sit down on a low wooden stool. Mr. Mohlwane knelt on the floor beside me. He took my left hand, cupped it in his own two hands and closed his eyes. Then he began to pray. The language was clearly North Sotho but as he progressed he began leaning down towards the floor and the words became unrecognizable. It wasn't long before his forehead was resting on the floor and he was babbling in unknown tongues. I could see by Peter's reaction that he could not make head or tail of what was being said. Holding my hand in a tightening vise-like grip Mr. Mohlwane's words flew from his lips at a furious rate. It seemed like I was listening to a recording that was being played back at very high speed. All the while his head remained on the floor. Beads of perspiration began appearing on his brow. After about three minutes he stopped, took a deep breath, released my hand and then rearranged himself in a squatting position on the floor in front of me. He looked up at the photograph of the ZCC church complex on the wall and said something in North Sotho, ending with, "Jesus Christus. Amen."

Then, very slowly, he began to speak to me. Word for word, everything was comprehensible to Peter and he interpreted for me. He said that I was suffering from a sickness in two places. Each one was on the opposite side of the body, just below my rib cage. The sickness had 'come into me' in two parts. He said I was a baby when the first one happened, and then about seven or eight years old when the second one occurred. The sickness had entered into my body through 'openings' in my flesh, first on my neck and then later at my right foot. After what the *sangoma* Mazia had told me during my *femba* a few years earlier in Swaziland I could not believe that I was hearing about something regarding my right foot again. Mr. Mohlwane went on to say that the sickness had been inside me ever since my childhood and that it was only recently that it had, as he put it, "become alive." Now my thoughts went to my nephrologist in Los Angeles who had asked me whether anything like a bite, sting or intrusion had ever occurred which may have triggered a toxic condition that might have lain dormant in my system for years. What was Mr. Mohlwane referring to?

He said he would prepare some sort of *muti* to help me but, even more importantly, he wanted me to purchase some tea leaves that he would 'bless' and that I should take back to America and use in a weekly ritual in a bath. Again a ritual. Again a bath. His healing paradigm was interesting but not quite that of the traditional *sangomas* that I had consulted previously. His methods encompassed essences of Christianity that were interwoven with a tribal African modality. I was totally intrigued. Turning to Peter he issued him with details about where I would find the tea leaves that I needed, what I had to do with them, what other *muti* he would prepare for me, what I should do in my hotel room that night and how I was to proceed with my healing ritual back home in California. Meanwhile he would prepare a mixture that he wanted to apply directly to my body. While he and his assistants did that I should go and procure the tea leaves. The first part of the healing session was over, and Peter and I left the outbuilding to join Diana at the eucalyptus tree trunk. She asked me to explain what had happened but I was at a total loss for words.

Our instructions were to go to the nearest trading store and buy a large packet of *Five Roses* tea leaves, one of the most popular tea brands in South Africa. After a ten- or twelve-minute drive we found a store, bought the tea and returned to Mr. Mohlwane's place. We settled ourselves on the fallen eucalyptus tree trunk again while we waited for him to appear. All the while I was going over and over what had happened earlier. I searched my memory banks to make sense of what Mr. Mohlwane had said but nothing came to me. And then, like wispy threads slowly metamorphosing out of a distant mist, I began to recall things.

When I was three years old I had been hospitalized with diphtheria. Had I not been rushed to hospital I would have died from suffocation. A surgical tracheotomy had to be performed. This consisted of cutting into my throat and making an incision in my windpipe to clear an obstruction to my breathing. Was this the first 'opening' that Mr. Mohlwane had described? As for the second one that he mentioned, could that have been the horrible accident that happened to me when I was seven years old? We were living in Kempton Park at the time. I was often the leader of the pack, taking the initiative to get into trouble while five or six of my buddies did my bidding. One day we grouped together outside my father's store on the main drag of town while I hatched plans to storm the house of an old woman who lived on her own. We all believed the dark single-story home that nestled behind the tall weeds and shrubbery of her front garden was haunted and that the old lady was a witch. To get to her place we had to scamper down the narrow lane dividing my father's business from the building next door. Beyond the lane lay an open field and on the other side of that was the street where the old witch lived.

After getting high on sugary candy from the corner cafe and milk bar we went whooping down the lane, with me sprinting in front. Halfway down the lane was a low brick wall, an easy object for a bunch of wild boys to scale. We had done it so often before. But what I didn't see that time was the broken glass bottle that lay buried in the weeds and grass on the other side of the wall. Clad in summer shorts and sandals and hell-bent on mischief I leaped over the wall. At first I sensed nothing but when I got to the end of the alley I felt my khaki shorts becoming very soggy and clinging to my right leg. When I stopped and looked down I saw a fountain of blood spurting from my right ankle. My shorts were soaked. By the time Rusty, Dave, Maish, Colin and Neville reached me I was saturated in blood. With their help I was taken to my dad's store. My mother shrieked hysterically and then called our family doctor. By the time Doc Garber and a nurse arrived in his large fawn-colored Plymouth the glass display counter on which I was perched was covered in blood. It was pouring over the sides like a waterfall, accumulating in a crimson pool on the floor. My mother was frantic while my father fussed and fiddled with cloths and towels to try to stop the bleeding. After our doctor loaded me into his car and drove Mom and I to his consulting rooms a mile or two away I was beginning to lose consciousness because of blood loss. In the examination room the nurse slapped a cloth soaked in chloroform over my face and I did pass out completely. Doc Garber went about his business and gouged two pieces of green glass shard from the fibular artery of my right foot, cleaned the wound, stitched it up and then sent me home. Was that the second 'opening' Mr. Mohlwane was referring to? He said I was seven years old when it happened. That corresponded exactly with my age at the time of the accident.

I mentioned all this to Diana and Peter as we waited for Mr. Mohlwane but they were as perplexed as I was. Then the old man appeared once again from the outbuilding. Two of his assistants were behind him. They were carrying the bucket that I had seen earlier on the little coal stove. It was steaming and its contents were slopping over the sides. When they reached me Mr. Mohlwane told me to stand up. Pulling a rag from the pocket of his overcoat he plunged it into the steaming brown liquid and began wiping my legs and feet with the vile-smelling stuff. It was so hot that I winced with pain but he continued to cover every inch of both legs and feet. Swelling of my legs due to the edema was quite bad that day, a direct result of my kidney disorder. When he had finished one of his assistants handed him a towel and he wiped me dry.

Mr. Mohlwane then invited Peter and I back into the little outbuilding. He took the package of tea that I had bought, tore a small hole into it, lit a candle, waved the packet over it as he prayed intensively in that rapid, babble-like unknown language again. Then he handed the tea to me and told Peter that it was now blessed with the power of his ancestors, almighty God and the Lord Jesus Christ. I was to think of my own ancestors and be grateful to God every time I added a few pinches of it to my ritual bath water back home in California. If I needed to have the tea reenergized in America all I had to do was to let Peter know and he would relay the message to him. Mr. Mohlwane would then send remote energy to it to assist with my healing. Then he reached into his other coat pocket, pulled out a small plastic bag containing a mixture of powders, crushed leaves and pulverized material. He told Peter that I was to take the stuff back to the hotel, pour it into jugs of lukewarm water and consume all of it before dawn the next day.

My first consultation with the amazing Mr. Mohlwane was over. When I offered to pay him for his services he refused saying that he was only an agent. God was the real healer. It was his pleasure to act as God's messenger. We argued briefly but I insisted he accept my money and I shoved a wad of bills into his coat pocket. We shook hands and Peter, Diana and I drove back to our hotel in Polokwane. I was at a total loss for words that evening as I contemplated one of the nicest and strangest human beings I had ever had the pleasure of meeting.

That night, to Diana's absolute horror, I drank all the powder he had given me. And I did not spend more than three minutes at a time away from the bathroom. My stomach and innards went into convulsions. My bladder emptied itself about fifteen times. At about 4am I collapsed into bed, drained, emptied and depleted. When I awoke at around seven I was starving. Feeling like a ghost awakened from the dead I stumbled into the hotel dining room and devoured plates of fruit, cereal, breakfast potatoes, fried tomatoes and toast. I could not satisfy my ravenous appetite. My head spun. But by that afternoon my energy level was peaking in a way I had not experienced in years. I felt as though I was running on steroids. It took about three days for me to begin feeling normal again. And when I did my edema was gone. All swelling in the legs had totally subsided. My bladder behaved perfectly. Something indescribable had happened. But to this day I have no idea what it was.

On my return to California I began amending my weekly bathing ritual. In addition to the red wine, I began adding three pinches of the sanctified tea to the bath water. Using my grandfather's walking stick with the tip thrust into the bronze ring with the initial 'Z' on it I swirled the water until all the wine and tea had been fully integrated. Then for ten minutes I immersed myself in the tub, silently thanking my ancestors and guides or whatever entities were keeping an eye on me. This became a ritual that was diligently reenacted once every week. As I sat immersed in the water I always thought of the ritual of the Hebrew *mikvah* or sacred bath. Then, of course, there was the baptism of Christianity. There was also the ablution ritual prior to prayer of Islam, the immersion in the River Ganges of Hinduism, the water purification processes of Zoroastrianism and Shintoism. All of them involved water. My bath was simply another form of an ancient phenomenon that had been practiced by humans since time immemorial. The custom came from something incalculably ancient. And I liked that.

I began to study the trailblazing work done by the Japanese researcher Dr. Masaru Emoto. He had demonstrated that human consciousness can have an effect on the molecular structure of water. His findings factored in perfectly with the findings of Dr. Robert Jahn and his work at the PEAR Lab at Princeton. It seemed likely that we humans are able to influence organic and inorganic matter, and to connect with nature on a superconscious or perhaps even subatomic level. Conventional physics has a long way to go to discern the inner complexity of the workings of nature and on how we humans are part and parcel of that process, regardless of whether we are in physical form or not.

Towards the end of 2006 my good friend Moses Shado Mahlabisane Dludlu, the *sangoma* I had met with Dave Cumes in South Africa, came to visit. He stayed with us for a week at our home in California. He had brought his beads, necklaces, cloths and divining bones with him so I was able to arrange for him to meet some of our friends and explain the intricacies of African traditional medicine and divining methods to them. One morning as we lazed on the porch in the back garden he asked me about my illness. I told him it was a chronic condition. It would never go away. The best I would ever be able to do was manage it or simply stay on top of it until I eventually succumbed to it. He said that with ancestral help I would find the process easier and that I should not give up. I told him about the walking stick P.H. had given me to establish a relationship with my deceased grandfather. But Shado said I should do more. He wanted to know about all of my grandparents.

"Do you consult with them too?" he asked. "Do you seek their help?"

I said that I was not sure whether my other ancestors were with me or not. Or indeed whether they would even want to bother themselves with me. Surely they had better things to do. Other than perhaps one aspect of my paternal grandfather's spirit that I had come to believe did in some mysterious way play a role in my life, I was always under the impression that once a person or any living being for that matter dies its essence, its consciousness, its spirit, its soul, call-it-what-you-will moves on. Maybe through my bathing, *muti* and walking stick ritual I was in touch with just a portion of what had once been my grandfather. To my way of thinking the greater soul continually incarnates, dipping in and out of the physical world accruing experiences that it needs for developing and improving itself. For me, its ultimate destination will always remain a mystery but that is something not for us to know.

"As far as I am concerned," I said to Shado, " Karma is a driving force that dictates how, when and where we reincarnate. I have always subscribed to the view that we are on a journey to improve, refine and perfect the soul. Perhaps the essence of what Mazia and P.H. had referred to as my grandfather was but a small part of a greater, infinitely more complex whole, much of which was beyond my grasp or understanding. Don't you agree?"

He nodded and then said, "Yes, there are no doubt more dimensions to what we call the soul than most people can imagine."

I immediately thought of the Kabbalistic or Hebraic concept of the soul being made up of three parts or levels, the *nefesh* (breath), *ruach* (spirit) and *neshama* (soul). I thought too of Plato's writing in his *Republic* that the soul or consciousness exists as a tripartite entity which he called mind, will and emotion.

I was also fascinated by numbers and numerology. I never knew why but the number nine always had special significance for me. And wasn't three the square root of nine? Did that mean anything? For some reason or another all of my passwords and padlock combinations ever since my childhood had been made up of a combination of nines and threes. According to Catholic doctrine God exists as a tripartite, namely the Father, the Son and the Holy Spirit. According to that same doctrine, on the physical plane humans manifest on three levels as body, soul and spirit. Does that provide insight into the nature or divisions of the soul, or into how we may view what constitutes our ancestors? It was an intriguing question. Shado and I tossed our thoughts around for a couple of hours. As the sun slowly drifted across the clear Californian sky we decided that perhaps one-third of the soul in any given incarnation is the part that lingers on as an ancestor while the greater portion of the soul reincarnates, once again made up of three parts. But the solution to these grander questions lay far beyond our understanding. All that really mattered, Shado told me, was that the ancestors prevail. And that it was our duty to recognize them. The conversation ended with him telling me that the time had come for me to find mine, to locate them wherever they may be in the ether, the metaphysical universe or on the Earth plane and to invite them to participate in the affairs of my life.

"But how do I do that?" I asked.

"Look for them," was his reply.

I told him that I had no idea where my paternal grandfather was buried. He died of typhus in Latvia in Northern Europe almost a century ago. The final resting place of my paternal grandmother was also unknown to me. She, together with most of my father's family, had perished at the hands of either Stalin's minions or the Nazis. I also had no idea where my maternal grandfather was buried. He had died in South Africa decades ago and my Ouma had remarried. But she, my beloved Ouma, was buried in a cemetery in what was once a rural farming district to the west of Johannesburg. She had passed away in 1962 when my parents and I were living in Northern Rhodesia.

"How am I going to find them all?" I wanted to know.

"We need to go to a place free of noise and people," Shado answered. "We need to call out to them so that they may hear us and respond."

When I asked him exactly what kind of environment he had in mind for this meeting, he suggested a park or forest.

And so it was that early the next morning Shado and I set out on the traffic-congested eight-lane Interstate 101 freeway from my home in Woodland Hills bound for Griffith Park in the Hollywood Hills. Griffith Park is huge, covering 4,310 acres slap bang in the middle of Los Angeles. It is one of the largest urban parks in the United States. Within its vast terrain are mountains, forests, paved and unpaved roads, a zoo, a railroad museum, a carousel, pony rides, miniature trains and the famous Griffith Observatory and planetarium. It is easy to get lost on its myriad winding dirt tracks and hiking trails. This is where we were headed, bound for a rendezvous with my ancestors. Shado wore his *sangoma* regalia and I was dressed in shorts and hiking boots. Naturally, I carried my grandfather's walking stick with me.

After parking the vehicle we followed a trail on foot into the wilderness, far from traffic and the multitudes. Using Grandfather's stick like an African *panga* or knife I swiped my way through bush and brush, wending my way deep into a heavily wooded canyon where Shado said he thought we might be able to do a ritual to summon my ancestors. It was grueling work. The Southern Californian sun beat down on us as we sweated our way through the boondocks. Insects swirled around as twigs and branches lashed at our naked legs and arms. When

I thought I could not go on any more Shado suddenly called out, "Here! This is the place!"

I stopped and collapsed into a needle-sharp grove of dry grass and chaparral. The canopy of a towering oak tree provided some welcome shade. We had not brought any water with us and I felt dehydrated. Nevertheless, Shado reached into a small leather bag he was carrying and pulled out a beaded necklace which he draped around my neck. Then he produced an African rattle made of seeds and cocoons tied by a thin leather thread to a little stick. He began to shake it and to call out in Zulu. After a few minutes he told me to say aloud my grandparents' names. There we were, two of us sitting in the dry grass, a barefooted black man in full *sangoma* regalia sing-songing words in Zulu and me, a white guy, calling out the names of my long-deceased grandparents. After about twenty minutes of this Shado reached out and grabbed my arm and told me to be silent. Leaning over to me he whispered, "They are here."

I looked around. I closed my eyes and breathed deeply. I tried desperately to feel that something—*anything*—had happened, that 'they' were indeed here. But try as hard as I could I sensed nothing. Shado could see that I was filled with doubt. He merely smiled.

"Don't worry," he said. "You cannot see, but they are here. Speak to them. Greet each one by name and ask them to follow you."

Shado got up to return to the vehicle. I softly called out the names of three of my grandparents. Unfortunately, I did not know the name of my maternal grandfather and so I merely referred to him as Oupa, the Afrikaans word for grandfather. Feeling slightly embarrassed I called out: "Welcome. Please, will you follow me?"

With Shado leading the way I trailed along, imagining that all four of my parental ancestors were following single file behind me.

"Keep on speaking to them," Shado called back to me. "Tell them not to be afraid. Tell them exactly where we are going and that they should please accompany you."

I did as he asked and when we got to the car Shado indicated that I should unlock the doors and respectfully usher the ancestors into the vehicle.

As we drove back on the busy 101 freeway he leaned over from the passenger seat and whispered, "Tell them you're happy. Thank them for coming along. Tell them everything is okay. Say that you're taking them to your home—*their* home."

I did as he asked and by the time we got back to my house I really did feel that there were four passengers seated in the back of my vehicle. Shado had me open the front door of the house, bid them welcome and show them upstairs to where I had my little shrine in their honor. Fortunately, Diana was not at home when all this was going on. I don't know what she would have thought if she was witness to it. Then Shado advised me to run a bath, add my African blessed tea leaves from Mr. Mohlwane and some red wine to it and then sit in the water and explain to my ancestors that I needed them to please remain with me, to protect me and help me to deal with my illness.

All this was duly done and that night I slept like a log, unequivocally believing that my ancestors were finally with me.

Twenty

By early 2007 my allopathic drug regimen was being regularly altered by my nephrologist. The cyclosporine medication was no longer working as well as it did earlier. I had now been put on a twice-daily dosage of *Prograf*, another potent immunosuppressant. Crazily fluctuating blood pressure from very low to excessively high was a constant problem. There was also the build-up of uric acid in my system. Not to mention chronic fatigue, loss of energy and a litany of other annoying maladies. I was now on 13 different medications daily. But I was still dodging the bullet and living a relatively normal life.

My doctors were amazed that I had escaped the worst of what my autoimmune-induced kidney disorder could have thrown at me. Naturally, they felt it was due entirely to the medications and the allopathic care I was receiving from them. But I instinctively knew there was more to it than that. Diet was playing a key role in keeping me alive. I am convinced that had I not been vegan I would have succumbed to kidney failure years ago. Without being able to discuss it with any of my medical caregivers, I also knew that metaphysical help supported by my African rituals and the influence of my ancestors were fundamental to the battle. In fact, as I inched closer to my 70th birthday I continued to travel, to work and to write.

"It's amazing," people were saying. "You're ill yet you look so well. How do you do it?"

It wasn't easy, of course. But it could be done. With psychic and supernatural assistance.

By 2014 the tea leaves that Mr. Mohlwane had blessed for me were all gone. I returned to South Africa to pay him another visit. This was eight years after I had first seen him. Sadly, by now he had become a very frail and ailing man. He had lost sight in both his eyes. Assisted by members of his family he could only shuffle around inside his house where he still interacted with patients. There were no longer bevies of assistants to help him and he relied on what I assumed were his elder sons and daughters. The minute I shook his hand he remembered me vividly. He instantly recalled my wife Diana and asked after her. Incredibly, he clearly remembered what I told him about all the members of my family during our previous meeting eight years earlier. He asked after each one of them. Then, as he lapsed into prayer in a big leather armchair in his sparsely furnished living room he began to offer advice, just as before. Once again with my friend Peter Tsheola acting as translator I was told that despite my illness I would be given the opportunity to deal with the affliction. Once more I was told that I needed items for him to bless for a ritual bath and so a trip to the local trading store was required. This time I was told to buy tea leaves, coffee granules, powdered milk and cocoa powder. Once these were brought back to Mr. Mohlwane's house one of his elder sons lit a candle for him and one by one he held each item above the flame while he blessed it. When he had finished he began babbling in that fast-paced strange language once again. Then he turned to Peter, and with glazed, unseeing brown eyes he declared that I also needed to take some 'sacred' African water back to America with me. He explained to Peter where it could be procured. It was sold by an elderly *sangoma* at the far edge of the Seshego residential area. The water had come from a stream high in the Waterberg mountain range. We should buy it from the old man and then return for it to be blessed.

What followed was something of a frenetic search for the *sangoma* and the special water. Fortunately, Peter's son Archie—an engineering student from Johannesburg currently visiting his parents—had a buddy who knew where the seller lived. We met up with him, and while Peter entertained me with stories about his work at the Department of Environmental Affairs in his comfortably furnished home, Archie dashed off with his friend in his dad's car to find the water. When he returned with it in a half-gallon plastic container an hour later we siphoned some of it off into a small empty plastic Coca-Cola bottle. That was the only way I would be able to carry the liquid back in my checked luggage to the United States. Then we raced back to Mr. Mohlwane's place with my little container of water. By late afternoon it had been held over a candle and sanctified. Armed with that plus my coffee, cocoa, tea and powdered milk I was taken back to my hotel. A couple of weeks later all the items were safely back at home with me in Los Angeles. In addition to the wine, my weekly bathing ritual now included pinches of all these new ingredients plus a few drops of the sacred water. An upgraded regimen had begun.

In 2017 my illness flared up yet again. I was no longer responding to the *Prograf* immunosuppressant. My long-suffering and hard-working nephrologist said that we had run out of oral medicinal options to stave off my overactive immune system. It was time to try something more radical, an infusion of a potent drug called *Rituxan*. In November that year I underwent two infusions of the drug administered directly into the veins of my left arm. Three months later there was no sign of the condition improving. By then the concoction of blessed coffee, cocoa, powdered milk, tea leaves and mountain spring water for my weekly ritual bath that I had received from Mr. Mohlwane had run out. I was desperate. I had to find yet another method. I raced to see my surgeon-*sangoma* friend Dave Cumes in Santa Barbara once again. After throwing the bones in his *ndumba* hut to confirm that the illness had indeed resurfaced he pottered around his large collection of *muti* and other bric-a-brac that he had brought home with him from his regular visits to South Africa. Then he handed me a plastic bag filled with dried medicinal plants, herbs, powders and grains of soil. I began adding these to my bath water. Within a few weeks my high blood pressure began to come down, my energy level improved and the loss of protein subsided. But I was by no means out of the woods. Then a friend suggested I talk to a South African physiotherapist based in Los Angeles who was trying a new holistic system developed in collaboration with NASA. It goes by the name of Amino Neuro Frequency Therapy. This modality relies on tiny round patches of charged particles applied directly to the skin. Each patch transmits a unique frequency through neurons in the body, relaying them directly to organs beneath the area where the patches are applied. This is believed to trigger a self-healing process. By improving the nervous system at the cellular level the efficacy of the treatment is said to have remarkable results. No drugs or chemicals are involved. It all sounded completely like 'black box' science to me, another hocus-pocus way of bilking the ill and the gullible out of money. But I was ready to try anything. I had dabbled in far weirder methods in the past. Why not this? I gave it a shot. For a month I went to see the practitioner every fourth day and every time I came away covered in little discs, all the way from my neck to my ankles. I looked like a pantaloon clown in a polka-dot outfit. It was quite an expensive, time-consuming and inconvenient process. It also hurt like hell every time I removed the spent patches as they tore at my body hair. Each patch was only effective for 72 hours. But as we saw no further improvement in my condition I reluctantly gave it up after four weeks.

And then something unbelievable started happening.

One morning I woke up to find my blood pressure had returned to pre-illness levels. Within days there was a complete absence of frothing in the urine, indicating that I wasn't losing any protein. The edema in both my legs had disappeared. And, best of all, as time wore on the tiredness that had been plaguing me for years dissipated.

What had done it? The Amino Neuro Frequency Therapy sessions? The allopathic *Rituxan* infusions? The mounds of medication that I was still taking? The *sangoma muti* in my weekly ritual baths? The influence of my ancestors? My twice-daily meditation sessions? My vegan diet? The sheer tenacity and expertise of my wonderful doctors? Perhaps all of them. By early 2019 my nephrologist pronounced that I was in complete remission. It was a miracle. But how long would it last? Would a relapse occur? Only time will tell. But this I do know. According to my nephrologist most of his patients who have suffered from my condition for as long as I have are either on dialysis or have perished from their illness, let alone stumble along with it for close on 25 years.

This much I also know: without the essence of Africa in my healing strategy I don't think I would have made it this far. I adamantly believe that the influence of Africa's traditional diviners and herbalists were fundamental to the curative process. Now, as I look back on my life I ponder. What is the take-away lesson of the past 75 years that I have lived on this planet? What have I learnt from it all?

I think the most important thing that life has taught me is the critical importance of maintaining an open mind. Coupled to that is the cruciality of being insatiably curious. We can never know enough. But there is a decidedly bleak side to what I have experienced because, sadly, what has happened to my beloved Africa leaves me in a somewhat somber state of mind. I am astounded at how right film makers Bernard and Michael Grzimek had been with their two films about the destruction of the continent's wildlife and environment that I saw as a teenager so long ago. Africa is groaning under the sheer weight of an ever-exploding human population. In 1960 there were approximately 285 million people on the continent. In 2018 that figure had more than quadrupled to 1.3 billion. Population density had risen from ten persons per square mile to 94 per square mile. According to the United Nations, Africa currently accounts for 27% of all worldwide births. This will increase to 37% by the year 2050. As early as 2025 there will be more Africans in the world than Chinese.

The World Bank reported that in 2018, 413 million people were living below the breadline in sub-Saharan Africa alone. Despite this appalling state of affairs many African leaders turn a blind eye to the need for birth control. In some cases they condemn it outright. In 2016 John Magufuli, the president of Tanzania, announced that overpopulation was not a problem at all. He reckoned that because government-run schools in his country had become free and open to everyone women should simply throw away their contraceptives and have more babies. He said that a large educated labor force would be essential for developing the nation. He proclaimed that Tanzania should not follow the trends of Europe because one of the inevitable side effects of family planning was a shrinking labor force. Curbing his country's population growth would mean that more immigrants would be needed to maintain its growing economy. But the fact is that Europe's fertility rate was 1.6 and its economies were doing fine, whereas Tanzania's fertility rate was estimated to be 4.9 and its economy not doing very well at all. Current statistical trends meant that each woman in that country would have an average of almost five children during her lifetime. Admittedly, figures were different for other African nations. Botswana's fertility rate of 6.6 in 1960 shrank to 2.6 in 2018. In 2018, 53% of married Kenyan women used contraception, up from 32% only fifteen years earlier. But that is no cause for complacency. There are deeply imbedded cultural and traditional realities to bear in mind when it comes to understanding Africa. A tribal man's wealth was always measured by the size of his herds and by the number of his children. In many rural areas this belief remains strong. It is still believed that the more children a tribesman has the richer he is, and the better he and his wives will be taken care of in their old age. But where are all these children going to live? Is there space to accommodate them? Where will they find jobs? Where will their food come from? Is there enough arable land and water resources to go around?

In many African countries once-thriving national parks are now empty. Most big mammals are long gone. Across the continent wild animals have been eaten out of existence. Travel the length and breadth of Angola or Nigeria and there is nothing but the imprint of humans everywhere. Fly on some of the smaller West African air carriers and there is a chance that you will find 'bushmeat' on the menu. This is meat from animals caught in the wild. Their slaughter is often cruel and barbaric, relying on methods like wire snares, leghold traps and even poisonous bows and arrows. Visit rural food markets in many African countries and you will invariably come across dead or living wild creatures for sale. These range from smoked chimpanzee and monkey carcasses to salted antelope and endangered river fish. One of the latest trends in East Africa is the sale of giraffe meat disguised as beef in supermarkets and butcheries. In March 2019 the government of Botswana was considering whether to cull its still healthy elephant population and turn their meat into pet food. Later that year the ban on hunting elephants as a trophy sport was lifted.

Africa has gone through a metamorphosis with very little of it good. Vast tracts of its mineral wealth and real estate have been sold off to foreign investors and plunderers, most often China. That country is now the world's biggest seller of arms to Africa and it has replaced the old colonial powers as the dominant economic force on the continent. China, Vietnam, Laos and Cambodia account for a major percentage of the destruction of Africa's fauna. Elephants are killed for ivory, pangolins for their scales, rhinos for their horns, lions for their bones and even domestic donkeys for their skins. With the exception of ivory—used mainly for carving trivial trinkets and bric-a-brac for wedding gifts—everything else is intended for traditional Oriental medicine. This demand is satisfied with little or no regard for Africa's people or animals.

As the global human population inches toward eight billion

we find ourselves living in an increasingly anthropocentric world. We believe that everything revolves around ourselves. All else is secondary. Sadly, in our brick, steel and concrete cities we have lost our connection with nature. We no longer cultivate respect for our fellow beings or for the planet that supports us. This tragic state of affairs is further exacerbated by the fact that the man America chose to occupy the White House in 2016 stubbornly refused to even recognize the threat of climate change. He simply dismissed the science of global warming as being a product of 'fake news.'

Events move too quickly nowadays. Modern technology has shrunk the planet. As people become more reliant on communication, information and entertainment powered by invisible ones and zeroes that zip along at the speed of light, we find little time for reflection, contemplation and introspection anymore. The winds of change blow through the corridors of history with such force that much of the past has already been swept from memory. Who under the age of 40 knows of Dunkirk, D-Day, the Holocaust, the Vietnam War, the Irish Potato Famine, Hiroshima, even 9/11? When we consider Africa will Nelson Mandela's memory be reduced to a forgotten pinprick in time? Will his example endure? How many young people today have even heard of him? The pace of modern life makes the past ever more remote. Some might even say it makes it irrelevant.

Equally troubling is the fact that a new form of apartheid is now taking root in South Africa. But this time the tables have turned. It is racism in reverse. Young white university and college graduates are finding it increasingly difficult to enter the labor market as opportunities favor blacks. The nationally-run airline—now bankrupt due to gross managerial ineptitude—prefers to employ black pilots and cabin crew rather than a mixture of races. But there is a dark side to that picture. Emancipation of the black man from the shackles of apartheid was celebrated around the world when Nelson Mandela was released from prison.

The general election of 1994 gave birth to the 'rainbow nation' and to one of the planet's most vibrant young democracies. Its constitution was light years ahead of any other. But the leaders who followed Mandela, namely Thabo Mbeki and the notoriously corrupt Jacob Zuma, paved the way to a morally and financially bereft future rather than foster methods for bettering the lot of the deprived black majority. Politicians' fingers have been raiding cookie jars left, right and center. They have been stealing from public coffers. The national power system, ESCOM (Electricity Supply Commission), is broke. Power outages are a regular occurrence. Unemployment is at a record high. Crime is rampant. Antiquated and overcrowded black townships or 'locations' around Johannesburg, Cape Town and Durban are now some of the most violent places on Earth. Fifty people are murdered in the country every day. Growing numbers of young black members of the so-called 'Born Free' generation are increasingly calling for the takeover of white-owned land and property without financial compensation. Even worse, isolated pockets of black extremists are calling for the total destruction of the white population. These demands sometimes take savage form such as an incident in December 2018 when a live sheep was brutally tortured, half-drowned and then torn apart on Cape Town's fashionable Clifton Beach by a chanting mob of hooligans. The innocent animal was used to represent the white population, its gruesome death a symbol of the 'cleansing' of the country of all whites. It is a sorry state of affairs.

And yet, I continue to have absolute faith in South Africa's future. Not everybody follows such savage behavior. An indomitable legacy of goodwill among the population prevails. The spirit of the average man or woman on the street is still a benevolent and positive one. You have to travel far and wide in the world today to find a more gregarious and friendly mix of people. Africa remains a wonderful place and I am mightily proud that it is an inherent part of who I am.

Epilogue

I constantly look back in amazement at the long road that has taken me from South African towns creaking under the immoral weight of apartheid to the boulevards and movie factories of Los Angeles. I know now too that the world is infinitely more mysterious and paradoxical than I could ever have imagined. It is filled with extraordinary and unknowably wonderous things. It is easy to get depressed about the state of international affairs but, for me, optimism and hope far outweigh the negative.

Sometimes I see our very existence as a gigantic Bumper Cars fairground attraction. With riders buzzing around in brightly-colored electrically-powered vehicles as they dodge and swerve into one another the experience creates fear, thrill and laughter. At the rear end of each of those cars is a whip-like antenna with a metal contact at its tip. The tip brushes along a wire mesh or grid suspended above the ride. It is from there that the electricity powers the car. I think in some way or another every single living entity—people, ponies, petunias—are all connected to a similar grid. But it exists on a level beyond the physical, beyond our capacity to see it. It is a vast force field that extends throughout the cosmos. We are all bound by it. It transcends time and place. But who or what controls the power? And what exactly is the purpose of the ride? I think those are the sort of questions that we are here to try to find out. It may take many lifetimes to discover even a tiny part of the answer. But it is the quest that is important.

Speaking for myself, the past 75 years have been a fantastic Bumper Cars ride, an incredible journey. And I think that somewhere in the background, far beyond the noise and the laughter and the fears I can sense my ancestors watching… and smiling…

BOOKS

O-BOOKS

SPIRITUALITY

O is a symbol of the world, of oneness and unity; this eye represents knowledge and insight. We publish titles on general spirituality and living a spiritual life. We aim to inform and help you on your own journey in this life.

If you have enjoyed this book, why not tell other readers by posting a review on your preferred book site?

The Holy Spirit's Interpretation of the New Testament

A Course in Understanding and Acceptance

Regina Dawn Akers

Following on from the strength of *A Course In Miracles*, NTI teaches us how to experience the love and oneness of God.

Paperback: 978-1-84694-085-9 ebook: 978-1-78099-083-5

The Message of A Course In Miracles

A translation of the Text in plain language

Elizabeth A. Cronkhite

A translation of *A Course in Miracles* into plain, everyday language for anyone seeking inner peace. The companion volume, *Practicing A Course In Miracles*, offers practical lessons and mentoring.

Paperback: 978-1-84694-319-5 ebook: 978-1-84694-642-4

Rising in Love

My Wild and Crazy Ride to Here and Now, with Amma, the Hugging Saint

Ram Das Batchelder

Rising in Love conveys an author's extraordinary journey of spiritual awakening with the Guru, Amma.

Paperback: 978-1-78279-687-9 ebook: 978-1-78279-686-2

Thinker's Guide to God

Peter Vardy

An introduction to key issues in the philosophy of religion.

Paperback: 978-1-90381-622-6

Your Simple Path

Find Happiness in every step

Ian Tucker

A guide to helping us reconnect with what is really important in our lives.

Paperback: 978-1-78279-349-6 ebook: 978-1-78279-348-9

365 Days of Wisdom

Daily Messages To Inspire You Through The Year

Dadi Janki

Daily messages which cool the mind, warm the heart and guide you along your journey.

Paperback: 978-1-84694-863-3 ebook: 978-1-84694-864-0

Body of Wisdom

Women's Spiritual Power and How it Serves

Hilary Hart

Bringing together the dreams and experiences of women across the world with today's most visionary spiritual teachers.

Paperback: 978-1-78099-696-7 ebook: 978-1-78099-695-0

Dying to Be Free

From Enforced Secrecy to Near Death to True Transformation

Hannah Robinson

After an unexpected accident and near-death experience, Hannah Robinson found herself radically transforming her life, while a remarkable new insight altered her relationship with her father, a practising Catholic priest.

Paperback: 978-1-78535-254-6 ebook: 978-1-78535-255-3

The Ecology of the Soul

A Manual of Peace, Power and Personal Growth for Real People in the Real World

Aidan Walker

Balance your own inner Ecology of the Soul to regain your natural state of peace, power and wellbeing.

Paperback: 978-1-78279-850-7 ebook: 978-1-78279-849-1

Not I, Not other than I

The Life and Teachings of Russel Williams

Steve Taylor, Russel Williams

The miraculous life and inspiring teachings of one of the World's greatest living Sages.

Paperback: 978-1-78279-729-6 ebook: 978-1-78279-728-9

On the Other Side of Love

A woman's unconventional journey towards wisdom

Muriel Maufroy

When life has lost all meaning, what do you do?

Paperback: 978-1-78535-281-2 ebook: 978-1-78535-282-9

Practicing A Course In Miracles

A translation of the Workbook in plain language, with mentor's notes

Elizabeth A. Cronkhite

The practical second and third volumes of The Plain-Language *A Course In Miracles*.

Paperback: 978-1-84694-403-1 ebook: 978-1-78099-072-9

Quantum Bliss

The Quantum Mechanics of Happiness, Abundance, and Health

George S. Mentz

Quantum Bliss is the breakthrough summary of success and spirituality secrets that customers have been waiting for.

Paperback: 978-1-78535-203-4 ebook: 978-1-78535-204-1

The Upside Down Mountain

Mags MacKean

A must-read for anyone weary of chasing success and happiness – one woman's inspirational journey swapping the uphill slog for the downhill slope.

Paperback: 978-1-78535-171-6 ebook: 978-1-78535-172-3

Your Personal Tuning Fork

The Endocrine System

Deborah Bates

Discover your body's health secret, the endocrine system, and 'twang' your way to sustainable health!

Paperback: 978-1-84694-503-8 ebook: 978-1-78099-697-4

Readers of ebooks can buy or view any of these bestsellers by clicking on the live link in the title. Most titles are published in paperback and as an ebook. Paperbacks are available in traditional bookshops. Both print and ebook formats are available online.

Find more titles and sign up to our readers' newsletter at http://www.johnhuntpublishing.com/mind-body-spirit

Follow us on Facebook at https://www.facebook.com/OBooks/ and Twitter at https://twitter.com/obooks